Literary Lives

This classic and longstanding series has established itself making a major contribution to literary biography. The books in the series are thoroughly researched and comprehensive, covering the writer's complete oeuvre. The latest volumes trace the literary, professional, publishing, and social contexts that shaped influential authors—exploring the "why" behind writers' greatest works. In its thirtieth year, the series aims to publish on a diverse set of writers—both canonical and rediscovered—in an accessible and engaging way.

More information about this series at
https://link.springer.com/bookseries/14010

Andrew Maunder

Enid Blyton

A Literary Life

palgrave
macmillan

Andrew Maunder
School of Humanities
University of Hertfordshire
Hatfield, UK

Literary Lives
ISBN 978-3-030-76331-2   ISBN 978-3-030-76332-9   (eBook)
https://doi.org/10.1007/978-3-030-76332-9

Cover illustration: AF Archive/Alamy Stock Photo

This Palgrave Macmillan imprint is published by the registered company Springer Nature Switzerland AG
The registered company address is: Gewerbestrasse 11, 6330 Cham, Switzerland

For Brian and Elizabeth Maunder

Acknowledgements

The production of this book has involved the help of a good many people. Particular thanks are owed to the following: Rosie Miles, David Rudd, Kari Dorme, Valerie Grove, Julius Green, Lizza Aiken, Margaret Grace and Mark O'Hanlon. I'd also like to thank Sarah Lawrance, Kristopher McKie, Josie Summer and the collections team at Seven Stories for arranging access and granting permissions to use Blyton-related material; likewise staff in the British Library reading rooms and London Metropolitan Archives; Alysoun Saunders, archivist for Macmillan Publishers International Limited and Springer Nature; Catherine Flynn, archivist at Penguin Random House; Hannah Lowery, archivist at Bristol University Special Collections and Jill Sullivan, Assistant Keeper at University of Reading Special Collections Department; to Alexandra Antscherl and Sharon Rubin at Hachette for permission to use Hachette and Hodder and Stoughton archive material, and to Rebecca Hinsley and Emily Wood at Palgrave. BBC copyright material is reproduced courtesy of the British Broadcasting Corporation (all rights reserved). Tony Summerfield of the Enid Blyton Society has very kindly answered numerous questions about Blyton and her writing and allowed me to use material from the Society's website. Finally, I am very grateful to the members of Enid Blyton's family, notably Sophie Smallwood and Sara Lane, who have also generously helped with queries and have allowed me to quote from Blyton's letters and make use of photographs and other material. Any errors in the book are my own.

Andrew Maunder

Contents

Abbreviations

Novels and Story Collections

AF	*The Adventurous Four* (London: Newnes, 1941)
AWC	*Adventures of the Wishing Chair* (London: Newnes, 1937)
CD	*Circus Days Again* (London: Newnes, 1942)
CK	*The Children of Kidillin* (London: Newnes, 1940)
CStC	*Claudine at St. Clare's* (London: Methuen, 1944)
FBH	*Five Go to Billycock Hill* (London: Hodder and Stoughton, 1957)
FC	*Five Go Off in a Caravan* (London: Hodder and Stoughton, 1946)
FFF	*Five on Finniston Farm* (London: Hodder and Stoughton, 1960)
FFStC	*Fifth Formers of St. Clares* (London: Methuen, 1945)
FRT	*Five Run Away Together* (London: Hodder and Stoughton, 1944)
FTI	*Five on a Treasure Island* (London: Hodder and Stoughton, 1942)
FTMT	*First Term at Malory Towers* (London: Methuen, 1946)
HC	*House-at-the-Corner* (London: Lutterworth Press, 1947)
HC	*Hurrah for the Circus!* (London: Newnes, 1939)
IA	*The Island of Adventure* (London: Macmillan, 1944)
IFMT	*In the Fifth at Malory Towers* (London: Newnes, 1950)
LTMT	*Last Term at Malory Towers* (London: Methuen, 1951)
MDC	*The Mystery of the Disappearing Cat* (London: Methuen, 1944)
MFT	*The Magic Faraway Tree* (London: Newnes 1943)
MTC	*The Mystery of Tally-Ho Cottage* (London: Methuen, 1954)
NGS	*The Naughtiest Girl in the School* (London: Newnes, 1940)
RA	*The River of Adventure* (London: Macmillan, 1955)
RoM	*The Rockingdown Mystery* (London: Collins 1949)

RuM   *The Rubabdub Mystery* (London: Collins 1952)
SBB   *The Six Bad Boys* (London: Lutterworth, 1951)
SC   *Six Cousins at Mistletoe Farm* (London: Evans, 1948)
SCA   *Six Cousins Again* (London: Evans Bros 1950)
SI   *The Secret Island* (Oxford: Basil Blackwell, 1938)
SK   *The Secret of Killimooin* (Oxford: Basil Blackwell, 1943)
SM   *The Secret Mountain* (1941; Oxford: Basil Blackwell, 1947)
SSD   *Shadow, The Sheep-Dog* (London: Newnes, 1942)
SSS   *Shock for the Secret Seven* (Leicester: Brockhampton Press, 1961)
TCSS   *Three Cheers Secret Seven* (Leicester Brockhampton Press, 1956)
TStC   *The Twins at St. Clare's* (London Methuen, 1941)
TYMT   *Third Year at Malory Towers* (London: Methuen, 1948)
UF   *Upper Fourth at Malory Towers* (London: Methuen, 1949)

Plays

FF   *Famous Five Adventure*. British Library Add Mss, Lord Chamberlain's Collection of Plays. 1955/67
NT   *Noddy in Toyland*. British Library Add Mss, Lord Chamberlain's Collection of Plays. 1954/17
Six   *Six Enid Blyton Plays* (London: Methuen, 1935)

Poetry

CW   *Child Whispers* (London: J. Saville, 1922)
RF   *Real Fairies* (London: J. Saville, 1923)

Magazines

EBM   *Enid Blyton's Magazine* (London: Evans)
SS   *Sunny Stories* (London: Newnes)
TW   *Teacher's World* (London: Evans)

Non-fiction

CL   *A Complete List of Books: Enid Blyton* (Edinburgh: John Menzies, 1951)
D   Diaries. Seven Stories, National Centre for Children's Literature collection EB/02/01/01-EB/01/01/23

Mac   The Archives of Macmillan and Company. Special Correspondence: Enid
        Blyton. British Library. Add Ms: 89262/1/5; 89262/1/6; 89262/1/7;
        89262/1/8
SML   *The Story of My Life* (London: Pitkins, 1952)

Secondary Sources

Smallwood   Imogen Smallwood, *A Childhood at Green Hedges* (London: Methuen,
              1989)
Stoney   Barbara Stoney, *Enid Blyton* (1974; London: Hodder and Stoughton,
              1992)

List of Figures

1

Introduction

On Friday 3 January 1969, there was a memorial service for Enid Blyton at St James-in-the Fields, the fashionable Anglican church in London's Piccadilly. Blyton, who had died the previous November aged seventy-one, had been a novelist, poet, magazine editor and teacher who, despite an unremarkable background, had become, as *The Times* noted, 'the most successful and most controversial children's author of the postwar period'. She was also one of the wealthiest and one of 'the most productive' with 'over 400 titles…to her name'.[1] Amongst those paying respects were Blyton's daughters, Gillian and Imogen, her grandchildren, her agent George Greenfield, and a small collection of those who had worked with and, in many cases, done rather well out of, Blyton during the course of her long career. These included her dubious business manager, Eric Rogers, who ran the company responsible for administering her work. There were also representatives of the many charities with which Blyton had been involved: the Sunshine Fund for Blind Babies and Young People, the Friends of the Centre for Spastic Children and the 'Busy Bees', the children's arm of the People's Dispensary for Sick Children for whom Blyton had been 'Queen Bee'. The tributes were led by publisher Paul Hodder-Williams whose company Hodder and Stoughton published the Famous Five, as well as many other books by Blyton. He spoke of Blyton's 'strength and vitality', her 'sympathetic nature', but above all her 'gift of storytelling' which had brought her 'friends in every corner of the world - children of all nationalities and of all backgrounds over several generations'. But Hodder-Williams expressed the sentiments shared by some of those who

© The Author(s), under exclusive license to Springer Nature
Switzerland AG 2021
A. Maunder, *Enid Blyton*, Literary Lives,
https://doi.org/10.1007/978-3-030-76332-9_1

knew Blyton when he hinted that she was a complicated woman who 'did not have a happy or safe childhood', whose desire to write became a 'compulsion' and who—so Hodder-Williams noted—'retained throughout her life a childlike wonder at her own success'.[2] Such comments seem patronising but Hodder-Williams had liked Blyton and explained privately that he had taken his speech as an opportunity to 'counteract some of the rather churlish things' which had been said about Blyton in the years prior to her death.[3] For a writer who disliked 'unpleasantness' some of them had been decidedly unpleasant.

Were she around today, Enid Blyton would be horrified at the interest which her personal life continues to generate while also being pleased but not surprised (she always had full confidence in her own appeal) that sales of her books remain at levels anyone would envy. In 2009 it was reported that they were still selling 11 million copies a year—more than J.K. Rowling.[4] By 2019 total sales of Blyton's books were reckoned to have reached 600 million.[5] Meanwhile, claims for her influence (she also liked being thought influential) continue to appear in a multitude of settings. Alongside Winnie-the-Pooh and Peter Rabbit, Blyton's characters have long been seen as part of Britain's 'national myth'.[6] In 1997 as a tribute to a writer who, according to its official statement, retained a 'timeless appeal and magic', the British Post Office issued commemorative stamps featuring scenes from Blyton's most popular series: the Famous Five, Noddy, the Secret Seven, the Magic Faraway Tree and the Malory Towers school stories.[7] In a 2015 poll to 'find' the fifty most 'inspiring' Britons of all time, Blyton was ranked nineteenth, sandwiched between Agatha Christie (eighteenth) and Queen Victoria (twentieth). Florence Nightingale and Winston Churchill came first and second.[8] The following year there was Gemma Whelan's turn as a singing and dancing Enid Blyton in CBBC's *Horrible Histories* 'Staggering Storytellers Song' (2016). Parodying the hit 'Black Magic' made famous by the group Little Mix, the sketch co-opts Blyton onto a team of other 'sisters'—Malorie Blackman, Beatrix Potter and Jacqueline Wilson—a preternaturally gifted girl-group of storytellers who rap and twerk as they celebrate their powers of making books 'fly off the shelves'.[9] Blyton has her feet in other camps, too: holiday companies offer breaks in 'Enid Blyton's Dorset', including trips to Corfe Castle (claimed as the inspiration for the Famous Five's Kirrin Island) and Swanage, where Blyton holidayed and in 1950 bought the Isle of Purbeck Golf Club. Theatregoers have been able to debate the playwright Michael Frayn's representation of a certain Enid Blyton (poet) who appears in his 1987 play *Balmoral* (revived by the Peter Hall Company (2009)) exiled along with other middle-brow 1930s authors to a commune following a commu-nist revolution. More recently there has been Glyn Maxwell's stage adaption, *The Secret Seven* (Storyhouse Theatre, Chester, 2017), Emma Rice's acclaimed theatre production based on the Malory Towers stories (2019) and Canadian television's, *Malory Towers* (2020). More than fifty years after her death, 'the great Enid', as publisher Harold Raymond mockingly termed her in 1957, remains very much part of the cultural landscape.[10]

These are not, however, the only guises under which Blyton appears. Indeed, in thinking about contemporary perceptions of Blyton it is difficult to ignore the extent to which the author and her universe have increasingly been invoked in ways that are *un*flattering. In 2009 the BBC portrayed Blyton's life on screen in *Enid*, part of a string of one-off film dramatisa-tions about prominent British figures or 'national treasures' which involved digging up secrets at odds with their public image: Margaret Thatcher, Frankie Howerd, Hattie Jacques, Barbara Cartland and Fanny Cradock all featured. In keeping with the series, the filmmakers came at Blyton from an unexpected direction, one that she would not have liked. Not only was there something sharp-edged about Enid Blyton who appeared on screen but, as portrayed by Helena Bonham Carter, she was characterised by her cruelty and her frozen emotional development. The film drew heavily on *A Childhood at Green Hedges* (1989), a memoir by Blyton's younger daughter, Imogen Small-wood, who while not unappreciative of her mother's achievements made the point that living with Blyton was not always the joyous experience one might have expected. The slow realisation on the part of the young Imogen that she was actually related to the woman with the typewriter who preferred to keep her confined in the nursery has since been repeated many times in tele-vision documentaries packaged up with allegations from other sources to do with Blyton's meanness (a sick gardener being charged for a basket of fruit), supposedly 'shocking' sexual adventures (nude mixed tennis; a lesbian affair) and a more general sense that Blyton must have had something to hide. For all her talent and enterprise, it has, thanks to various "exposés", been increas-ingly popular to cast Blyton as a tyrant who could be ruthless and self-serving: a vindictive hypocrite whose 'real' personality was far from being the straight-forward, kindly person she pretended to be in public. "'I was attracted to the role because she was bonkers'", explained Bonham Carter to *The Daily Mail*. "'She was an emotional mess and quite barking mad…She was allergic to reality - if there was something she didn't like then she either ignored it or re-wrote her life'". Unsurprisingly the idea of Britain's most successful chil-dren's author functioning somewhere between chaos and restraint was taken up by the media and Bonham Carter's performance gained her a good deal of praise. Enid Blyton was 'appealing and appalling' and Bonham Carter relished the chance to act out the less heroic bits of the subject's life.[11] What Blyton did *not* appear to be was a role model or 'foremother' for living women of the kind feminist film-makers and biographers have often looked for.[12] A similar point was made again in 2014 when Julia Davis took on the role of Enid Blyton in *Psychobitches*, Sky Arts' comedy sketch show that sees some of history's most (in)famous women psychoanalysed by a therapist and in which saying the unsayable is part of the package. In keeping with the rest of the series, the scriptwriters did not shirk in depicting as their subject as a tightly wound collection of neuroses and prejudices. When Davis's chain-smoking Blyton began a diatribe against goblins ('crafty', 'uxorious', 'insular') and extended it to incorporate Jews it was assumed that viewers did not need to have it explained to them.[13] Blyton's racism and the moral failure it encompasses was shared by many writers of her generation but it has been mentioned repeatedly since her death as the thing which defines her.

In thinking about Blyton's life, such representations have proved important because they mirror what Angela V. John has noted as a tendency in biographical studies 'to reduce the subject to hero or villain status' and recent accounts of Blyton have veered towards the latter.[14] Suffice to say, such tags are difficult to shake off. Sales of Blyton's books remain strong, but her reputation has taken a hit. Even as her supporters champion Blyton's cultural significance, they too cannot help sounding a little bit apologetic as if she is beyond what is acceptable. Blyton, in spite of her influence on twentieth-century reading habits, tends to be seen as a xenophobic 'little Englander' and this, together with her occasional snobbishness, has been held up as the reasons why her books should be consigned to the dustbin. In 2019 it was precisely this sense of Blyton that lay behind the Royal Mint's decision not to issue a commemorative coin in her honour. Accompanying this is an appropriation of Blyton as a symbolic figure, someone whose work and vision are not to be taken seriously. When, in 2015, the Green Party published their manifesto in readiness for the General Election, Boyd Tonkin was struck by how the 'utopia' it evoked was full of fantastical vintage detail: a Green government would provide 'a fortnight's camping holiday in Cornwall with cheap train tickets and a pre-Beeching rail network'. During the rest of the year, the focus would be on 'low-key, small-scale community life'. This 'numbing dose of nostalgia' and the vision of Britain it presented was 'pure Enid Blyton', comforting but simplistic.[15] Tonkin's analysis had the effect not only of skewering the Greens but of reminding people—if they didn't know already—that Blyton was pretty low level—facile and not very realistic. It's an idea political sketch writers, in particular, have long been prone to take up. In 2012's 'Lashings of enthusiasm for Uniting the Kingdom', Ann Treneman's attention was taken by the 'perky' but, as she saw it, politically inexperienced, Tory transport minister Justine Greening, her 'bobbed hair swinging', and 'as wholesome as if she had escaped from an Enid Blyton book'.[16] That there is an Enid Blyton 'look' was likewise apparent on the occasion of Queen Elizabeth II's Golden Jubilee which took place in the same year. The televised celebrations were the cue for massed ranks of television presenters 'with preternaturally bright eyes and jingling voices reading autocues that sound[ed] like they were written by Enid Blyton'.[17] It was not a compliment. Nor do sportsmen escape. It seemed to *The Independent's* Stephen Brenkley, who was in sarcastic mood in 2012, that the England cricket team, after a day trying to read their Pakistan opponents (without much success) had made 'progress from Janet and John but only as far as, say, Enid Blyton's less cerebral works'. The intellectually-limited players worked 'doggedly without supplying firm evidence that they quite understood what they were dealing with'.[18]

Conversely, it says a lot about British media outlets that for some of them there is still something idyllic and magical about the Blyton world. It formed part of Matthew Dennison's tribute published in *The Daily Express* in 2017 to mark the seventy-fifth anniversary of the first appearance of the Famous Five. Noting that 'British readers buy one of Enid Blyton's books every minute', Dennison extolled the lost world inhabited by Blyton's child adventurers and their dog: 'freedom and lots and lots of fresh air' coupled with 'unspoilt beaches' and 'rolling green countryside'. Such a 'magical' kinship with nature was not something that many of today's children would ever experience.[19] This vision of Blyton as someone associated with the unspoilt glories of the precious English countryside is her acceptable face. When the COVID-19 epidemic arrived in Britain in early 2020, it appeared as if Blyton's time had come again as travel writers, unable to go abroad, evoked her in extolling the benefits of 'wholesome' camping and kayaking in Britain: 'How to have an Enid Blyton summer: jolly outdoor adventures for all the family' was the tagline deployed by *The Daily Telegraph* in June 2020.[20] Amongst all this, definite patterns have emerged. Most obviously it is that in Britain it can be quite difficult to close one's eyes and ears to all this (often lazy) referencing of Enid Blyton and her characters. But it is also the case that Blyton has been—and continues to be—so much a part of the cultural landscape that the assumption is always that readers will 'get' the reference. This is so much so that Blyton's most famous characters, the Famous Five, are even evoked to illustrate scientific debates down to whether the reason the Five had so much energy was because their sugar intake (via the 'lashings' of ginger beer) caused them to be hyperactive.[21]

I cite this long list of examples because one of the issues considered in this book about Blyton's literary life and career is her reception history and her meaning for different generations of readers—from the 1920s to the 2000s. Despite—or perhaps because of—the 'old-fashioned' attitudes, there is a sense in the minds of many people that Blyton's stories contain a time-less appeal. There is also an idea that her works are infinitely adaptable and accommodating. While one section of current critical opinion presents (and defends) Blyton's works as historical curiosities 'of their time', another cites Blyton and her 'dreamscape' as a way of speaking to the anxieties and desires of the twenty-first century. In 2019 when she was publicising her much-admired stage production based on the Malory Towers books, the theatre director Emma Rice was quoted as saying that Blyton's schoolgirls are positive role models for today's anxious children: 'strong female characters' driven by their nascent 'feminism'.[22] Such a stance echoes the one taken in the *Horrible Histories* sketch cited above in which Blyton and her fellow authors are billed as '(s)heroes' who wanted more than being told 'cooking was all we could do'.

But are Blyton's characters really models for today?How does Blyton belong to us? What meanings do her stories carry? What is her signifi-cance? Answers to these questions fluctuate considerably. There is Blyton the publishing phenomenon who is taken as embodying children's literature, at least as it existed in the early and middle parts of the twentieth century. There is another Blyton who is spoken of in pejorative terms with a feeling that she is not altogether a good thing for children's literature, a writer of 'stubby prose' who has long been regarded with derision by people who worry about what children read.[23] This is the Blyton whose stories have long been likened to sweets; in other words as examples of the kinds of things children shouldn't be given—and prompts the idea that if anything is to be learnt from her life and career, it is that to be a successful writer does not depend on being good at writing. There is also, as we have seen, Blyton the racist reactionary whose stories articulate bigoted fears of people of different races and creeds. Then there is a writer who deals in hope and aspiration and has always given her readers 'furniture for dreams' as Alan Coren put it.[24] It is this Blyton, for example, who garners support from readers (later writers) who grew up in the grey Britain of the 1940s and 1950s. She forms part of what Nicholas Saun-ders has termed the 'memory bridge' connecting successive generations to their pasts and also to each other.[25] 'Blyton taught me what books could do', recalls Susan Hill (b.1940) of her time growing up in Scarborough. 'Yes, her prose is bland….But Blyton had the secret, the knack…Enid Blyton excited us…'.[26] Ian McEwan, born in Leicester in 1948, has explained how by the age of eleven he had read 'probably every word that Enid Blyton had written to date'.[27] Most strikingly perhaps, the former Labour Home Secretary, Alan Johnson, born in 1950 into poverty in Notting Hill, writes affectionately in his memoir *This Boy* (2013) of the 'wonderful escapism' and the 'genuine comfort' which 'Blyton-land' provided in 'dark days'.[28] Whatever one's take on her it is certainly true is that these different views of Blyton—both woman and writer—have set the terms for a critical debate that is still being played out.

Who Was Enid Blyton?

Who was Enid Blyton and how might we approach her literary life? It is true that despite being the subject of a fair amount of biographical investigation including books and television and radio documentaries—and despite the existence of letters and some diaries—the person who was Enid Blyton remains an indeterminate and often obscured figure. This is so much so that it has become usual to preface accounts of her life with the provisos that she was 'reticent', 'secretive' or even an 'enigma'. Her early life has proved particularly challenging, a period about which Blyton appears to have been prone to distorting.

The different phases of Blyton's life will be examined in detail in later chapters but it is worth briefly introducing the key points. What do we know about her? She was born Enid Mary Blyton in a flat above a shop at 354 Lordship Lane, East Dulwich, South London, on 11 August 1897 where her father, Thomas Carey Blyton (1870–1920), worked for his family's wholesale cloth business (the 1901 census describes him as a mantle manufacturer/tailor). Her mother Theresa (née Harrison, 1874–1950) devoted herself to household matters—and the bringing up of the children who followed Enid: two boys, Hanly (b.1899) and Carey (b.1903). Soon after Enid's birth, the family moved to a semi-detached house in Chaffinch Road in the suburb of Beckenham, Kent, where their neighbours were a mixture of clerks, builders, cab drivers and fishmongers. The remainder of Enid's childhood would be spent in the town, although the family moved several times. The 1911 census shows them at a larger house at 31 Clock House Road, a more middle-class street (the census gives the occupations of these neighbours variously as bank and civil service clerks, and insurance agents). By this time, the family was able to afford a live-in servant, an indicator of their aspirations to gentility. By all accounts Thomas Blyton was a lively personality and the focal point of his young daughter's emotional life and early education, taking her for nature rambles and encouraging her to read.[29] The young

Enid was devasted in 1910 when her father left to set up home with another woman, Florence Delattre, with whom he had two further children, Florence and Gebir.

Although Blyton maintained some contact with her father, meeting him at his office in London, the family home in Beckenham became a much less congenial place. The standard account is that as an offshoot of her father's departure, Blyton had turned against Theresa Blyton, an antagonism exacerbated by the latter's apparently limited interests: housework, penny-pinching and respectability. Barbara Stoney has constructed an environment which provoked the young Enid to outbursts of temper and violence, constantly disappearing upstairs to write her diaries and poems, or escaping to the house of a friend's aunt, Mabel Attenborough. It was Attenborough who seems to have helped encourage the belief that Enid was destined for better things than Beckenham, who took the honorary title, 'Mums', and in whose family home the eighteen-year-old Blyton chose to live as a lodger rather than remaining with her mother and brothers. In Theresa Blyton's defence, we might say that her irritation is not difficult to understand. Rather than Enid's spending her time reading or scribbling in her small box bedroom, Hanly Blyton recalled how 'not unnaturally her mother thought that she would be better occupied coming down and doing some domestic work which of course was expected of a girl in those days'.[30] The relationship between exasperated mother and ambitious daughter did not improve, at least on Enid's part, and from the time she left home in 1915 to the time of Theresa Blyton's death in 1950, the two women had limited contact. Blyton did not attend her mother's funeral.

By this time, the young Enid had also begun her education and from 1907 attended St Christopher's School for girls. Her drive and determination led to her becoming head girl, captain of tennis and lacrosse. Blyton's classmate—and sometime collaborator—Phyllis Chase, recalled her as being 'awfully good-natured…brilliant…sickening… quite good at art…[T]here was nothing she didn't excel at'.[31] But Blyton's favourite subject remained English; she thrived on essay-writing and 'composition' and she remembered that as she grew older she continued to 'read a great deal' (*SML*, 68). Blyton and her classmates studied passages from Shakespeare and the Bible, and memorised poems for recitation. It was a challenge Blyton met easily and she retained the ability to quote what she had learned long after. The young Blyton was also a talented pianist and her parents had plans for their daughter to follow in the footsteps of an aunt, May Crossland, a professional musician, and enter the Guildhall School of Music. In an interview broadcast on the BBC radio programme, *Home for the Day* in 1963, Blyton, then aged sixty-five, remembered how 'at six years old, I had to begin to learn to play the piano and all through my childhood there was practice, practice, practice, till I was in my teens and I was doing four hours a day...[I]f you have to work at something that you have really no desire to achieve anything great in, it becomes a terrible bore'.[32] Blyton did not take up her place at music college. She discovered a love of teaching after helping her friend Ida Hunt at a Sunday school. Consequently, Blyton seems to have fixed upon the idea that training for the latter would help her achieve her ambition to write (this was true as it turned out). By the time she left St Christopher's in 1916 to take up a place on a Froebel course at Ipswich High School, the teenage Enid had transformed into a vivacious and striking young woman, standing five feet, four inches, somewhat sheltered (as most girls of her class were) but in her own words 'headstrong' and full of 'independence', possessing an irrepressible sense of her artistic destiny (*SML*, 77). 'I knew what I ought to do. I knew it without a single doubt. I wanted to be a writer for children' was how she remembered this period (*SML*, 75).

The socio-economic status of the Blyton family meant that Enid was obliged to earn her living. The women who had lived in her street as a teenager were variously dressmakers, shop assistants and clerks but Blyton, clever and ambitious, aimed higher. When in 1918 she graduated from her teacher-training course she dutifully obtained a teaching post at a small private boys' school, Bickley Park, in Bromley, followed eighteen months later by a post as governess to the Thompson family who lived at 'Southernhay', in Hook Road, Surbiton, a role she held for the next four years. It was here that she ran what she later described as her own school but was really Blyton teaching classes made up of seven or eight of the neighbours' children (all under ten years of age) alongside the Thompson boys (David, Brian, Peter and John). By all accounts, Blyton was an engaging teacher able to establish a rapport with her pupils. One recalled her '"deep, throaty laugh"' and willingness to have fun despite the full curriculum she imposed (Stoney, 42). Blyton also studied her pupils, as well as testing out stories, poems and plays on them, which she continually to tried to get published. Her school-friend, Phyllis Chase, illustrated many of them. Together and individually they had pieces accepted sporadically but in 1922 their careers got a boost when *Teacher's World* began taking their work. The magazine spotted Blyton's potential and offered her a weekly column (1923–1945). In 1922 Blyton's first book of poetry, *Child Whispers* appeared.

In 1924 Blyton's professional and personal life took an unexpected direction when she had her first emotional meetings with the man who would become her husband and mentor, Hugh Pollock (1888–1971), a book editor at the important publishing firm George Newnes Ltd. Pollock, charming and worldly, appreciated hero-worship and in Blyton, a young woman who was perhaps likely to form passionate attachments to dynamic, older creative men, he found a perfect (and seemingly willing) candidate—and one who was beginning to make a name for herself. When, in August 1924, the couple were married, they moved into a flat in Chelsea. Blyton, who had relinquished her teaching post, wrote full-time. She was partly guided in her choice of projects by her husband and, in 1926, took on the editorship of *Sunny Stories,* which she would supply single-handedly with material for the next twenty-seven years (to 1953). That same year the couple moved to 'Elfin Cottage', Beckenham, and in 1929 to 'Old Thatch' in Bourne End, Buckinghamshire, where their two daughters were born: Gillian in 1931; Imogen in 1935.

This part of Blyton's life is where we have a lot more information about her, partly because of her diaries and (from the early 1940s) letters. She and her husband established what witnesses described as 'an ideal partnership', which depended on Blyton's compulsion to write being given free rein.[33] Somehow Blyton also found time to make an active social life for herself, a comfortable whirl of cocktail parties, bridge, tennis and later golf. Hugh Pollock also moved in influential circles and knew some of the most eminent writers and politicians of the time, including Winston Churchill, whose books he helped edit. But when in 1938 the family moved again—to 'Green Hedges', a large house in Beaconsfield—the marriage was under strain, compounded by the outbreak of war in 1939 and Pollock's enlisting in his old regiment, the Royal Scots Fusiliers in 1941. The marriage did not survive and Blyton divorced Pollock in 1942. By this time she had begun a relationship with Kenneth Darrell Waters (1892–1967) whom she married the following year. Blyton's daughters were encouraged to regard Waters as their father. This was also the period in which Blyton appeared most 'Stakhanovite', as some observers described her immense productivity (the term took its name from Aleksei Stakhanov, a coal miner in communist Russia who was lauded as a hero by the state for vastly exceeding his quota). Thirty or more books a year were not unusual. It was partly this over-production that made her the perfect candidate for the critical disdain directed at her at the end of her career.

It is here that we get most sightings of her, for example via George Greenfield (1917?–2000) who, in 1953, became her agent (prior to this she dealt with business matters herself). Greenfield was part of the John Fahquarson Agency; his other clients included the mountaineer, Edmund Hillary, the plastic surgeon Harold Gilles and the showjumper Pat Smythe. He was used to dealing with successful people with large egos. When Greenfield met Blyton, she was in 'her full stride', and the agent who liked and became protective of his client recalled her as 'a professional to her fingertips, friendly – when things went well – and tough as a dried pemmican underneath it all'. As he noted, '[h]er idea was to catch them [children] young and keep them enthralled as they grew older'. What Greenfield also realised was that Blyton the person (as opposed to 'Enid Blyton' the literary character) was not the naïve figure people liked to imagine from her writings and manner: 'She knew exactly what she was doing', he recalled. As a worker she was 'indefatigable'; she was assiduous in keeping in touch with her publishers and readers.[34] She did not appear charismatic at public appearances but she could silence a room of children and keep them entertained effortlessly.

In the late 1950s, Blyton's health began to fail and it has been suggested that she was a victim of dementia from the early 1960s. Although her workload remained spectacular by most people's standards, her pace slowed. She toiled at the writing and editing of her biggest project of the decade, *Enid Blyton's Magazine* (launched in 1953) but was forced to close it down in 1959. Blyton's last adventure story, *Fun for the Secret Seven,* was written in early 1963. This was the same year that the twenty-first Famous Five title, *Five Are Together Again,* was published—also the last in the series. In 1967, Kenneth Waters died, leaving Blyton to be cared for by domestic staff. By this time, her memory had visibly started to fail and to observers like George Greenfield, she seemed to live in the past. In September 1968, Blyton was admitted to a Hampstead nursing home where she died aged seventy-one on 28 November. The obituaries were respectful, although their writers invariably suggested that it had been enough for Blyton to have been in the right place at the right time—and to have a knack for connecting with children. What the obituaries also noted was that while Blyton had been a public figure for more than forty years, many aspects of her life and personality remained unanswered. As *The Times* noted, the author herself had 'over the years' become 'as cagey as Marie Corelli about herself and her affairs'.[35] The newspaper's older readers would presumably have recognised the reference to Corelli (1855–1924), the best-selling novelist of the generation of writers just prior to Blyton's own, whose expertise in self-presentation and promotion but also obfuscation, hiding the truth about her origins was legendary. Was it the case, asked *The Guardian,* that Enid Blyton with her 'easy popularity' and her determination to avoid anything 'sordid' had had a life which was, well, sordid?[36] These questions continue to be asked today. Why was Blyton driven to write so much—what lay behind her apparently uncontrolled outpourings? Did she have a double life? Did she have a love affair with another woman? Was she a monster? I cite these questions not because they are the most useful ones to ask but because they are examples of the speculation Blyton's life often provokes, much of it tied up with the dissonance between her public image as a kindly auntie and the more complicated woman underneath. Since Blyton's death, a good deal of biographical information about her has come to light thanks to works by Barbara Stoney, Imogen Smallwood, Tony Summerfield, Duncan McLaren and David Rudd (amongst others). It is clear, however, that there is more to be discovered about Blyton's life and career.

Studying Blyton

There have been many different approaches to Enid Blyton and Chapter 2 surveys some of them. The present book is based on three main assumptions. The first is that although it would be misleading to offer an account of Enid Blyton's life and work without talking about her most famous series: the Famous Five, the 'Noddy' books, the Secret Seven and Malory Towers, Blyton's achievements as a writer do not rest solely on these works. As we shall see, Blyton had a long career as a poet, journalist, playwright, magazine editor and a storyteller (her phrase for herself). It began during the First World War and continued until—or even—after her death in 1968. While it is impossible to do justice to all her writing, one of the aims of this book is to reveal something of Blyton's diversity in terms of genre, form and subject matter, thereby suggesting that she is not as easy to sum up as she first seems and is certainly more complex and thoughtful than she is given credit for being. It is also worth noting that one of the reasons why Blyton is rarely treated as a serious writer is because there is an assumption that she is too popular to be good. She is an example of a bestselling author who achieved her status because of 'popular consent', as Mortimer Adler puts it. Blyton was not the choice of 'a special elite'. She was also a writer for children, an occupation which has traditionally brought with it its own 'stigma'.[37]

The second main assumption is that Blyton's achievements as a professional writer are deserving of more attention than they have received. Blyton's knowledge of the publishing industry and its workings were a central part of her career. She was interested in the fabric of her books, their illustrations, their covers, their typography, but also in their price and their marketing and in ways they reached the public in Britain or abroad via magazine or newspaper, serialisation, reprint, broadcast. As her career progressed, she looked to new ways to sell what she had written and sought to adapt stories for the theatre. A focus on Blyton's professional life thus seems appropriate. In the early 1970s when discussions about a biography of Blyton started to circulate, one reason why publisher Paul Hodder-Williams was sceptical was that it seemed that her personal life had been largely uneventful. As he explained: 'she [Blyton] devoted her whole free time to her writing, so that the story of her life is so often the story of the stories, poems, nature study articles etc. on which she was working'.[38] This was not strictly true, of course. However, it was the case that Blyton kept people at arm's length partly so she could focus on being a professional wordsmith. 'I am a very busy person' she told the illustrator Marjorie Davies, adopting the regal tone she sometimes deployed. 'I do not like working with anyone slack'.[39] The overriding impression, of course, is often that Blyton *never* stopped working. Her fiction, too, is full of people working. Thus, one of the concerns of the present book is also work—the importance of work but also the pressure of work.

As we shall also see, one of the things that makes Blyton so hard for biographers—and even her family—to follow (in the sense of understanding the 'real' woman beneath) was the ways she compartmentalised her life or 'lives' as she put it (Mac, 11 January 1950). There are tensions between different versions of Blyton—the dynamic, ambitious writer who wielded considerable power in a male world but who also espoused the values of home and husband. For thirty years she lived in Beaconsfield, a town in the Home Counties, where she was seen proudly adopting—and enjoying—a domestic, feminine lifestyle, attending to her flowers and organising meals. Yet while she lived this largely private life, she also cultivated a uniquely close relationship with her readers. She gave generously to charities, particularly those connected to children and animals, but she could be mean-spirited, and one of her daughters felt neglected. Like other celebrated exponents of writing for children—Rudyard Kipling, Kenneth Graeme—she has been labelled emotionally immature and 'child-like' and this has been given as a reason for her success, but she was also, as her daughter Imogen recalled, 'incredibly, beautifully organised and controlled, self-controlled and very happy like that'.[40] At the height of her career, she could also feel torn between the competing demands on her time and the different obligations she put herself under. Blyton was a housewife and mother, but her life was also about her work; the next book and the next project.

The third assumption governing this book is that the responses of Blyton's own contemporaries to her and, the twentieth-century historical and literary contexts and conditions in which she published her works, are central to any understanding of them. Blyton's life coincided with some of the major transformations not only in publishing, but also of British society more generally; hers is what Barbara Caine has described as 'the capacity of an individual life to reflect broad historical change'.[41] During Blyton's seventy-one years she lived through the First World War, the economic depression of the 1920s and 1930s, the rise of Fascism, the Second World War, the emergence of the welfare state and the dawn of the 'swinging sixties'. So, this book argues for the significance of the initial contexts of Blyton's work, as a writer who (surprisingly) can seem much more socially, politically and culturally engaged than is often imagined—and also more sensitive—something which becomes more noticeable when we are willing to move beyond the realms of Noddy et al. and admit the existence of other fictional, dramatic, poetic and journalistic work. The potential of this approach is described in more detail in Chapter 2. There are still difficulties in 'knowing' Blyton but what such investigations also reveal is the tension noted earlier, between different versions of Blyton the writer—between the Blyton who can seem modern and 'relevant' to the twenty-first century and the Blyton whose varied output is bound up in specific historical circumstances and the middle-class, Anglo-centric attitudes which Blyton carried around with her.

This book will also suggest that Blyton is occasionally a more complex writer than she appears. Although she is popularly remembered as a conservative who possessed 'outsize social prejudices', as Nicholas Tucker puts it, one of the characteristics of some of her writing is its polyphony and its potential to resist fixed readings.[42] Despite Blyton's obvious conformity and place within the culture of her time, her writings—and also her life and career—are interesting for the ways in which they can sometimes be read as entering into a challenging relationship with the cultural values they appear to propagate so happily. Blyton's stories seem to encourage conformity, but themes of transgression, rebellion and secrecy also appear, alongside a fascination with disguise, escape, and alternative selves and choices. Blyton's adoption of a pseudonym 'Mary Pollock' for some of her works perhaps also suggests her own interest in assuming another identity.

In a book of this length focused on someone who wrote so much it is necessary to be selective and in deciding what issues and texts to concentrate on, notice has been taken of David Rudd's observation that '[t]here are in fact a number of "Blytons" out there, just as there are different versions of her most famous characters' and it is impossible to capture all of them.[43] The chapters which follow are broadly chronological and discuss selected issues in relation to Blyton's life and a range of different writings produced at different points in her career. By its very nature, a study of this kind dealing with such numerous, varied and multivalent texts (the work of a person who was herself complicated and contradictory) can only offer a partial view, but the discussions offered here of particular series, novels and poems are intended to whet the reader's appetite. Of the texts chosen, some like *The Famous Five* (1942–1963) and the *St Clare's* series (1941–1945) have been the focus of a good deal of criticism, particularly as examples of genre fiction; others like *The Adventurous Four* (1940), *House-at-the-Corner* (1947), *Six Cousins at Mistletoe Farm* (1948) and *The Six Bad Boys* (1951) have received very little attention.

Chapter 2 traces some of the developments in Blyton's critical fortunes and explores some of the ways in which critics have sought to explain Blyton the person and her work. Chapters 3 and 4 consider the early part of Blyton's career in the 1920s and 1930s; they trace the emergence of what would become recognisably Blyton subjects—fantasy, animals, adventures, circuses—as well as looking at some of the ways in which Blyton as a writer within the literary marketplace also works within the narrative structures and traditions peculiar to different fictional sub-genres of her day. Chapters 5, 6, 7 and 8 demonstrate some of the ways in which Blyton's texts engage with issues which had special relevance in the period in which she was at her most dominant, 1939–1955: the Second World War, nationhood and Englishness, empire, juvenile delinquency, the family. Read alongside these contexts, these works begin to take on new dimensions, emerging as records of social crisis and but also resolutions. Chapter 9 continues this theme by considering Blyton's stance in relation to debates surrounding women's roles and the extent to which her stories can be said to dramatise some of the feminist arguments of their day as well as embodying a conservative viewpoint. Chapter 10 considers Blyton's thorny reputation in the 1950s and her creation of another popular but highly controversial (and, some would argue, idiotic) series, *Noddy in Toyland*. Chapter 11 looks at Blyton's forays into television but more especially theatre—and the success of her stage adaptations in the 1950s of the Noddy stories and of the Famous Five adventures. Chapter 12, 'Final Years' looks at Blyton's work leading up to her death in 1968. The intention is that what emerges is an Enid Blyton who is more varied, more impressive, more creative and socially aware than many critics have allowed for.

Notes

1. Unsigned Article, 'Miss Enid Blyton: Froebel Teacher Who Became Best-Selling Children's Author', *The Times* (29 November 1968), 12.
2. Paul Hodder-Williams, 'Enid Blyton Memorial Service', London Metropolitan Archives/Hodder and Stoughton Archives, M.16352A. See also Paul Hodder-Williams, 'Enid in Toyland', *Sunday Telegraph* (1 December 1968), 15.
3. Paul Hodder-Williams to George Greenfield, 8 January 1969, London Metropolitan Archives/Hodder and Stoughton Archives, M.16352A.

4. David Rudd, 'In Defence of the Indefensible? Some Grounds for Enid Blyton's Appeal', in *Children's Literature: Approaches and Territories*, eds. Janet Maybin and Nicola J. Watson (Houndsmills: Palgrave Macmillan, 2009), 168–82 (168).

5. Joe Sommerlad,'World Book Day:10 Best Children's Books by Enid Blyton', *The Independent* (7 March 2019). https://www.independent.co.uk/arts-entert ainment/books/features/world-book-day-enid-blyton-books-best-series-famous-five-secret-seven-a8810566.html. Accessed 26 June 2021.

6. David Holloway, 'Enid Blyton, Creator of Noddy and Big Ears', *The Daily Telegraph* (29 November 1968), 29.

7. First Day Cover Insert, 9 September 1997.

8. Boudicca Fox-Leonard, 'The 50 Greatest Britons Revealed', *Daily Mirror* (22 September 2015). https://www.mirror.co.uk/news/uk-news/50-greatest-britons-revealed-wills-6495706. Accessed 23 June 2021.

9. Steve Connolly (director), 'Staggering Storytellers' Song', *Horrible Histories, CBBC* (11 July 2016) https://www.bbc.co.uk/cbbc/watch/staggering-sto rytellers-special-sneak-peek?collection=international-womens-day. Accessed 13 March 2021.

10. Harold Raymond to Norah Smallwood, 17 July 1957, University of Reading, Special Collections, CW169/1, Raymond 865486.

11. Lisa Seward, 'Naked Tennis, a Lesbian Affair with the Nanny: There Was More to Enid Blyton than Midnight Feasts and Ginger Beer: New TV Drama Reveals Her as a Barking-Mad Adulterous Bully', *Daily Mail* (13 November 2009), 63.

12. Marcia Citron, *Gender and the Musical Canon* (Urbana: University of Illinois Press, 2000), 226.

13. Jeremy Dyson (dir.), 'Enid Blyton', *Psychobitches* Series 1: 2, Tiger Aspect Productions/Sky Arts, 6 June 2013. https://youtu.be/nX3LPe9jd7U. Accessed 13 March 2021.

14. Angela V. John, *Turning the Tide: The Life of Lady Rhonda* (Cardigan: Parthian, 2013), 20.

15. Boyd Tonkin, 'Britain Was at Its Best in…?: Each Party Has a Different Take', *The Independent* (17 April 2015), 36.

16. Ann Treneman, 'Lashings of Enthusiasm for Uniting the Kingdom', *The Times* (13 January 2012), 15.

17. Harriet Walker, 'Duty Keeps Calling', *The Independent* (6 June 2012), 20.

18. Stephen Brenkley, 'DRS Has Changed the Way We Have to Play Spin, Admits Cook', *The Independent* (27 January 2012), 65.

19. Matthew Dennison, 'The Famous Five Are 75', *Daily Express* (11 May 2017), 13.

20. Hattie Garlick, 'How to Have an Enid Blyton Summer: Jolly Outdoor Adventures for All the Family', *The Daily Telegraph* (6 June 2020). https://www.telegr aph.co.uk/family/life/have-enid-blyton-summer-jolly-outdoor-adventures-fam ily/. Accessed 13 March 2021.

21. Chris Green, 'Lashings of Ginger Beer Could Lead to a Sticky End', *The Independent* (12 June 2014), 23.

22. Emma Rice, 'Society Needs to Rediscover the Values of Enid Blyton's Malory Towers', *The Daily Telegraph* (26 June 2019). https://www.telegraph.co.uk/the atre/what-to-see/emma-rice-society-needs-rediscover-values-enid-blytons-mal ory/. Accessed 13 March 2021.

23. Mary Sullivan, 'Land of Noddy', *The Sunday Telegraph* (25 July 1982), 14.

24. Alan Coren, quoted in *Queen of Adventure: Enid Blyton*, BBC Radio 4 (31 July 1997), 03.32. https://www.bbc.co.uk/archive/queen-of-adventure-enid-blyton/ zjjcpg8. Accessed 14 March 2021.

25. N.J. Saunders, 'Apprehending Memory: Material Culture and the War, 1919–1939', in *The Great World War, 1914–1945*, eds. J. Bourne, P.H. Liddle and H. Whitehead (London: HarperCollins, 2001), 476–88 (477).

26. Susan Hill, *Howard's End Is on the Landing* (London: Profile Books, 2009), 24.

27. Ian McEwan, 'An Only Childhood', *The Observer* (31 January 1982), 41.

28. Alan, Johnson, *This Boy. A Memoir of Childhood* (London: Corgi, 2014), 118.

29. Whether Thomas Blyton was, as he seems to have claimed, a published author remains less clear. There is no evidence to back up a story which Blyton trotted out in a *Daily Express* interview in 1952 that her father's literary work appeared alongside that of Oscar Wilde and Aubrey Beardsley in the celebrated avant-garde magazine, *The Yellow Book,* in the 1890s. See Nancy Spain, 'Saturday Outing with Nancy Spain', *The Daily Express* (27 September 1952), 4.

30. Hanly Blyton quoted in *A Child-like Person*, dir. Roger Thompson BBC Radio 4 (19 August 1975), 07.33. https://www.bbc.co.uk/archive/a-childlike-person/ zvvt8xs. Accessed 14 March 2021.

31. Phyllis Chase quoted in *A Child-like Person*, 06.35–06.45.

32. *Home for the Day: Enid Blyton*. Interview with Marjorie Anderson, BBC Light Programme 13 January 1963, 00.58–01.18. https://www.bbc.co.uk/archive/ home-for-the-day--enid-blyton/zvy6kmn. Accessed 1 March 2021.

33. Dick Hughes quoted in 'A Child-like Person', 15.51.

34. George Greenfield, *A Smattering of Monsters* (1995; London: Little Brown and Company, 1997), 11, 110, 112, 115.

35. Unsigned Article, 'Enid Blyton: Froebel Teacher Who Became Best-Selling Children's Author', 12.

36. Unsigned Article, 'Enid Blyton', *The Guardian* (29 November 1968), 22.

37. Mortimer Adler, *Reforming Education: The Opening of the American Mind* (1977; New York: Macmillan, 1988), 320.

38. Paul Hodder-Williams to Michael & Elsie Herron, 26 November 1973, London Metropolitan Archives/Hodder and Stoughton Archives, M.16352A. Williams also advised George Greenfield that a biography would be a terrible idea; prying into Blyton's life would 'only harm her sales & her image'. Paul Hodder-Williams to George Greenfield, nd, 1970, London Metropolitan Archives/Hodder and Stoughton Archives, M.16352A.

39. Enid Blyton to Marjorie Davies, 25 January 1950 and 28 January 1950, quoted in Sally Varlow, *A Brush with Enid Blyton: The Life and Work of Marjorie L. Davies* (Lewes: Pomegranate Press, 2011), 89.

40. Imogen Smallwood, quoted in *The Blyton Legacy* (Seven Stories, 2013), 0.37–1.24. https://youtu.be/lTEjM2xLtTM. Accessed 3 March 2021.
41. Barbara Caine, *Biography and History* (London: Palgrave 2010), 5.
42. Nicholas Tucker, 'Introduction', in *Enid Blyton. A Celebration and Re-appraisal. NCRCL Papers 2*, eds. Nicholas Tucker and Kimberley Reynolds (London: National Centre for Research in Children's Literature, 1997), vii–xiv (xii).
43. David Rudd, 'Blytons, Noddies and Denoddification Centers: The Changing Construction of a Cultural Icon', in *Change and Renewal in Children's Literature*, ed. Thomas van der Walt (London: Praeger, 2004), 111–8 (111).

Bibliography

———. *Home for the Day: Enid Blyton*. Interview with Marjorie Anderson, BBC Light Programme 13 January 1963, 00.58–01.18. https://www.bbc.co.uk/archive/home-for-the-day--enid-blyton/zvy6kmn. Accessed 5 April 2021.

Benton, Michael. 2009. *Literary Biography. An Introduction*. Chichester: Wiley Blackwell.

Caine, Barbara. 2010. *Biography and History*. London: Palgrave.

Citron, Marcia. 2000. *Gender and the Musical Canon*. Urbana: University of Illinois Press.

Greenfield, George. 1995; 1997. *A Smattering of Monsters*. London: Little Brown and Company.

Hill, Susan. 2009. *Howard's End is on the Landing*. London: Profile Books.

Hunt, Philip. 2001. *Children's Literature*. Oxford: Blackwell.

John, Angela V. 2013. *Turning the Tide. The Life of Lady Rhonda*. Cardigan: Parthian.

Johnson, Alan. 2014. *This Boy. A Memoir of Childhood*. London: Corgi.

Rudd, David. 2004. 'Blytons, Noddies and Denoddification Centers: The Changing Construction of a Cultural Icon'. In *Change and Renewal in Children's Literature*, edited by Thomas van der Walt: 111–8. London: Praeger.

———. 2009. 'In Defence of the Indefensible? Some Grounds for Enid Blyton's Appeal'. In *Children's Literature: Approaches and Territories*, edited by Janet Maybin and Nicola J. Watson: 168–82. Houndsmills: Palgrave Macmillan.

Saunders, N.J. 2001. 'Apprehending memory: Material Culture and the War, 1919–1939'. In *The Great World War, 1914–1945*, edited by J. Bourne, P.H. Liddle and H. Whitehead: 476–78. London: HarperCollins

Seven Stories. *2013. The Blyton Legacy* https://youtu.be/lTEjM2xLtTM. Accessed 3 March 2021.

Stanley, Liz. 1995. *The Auto/biographical I: The Theory and Practice of Feminist Auto/biography*. Manchester: Manchester University Press.

Thompson, Roger. Director. 1975. *A Child-Like Person.* BBC Radio 4 (19 August). https://www.bbc.co.uk/archive/a-childlike-person/zvvt8xs. Accessed 14 March 2021.

Tucker, Nicholas and Kimberley Reynolds. Editors. 1997. *Enid Blyton. A Celebration and Re-appraisal. NCRCL Papers 2.* London: National Centre for Research in Children's Literature.

Varlow, Sally. 2011. *A Brush with Enid Blyton: The Life and Work of Marjorie L. Davies.* Lewes: Pomegranate Press.

Wagner Martin, Linda. 1994. *Telling Women's Lives: The New Biography.* Rutgers: Rutgers.

2

Blyton and the Critics

Enid Blyton's reputation has fluctuated a good deal. At the peak of her career in the 1940s and early 1950s, Blyton was widely regarded as an iconic figure, a 'national institution' and an expert in all things related to children for whom she was an 'idol'.[1] An Enid Blyton book was 'a passport to happiness for millions of children' declared Peter Hawley in 1947. There was also a feeling that the author's vast output and her 'cult of simplicity' had helped change the landscape and possibilities—including commercial ones—of children's literature.[2] 'Enid Blyton is a good thing' explained bookseller John Piper in 1951. 'She keeps children – and their parents - coming into bookshops. She encourages children of *all ages* to read'. It was, he added, 'up to rival authors to write something more entertaining if they want to compete'.[3] The diversity of Blyton's work meant that she was compared to Robert Louis Stevenson, Beatrix Potter, Edith Nesbit and J.M. Barrie. But Blyton was more than a children's writer. She intervened in public debates and was taken seriously by important people. A headline in 1949 yelled 'Working - Mother Plan "Disastrous for Nation" – Authoress', a response to Blyton's much-publicised participation in a campaign to 'safeguard' home life in the face of the Labour government's attempts to encourage more women to take paid work.[4] Yet in the years leading up to and following her death in 1968, Blyton was re-cast a writer of dubious merits and little credibility—'a ruthless writing machine' producing 'easy pap' as David Holloway described her in 1974.[5]

It is not possible to tell the whole story of Blyton's reputation here, but a useful starting point is the publication in the late 1950s and 1960s of a series

© The Author(s), under exclusive license to Springer Nature
Switzerland AG 2021
A. Maunder, *Enid Blyton*, Literary Lives,
https://doi.org/10.1007/978-3-030-76332-9_2

of attacks by prominent librarians, educationalists and journalists.[6] These helped create a picture of Blyton as a self-important, over-indulged figure who had been given free rein over children's literature for long enough. A notable example of this was Colin Welch's scathing (and supercilious) article, 'Dear Little Noddy' (1958). This attacked Blyton as an ill-qualified 'former school teacher' and self-pronouncing missionary with 'A Message' who was exploiting the nation's families while making herself so rich that she had become 'the highest paid woman in the British Isles'. By this time Blyton's pride in the vast number of books bearing her name was well-known (it was always mentioned in interviews). For Welch, it was something which 'naturally' prompted suspicion and he returned to a rumour which had circulated for some years: whether Blyton wrote all these books herself? If 'yes', how was it possible, given the rapid rate at which they spilled out, that they could be any good? Even if she did write her own books Blyton's lack of intellect was, for Welch, all too obvious, and she would not be worth taking seriously were it not for the fact that children were entranced by her. Much of Welch's ammunition was aimed at Noddy, the wooden nodding boy, whose 'imbecility' he judged 'almost indecent' and who was 'the most egocentric, joyless, snivelling and pious anti-hero in the history of British fiction'. It did not reflect well on anyone, least of all Blyton, that '[i]n this witless, spiritless, snivelling, sneaking doll the children of England are expected to find themselves reflected. From it they are to derive ethical and moral edification'. As a personality, Noddy was 'querulous, irritable and humourless', 'unnaturally priggish' and 'a sneak'. Nor was Blyton redeemed by her writing style which was dependent on dumbing so far down that the reader's abilities were never stretched. The result was that '[b]y putting everything within reach of the child mind', her books 'enervate and cripple it'. Older children fared little better. How was it possible, Welch asked, that 'a diet of Miss Blyton could help with the 11-plus or even with the Cambridge English Tripos'? Welch also included evidence from a town librarian who reported that 'Only not-so-bright children like Enid Blyton'. Faced with this, Welch looked back fondly towards the children's books of the Victorian age which 'often involve long words and quite complex intellectual and moral problems'.[7] Although it is not difficult to spot Welch's own biases—he is snobbish and has trouble reconciling the fact that a well-paid and influential author can be a woman of lower-middle-class origins—his intentions are clear enough. He seeks to make Blyton look self-serving and third-rate and does so by insulting her and her readers. By emphasising the dangers to a child's education—even if the child is pre-school—Welch is able to present Blyton as a pernicious presence, lacking in subtlety and obsessed by a need to dominate.[8]

Another turning point was the news which reached Britain in 1960 that Blyton's books had been banned from New Zealand's libraries. Whether or not this was a decision influenced (as some claimed) by Welch's article and his argument that Blyton's stories did nothing to help a child's literacy, it was surprising enough to be widely reported. As wags were prone to point out, being banned was a distinction Blyton shared with the 'pornographic' American author Henry Miller. In the years that followed, several municipal libraries in British cities made similar headlines by following suit or adopting a policy of not replacing their stocks of Blyton's books. These decisions were reported melodramatically. 'City turns out Noddy and friends' was how *The Daily Mirror* in 1964 described Nottingham's cruel actions; the city council had 'ordered out' little Noddy as well as 'most other books by their creator' on the grounds of their 'limited appeal'. The paper carried a statement from Kenneth Darrell Waters (who had presumably been rung up at Green Hedges) who told the reporters that '[t]hese librarians don't like books being popular. They try to force the classics on to the children, but the children won't read them'.[9]

It is often assumed that by this point it was the racism in some of Blyton's stories which was being put forward as the reason why she should no longer be read or stocked (see p. 38), Yet in the 1960s it was more often the case that when detractors went after the veteran author the issue was the apparent lack of 'grit' and realism in her stories, and what was seen (unfairly) as her simplistic, pastel-shaded view of children. This is apparent in another take on Blyton: 'Women of Influence', published in 'The Women's Mirror' (part of *The Daily Mirror*) in September 1964. Here, in a rather confused attempt to find out about 'the personalities behind the power', a group of well-known 1960s women (television producer, Hazel Adair, novelist Barbara Cartland, gossip columnist Betty Kenward, TV cook Fanny Craddock) were quizzed about their views on the modern woman and her opportunities for making a mark. Blyton was also interviewed and was quoted as saying 'I think I've had an influence – as all good teachers have – by bringing out the musical and artistic sense in children, and also their curiosity'. It was familiar Blyton stuff. Then, however, the magazine—rather ungraciously—brought in a psychiatrist who offered a damning assessment. He explained that:

Enid Blyton's work...reflects the over-feminisation of society. Men come off especially badly in her books. Noddy is an educationally subnormal nit who is easily led astray. His companion, Big Ears, is a ridiculous dwarf. The girls, by comparison, are terribly pretty and rather clever – and there are few, if any, witches.

Mothers like the stories and that's why they sell well. They hate to think of their children, especially boys, having violent feelings – but boys need to release aggression.

After this, the article's author, Steve Young, moved onto Barbara Cartland (1901–2000), almost an exact contemporary of Blyton. His verdict was similarly damning: 'Barbara Cartland's novels are a logical progression from Enid Blyton's stories. Love tends to be an anaemic, gutless game that reaches suffocatingly unreal climaxes under a full moon'.[10] The flip side of this was that while such revisionist takes gained some traction with some parents and teachers, they did not really dent Blyton's sales. Her books—like those of Cartland—continued to sell in quantities most writers only dreamt of. In 1967 the paperback reprint of *Five on a Treasure Island* sold 72,688. In 1968 *The Secret Seven* managed 41,250.[11] It was thus a source of considerable irritation to her detractors that the Blyton brand appeared to go from strength to strength; it was as if they were making no impression at all. 'Are your children addicted to Enid Blyton and what, if anything do you do about it?' asked Edward Blishen wearily in 1967.

Whilst there is no single explanation as to why Blyton became so little regarded, it is clear that the decline in her reputation mirrors the kinds of shifts and changes in taste and understanding that Hans Robert Jauss describes in *Towards an Aesthetic of Reception* (1982). Using Jauss's framework, the emerging dislike of Blyton can be attributed to a change in the 'horizon of expectations' and an 'altered aesthetic norm' that causes 'the audience [to] experience formerly successful works as outmoded and [to] withdraw its appreciation'.[12] The fact that Blyton's achievements seemed to be reducible to tales about pixies, golliwogs and talking animals made it easy to dismiss her as too banal and too out of date to have any value. Nor did it help that for much of her lifetime she was recognised as the voice of Home Counties England, pouring out 'sub-Ransome' stories in 'endless profusion', all populated by clean-limbed, middle-class children speaking received-pronunciation and attending boarding school, as *The New York Times* reported in 1960.[13] The bias displayed by editors towards such work—especially if ponies made an appearance—was well-known. Blyton benefited from a 'tolerant deafness' on the part of publishers who inhabited a 'self-satisfied…small world' and were happy to have her write the same kinds of stories despite how socially glib and out of touch they were.[14] By the time the slow cultural and political turn begun in the 1960s reached the 1970s Blyton (who had died in 1968) had become an easy person to disparage. 'We do not now want our children to be as Enid Blyton wanted them to be: we do not indeed believe that they are as she said they were', announced the novelist

Gillian Tindall in 1974 as she surveyed Blyton's 'priggish, snobbish, mini-folk'. In a demonstration of how the different criticisms which had gathered around Blyton ran into each other, Tindall also explained that Blyton was unsuitable because she had 'the mental outlook and tastes of a particularly unsophisticated nursery governess – as well as some of the abilities'. Blyton's long-running success was largely due to the fact that in her lifetime she had managed to convince everyone that she was both talented and trustworthy by dint of her management of a 'carefully-cultivated public persona'.

Elsewhere a sense of Blyton as what Jane Gallop would call a 'phallic mother' whose influence needed to be shaken off, also took hold, particularly amongst younger writers.[15] In 1962, Alan Garner (b. 1934), author of the acclaimed *The Weirdstone of Brisingamen* (1960) was unapologetic in telling interviewers that Blyton made him 'squirm'.[16] Older writers, meanwhile, had for a long time felt irritation and envy at Blyton's success and, following her death, several were prepared to give vent to their feelings. Alison Uttley, famous for her stories about Little Grey Rabbit, and a neighbour in Beaconsfield, declared that the best place for Blyton's books 'was a sale of work'.[17] Blyton's tendency to hold herself separate, her presentation of herself as superior, not just in what she said, but in her manner was also disliked, as was her sense that she was different from others in the 'special' connection she had achieved with the nation's children. Geoffrey Trease, another for whom the Blyton cult provoked irritation coupled with bewilderment, described Blyton's egotism. For him, one way this manifested itself was in Blyton's dislike of sharing the limelight with other authors and possible rivals. She 'learned that I also was invited', Trease recalled of one literary event, 'and made my removal a condition of her own acceptance. She was almost incredulous, the organisers informed me, when my invitation stood'. Reflecting on Blyton's magnificent career, Trease added that he—rather like Colin Welch and Gillian Tindall—thought her success was a clever con trick: 'Whether or not Enid Blyton knew, as she claimed, exactly what children wanted, she certainly knew how to convince them that it was what she was giving them'.[18] What becomes apparent is that Blyton could simultaneously be an object of irritation and wonderment and the topic of catty comments but as a 'serious' or 'literary' subject she was not very interesting. The idea that anyone would want to write a book about her seemed remote. It was partly what made the publication in 1974 of Barbara Stoney's biography of Blyton all the more surprising.

At the same time, it was also apparent that Blyton was a frustrating figure to categorise because she had clearly done *some* good during her career. Peter Wait, who worked for Methuen, remembered Blyton as '[a] nice little woman…kind and good…a highly competent storyteller, moral, good middle-class moral standards and…she made children want to read books'.[19] Wait's terms of reference sound old-fashioned but his last point is important: Blyton's skill in getting young people of all classes to read on their own, together with her sales and her reach, was simply too powerful to be disregarded. This was partly the image Blyton had constructed of herself in her own lifetime. As M.S. Woods pointed out shrewdly in 1974, her success was the result of 'by-passing the literary middle-men – the teachers, librarians and critics who aim to shape children's literary tastes – and selling directly to the consumers'.[20] The accessibility of Blyton's stories was also why, in 1960, Walter Allen felt she was such a 'phenomenon', and why, in the 1980s, as discussions about Britain's National Curriculum took place, there were calls led by Roald Dahl for her to be included.[21]

The hard work of Blyton's rehabilitation took a long time. In spite of Dahl's advocacy, it was not until the 1990s that Blyton began to be viewed more favourably by professional critics and her work seen as deserving a 'serious, culturally respectful' reading, as Peter Hunt put it in 1995. For Hunt, attempting to overturn the 'stigma' surrounding children's novels, namely that these are texts 'not capable of being read in what we might call a literary or worthwhile (or intergalactic) way', Blyton was a peculiarly suitable case for treatment. She was still selling more than eight million books a year, most of which were labelled '"trash"'. The central issue for Hunt was the danger of falling into 'the trap' laid by popular ideas of what '"Literature"' and 'literariness' are and the ways in which people are encouraged (wrongly) to regard certain kinds of writing—books for Blyton being a notable example—as '"inferior"' or '"unrewarding…."' Her books never got 'the full "literary" (serious, considered, culturally respectful) reading'. Hunt thus issued a challenge: 'Suppose we approached Blyton with the same reverence, the same expectation of excellence that we do *The Wind in the Willows* - What would we find?' The answer according to Hunt was writing 'which balances dark and light, security and violence, power and helplessness, which explores (often with the crudity and directness of childhood) insider and outsider, and class and race and sexual distinctions'.[22]

Thanks in part to Hunt's encouragement, the easy labelling of Blyton as someone whose strengths were the ability to tell a formulaic, escapist story in 'repetitive prose' has to an extent been slowly broken up.[23] An interest in the historical and cultural frameworks of Blyton's work and its links to a range of contemporary discourses has formed the basis of criticism by David Rudd, David Buckingham, Philip Gillett and Fred Inglis—the last arguing that Blyton was an 'agent of culture' whose writing sought to pass on a particular sense of 'Englishness'.[24] The emergence in the 1990s of critics interested in gender and identity politics as they are played out in Blyton's stories added to the number of critical positions. Some, like Catherine Belsey, who in 1998 analysed Daphne Du Maurier's romance *Frenchman's Creek* (1941) alongside *Five on a Treasure Island* (1942), sought to suggest that Blyton was more radical than might be assumed. What messages, Belsey asked, did these texts—judged 'a waste of time' by 'serious' critics—send to their readers? Did the adventures of 'tom-boy', George, offer 'an imaginary alternative to the responsibilities assigned to women'?[25] Others, like Liesel Coetzee, have detected subversive or 'contradictory' meanings hidden within the 'dominant discourse' of gender as Blyton seeks to reveal different possibilities for girls beyond the role of housekeeper.[26] Elsewhere Barbara Wall has highlighted the importance in Blyton's writing of 'the relationship of narrator to narratee' and her narrator's powerful use of the 'single address', that is, speaking directly to children, an innovation that seemed modern at the time.[27] Meanwhile Dennis Hardy has discussed Blyton as a writer of utopian fictions. Kristin Bluemel has suggested another guise for Blyton: as an 'intermodernist' writer, part of a loosely defined collection of authors of the 1920s and 1930s, who were not high modernists; that is to say, they were not T.S. Eliot, Virginia Woolf or Katherine Mansfield. This interesting idea of seeing Blyton as potentially part of a bigger creative group rather than as a lone author and defined by a commitment to 'middle-brow' or 'mass' genres and who have been judged as 'too popular to be good' adds to the number of critical approaches.

What has also been recognised is that despite being all but dismissed from the canon of children's literature, Blyton's output is more impressive and wide-ranging than is often presented—something which Tony Summerfield's four-volume *Enid Blyton: An Illustrated Bibliography* (2002–2005) has made apparent. Blyton's first collection of poems, *Child Whispers*, was published in 1922, followed by *Real Fairies* in 1923, the same year in which she was awarded a weekly column in the magazine, *Teacher's World*, a commission she held until 1945. In 1924 she published *The Zoo Book* and *The Enid Blyton Book of Fairies*, both with George Newnes Ltd. and began a long association with the company. This included, in 1926, the launch of *Sunny Stories for Little Folks*; it was announced as 'edited' by Blyton although she was in fact responsible for writing all its contents in its different manifestations for the next twenty-six years; in 1937, its name was changed to *Enid Blyton's Sunny Stories* before being changed back to *Sunny Stories* in 1942. In 1953 Blyton resigned as editor in order to launch a more ambitious project, *Enid Blyton's Magazine* (–1959). Alongside this, Blyton was in constant demand from other magazines and annuals. To begin with, she concentrated on short stories and poems but in 1927 published her first long adventure story, *The Wonderful Adventure* (1927), which led to more stand-alone books and series, notably: *The Secret Island* and sequels (five titles; 1938–1953), The Famous Five series (twenty-one titles; 1942–1963), The Find-Outers series (fifteen titles; 1943–1961), the '--- of Adventure' series (eight titles; 1944–1955), The Caravan Family (six titles; 1945–1951), The Secret Seven series (fifteen titles; 1949–1963), the Barney mysteries (six titles; 1949–1959) and the fantasy tales, *Adventures of the Wishing Chair* (1937), *The Enchanted Wood* (1939) and *The Magic Faraway Tree* (1943). Many of these texts appeared initially in instalments, sometimes in Blyton's own magazines but also in other periodicals and newspapers and, as Victor Watson notes, they had the effect of helping 'define for the general public what children's books were and how they were to be perceived'.[28] Between 1940 and 1951, Blyton turned her hand to boarding school stories which also became series, including *The Naughtiest Girl in the School* (three titles; 1940–1945), the novels set at St. Clare's (six titles; 1941–1945) and Malory Towers (six titles; 1946–1951). Blyton's readiness to experiment with different sub-genres included circus stories, beginning with *Tales of the Circus* (1927) but more ambitiously with *Mr. Galliano's Circus* (three titles; 1938–1942), and stories of farm life beginning with *The Children of Cherry Tree Farm* (three titles 1940–1943) and followed by *Six Cousins at Mistletoe Farm* (two titles; 1948; 1950). These last sets of novels were also part of a move into so-called 'Family Books' which focused on the challenges and tribulations thrown at apparently ordinary families, including divorce, unemployment and juvenile delinquency, examples of which include *The Family at Red-Roofs* (1945), *House-at-the-Corner* (1947) and *Six Bad Boys* (1951). The celebration of the countryside was a familiar Blyton motif and formed the basis for those works of non-fiction in which the teacherly aspect of Blyton was much to the fore: *Enid Blyton's Nature Lessons* (1929), *Round the Year with Enid Blyton* (1934) and *Hedgerow Tales* (1935), to name but three examples. More prestigiously, she worked with the distinguished editor of *Nature* magazine on thirty-six *Nature Readers* (1945; 1946), and, in 1949, Blyton, now seen as a writer with a sense of social and moral purpose, was invited to re-tell Biblical stories in *The Enid Blyton Stories Old Testament Book* (in fourteen parts), followed by the *New Testament* presented in a similar format; she had already published *The Children's Life of Christ* in 1943. Alongside this work were re-tellings of other 'classic' tales taking in figures who were public property, like Robin Hood, and others who were not (Brer Rabbit and Babar the elephant), as well as assorted stories for much younger children, including those featuring Mary Mouse (1942;

twenty-six books), 'Amelia Jane, the naughty doll' (1939; three books), and the doll, mouse and rabbit, Jose, Click and Bun (1940; five books). Notable later projects included the collaboration in 1949 with the Dutch illustrator Eelco Martinus ten Harmsen van der Beek on the first Noddy book, *Noddy Goes to Toyland*. By the time of Blyton's death, there were 154 titles featuring the same character, who also sparked a mass of Noddy-related products, a television series and a long-running West End pantomime (also written by Blyton), which ran for five successive Christmases from 1954. Alongside this are the hundreds of stories and poems written for magazines and newspapers which were invariably collected into Enid Blyton 'Readers', 'Bedtime' and 'Holiday' books. As 'Mary Pollock', Blyton wrote six books: *The Children of Kidillin* (1940), *Three Boys and a Circus* (1940), *The Secret of Cliff Castle* (1943), *The Adventures of Scamp* (1943), *Smuggler Ben* (1943) *and Mischief at St. Rollo's* (1943). This summary represents the tip of the iceberg; and along-side the titles listed in Summerfield's *Bibliography*, new ones continue to be unearthed. The quality of this writing varies enormously but the diversity and scale of these achievements are, as Summerfield has pointed out, another reminder that Blyton is a figure who cannot be conveniently classified with a single label.

Approaches to Blyton

The impressive range of Blyton's work will hopefully become clear in the following chapters. Before then, it is worth exploring further some of the popular ways in which Blyton has been approached. In terms of Blyton the person, there are the challenges (often expressed by feminist biographers) in making ambitious, successful women—and Blyton falls into this category—'understandable rather than monstrous'.[29] She was not as straightforward a character as is sometimes assumed. As has been seen, Peter Hunt has championed the idea in respect of Blyton's writings of a 'complexity of ideas beneath the apparently simple surface'.[30] There is also the idea (in respect of Blyton the person) of a 'tension between sunny surface and welling undercurrent' as David Rudd puts it. This depends on a reading of Blyton as a woman who assumed different identities, and for much of the time successfully covered up her emotional turmoil and sense of insecurity.[31]

Rudd's comments point to one of the recurrent features of Blyton studies which is the persistence of a tendency to read her stories as having auto-biographical elements. It is an assumption often made of female authors—what Mary Jacobus termed the 'autobiographical fallacy'—whereby women's writing is viewed as closer to personal experience than men's, and their texts are thus viewed as 'dramatic extensions of the female author's consciousness'.[32] The occasional parallels between Blyton's own life and her stories and poems have helped make them intriguing works, both for the inquisitive reader and for critics concerned with the origins of Blyton's creativity. The publication in 1974 of Barbara Stoney's biography of Blyton played a part in this, not least in her summation of Blyton as 'a very insecure, complex and often difficult, childlike woman' whose insecurities began in childhood (Stoney, 191). This analysis helped begin a trend according to which the break-up of her parents' marriage and her father's departure from the family home was a kind of conversion experience for the young Enid who in *The Six Bad Boys* (1951) revisited the negative effects it had on herself and her two younger brothers.[33] It is certainly the case that critics find it very easy to think of Blyton as someone divided, having a sunny public face and a dark, private inner-life. Duncan McLaren, in his idiosyncratic *Looking for Enid* (2007), presents Blyton as an insecure genius in search of a surrogate father (her own having left). Initially, she found such a figure in Hugh Pollock, the book editor whom she married in 1924.[34] Elsewhere, George Greenfield writes in *Enid Blyton* (1998) of how the author 'in her stream of consciousness approach to creative writing' redesigned elements of her own life. In *First Term at Malory Towers* (1946) Blyton takes her second husband, Kenneth Darrell Waters—re-christened 'Rivers' in the book—as the model for the surgeon father to the heroine (Darrell) and her sister, characters who it is suggested were modelled on Blyton's own schoolgirl daughters, Gillian and Imogen. Greenfield takes this as a sign of how far Blyton had, in her own mind, 'obliterated the real father of her children, Hugh Pollock' after having divorced him in 1942.[35] What is also true is that these responses are, in a curious way, a critical throwback to those adopted by Blyton's early reviewers, some of whom often claimed to discern Blyton's 'real' personality in her stories via their 'Nanny narrator'.[36] Coming away from a Blyton book it was possible to feel like one had been 'governessed' as a reviewer for *The Times Literary Supplement* put it (possibly snobbishly) in 1938.[37] For another reviewer, writing in 1954, *The Mystery of the Disappearing Cat* and *The Mystery of Tally-Ho Cottage* both displayed evident traces of their author's 'clear-cut ideas of right and wrong' and also her penchant for 'fun'.[38] In 1974 William Feaver also suggested that Blyton could be spotted in the character of Uncle Quentin from the Famous Five series: 'secretive, insecure and irritable'.[39] Although Blyton always denied her writing was autobiographical or a form of therapy—'I do not write, as I know some authors are forced to do, to express some side of myself repressed in ordinary life' she announced testily—it is added grist to the mill that in her own life Blyton—like many others of her generation—was guarded about her emotions.[40] In reading Blyton's stories, it is perhaps inevitable that critics assume that the narrator is the author or that a particular character is a 'mouthpiece' for Blyton or that a scenic description of a lighthouse or rushing water is a psycho-sexual slip. The limitations of these kinds of readings become evident as the extent and variety of her achievements are recognised more fully.

Rosemary Dinnage's profile of Blyton in *Alone! Alone! Lives of Some Outsider Women* (2004) is an example of this kind of approach in its most extreme form. Dinnage's book with its Blytonesque exclamation marks also takes in Katherine Mansfield, Marie Stopes, Gwen John, Clementine Churchill and Rebecca West (amongst others), and is traditional in categorising these women 'who, especially acutely, felt alone', as strange but modern in their achievements. The harsh verdict on Blyton is that she was 'a tiresome, insecure, Margaret Thatcher-esque queen of kitsch'. But Dinnage's work also exemplifies the way in which cod-psychoanalysis has been used to explain Blyton's 'fixation' with 'pixies, bunnies and teddies' and her 'compulsive fantasizing'. Blyton is dealt with in a chapter alongside a contemporary, Angela Brazil (another prolific writer of school stories). Dinnage tells the reader that '[w]ith the Brazils and Blytons we feel that at some point in childhood they were not *noticed* enough and so there they stuck and blew up their fantasy balloons'. Her father's decision to leave home 'and live in sin' haunted Blyton and it is for this reason that for years she stuck with tales of Toyland and *Sunny Stories* because they 'must have been devitalized substitutes for memories of a real childhood that was both denied and preserved'. For Dinnage, this poses the interesting question: how was it possible for a mentally 'impoverished' woman with a 'dissociated talent' and a 'dull' and 'depleted' personality to sustain her literary career for so long? Blyton's early 1920s columns for children in the magazine *Teacher's World*, in which she talks of playing with conkers and making snowmen, are chosen by Dinnage as places which can be picked apart to show Blyton's difficulties in growing up but, by the same token, of course, her ability—and compulsion—to connect with children (apart from her own). All this was helped by a sense of emptiness, proof that '[w]hen there is such a sense of void at the centre, all the stronger is the stockade that protects it'. Thus Blyton 'successfully stifled any misgivings under an unstoppable flow of words'.

In her reading of Blyton, Dinnage analyses what she takes to be Blyton's 'oddities', including the successful author's famous description (given in interviews) of how she wrote her books whereby she closed her eyes and characters would 'take on movement and life' before her while she then typed out their talk 'like a secretary taking dictation'. Although Dinnage wonders if making fun of Blyton has somehow become 'inevitable', she recognises that the truth is not so simple:

> To become the fantasists they were [Blyton is coupled with the birth control pioneer Marie Stopes here], they had to be isolates; the oddity is that through a different part of their personality they became extremely successful women rather than bag ladies. They could put their self-deluding inner-life into the service of others or, in Blyton's case, into making money.

The other question Dinnage poses is whether Blyton, like other women, 'sacrificed' herself, possibly willingly, either 'to other people's needs' and/or to her 'art'. Was she one of those women who 'built entire fantasy worlds that got them through life but nevertheless estranged them somewhat from ordinary humanity'?[41] For Blyton, life was a struggle and it is—so the argument goes—the resulting work which shows us what was really going on.

Whether Blyton was able (or not) to free herself from her past is a question likely to remain unanswered but Dinnage's approach is, of course, not uncommon. Identifying a trauma in a famous woman's life which led her to act as she did is a popular pastime amongst biographers. So, too, is the tendency to see the female subject as someone's daughter: what father, it is asked, was responsible—directly or indirectly—for this woman's achievements? Another of the striking things about Dinnage's book is, of course, the tendency to make it seem that Blyton's success turned her into a 'monster' (that term again). This is also partly true of other re-considerations of the author, notably Imogen Smallwood's *A Childhood at Green Hedges* (1989), which points to similar negotiations needing to be made around stereotypes of expected behaviours for women. As Iris Marian Young puts it, the notion of home expresses 'a bounded and secure identity....where a person can be herself'.[42] Blyton's home 'self' at Green Hedges, as Smallwood portrays it, is that of a distant, self-centred woman preoccupied with her career and her public image. The effect is to retain admiration for Blyton's work ethic but also make her appear unappealing. It also reiterates the idea that one of the reasons that Blyton is so hard for biographers—and even her daughters—to follow (in the sense of understanding the 'real' woman beneath) is precisely the way she compartmentalised her life. She was a public figure (as the fan mail and interviews testify) but her public self was also a performative one.[43] 'Enid Blyton' the literary character and Enid Blyton the person were not the same. When Smallwood's book was published in 1989 some readers felt betrayed that the author they admired was apparently so nasty—or at least indifferent—to her children. The fact that Blyton was female ensured that the dismay was increased. While many men have behaved equally objectionably to their families—Charles Dickens is a notable example—revelations about their home lives provoke far less lasting damage to their literary reputations. More than Dinnage's essay, Smallwood's reading has proved the most provocative analysis of the relationship between text and author's life and certainly one very different from those which appeared during Blyton's lifetime.

The Story of My Life (1952)

Whilst it is over-simplistic to amalgamate Blyton's life and work and see her texts as examples of involuntary self-revelation, as a critical habit it has proved remarkably difficult to shake off. It is encouraged by the fact that while Blyton left a number of written versions of herself—including diaries and letters—she tended not to give much away. Yet she was certainly aware of stories told about her, complaining in private that most were 'wide of the mark' (Mac, 8 September 1944). It was partly to counter such gossip that in September 1952, aged fifty-five and at the peak of her popularity, she published *The Story of My Life*, an attempt to demonstrate what she always said, namely, that '[w]riting'—and nothing else, 'is my ordinary life – writing for all ages of children, taking a score of different themes as varied as a child's needs'.[44]

Since *The Story of My Life* is referred to at various points in the present book—as well as being the nearest we get to a Blyton autobiography—it is worth paying some attention to it. For example, while the book was the result of Blyton's wariness about her public image it was also, as David Rudd has noted, produced out of unfinished childhood business.[45] Like much of what Blyton produced, it is also a text which appears artless. Partly this is because it was (ostensibly) written for Blyton's young fans and it is to them that Blyton gives innocuous details of 'My Home: Green Hedges', 'Another Home: Old Thatch', 'My Very First Garden', 'Pets I Have Had' and 'My Little Family', explaining that in writing the book 'I have tried to answer all the questions you [her fans] have asked me for the last ten or twelve years' (*SML*, 6). What is striking, however, are the number of gaps and silences. There are no dates provided—an omission justified perhaps on the grounds that they might confuse younger readers. But as David Rudd has noted, throughout Blyton rarely refers to her mother. Nor does she mention her brothers or her first husband, Hugh Pollock—the father of Gillian and Imogen, who *do* figure prominently, the latter shown riding her pony.[46] Pollock's removal from the record obviously had a purpose behind it: he was a painful reminder of a

marriage that had not worked. Removing him also allowed Blyton to camou-
flage the arrival of her second husband Kenneth Darrell Waters, elevating his
importance and leaving readers to assume he was the girls' father (This was a
sleight of hand Blyton also deployed in newspaper interviews throughout the
1950s).

In contrast, Blyton's own father, Thomas, is very much present; the impression given is that he was part of his daughter's home for her entire childhood,
rather than leaving for another woman. Much is made of Thomas's cultural
and intellectual interests and their influence on his daughter's early life.
Thomas gave his young daughter access to his large library ('hundreds of
books…on every subject under the sun' including works on botany [one
of Enid's passions], alongside volumes of poetry and drama, and works
on astronomy [Thomas also had a telescope] [*SML*, 51]). It was in order
to impress her father that the young Enid—a child prodigy—read 'every
book' from her Francophile father's collection. She claims to have taught
herself French, mastering the language by picking up a dictionary and slog-
ging through Alphonse Daudet's comic novel *Tartarin de Tarascon* (1872).
The importance of self-improvement—a favourite Victorian mantra—looms
large.

As part of this theme, Blyton also writes of the impact on her in childhood
of Arthur Mee's *Children's Encyclopaedia*. This was a serial publication tailored
for the aspirational Edwardians which was launched in March 1908 and
appeared at fortnightly intervals (until February 1910). Each issue contained
different sections ('divisions of knowledge') under headings such as 'Literature', 'Plant Life', 'Countries of the World', 'Stories: the great stories of
the world that will be told forever'.[47] 'It gave me my thirst for knowledge',
Blyton writes of the *Encyclopaedia*, recalling that it had the effect of sending
her 'questing through my father's vast array of book-cases for other book-
s…There were many volumes above my head that I found and read because I
*had t*o know more…' (*SML*, 49). It was Arthur Mee who gave the fourteen-
year-old Blyton her first experience of being published when, in 1911, she
won the *Encyclopaedia's* poetry competition for children. 'I could have cried
for joy', she writes, especially when Mee wrote back inviting her to send
other things (*SML*, 70). Undaunted by her family's warnings not to become
big-headed, Blyton then describes how she resolved to carry on writing and
nightly prayed for Mee's success and soul. In a chapter entitled 'Struggling
Along', Blyton celebrates persistence (notably her own) and also raises the
dilemma of personal ambition versus loyalty to one's parents. 'I didn't want to
upset my parents', she writes of her youthful decision to abandon music and
take up teaching, but her father, she explains, 'liked my independence.…He

probably recognised the same things in himself' (*SML*, 76; 77). There is, as had become usual, no mention of her mother's reaction. As a middle-aged woman living in a mock-Tudor mansion with servants, and as a fêted author, Blyton in 1952 was far removed from the angry young girl in Beckenham who poured her emotions into short stories which got rejected. Now she could savour her success and remove as far as possible those, like her mother, who had hindered it.

Several other observations can be made about *The Story of My Life*. The most notable is that Blyton's passionate response to reading and writing is virtually the only aspect of herself about which she was prepared to be open. She disliked much of the material she was given as a child, remembering many of the children's books as 'deadly dull...there were no real children as characters...no lively conversation' and 'it was children I badly wanted to read about...' (*SML*, 48). She wrote enthusiastically of her encounters with Lewis Carroll's *Alice's Adventures in Wonderland* (1865) and *Through the Looking-Glass* (1871) and of her young self being bewitched by the heroine's meetings with talking animals. Despite her status as a child, Alice is also, of course, a reckless adventurer and shapeshifter who strikes out on her own. There was a similar attraction in George MacDonald's fantasy novel *The Princess and the Goblin* (1872), notable for another plucky, eight-year-old heroine, as well as for its secret staircases and malignant gnomes living underground. Blyton also liked Charles Kingsley's *The Water-Babies* (1863) and R.M. Ballantyne's *The Coral Island* (1857) and Anna Sewell's *Black Beauty* (1877), 'which I *loved*, though some of it was too sad' (*SML*, 48). If we allow that childhood reading represents the 'furnishings of a mind', as biographers often maintain, then Blyton's choices can be viewed as significant especially given how her career panned out.[48] They remind us that as with all lives, Blyton's attitudes were influenced by the times in which she grew up. She was a product of its forces and this included her literary encounters. Secondly, and with an eye to posterity, she was seeking in 1952, to align her own career within the classic traditions of children's literature.

All this points to another challenge which frequently present itself to students of life-writing: how far do we accept or reject the subject's *own* presentation of themselves? It is a challenge tied up with the idea that there is a secret self that the subject tries to keep hidden. In *The Story of My Life*, which is the 'official version' of Blyton, one result is that all Blyton's 'lives', past as well as present, become 'her own, controllable construction'.[49] *The Story of My Life* presents Blyton as she wanted to be seen: a professional author and literary figure. Indeed, as Rudd points out, what is particularly striking about the book is that while Blyton seems to be telling her own story, she presents herself almost entirely as a writer.[50] Eight of the nineteen chapters are about how she produces her stories: 'How the Story Comes', 'Which of My Characters are Real' and 'Why I Write So Many Books' (a question many people had begun to ask in 1952). The pages detail her pride in her success, convey a sense of writing as vocation and reveal an appreciation of her audience, something which she was always conscious of needing to express. 'I belong to all of you', she explains, 'I am your storyteller' (*SML*, 6).

Blyton's decision to be selective in what she told the public or to distort events was not exceptional, of course. Few people who write autobiographies put everything in. Moreover, as Liz Stanley notes, there is generally an acceptance that 'the self who writes' does not have a straightforward access to the 'self who is past': 'memory is necessarily limited, and fictive devices are always necessary in producing accounts of ourselves'.[51] It is also the case that in 1950s Britain, this kind of approach to autobiography was not unusual, something which becomes apparent if we compare Blyton's autobiography with those of other celebrities who were also publishing in 1952. In *Tallulah*, the actress Tallulah Bankhead boasted of having 'lived to the hilt' and of having 'soared in the clouds and touched bottom', but this kind of frankness was unusual—and Bankhead was American.[52] Cecil Beaton's *Photobiography* is gossipy but is equally concerned to explain his working methods. *Matty* by A.E. Matthews is a celebration of sixty years of the veteran actor's life but offers little in the way of soul searching. John Masefield, *So Long to Learn. Chapters of an Autobiography*, is typically elegiac and lyrical.[53] Interestingly, the text to which *The Story of My Life* comes closest in tone and in its focus on a career well done is the autobiography of another 1950s icon, Stanley Matthews, whose book, *Feet First Again*, was reprinted in the same year. Matthews writes of his passion for football in much the same tone as Blyton describes her writing: 'Soccer is life to me. If I ever did quit the game I love, I should age suddenly and fade away'.[54] Thus *The Story of My Life* might usefully be seen in terms of these other studies of achievement and service, which are more about how their subjects accomplished their feats rather than how they actually experienced the past. What also makes the text valuable for the purposes of the present study is that, as David Rudd notes, it 'provides some revealing insights into the *persona* "Enid Blyton"' who, by 1952, is able to 'fashion her own ideal family tree pruned and disentangled of unsightly roots'.[55] The book's title with its definitive 'The' hints that this is the only true account, although the use of the word 'story' in a book by someone specialising in make-believe, also looks like further careful positioning.[56]

Blyton in Context

In what other ways might Blyton be approached? As noted earlier, one important development since the 1990s has been that while many critics continue to find a good deal of mileage in psychoanalytic readings, others adopt a socio-cultural or historicist approach. There is the same recognition of the difficulties in pigeonholing Blyton, but it manifests itself in a greater emphasis on Blyton's centrality within the history of twentieth-century ideas and anxieties. This is partly the case with Peter Hunt's aforementioned 'How Not to Read a Children's Book' (1995). Like Rosemary Dinnage, Hunt is interested in the sources of Blyton's creativity and inspiration as a writer but, whereas Dinnage is obsessed with Blyton's works as evidence of personal neuroses, Hunt is interested in reading Blyton's stories 'contextually'. This might mean reading Blyton texts alongside other stories but also thinking about the texts at the moment of their production—for example, the ways in which Blyton's texts respond to some of the anxieties of her time, particularly in the 1940s. This was a period in which war-time restriction was tied up with the physical bombing of Britain's cities, along with over-crowding, rationing, the blackout, poor standards of national health, fears about youth crime and rising divorce rates. In 1945, a purposeful national mood saw Clement Attlee's Labour government sweep to power and embed the welfare state but Britain's loss of Empire, the emergence of the Cold War and continued food and fuel shortages led to the sense that exhausted post-war Britain was on the verge of becoming 'destitute', as David Childs puts it.[57] Read alongside these contexts, the bicycles, picnics, country lanes, unlimited food and lemonade, and the middle-class children, 'innocently free and empowered' who emerge victorious against kidnappers, robbers and smugglers begin to take on new dimensions. As Hunt notes, Blyton's works of the 1940s, specifically, though not exclusively the Famous Five series, can be viewed '[i]n the context of post-Second World War literature' and that period's 'ruralist, pacifist, nostalgic trends', including the aching desire for 'a lost, golden, idyllic world'.[58] With society in flux, it is hardly surprising that readers—whether they were at home or had been evacuated—embraced Blyton's fictional world so readily.

This idea that Blyton's writings can be read as responses to specific anxieties faced in Britain in the middle part of the twentieth century stems from the idea that literary texts should be understood within history. Although Blyton's writings are aimed primarily at children—and are most obviously concerned with what Peter Hollindale terms 'childness' namely 'the quality of being a child'—any texts can be examined in this way.[59] The troubled and transitional states of war-time and post-war society within which Blyton writes, together with her own interest in education, instruction, nationhood and social behaviour, offer potential for this kind of approach. Some of Blyton's works—*The Caravan Family* (1945) and *The Six Bad Boys* (1951) being notable examples—were very obviously prompted by specific challenges (the housing shortage; the rise of juvenile 'delinquency') seen from the point of view of children. The same claim has also been made of the Noddy stories launched in 1949, wherein Blyton's deployment of golliwogs has been held up as embodying her racist anxieties about 'coloured immigration', as it was termed in the 1950s and 1960s, and the accompanying feeling that Britain was experiencing 'a colour problem'.[60] In 1965 there was also a furore surrounding Blyton's *The Little Black Doll*. This was a tale in which the life of the title character ('Sambo') improves immeasurably when the rain washes him white. The idea that Blyton was 'an aggravator of the colour question' was seized on by sections of the press. Blyton was quoted in *The Daily Mail*, saying that she thought the fuss made about golliwogs 'ridiculous….I have golliwogs myself, I adore them. it's fantastic to say any child could have a colour prejudice about a doll - or be made colour-conscious by this kind of story'.[61] 'I have' she explained, 'run a school for children myself so I can say for a certainty that this book would have no adverse effect on young children'.[62] Blyton's racism has been discussed extensively by critics such as Bob Dixon and David Rudd and it is one reason why her reputation has suffered.[63] One way of approaching this issue might be to follow Ania Loomba's recommendation about literary representations of race which is 'to go beyond identifying "positive" or "negative" images' and instead view Blyton's texts as 'indices of cultural complexities' or as entry points into the assumptions of the culture. What cultural assumptions do they make? How have they come about? To what extent does the text accept (or not) those assumptions?[64]

The same approach can be applied to other discursive contexts. For example, as we shall see in Chapter 9, Blyton often draws attention to her female characters' positions within a society which has very definite expectations as to how they should develop as individuals. There are links here to the urgency with which commentators of the 1940s and 1950s debated the figure of the middle-class woman and the duties and expectations placed on her—and her daughters. When in 1918 the right to vote was awarded to women over thirty, it coincided with what Elizabeth Maslen describes as 'the growing aspirations of girls to go beyond domesticity'.[65] Blyton's seemingly unresolved stance on this (despite her own career) makes her an interesting subject for analysis. To this can be added other important critical frameworks for thinking about the representation of women such as that offered by Toril Moi in *Sexual/Textual Politics* where she notes society's habit of 'imposing certain social standards of femininity on all biological women, in order precisely to make us believe that the chosen standards for "femininity" are natural, that a woman who refuses to confirm can be labelled both unfeminine and unnatural'.[66] A question to be asked is whether Blyton's books are 'instructional' in this way, offering the reader examples by which she—or he—should behave. In some instances, the answer is clearly 'yes': *The Family at Red-Roofs* (1945) is a prime example of this. But does Blyton always perpetuate some of the stereotypes of women dominant in the early-mid-twentieth century or does she in fact undermine them?

Thus, as well as focusing on Blyton the professional writer, what the present study is interested in is the extent to which Blyton's works, like other texts written in the same period, can be said to have been shaped by the social structures and sources of their times. All Blyton's stories are part of Britain's historical record as it played out in the middle of the twentieth century.

Before turning in the following chapter to Blyton's early attempts in the 1920s to carve out a literary career, it is worth considering some final points about the critical responses to her. Firstly, it is apparent from the examples of criticism and biography discussed in this chapter and the previous chapter that several constructions of Blyton have emerged. Some of these were the result of Blyton's attempts to control her own image. Secondly, this means, of course, that the directions in which discussions of Blyton tend to go are numerous. There is still a tendency for some critics to focus on the biographical or psychoanalytic potential of the texts and their author's 'arrested' development. Yet others have suggested ways of moving the discussion forward to offer a more expansive version of Blyton. This is afforded by being more alert to her involvement in the creation of social discourse and to contemporary anxieties to which Blyton's writings sometimes respond and occasionally offer solutions. Subsequent chapters will consider some of these in greater detail, especially as they relate to issues of gender, criminality and nationhood. However, what this book is also interested in are the literary and economic milieus in which Blyton's writings were produced—that is the literary fields of the 1920s, and later the 1930s, 1940s and 1950s— as well as the sub-genres (adventure novels, school stories, animal stories, nursery poetry) within which she worked. What will become apparent is that whilst for Blyton writing was a vocation it was also a career. Her letters and diaries reveal that her writing was a business and what she published (and how) was governed by these facts—and also by her desire to do 'better' than contemporaries like A.A. Milne, Rose Fyleman and Arthur Ransome.

Notes

1. David Malbert, 'Enid Blyton', *Illustrated* (27 December 1952), 33.
2. Peter Hawley, 'Twenty Books a Year', *The Reading Lamp* (1 July 1947), 13.
3. John Piper, 'Over My Counter', *W.H. Smith's Trade Circular* (22 September 1951), 23.
4. Unsigned Article, 'Working—Mother Plan "Disastrous for Nation"—Authoress', *Coventry Evening Telegraph* (23 November 1949), 16.
5. David Holloway, 'Enid Blyton: A Less Than Sunny Story', *The Daily Telegraph* (3 October 1974), 10.
6. For a fuller discussion of this see, for example, Sheila Ray, *The Blyton Phenomenon* (London: Deutsch, 1983); David Buckingham, 'The Blyton Enigma: Changing Critical Perspectives on Children's Popular Culture'. https://davidbuckingham.net/growing-up-modern/the-blyton-enigma-cha nging-critical-perspectives-on-childrens-popular-culture/. Accessed 28 March 2021.
7. Colin Welch, 'Dear Little Noddy: A Parent's Lament', *Encounter* (January 1958), 18–22 (22).
8. The idea that a diet of Blyton did little to help children develop their reading—and even held them back—became a popular complaint. '[S]he and others think that children are taxed too much if they are confronted by so much as a polysyllable', wrote Margery Fisher in her important book, *Intent Upon Reading: A Critical Appraisal of Modern Fiction for Children* (Leicester: Brockhampton Press, 1961), 28.
9. Unsigned Article, 'City Turns Out Noddy and Friends', *Daily Mirror* (6 February 1964), 16.
10. Steve Young, 'Roving Commission: A Young Man Interviews Women of Influence', *The Woman's Mirror* (26 September 1964), 25; 26.
11. 'Knight Book Minutes', London Metropolitan Archives/Hodder and Stoughton Archives, M 16,394.
12. Hans Robert Jauss, *Toward an Aesthetic of Reception* (Minnesota: University of Minnesota Press, 1982), 27.
13. Walter Allen, 'A London Father Tells of His Children's Literary Tastes', *The New York Times* (13 November 1960), CBS 30.
14. Robert Leeson, *Reading and Righting: The Past, Present and Future of Fiction for the Young* (London: Collins, 1985), 123.
15. Jane Gallop, *The Daughter's Seduction* (New York: Cornell University Press, 1982), 77–8.
16. Denis Hart, 'Sorcerer's Apprentice', *The Guardian* (9 April 1962), 14.
17. Quoted in Dennis Judd, *Alison Uttley: The Life of a Country Child* (London: Michael Joseph, 1986), 169.
18. Geoffrey Trease, *Laughter at the Door: A Continued Biography* (London: Macmillan, 1974), 158.

19. Quoted in Maureen Duffy, *A Thousand Conspicuous Chances: A History of the Methuen List, 1889–1989* (London: Methuen, 1989), 90.

20. M.S. Woods, 'The Uses of Enid Blyton', *New Society* 29 (19 September 1974), 731–3.

21. Walter Allen, 'A London Father Tells of His Children's Literary Tastes', CBS30.

22. Peter Hunt, 'How Not to Read a Children's Book', *Children's Literature in Education* 26 (1995), 231–40 (233; 238; 238).

23. Nicholas Tucker, 'Introduction', in *Enid Blyton. A Celebration and Re-Appraisal: NCRCL Papers 2*, eds. Nicholas Tucker and Kimberley Reynolds (London: National Centre for Research in Children's Literature, 1997), vii–xiv (xii).

24. Fred Inglis, 'Enid Blyton, Malcolm Saville and the Good Society', in *Enid Blyton: A Celebration and Reappraisal*, 127–33 (133).

25. Catherine Belsey, 'Popular Fiction and the Feminine Masquerade', *European Journal of English Studies* 2:3 (1998), 343–58 (344–5).

26. Liesel Coetzee, 'Empowering Girls? The Portrayal of Anne and George in Enid Blyton's Famous Five series', *English Academy Review*, 28:1 (2011), 85–98.

27. Barbara Wall, *The Dilemma of Children's Fiction*, 40; 42, quoted in David Rudd, 'The Development of Children's Literature', in *The Routledge Companion to Children's Literature*, ed. David Rudd (London: Routledge, 2010), 1–13 (9).

28. Victor Watson, *Reading Series Fiction* (London: Routledge, 2000), 85; 100.

29. Linda Wagner Martin, *Telling Women's Lives: The New Biography* (New Brunswick: Rutgers, 1994), 18.

30. Philip Hunt, *Children's Literature* (Oxford: Blackwell, 2001), 38.

31. David Rudd, *Enid Blyton and the Mystery of Children's Literature* (Basingstoke: Macmillan, 2000), 1.

32. Mary Jacobus, 'Review of *The Madwoman in the Attic*', *Signs* 6:3 (1981), in *Essays on Life Writing: From Genre to Critical Practice*, ed. Marlene Kadar (Toronto: University of Toronto Press, 1992), 165.

33. This is also the line taken by Hugh Cragoe, 'Enid Blyton: The Greatest Adventure of Her Life', in *Utter Silence: Voicing the Unspeakable*, eds. Alice Mills and Jeremy Smith (New York: Peter Lang, 2001), 157–82. According to Cragoe, 'the most fruitfu level of analysis for Blyton's work is a psychological one, in terms of her (and our) emotional development in early childhood' (158).

34. Duncan McLaren, *Looking for Enid: The Mysterious and Inventive Life of Enid Blyton* (London: Granta, 2008), 234.

35. George Greenfield, *Enid Blyton* (Stroud: Sutton, 1998), 77.

36. Victor Watson, *Reading Series Fiction*, 85; 100.

37. Unsigned Article, 'Christmas Books', *The Times Literary Supplement* (10 December 1938), 789.

38. Unsigned Article, 'For the Children', *The Morpeth Herald* (13 August 1954), 1.

39. William Feaver, 'Naughtiest Girl in the Library', *The Listener* 92 (29 September 1974), 415.

40. Enid Blyton, 'Writing for Children', *The New Statesman* (9 May 1959), 649–50 (649).

41. Rosemary Dinnage, *Alone! Alone! Lives of Some Outsider Women* (New York: New York Review of Book, 2004), xv, 165, 169, 277, 278.

42. Iris Marian Young, *Intersecting Voices: Dilemmas of Gender, Political Philosophy and Policy* (Princeton: Princeton University Press, 1997), 157.

43. Linda Wagner Martin, *Telling Women's Lives*, 7.

44. Enid Blyton, 'Writing for Children', *The New Statesman* (9 May 1959), 649–50.

45. David Rudd, 'Froebel Teacher to English Disney: The Phenomenal Success of Enid Blyton', in *Popular Children's Literature in Britain*, eds. Julia Briggs, Dennis Butts, and M.O. Grenby (Aldershot: Ashgate, 2008), 251–69.

46. David Rudd, *Enid Blyton and the Mystery of Children's Literature*, 27; 29.

47. Kristen Thornton, 'Arthur Mee's, 'Children's Encyclopaedia'. https://www.deakin.edu.au/library/special-collections/collections/mee-encyclopaedia. Accessed 10 March 2021.

48. Richard Oram, 'Writers' Libraries', in *Collecting, Curating and Researching Writer's Libraries*, eds. Richard W. Oram and Joseph Nicholson (Lanham: Rowman & Littlefield, 2014), 1–28 (3; 2). On Blyton's childhood reading see also: Robert Houghton, 'The Railway Children and The Family at Red-Roofs', *The Enid Blyton Society Journal* 54 (Summer 2014), 4–10; Anita Bensoussane, 'Enid Blyton and Edith Nesbit', *The Enid Blyton Society Journal* 66 (Summer 2018), 50–66.

49. David Rudd, 'Froebel Teacher to English Disney', 251–69.

50. David Rudd, *Enid Blyton and the Mystery of Children's Literature*, 26–7.

51. Liz Stanley, *The Auto/biographical I: The Theory and Practice of Feminist Autobiography* (Manchester: Manchester University Press, 1992), 62.

52. Tallulah Bankhead, *Tallulah* (London: Victor Gollancz, 1952), 279.

53. Cecil Beaton, *Photobiography* (London: Odhams Press, 1951); A.E. Matthews, *Matty* (London: Hutchinson, 1952); John Masefield, *So Long to Learn: Chapters of an Autobiography* (London: Heinemann, 1952).

54. Stanley Matthews, *Feet First Again* (1948; London: Nicholas Key, 1952), 136.

55. David Rudd, *Enid Blyton and the Mystery of Children's Literature*, 29–30.

56. Ibid.

57. David Childs, *Britain Since 1945: A Political History* (London: Methuen 1979), 23.

58. Peter, Hunt, 'How Not to Read a Children's Book', 237, 238.

59. Quoted in David Rudd, 'The Development of Children's Literature', 11.

60. Peter Hennessy, *Having It So Good: Britain in the Fifties* (2006; London Penguin 2007), 223.

61. Unsigned Article, '"I Love My Golly" Says Enid Blyton', *Daily Mail* (3 December 1965), 3.

62. Unsigned Article, 'By Golly! Children's Tale Starts a Fuss', *The Birmingham Daily Post* (29 January 1966), 32.

63. See for example, Bob Dixon, 'The Nice, the Naughty and the Nasty: The Tiny World of Enid Blyton', *Child Literature in Education* 5 (1974), 43–61. See also David Rudd, 'Gollywog: Genealogy of a Non-PC Icon', *Studies in Children's Literature, 1500–2000*, eds. C. Keenan and Mary Shine Thompson (Dublin: Four Courts, 2004), 70–7.

64. Ania Loomba, *Shakespeare, Race and Colonialism* (Oxford: Oxford University Press, 2002), 73.

65. Elizabeth Maslen, *Political and Social Issues in British Women's Fiction, 1928–1968* (Basingstoke: Palgrave, 2001), 35.

66. Toril Moi, *Sexual/Textual Politics: Feminist Literary Theory* (London: Methuen, 1985), 65.

Bibliography

Bankhead, Tallulah. 1952. *Tallulah*. London: Victor Gollancz.

Beaton, Cecil. 1952. *Photobiography*. London: Odhams Press.

Belsey, Catherine. 1998. 'Popular Fiction and the Feminine Masquerade'. *European Journal of English Studies* 2(3): 343–358.

Bensoussane, Anita. 2018. 'Enid Blyton and Edith Nesbit'. *The Enid Blyton Society Journal* 66(Summer): 50–66.

Bluemel, Kristen, ed. 2009. *Intermodernism: Literary Culture in Mid-Twentieth Century Britain*. Edinburgh: Edinburgh University Press.

Buckingham, David. 'The Blyton Enigma: Changing Critical Perspectives on Children's Popular Culture'. https://davidbuckingham.net/growing-up-modern/the-blyton-enigma-changing-critical-perspectives-on-childrens-popular-culture/. Accessed 28 March 2021.

Childs, David. 1979. *Britain Since 1945: A Political History*. London: Methuen.

Coetzee, Liesel. 2011. 'Empowering girls? The Portrayal of Anne and George in Enid Blyton's Famous Five Series'. *English Academy Review* 28(1): 85–98.

Cragoe, Hugh. 2001. 'Enid Blyton: The Greatest Adventure of Her Life'. In *Utter Silence: Voicing the Unspeakable*, edited by Alice Mills and Jeremy Smith, 157–82. New York: Peter Lang.

Dinnage, Rosemary. 2004. *Alone! Alone! Lives of Some Outsider Women*. New York: New York Review of Books.

Dixon, Bob. 1974. 'The Nice, the Naughty and the Nasty: The Tiny World of Enid Blyton'. *Children's Literature in Education* 5(3): 43–61.

Duffy, Maureen. 1989. *A Thousand Conspicuous Chances: A History of the Methuen List, 1889–1989*. London: Methuen.

Fisher, Margery. 1961. *Intent Upon Reading: A Critical Appraisal of Modern Fiction for Children*. Leicester: Brockhampton Press.

Gallop, Jane. 1982. *The Daughter's Seduction*. Basingstoke: Macmillan.

Greenfield, George. 1998. *Enid Blyton*. Stroud: Sutton.

Hardy, Dennis. 2000. *Utopian England: Community Experiments 1900–1945*. London: Routledge.

Hennessy, Peter. 2007. *Having It So Good: Britain in the Fifties*. London: Penguin.

Houghton, Robert. 2014. 'The Railway Children and the Family at Red-Roofs'. *Enid Blyton Society Journal* 54 (Summer): 4–10.

Hunt, Peter. 1995. 'How Not to Read a Children's Book'. *Children's Literature in Education* 26: 231–240.

———. 2001. *Children's Literature*. Oxford: Blackwell.

Jauss, Hans Robert. 1982. *Toward an Aesthetic of Reception*. Minnesota: University of Minnesota Press.

Judd, Dennis. 1986. *Alison Uttley: The Life of a Country Child*. London: Michael Joseph.

Kadar, Marlene, ed. 1992. *Essays on Life Writing: From Genre to Critical Practice*. Toronto: University of Toronto Press.

Leeson, Robert. 1985. *Reading and Righting: The Past, Present and Future of Fiction for the Young*. London: Collins.

Loomba, Ania. 2002. *Shakespeare, Race and Colonialism*. Oxford: Oxford University Press.

Masefield, John. 1952. *So Long to Learn: Chapters of an Autobiography*. London: Heinemann.

Maslen, Elizabeth. 2001. *Political and Social Issues in British Women's Fiction, 1928–1968*. Basingstoke: Palgrave.

Matthews, A.E. 1952. *Matty*. London Hutchinson.

Matthews, Stanley. 1952. *Feet First Again*. London: Nicholas Key.

McLaren, Duncan. 2008. *Looking for Enid: The Mysterious and Inventive Life of Enid Blyton*. London: Grant.

Moi, Toril. 1985. *Sexual/Textual Politics: Feminist Literary Theory*. London: Methuen.

Oram, Richard. 2014. 'Writers' Libraries'. In *Collecting, Curating and Researching Writer's Libraries*, edited by Richard W. Oram and Joseph Nicholson, 1–28. Lanham: Rowman and Littlefield.

Ray, Sheila. 1983. *The Blyton Phenomenon*. London: Deutsch.

Rudd, David. 2001. *Enid Blyton and the Mystery of Children's Literature*. London: Palgrave.

———. 2004. 'Gollywog: Genealogy of a Non-PC Icon'. In *Studies in Children's Literature, 1500–2000*, edited by C. Keenan and Mary Shine Thompson, 70–7. Dublin: Four Courts.

———. 2008. 'Froebel Teacher to English Disney: The Phenomenal Success of Enid Blyton'. In *Popular Children's Literature in Britain*, edited by Julia Briggs, Dennis Butts, and M.O. Grenby, 251–69. Aldershot: Ashgate.

————. 2010. 'The Development of Children's Literature'. In *The Routledge Companion to Children's Literature*, edited by David Rudd, 1–13. London: Routledge.

Scholes, Robert. 1985. *Textual Power: Literary Theory and the Teaching of English*. London: Yale University Press.

Stanley, Liz. 1992. *The Auto/biographical I: The Theory and Practice of Feminist Autobiography*. Manchester: Manchester University Press.

Thornton, Kristen. 'Arthur Mee's "Children's Encyclopaedia"'. https://www.dea kin.edu.au/library/special-collections/collections/mee-encyclopaedia. Accessed 10 March 2021.

Trease, Geoffrey. 1974. *Laughter at the Door: A Continued Biography*. London: Macmillan.

Tucker, Nicholas, and Kimberley Reynolds, eds. 1997. *Enid Blyton. A Celebration and Re-Appraisal: NCRCL Papers 2*. London: National Centre for Research in Children's Literature.

Wagner Martin, Linda. 1994. *Telling Women's Lives: The New Biography*. New Brunswick: Rutgers.

Watson, Victor. 2000. *Reading Series Fiction*. London: Routledge.

Welch, Colin. 1958. 'Dear Little Noddy: A Parent's Lament'. *Encounter* (January): 18–22.

Woods, M.S. 1974. 'The Uses of Enid Blyton'. *New Society* 29 (19 September): 731–3.

Young, Iris Marian. 1997. *Intersecting Voices: Dilemmas of Gender, Political Philosophy and Policy*. Princeton: Princeton University Press.

3

Blyton's Early Career

'I always wanted to write for children, but it never occurred to me as a child that I would ever be famous'.[1] So began one of Blyton's familiar anecdotes recorded towards the end of her life in a 1963 BBC radio interview. It expressed the good luck that Blyton—and some critics—felt had accompanied her career but conveyed, too, the idea of someone who, more than any other twentieth-century writer, had always known her own mind—and her audience's—someone who was quick to learn, and who knew what children wanted. But Blyton's success was not an accident. She began to make her way as an author in the literary field of the 1920s and in this chapter I consider some of the different ways of constructing and explaining her early career and the professional, personal and cultural contexts in which it took shape—the first two of these necessarily involve thinking about the role of Blyton's husband, Hugh Pollock, whom she met in 1923. I will also examine some of the most significant texts that she published at this time. These works—*Child Whispers* (1922), *Real Fairies* (1923), the 'From My Window' columns in the magazine *Teacher's World* (1923–1927) and her work for *Sunny Stories* (1926)—can be taken as examples of Blyton's early ability to exploit trends that were popular and mainstream (she was very good at this). They also demonstrate something of her versatility and her ability to work within different genres. *Child Whispers* and *Real Fairies* are books of 'nursery poetry' and celebrations of childhood innocence. The 'From My Window' columns are examples of what magazines termed 'middle articles'. They show Blyton adopting a distinctive form of personal journalism directed at both

© The Author(s), under exclusive license to Springer Nature
Switzerland AG 2021
A. Maunder, *Enid Blyton*, Literary Lives,
https://doi.org/10.1007/978-3-030-76332-9_3

children and 'grown-ups'. All these writings can be seen as apprenticeship works written when Blyton was trying to secure a role for herself in the midst of the opportunities and constraints of 1920s publishing markets. As a character puts it in Blyton's *House-at-the-Corner* (1947): "'You have to make your own name, you know, and you can only do that by trying again and again, finding out what you can write best, what people want to read, and so on'" (*HC*, 79).

* * *

The historical and cultural factors shaping the emergence of Blyton as a professional writer include changes to the early-twentieth-century publishing industry, increased opportunities for women, the rise of celebrity culture, together with new ideas relating to children and the cult of the child. To take the first of these, when Blyton began to establish herself as a writer in the early 1920s, the legacy of the First World War (1914–1918) loomed large. Of the 5.2 million men who served in the army, 2.3 million had been killed or wounded.[2] (Blyton's family was unusual in seeming to escape unscathed.) The British economy was debt-ridden. Returning soldiers faced unemployment and uncertainty. However, the publishing industry was booming. It expanded rapidly out of the restrictions of the War back into mass production where it sought to fill the demands of a population for whom reading had become an important part of their leisure. The expansion of education in Victorian Britain had already made itself felt before 1914, creating a larger literate public. As the 1920s progressed H.A.L Fisher's Education Act (1918), which raised the school leaving age to fourteen, took effect. In 1932 Q. D. Leavis reported in her classic study *Fiction and the Reading Public* how '[i]n twentieth-century England not only everyone can read, but it is safe to add that everyone does read'.[3]

Something of the scale of the expansion which the publishing industry underwent is evident in statistics relating to the book trade, indicating that the number of books published increased every year between 1919 and 1937.[4] For those readers who could not afford to buy books, there was, in the wake of the Public Libraries Act (1919), increased free library provision with a corresponding increase in books (from 15 million in 1924 to 42 million in 1949).[5] The publishing world was also growing more interested in books for children and in 1921 *The Times* reported a massive expansion rivalling that of adults, and a new 'rich array of children's books now pouring…from our own presses'.[6] There was a corresponding increase in the sales of daily newspapers: from 3.1 million copies a day in 1918 to 4.7 million in 1926 to 10.6 million in 1938.[7] This went hand in hand with the start of a 'magazine boom', as

Q.D. Leavis termed it.[8] This was partly the result of publishers' efforts to reshape existing magazines (of which there were already a large number) and also their decisions to create new ones in the search for mass circulation and the attention of the 'common man'—or woman.[9]

This last point is significant for although in literary terms the 1920s are often associated with Modernism—T.S. Eliot's famously 'difficult' poem, *The Wasteland*, published in 1922, or James Joyce's even trickier *Ulysses*, published in Paris in the same year—there was not (as is often supposed) a sprint towards 'high' art. As D.J. Taylor points out, to be 'fond of reading' was more likely to mean a liking for romantic fiction, detective and spy stories, comic stories, or 'shockers' (or, indeed, poems about fairies, one of the topics of Blyton's *Child Whispers*, also published in 1922).[10] It was partly for this reason that Q.D. Leavis associated the decade not with Modernism and its ambitious new ways of writing, but with a general dumbing down of culture as writers happily admitted tailoring their works to meet the tastes and reading levels of a mass readership.

This description of developments in the publishing industry is necessarily brief but the details are significant in thinking about the contexts which allowed Blyton to become a professional writer. A corollary to the country's 'reading habit' was, as Nicola Humble notes, 'a clear sense' amongst writers and those who wanted to write that a 'lucrative market had opened up'.[11] Many publishing houses were expanding and it seemed a good time to be an author. One expression of this came in December 1922 when a writer signing himself 'R.A.B.' complained to *The New Statesman* that too many 'women who ought never to have been allowed to put pen to paper…and who in any period of English literary history would…have found no publisher' were now finding their way into print.[12] He—we can assume it was a 'he'—was responding to a boast made the previous week by Rebecca West in which she had noted 'a notable preponderance of the names of women' in the literary pages of newspapers, 'all writers of a certain horsepower'. Virginia Woolf, Katherine Mansfield, Jean Rhys were on West's list, but so, too, were Clemence Dane, Sheila Kaye-Smith, Eleanor Farjeon, E.M. Delafield, F. Tennyson Jesse and Rose Macaulay. This new 'mass' of female writers was taken by West to be 'one of the consequences of the war'; the loss of so many men under thirty-five which had left 'fiction…at the present moment largely in women's hands'.[13]

No one registered it but Blyton, then aged twenty-five and a governess working in Surbiton, was part of this 'class of '22'. Her *Child Whispers* had been published in June of that year. She was, moreover, part of a generation of young women experiencing a different world from that of their mothers.

These were young women who wanted to write professionally and also valued their 'independence' (Blyton's description of herself [*SML*, 72]). Although the Sex Discrimination (Removal) Act of 1919 had opened doors to the professions (law, medicine, engineering), most women who needed to work remained stuck in familiar grooves: teachers, shop assistants, clerks, waitresses, factory workers. Authorship seemed to be one occupation where women could move freely and compete on 'terms of greater equality…than in other important professions'. This, at least, was the message of the manual *Careers for Girls* (1928), another voice espousing the idea that the War had changed things, although would-be authors were counselled that it was important to choose one's subject matter carefully: 'the reading public want a *story*, and a real human drama will never fail to interest'. The guide warned that there was little to be gained by going in for 'the morbid, unhealthy psychological fiction which has flooded the world since the war'. 'A taste for rummaging dustbins and the unsavoury scrapheaps of life is not a sigh of strength'.[14] This, of course, would never be Blyton's style.

Another changing aspect of the publishing industry relevant to Blyton is the one outlined by Christopher Hilliard in his important book *To Exercise Our Talents: The Democratization of Writing in Britain* (2006), in which he analyses the tendency in the 1920s amongst newspapers and magazines— points of entry for aspiring writers—to encourage the idea that anyone—even those who were not from advantaged backgrounds or who, like Blyton, were born above a shop in East Dulwich—could be trained to become an author and make money from it.[15] 'It is the day of opportunities' announced *John o'London's Weekly* on 12 April 1919. 'The gates of the new world have been thrown wide open to the young and ambitious. Our old-time class prejudice, hallowed privileges, and conceits of every kind have been swept away in the great upheaval'.[16] Magazines were full of adverts for writing schools and correspondence courses which explained that 'Everyone Can Write'.[17] Students were promised instruction from 'tutors' who were well-known literary personalities: the 'ABC Writers Course' boasted that Stacy Aumonier, Gilbert Frankau, 'Sapper' (Herman Cyril McNeile) and Henry de Vere Stacpoole were part of its staff. There were also articles such as 'How I Write: Secrets of Authorship. By Famous Novelists' in which well-established writers such as John Galsworthy and Arnold Bennett offered tips, and others in which successful graduates of writing schools—or people pretending to be—explained that it was possible not simply to get published but just as crucially, to make a living out of it.[18] In 'My Literary Career', a former domestic servant, Jessie Stephen, explained that having caught 'scribbling fever' she had completed a course and had since written 'many stories and novelettes', all of which had been published.[19] Another 'graduate', K.P. Hunt, told readers that having started writing for *Tit-Bits*, he had now graduated to being paid up to £10 per article and that freelance work could bring in up to £1500 a year.[20] Not everyone was convinced. 'The thing is becoming a cult', noted *Punch* in 1924 in response to all these writerly aspirations on the part of suburban clerks, housewives and teachers busily churning out 'light literature' for profit.[21] The publisher Michael Joseph thought that many of those who formed part of this 'invading army' of authors were being misled or were writing for the wrong motives; that is to say, they wanted fame, money and celebrity (preferably all three) and sought to 'gratify their vanity by publication' by catering to 'the needs of the mutton-headed public'. He issued a stark warning: few authors could hope to earn more than £25 a year from writing.[22] How successful the majority of the new writers were is unclear but it is evident that all the changes—new readers, new authors, new outlets—combined to give an experience of publishing that was if not completely brand new, felt like it was, both in its scale, its capacity to amalgamate so many different forms of writing and the options it offered people who were not university graduates or socialites with connections. As Hilliard points out, another way of looking at the phenomenon, and perhaps one reason why it was disapproved of by 'elites', is to see it as part of a wider 'democratization of culture' that took place after the First World War and manifested itself most obviously in efforts to find working-class authors. There were, as Hilliard notes, opportunities whereby 'respectable, unostentatious people [young women like Blyton] could pursue creative ambitions, and fashion themselves as creative, special, people, without renouncing their normal lives'.[23]

As a teenager, Blyton found solace by escaping into the tales of derring-do and girl-meet-boy stories offered by the popular magazines of the time including *The Strand, The Windsor Magazine* or *Pearson's*. The idea that she, too, might write for them (and get paid for it) was exciting. Everyone knew that magazine editors had launched some writers on extremely successful careers, including people who at best were only modestly talented: Florence Barclay, Jessie Pope and Berta Ruck had all become household names. Moreover, as an avid reader of *Nash's and Pall Mall Magazine*, the young Blyton who, as she would later explain, already saw herself as a storyteller, would doubtless have seen this announcement which appeared in its pages in 1915:

NEVER was there such a demand [for writers]....In the last few weeks reputations have been made almost in a day; young writers have acquired fame and fortune because they know what to write, how to write it, and where to sell it when written....[T]he public wants...to read the little human incidents, the little side-lights, the comedies, as well as the tragedies of this terrific epoch.

The writer then made a call to those readers who were also potential writers, to join the modern democracy of letters:

> War is the mightiest stimulus. Old organizations are shaken up; dull, tiresome writers give place to newcomers and it is in this general shake-up and readjustment that occur splendid opportunities. Readers don't care whether you come from Oxford or Girton - whether you use split infinitives or bay-rhum; but they care very much that you have something to say and say it interestingly.
>
> The men and women who matter in this new writing-for-the-people business are just ordinary folk, gifted with common sense and initiative.[24]

What was set out for Blyton in 1915, busily writing in her box-room bedroom in 'dull' Beckenham was a vision of the ways in which a modern, democratised and commercialised literary market might work not only in war-time but afterwards. This rallying cry for fresh voices clearly struck a chord and it was to *Nash's*, while undertaking her teacher-training course, that, aged twenty, Blyton submitted some poems, two of which the magazine published in 1917: 'Have You--?' (March) and 'My Summer Prayer' (August) and a third, 'Do You--?' in September 1918. In 'Do You--?', Blyton, as she liked to do, presented nature through the lens of the changing seasons: 'the cuckoos calling thro' the quivering noon-tide air' and the 'sleepy summer clouds' (445). Although Blyton is not usually thought of as a war poet, her verses, like many others written during the years 1914–1918, convey an image of an England of green fields and rolling hills—something worth fighting for.

After qualifying as a teacher, the young Blyton secured a post at Bickley Park School in Bromley where she stayed until 1920, when she took up a post as governess to the Thompson family in Surbiton, where she stayed until 1924. Alongside this, Blyton attempted to follow some of the other recommended new routes to establishing a writing career. She purchased writing manuals (popular titles included George Magnus's *How to Write Saleable Fiction* (fifteen editions between 1904 and 1925) and Michael Joseph's *Short Story Writing for Profit* [1922]). In 1920 she joined a creative writing group, the Quill Club (a 'co-operative organization' for 'the unfledged author and literary student') which published her poem 'Sonnet' in their anthology *Singers in the Crowd* (1921).[25] As a collection put together by ambitious students, *Singers in the Crowd* (its title perhaps indicates the sheer number of aspirant writers looking for a 'break') is a very disparate one, an example of how at any moment in literary history a range of influences are likely to be circulating. Some of those publishing in the volume were taken by the avant-garde styles of the times, notably the Imagist and Modernist movements and Ezra Pound with his call to 'make it new!'[26] But for other contributors, Blyton included, these changes were not of much interest. Like her earlier contributions to *Nash's*, Blyton's poem sticks to traditional ground and conveys the poet's 'exultance' at wandering through the English countryside.[27] Blyton had a belief—shared by many at the time—in the value of poetry that was accessible—and therefore saleable. As Hilliard notes, poetry was popularly seen as an outlet for powerful (personal) emotion rather than for ('pretentious') technical display, a genre 'animated by the spirit' and 'a way of honouring or consecrating feelings'.[28]

Accessibility also tended to be the advice given by creative writing 'experts' when they discussed how best to get published and talked about 'style.' W. Somerset Maugham advised that the best stories were 'strongly plotted' and he attacked the emerging batch of Modernists for writing plot*less* stories using atmosphere to 'decorate a story so thin that it could not exist without its trimmings'.[29] As a piece of advice to would-be storytellers, this was frequently reiterated and taken up—successfully in Blyton's case. Later, as a successful author herself, she would almost always say the same thing whenever she was asked for guidance: action—or story—was preferable to a focus on character. She registered, too, the demand for escapist stories which would 'transplant' readers' out of their own homes 'to scenes and places over which there is still for them the glamour of romance'. This was the recommendation of Louise Heilgers in *How to Write Stories for Money* (1920) who explained that '[m]en and women do not want to read stories that reflect their own daily life....They want to be taken out of themselves...'.[30]

By the time *Singers in the Crowd* was published, Blyton's dreams of a literary life were under strain. There were 'at least five hundred things sent back to me', she recalled of her early submissions to publishers. 'I had no success at all' (*SML*, 72). For Blyton, as for another contemporary, Richmal Crompton (b.1889), the best chance was to place work in some of the monthly or weekly magazines and story papers derided by Q.R. Leavis and with which the country was being 'flooded', as *The Bookman* put it in January 1920.[31] Crompton got herself on this path when, in 1919, *Home Magazine* paid the (then) unknown classics teacher three pounds for 'Rice Mould Pudding', the first of her comic tales featuring William Brown and his long-suffering family. She continued to supply the magazine before the same stories were collected in book form as *Just William* (1922) and published by George Newnes Ltd. Crompton recalled the 1920s as 'easy days for writers' in which 'a host of no longer existing magazines (*Strand, Windsor, New Red, Novel, Quiver, Pearson's, Home, Happy* and many others) offered a ready market for the beginner'.[32] Blyton, too, followed this route, sending off stories and verses to similar middle-brow magazines: 'Vantage In' appeared in *The Bystander*, an up-market illustrated magazine which ran short stories, theatre reviews and 'Society' gossip, on 28 September 1921. 'Trumped', which was published in *The Londoner* (22 October 1921) was a comic story (unsigned) about a writer taking revenge on an annoying acquaintance by incorporating him in a story, only to find that the spiteful gesture back-fires when acquaintances think the character depicted is a self-portrait. This was followed by 'Aunt Jershua's Earwig' (*The Londoner*, 22 October 1921) and 'The Reward of Virtue' (*The Passing Show*, 20 May 1922). 'Quite Incomparable' signed 'E.B.' (*Bystander*, 1 January 1922) was another humorous tale about mistaken identities on a train. On 23 August 1922 *Punch* published (uncredited) Blyton's poem 'Pretending' one of the first instances in which she adopted a child's voice ('I've got a book of history that tells of queens and kings/Of crowns and thrones and battles and all kinds of thrilling things' [180]).

There is a sense when reading these early pieces that Blyton was still following the advice of writing guides. Women, in particular, were often told that they could become successful if they deployed their innate 'sprightliness' and 'observation'. They were advised to take note of what their neighbours were doing or listen to conversations on buses or trains, something Blyton (a commuter) did. In this scenario, a woman's entry to an alternative world of economic independence and career was dependent on her retaining some essential elements of her domestic, 'feminine' self. There was also good scope for getting such work published, especially if given a female slant. The number of magazines aimed at women was increasing. In 1928, *The Newspaper Press Directory and Advertisers Guide* listed sixty-seven, a three-fold increase on numbers before the War.[33]

This perhaps explains 'The Man She Trusted', a limp romantic short story by Blyton published unsigned in *Home Weekly* (7 October 1922). The tale had the tag line 'A Complete Story of a Romance that began in the Blue Mist of an October Morning'. As a location for this kind of work *Home Weekly* (price 2d) was clearly suitable: a mass market, general-interest publication targeted at young working women (typists, waitresses, shop assistants) and lower-middle-class housewives.[34] The 1920s are remembered mythically as glamourous 'roaring', years: Hollywood films featuring 'it' girls like Clara Bow, aviatrixes like Amy Johnson, a jazz soundtrack, cocktails and nightclubs populated by 'bright young things', Fritz Lang's expressionist film *Metropolis*, entertainments in Paris featuring Josephine Baker and *La Revue Negre*, and women shingling their hair or adopting Eton Crops. But for most women it was a case of reading about such things rather than being part of them: a trip to the British Empire Exhibition at Wembley, tea at a Lyon's café, a trip to the pictures and shopping in Croydon (all of which Blyton's diaries record her doing in 1924) represented the kinds of low-key, frequently mundane, activities which interspersed themselves amongst the competing demands of jobs and obligations to family. These were some of the concerns addressed by *Home Weekly* in its features on dressmaking, health (what to do if feeling 'run down'), childcare and cooking ('What is nicer than a tasty stew?'). But it also provided lots of escapist stories and serials about romantic entanglements, usually involving an ordinary—and therefore recognisable—young woman in a lowly paid job, who finds herself attracted to one or more men of varying degrees of suitability. Thus Dorothy, Blyton's heroine in 'The Man She Trusted', is a callow young woman of marriageable age who, while on a country walk, encounters an attractive man carrying a sack. She is piqued that he has spoiled her solitude, but he wins her over and they arrange to meet again. However, she comes to suspect that he has robbed a neighbouring house and when she next encounters him (on the top deck of a London bus) she shuns him, thinking he has made a fool of her: 'Her mind had weaved an aureole of romance around their meeting…and to have the romance so rudely shattered, and her self-respect dealt such a hard blow, was an experience Dorothy found it hard to forget'.[35] When his innocence becomes obvious she is willing to resume their flirtation which—it is hinted—will lead to courtship and (eventually) marriage. The story is a poor effort; there is no new ground being broken and for a decade in which readers were being thrilled by the film of Ethel M. Dell's *The Sheik* (1921, with Rudolph Valentino), it seems too anodyne and decorous to have ever been exciting. But possibly that was the intention. Instead 'The Man She Trusted' is indicative of the way in which, as Hilliard has explained, a 'greater homeliness came to mark "escapist" periodical fiction' in the 1920s.[36] The men held up as objects of desire in the pages of *Home Weekly* were, for the most part, sporty, reliable chaps likely to make good husbands and with enough income for their wives not to have to work after marriage. And while critics, then as now, would baulk at calling the *Home Weekly* a 'literary' magazine, what begins to emerge is that Blyton's story appeared in a magazine in which literary discourse—stories and serials—was used in a very particular way (a pattern Blyton would later follow when she had control of her own magazines). Literary discourse represented commitment to entertainment, but it was also a means of regulating readers' access to knowledge, providing them with advice, a social location, models of behaviour and a context for issues related to their own lives. Blyton's central character was someone whom some young female readers in 1922 could imagine themselves being; there is an implicit assumption that they are familiar with young men and what men might be 'after' sexually, and that choices connected to romantic relationships are often more complicated than they might at first appear.[37]

If it is possible to pick out false starts from amongst Blyton's early works and a lack of direction, it is also the case that 1922 marked a turning point. Partly this came about by following the adage 'write about what you know'. As someone working as a nursery governess, who spent her days observing her pupils, telling them stories and planning nature lessons, what Blyton 'knew' were young children and their interests. There was already a heightened awareness of the opportunities on offer in writing for children. As Peter Hunt notes, 'the potential market was perhaps greater than ever before'.[38] There was a recognition of child readers as a distinct entity with their own likes and dislikes and Blyton began her career just as publishers were doubling their efforts to build on the concept of 'the new empowered child', youngsters who were 'peers, not inferiors', many of whom had pocket money to spend on reading material: magazines, comics and even books.[39] In 1921 *The Times* reported admiringly of attempts by publishers to expand provision and corresponding moves in bookshops to set up designated sections for children.[40] Things continued apace: by December 1924, *John o'London's* was able to claim that 'in no other branch of literature has the swing of the pendulum wrought so great a change'.[41] The following Christmas, the magazine returned to the subject, noting wistfully how '[i]t must be delightful to be a child these days with so many wonderful people writing books for one'.[42] These people included such household names as E. V. Lucas, whose *Playtime and Company* (with drawings by Ernest Shepherd) received especial praise for succeeding in the 'difficult art of looking at things through a child's eyes', Hilaire Belloc author of *The Bad Child's Book of Beasts* and Angela Brazil, who had made her name writing school stories, 'an author for girls with a big and faithful public'.[43] It was the new richness of such work that struck Eleanor Farjeon in a 1926 article 'Child's Luck', in which she reviewed such 'delicious' titles as *Winnie-the-Pooh*, by A.A. Milne, *Doctor Dolittle's Zoo*, by Hugh Lofting, *Made-To-Order Stories*, by Dorothy Canfield and *But We Know Better*, by Annabel Williams-Ellis.[44]

A survey of these and other review columns clearly registers the inroads writers of children's literature were making, although it is hard not to be struck, as reviewers of the 1920s were, by the fact that for all the liveliness of their works, writers continued to remain within fairly narrow boundaries: subject matter framed on boarding schools, adventures on the high seas, animals and fairies. While writing manuals were quick to point out that the 'best' writers for children had long been men, notably Lewis Carroll, J.M. Barrie, Kenneth Graeme, A.A. Milne—'Where', asked one, 'are the works by women to set beside these?'—there was some acceptance that this was an area in which women, especially if they were mothers, were beginning to demonstrate some 'natural aptitude'.[45] (The success of Edith Nesbit, Beatrix Potter and Frances Hodgson Burnett was, of course, being overlooked here.) At the same time, manuals such as *Hints on Writing Juvenile Literature* published by F. Warne & Co. (who were Potter's publishers) warned that to produce really good work was not easy: 'Anyone can write trash of course, and unfortunately some of it finds its way into print…but to write stories for the young requires just as much sincerity of work as any other branch, and it has a technique of its own'.[46]

It would have been difficult in the 1920s for anyone thinking about writing as a career *not* to have seen this 'new' impetus, and as well as being ambitious, Enid Blyton was nothing if not observant. She also started to feel that she had at least some serviceable talent when, in January 1922, she was commissioned by the influential firm George Newnes Ltd. to supply material for the magazine *Merry Moments*. At the same time, she began to have material published in some of the annuals for young children which pervaded the market: a story about 'Waddles' (a tortoise) appeared in a collection for the 'Playtime Story Book Series' and another, 'The Adventures of Bobs Bunny' in *Nursery Stories* (both published by Dean and Son, 1922). In 1922, forty-one (of fifty-two) issues of *Merry Moments* published that year contained work by her. Her contributions to the 4 November issue were typical: a story, 'The King Who Couldn't Laugh', set somewhere in 'fairy-land', as well as some jaunty verses on 'Guy Fawkes Day'. It was here that her lifetime habit of over-producing stories about elves, brownies and sprites also seems to have begun along with another realisation that 'festival' days in Britain's calendar made appealing topics. (Earlier, 'A Fairy Easter Egg' (15 April 1922), had managed to combine the popular (pagan) interest in 'little folk' *and* the Christian religious festival.) In 1922 the progress of her career continued when Blyton sold similarly themed stories to a rival magazine, *Fairyland Tales*, owned by John Leng & Co., where 'Flopperty Castle', 'The Wizard's Necklace' and 'Fanny in Fairyland' appeared (again uncredited) in October.[47] She had more work published in November 1922 when a provincial newspaper, *The Leicester Advertiser*, took a story ('A Wonderful Recovery') and three verses ('Suppose', 'Our Band', 'Those Pigs!'), all small-scale and rather twee and illustrated (like much of her early work) by her schoolfriend, Phyllis Chase.[48] All this led to a realisation, she later recorded, that she was able to write at least two kinds of saleable things: those 'that were very like nursery rhymes' and 'verses that tried to describe the small things I loved, such as the daisy, the field-mouse, the drops of rain running down the window....Anything that I thought was lovable or beautiful I tried to catch...'.[49] Both sorts were suitable for children and in *Child Whispers* and *Real Fairies*, she would try to persuade the public of this as well.

Child Whispers and Real Fairies

Child Whispers was the first book Blyton wrote (at the age of twenty-four) and which was accepted for publication (by J. Saville and Company). It was published in June 1922 priced 2/6 (a second edition followed in 1923). *Real Fairies*, her third book (her second was *Responsive Singing Games* [1923]), was published by the same firm in July 1923 and illustrated by Phyllis Chase.

To date, however, these books have received very little attention and their contents do not (at first glance) repay much analysis. However, they did—do perhaps—have charm of a kind. Through twenty-eight poems in *Child Whispers* and thirty-three in *Real Fairies*, fairies living in suburban gardens variously 'frolic', dance, swing in hammocks, play musical chairs (using toadstools), torment the children's nanny, practise cricket and get a soaking when a little girl waters some pansies under which they are sheltering. These 'little folk' it seems, are everywhere; even 'A Queer Butterfly', caught in a net, turns out to be a fairy. Other poems—'The Little Folk on the Hill', 'The Fairy's' Bedtime', 'Before Breakfast'—continue the magic, reminding readers (as Blyton explained in her Preface to *Real Fairies*) that 'the little child, with his wondering, sensitive mind' is full of fairies (and pixies and goblins) whom adults ('Mummy and Daddy, and Nannie and Cook' cannot see but the child (and his pets) can (*RF*, 7; 9).

In choosing to write about fairies and children, Blyton was trying to exploit one of the crazes of the 1920s. Indeed, it is difficult to appreciate how unprecedentedly popular writings about fairies, in particular, could be. One famous example is Rose Fyleman's poem 'There are Fairies at the Bottom of our Garden' (*Punch*, 1917) which was later set to music. The widespread sense of loss of innocence following the slaughter of the First World War had something to do with the appeal, along with the corresponding idea that children were precious, their psychology needed to be understood, and their innocence celebrated. To immerse oneself in fairyland was to be transported back to a more innocent world devoid of adult cares, to indulge in a kind of escapism that was doubly powerful in the years following the trauma of the conflict. The existence of fairies also suggested that there was another world—an afterlife—comforting to those who were mourning sons or brothers. It was partly for this reason that when, in 1920, news broke of fairies photographed by two girls in their garden in Cottingley near Bradford, many people, foremost amongst them, Arthur Conan Doyle (himself a grieving father), were willing to believe that the pictures were genuine. But Doyle believed, too, that the recognition of fairy 'existence' could act as an antidote to modern cynicism; the world of the fairies, like that of children, was pure and unsophisticated at a time when being 'impure' and sophisticated was all the rage amongst cocktail-quaffing adults, obsessed with the cinema and nightclubs. There was also something elegiac in all this, particularly where children were concerned, and this manifested itself in the widespread tendency, as Kimberley Reynolds has noted, 'to lament the need for children to grow up and move into the future'.[50] The level of enthusiasm expressed by Lydia Miller Mackay, writing in *Time and Tide* in December 1921 where she reported on several 'delectable fairy-books' full of 'dear little pixies', was typical.[51] In *John o'London's* in 1923, Philip Sidney was only slightly more restrained when he reviewed an assortment of titles including *The Dodo's Egg*, *The Pearl Fairy Book*, *The Emerald Fairy Book*, *The Flower Fairies*, *The Seed Fairies*, *Good Night Rhymes* and *Star Dust*. 'Children', he explained, 'speak in many tongues but there is a happy phase of childhood during which they think in terms of one universal language, the language of the fairy'.[52] In 1928, Naomi Mitchison surveyed a long list of titles for younger readers in which 'fatuous' fairies and 'an especially idiotic kind of animal' featured. She decided it was all to do with parents envisioning their children as 'innocent and pretty' and wanting them to stay that way. In turn, as Mitchison explained, publishers had cottoned onto this and pushed titles in ways akin to 'dope' dealers selling cocaine: 'They are early thrust into a child's gaping paw: parents and others consider them safe food; they will always sell'.[53]

The trajectory Blyton set herself whereby she put the same subjects—fairies and children—front and centre can thus be understood in these contexts. Moreover, the reviewers on whose desks these slim books landed, seem to have liked them. *The Bookman* praised the 'simplicity' of the 'light, lilting, happy tales' which made up *Child Whispers* (quoted in Stoney, 48). Meanwhile, *The Schoolmistress* waxed lyrical about the '[w]itches, fairies, goblins, flowers, little folk, butterflies and other delights [which] all live between its pages' (quoted in Stoney, 49). Whether what Blyton wrote was also 'poetry' was another question, but these volumes convinced critics that Blyton was capable of producing distinctive effects even if these and her subsequent efforts generated some twee responses:

If only we are wearing the right kind of spectacles fairies, gnomes elves and pixies are to be all round us, peeping between the petals of flowers, out of half-opened leaves, and using mushrooms sometimes for shelters, and sometimes for tables, and we are of the opinion that Miss Enid Blyton is the happy possessor of a very good pair, for she is able to see them at their work, at their play (which might sometimes be called mischief), and in their dear little houses, such as those made of tiddlywinks...Fairies wondrous busy in their noisy market-place, and up to all kinds of pranks, are seen here in this delightful volume.[54]

It was this ability to turn the tap on when something 'frolicsome' or 'winsome' was required that began to make Blyton useful to publishers tired of the same old middle-aged voices. She also gave the impression of seeming fully and sincerely taken up by the whole fairy business. At the same time, the poems in *Child Whispers*, *Real Fairies* and in later collections, *Silver and Gold* (1925) and *Wake Up!* in 1927, were early evidence of Blyton's—and others— belief in the importance of things being presented 'from the child's point of view and not from the "grown-up's"—a very different thing' (*CW*, 2). The 'wondering' child's perspective, quirky, cute or misapprehending, was seen to be an attractive ingredient, a point made by Lydia Miller Mackay, in *Time and Tide* in 1926. It conveyed something unspoilt and truthful and even magical: 'To the child every wood is an enchanted wood, whether he discovers in it a fairy, a squirrel's nest, or a house made of chocolate'.[55] As Blyton later explained, she, too, had always been determined to write 'of things in a child's own world'.[56] Given her own environment and the pupils in her care, it was, unsurprisingly, an unapologetically safe, middle-class environment of garden parties, trips up to London, taxis, and visits to the Zoo. The events in *Real Fairies* are conjured up in sprightly fashion by a well-mannered albeit self-engrossed child narrator (aged eight), curious and combining an unshakeable belief in the exotic (fairies) with an intense love for the natural world. This world is populated by adorable creatures: 'In my garden every day/A little squirrel came to play' [*RF*, 34]), bumble-bees who, dressed in 'uniform of velvet brown and gold' 'fumble' and 'tumble' round the flower beds (*RF*, 51), and the rabbits who 'lolloped' in 'Cuckoo Wood' (*RF*, 53). In this environment of 'small things' the grown-ups are friendly and protective, irrespective of social status (nannies, gardeners, workmen, taxi drivers), even if their adherence to prescribed rules of social behaviour seems odd to the child. Getting older puts paid to all this, of course, a point made in the final poem in *Real Fairies*, 'Little-Place', which ends with the destruction of the child narrator's innocent illusions. She discovers the woodland floor covered in litter left by picnickers and realises she can never return to this Edenic place: 'For never would it feel again as it had felt before' (*RF*, 55). The contents and tone of these verses led to comparisons with Rose Fyleman (1877–1857) and A.A. Milne (1882–1956), authors who had made their reputations—and fortunes—by creating similar worlds where the realities of adulthood were kept at bay. Milne's mixing of toy animals and woodland settings, in the middle of which was his young son, Christopher Robin (a celebrity with his smock and floppy fringe), was hugely popular. It is tempting to see the Enid Blyton of this period as someone jumping on the bandwagon of 'Christopher Robinism' as it was termed.[57] Yet Blyton's young protagonists are not quite the same. They are always better behaved—there are few discordant voices—no Mary Jane having a tantrum at being told to eat up her rice pudding as there is in Milne's *When We Were Very Young*. Moreover, Milne and Fyleman were far from being the only exponents of 'nursery verse' (as it was called), nor were theirs the only post-war voices celebrating the child as truth-teller. Barbara Euphan Todd's poem 'Sign Posts', which begins her collection *The Very Good Walkers* (1925), has a similar anti-authoritarian edge, urging children to follow '[t]he swallows who flash and flicker' as opposed to 'the hot and dusty roads where grown-up people go'.[58] There are other numerous examples. It is worth noting, too, that Milne's first book of verse, *When We Were Very Young*, was not published until 1924, by which time Blyton's first two volumes of 'poetry' were already published. Thus, rather than seeing Blyton's early books as a species of 'Milne-lite', it seems more accurate to situate *Child Whispers* and *Real Fairies* and their successors as part of a wider 1920s trend whereby the individualised experiences of children and their sayings and doings were deemed worthy of rapt attention.

Teacher's World

Blyton's interest in fairies and children recurs throughout the 1920s—and indeed beyond. However, the publication which helped Blyton make a big jump to professional writer was the weekly magazine *Teacher's World*, which published her story 'Petronel and His Pot of Glue' (15 February 1922). Blyton had had the idea of sending her work to magazines aimed at other teachers. Titles such as *The Teacher's Times* and *The Schoolmistress* carried a good deal of fiction and poetry for children, the idea being that teachers could use such material as resources in class; pupils could be read to or be asked to recite. Priced at three pence, *Teacher's World* was a lively fifty-page miscellany. It offered articles about education and pedagogical theory by prominent figures alongside regular features ('Diary of an Educationist', 'Secondary School News', 'Confessions of an Inspector') together with book reviews, interviews with literary celebrities, a problem page and classroom resources ('Britain's History at a Glance').

In what proved to be an enormous piece of good fortune, the magazine's young deputy-editor, Hilda Russell-Cruise, was very taken with Blyton's work and encouraged her to submit more. Blyton, in turn, was delighted to be asked. The resulting efforts—tales with light-hearted but moral endings and (apparently) sincere verses with neat little rhymes and set-piece descriptions as their determining qualities—were judged very serviceable—presumably teachers told the editors this as well. The poems were certainly not in any way peculiar or experimental and Blyton clearly hated free verse. *Teacher's World*, thus took hundreds of them, all similarly accessible. 'A Lively Horse', 'My Chicken' and 'The Railway' (all published on 5 January 1923 edition) took their subject matter from daily life while others moved into the realm of fantasy but the result was poetic work which was almost always ostentatiously down-to-earth and had a directness which Blyton felt sure children would understand: 'They puff so loudly as they go,/They sound quite out of breath,/And just as if the driver-man,/Was working them to death', is her description of steam engines ('The Railway', 708). Writing so many poems enabled Blyton to crystallise and to develop what might be called her own aesthetic (as opposed to that of the poems of *Child Whispers* which, it might be argued, are not distinctively 'Blytonian', so much as nakedly commercial). There is a sense of Blyton following the recommendations of forward-looking educationalists of the 1920s who advocated that poetry tailored for children should reflect 'the rhythms of our growing life'. This, at any rate, was the advice of George Sampson writing in *Teacher's World* in 1923, who added that teachers should 'not offer children poetry that is too hard for them…moving in regions of experience where the feet of children cannot tread'. Rather than making poetry 'alien by remoteness', children should be offered 'poetry that belongs to their own life and time and ways of thought and speech'.[59] Such views were part of the democratic educational ethos on which *Teacher's World* prided itself, one which championed education as 'part of the heritage of every human being' and 'as much his due as the conditions of a healthy life'.[60] Blyton believed this too.

In some instances, it was easier for children to learn playfully via Blyton's verses than to read a dry, old-fashioned textbook. In 1924, *Teacher's World* accepted Blyton's poems inspired by the British Empire Exhibition, which took place at London's Wembley Park (April 1924 to October 1925). Like the exhibition, the poems ('South Africa', 'Canada', 'Ceylon', 'An India Day') sought to convey the glamour of the colonial project and, via impassioned evocations of far-flung places, suggested that the British empire was a passport to adventure: 'Oh come with me to Burma, to the land of pleasant ways/Where a laughter-loving people dance adown the sunny days' (TW, 4 April 1924, 79). All this was at a time when the empire, as schoolroom maps demonstrated, occupied two-thirds of the world and, although Britain faced various challenges to its imperial dominance, notably from the United States, it was still (just) possible to believe in Britain's right to be in charge. While Blyton was not a traveller, she had a feel for what was wanted and the poems are in keeping with other popular representations of the time in films, novels and plays in which imperialistic loyalties tended not to be questioned (E.M. Forster's *A Passage to India* (also 1924) is one of the few exceptions). It was clearly easier to digest the poems in 1924 than now, but their ideological appeal is not hard to understand. Stylistically they also did what *Teacher's World* demanded of them and had a simplicity, an eye for detail and an immediacy that was liked. It was partly her apparent ability to produce verses to order which made Blyton an appealing prospect to Hilda Russell Cruise, who turned Blyton into the magazine's unofficial resident poet. Here, it is easy to forget, Blyton was in exalted company: Rudyard Kipling, Walter de la Mare and John Masefield all published in the magazine and Blyton's writings appeared with equal billing alongside theirs.

What happened next seems thoroughly lucky. In 1923, *Teacher's World* offered Blyton a weekly column, 'From My Window', which ran from July 1923 to August 1927 (at which point Blyton began a weekly 'Letter' to children). The idea was not entirely new: *Teacher's World* had run similar features ('A Weekly Page for the Infant School', 'A Number of Things: A Weekly Page for Boys and Girls'). However, with Blyton, the idea was for her to write more widely and produce 'light essays', staples of the newspaper and magazine industries in the 1920s and 1930s. In *The Prose Factory: Literary Life in England Since 1918*, D.J. Taylor notes that such pieces tended to follow a recognisable format: '[b]etween 800 and 1500 words in length, meditative, sometimes topical, nearly always humorous...varied in subject matter...about practically anything'.[61] Blyton was given free rein to write about education but also about books, children, theatre, nature—whatever took her fancy.

This part of Blyton's work for *Teacher's World* is notable because it was here that she was allowed space to develop her craft. From a biographical standpoint, the pieces are important because they reveal something of what the young adult Blyton thought about things, what she admired and what she read. For instance, Blyton's 1922 contributions (when she was twenty-five) show her discussing the application of the theories of the psychologist Émile

Coué to the classroom, in particular, his advocation of autosuggestion (26 April 1922, 180) (Blyton had earlier introduced the idea into a school story, 'The Making of Merriden Major' [12 April 1922, 88]) alongside statements of her conviction that one of the duties of a teacher was to encourage the development of 'moral character' and the 'higher spiritual life'. Her review of James Simpson's study of world history, *Man and the Attainment of Immortality* (1922), praises the clarity of the way the author has shown 'the trend of evolution, leading up to that great and unique personality in history, Jesus Christ', suggesting a belief in conventional forms of worship as well as an interest in zoology (15 August 1923, 942).[62] Other columns express Blyton's literary likes and dislikes; she references Andrew Lang's series of *Fairy Books* (1889–1913); in 1923, she was full of praise for the tragic 'grandeur' of Arnold Bennett's realist study of a miserly bookshop owner, *Riceyman Steps* (5 December 1923, 527). Later in 'A Queer Fashion' (1925), she complained vaguely about 'highbrow' culture, which she thought too gloomy: '[W]hy, why, why do so many poets, novelists, singers and composers imagine that the public like to read or listen to doleful, morbid or sad things?' she asked. 'I'm young and normal, and I prefer something more wholesome'. As she explained flatly:

> Most new novels, as they come out, find their way to my desk, and I read them. But so many of them are depressing. I think it is that they are getting too introspective, and, of course, some proportion are quite definitely nasty. It seems to be the fashion to be unpleasant in some way, and then get the publisher to label your book 'True to Life.' What it *really* ought to be labelled is 'True to a tiny corner of life, and a dusty depressing one at that'. (*TW*, 15 April 1925, 155)

Blyton wrote this in 1925, a moment at which the literary exponents of High Modernism—Virginia Woolf, T.S. Eliot, Katherine Mansfield—were ramping up suggestions that 'new expressions, new moulds for our thoughts & feelings', as Mansfield put it, were the way forward.[63] As has been seen, Blyton's sympathies lay away from writers who made things 'difficult' for their readers and the impression given in the 'From my Window' columns and elsewhere, is that her inclinations, like that of many people of her class, education and generation, not to mention the readers of *Teacher's World*, fell more naturally into the category of so-called 'middle-brow'. Middle-brow readers were popularly regarded as correspondingly middle-class and suburban; they held 'average' tastes, a large proportion of them were women and they made up the bulk of book buyers and subscription holders at W.H. Smith's and Boots' lending libraries. Thus Blyton, for one, liked detective stories and the novels of Joan Butler (Robert Alexander [1905–1979]), a comic novelist whose characters and settings were frequently likened to those of P.G. Wodehouse. She was a fan, too, of Angela Thirkell's gentle satires of provincial life. These were indeed the kinds of middle-brow authors derided by Virginia Woolf and other 'highbrow' figures, people 'of middle-bred intelligence', the literary qualities of whose writings were not challenging or demanding but conventional, safe and 'second-rate'.[64] Blyton's praise for Arnold Bennett, whose work was particularly singled out for criticism by Virginia Woolf in her essay 'Mr Bennett and Mrs Brown' (1924) also suggests on which part of the critical divide she stood.

The aim here is not to belittle Blyton or her published opinions—she read a great deal and her private letters occasionally reveal more obviously challenging fare (Bertrand Russell, for example [Mac, 14 February 1947])—but to think about the scope of her journalistic work (which is what these pieces are) and the relationship they secured her with readers of *Teacher's World*. As has been noted, the magazine was forward-looking in its views on pedagogy. In her columns, Blyton takes it for granted that readers will agree with her on the importance of encouraging the 'questioning, wondering mind' of the child and the Froebel-inspired belief that 'a child is always seeking to express himself' and should not be deterred from doing so.[65] Central to the Froebel philosophy was a focus on what psychologists call 'educational progressivism' which manifested itself in an emphasis not only in the central role of 'play' but in learning-by-doing and in face-to-face encounters with new sights and objects. This ethos represented a move away from behaviourism—which stressed the importance of regularity, obedience and corrective discipline.[66] As the 1920s progressed, these ideas gained new ground as part of wider revolution in child studies led by figures such as Susan Isaacs. She explained that '[w]hat helps most…is the ability to enter into the child's own world with an informed sympathy, the general sense that his problems are problems of growth, and a patient and friendly interest in the ways of that growth'. Isaacs also advocated the importance of play ('Nature's means of individual education') as the means by which the child's 'growth' would develop.[67] To Blyton in the 1920s, this kind of thinking *felt* right, and these ideas would creep into much of her early writing.

Elsewhere, the picture of 'Enid Blyton' that emerges—at least as she presents it in print—is of someone susceptible to whimsy, a trait given full rein in *Child Whispers* and *Real Fairies*. There continued to be a good deal of material relating to fairy folk living at the bottom of the garden. She also incorporated into her columns the idea of herself as someone well-mannered and good-humoured, but at the same time constantly torn between the 'thrilling heights of romance' and the 'level plain of the practical'. 'All my life long I have lived the legends of Merlin and of King Arthur and his Knights', she writes in August 1923.[68] Like many others, she looked for romance at the cinema and the theatre. She was swept away by a lavish production of James Elroy's Flecker's *Hassan* in London in November 1924, finding its 'passionate intensity…almost too much to be borne….I could not rid my mind of the feeling of excitement, nor my eyes of the splendour of colour and light. Anyone at all alive to the spirt of poetry must have felt the same'.[69] But she also found joy in being outdoors and vividly observing the natural world close at hand. On a beach holiday, she describes in detail the occupants of a rock pool, the sea anemones 'looking for all the world like squat chrysanthemum blossoms' and she feeds them baby mussels and pebbles.[70] She comes across as defiantly—but perhaps misleadingly—unsophisticated and there is an element of pride in being able to take pleasure in simple things. She explains that as a child she loved her toys 'with a deep love' and '[w]hen I became a woman, I did not put away childish things'.[71] In London, she likes the spectacle provided by Punch and Judy shows and the Lord Mayor's procession and with them the feeling of being part of a shared experience as she takes her place amongst the 'hustling, bustling' crowd.[72] But she also wants to assume a more detached role, that of the *flâneuse*, who walks the capital's streets, and who people-watches from the top of an omnibus as she travels between Surbiton and Beckenham.[73] Like other young women inclined to be fashionable, she goes shopping for clothes and visits the hairdressers (her adoption of the popular shingle hairstyle is, she admits, a big decision). There she reads magazines detailing the 'thrilling' doings of rich people in 'Society', 'Beautiful Lady-So-and-So in her yacht'—stories which she professes to envy but is also inclined to mock for she knows that this will never be her world nor that of her readers.[74] Overall, and assuming the 'Enid Blyton' who regales the readers of *Teacher's World* with trivia about her daily life has some resemblance to the Enid Blyton working as a teacher in Surbiton, the picture emerges of a capable, emancipated young woman, not cynical or easily troubled, lively and enjoying modern life and open to the intellectual and cultural experiences that came her way, albeit mostly within the confines of the suburban world she knew.

Professionally, Blyton's production for *Teacher's World* of these 'middle articles' had the result of putting her (in a small way) in the same business as well-known contemporaries like J.B. Priestley, Hilaire Belloc, E.V. Lucas, Robert Lynd and G.K. Chesterton, men who had columns in mass circulation newspapers like *The Daily Express* or *The Daily News*. These writers were a recognisable 'type'. Leonard Woolf described them as 'impeccable journalists who every week...turn out an impeccable essay...like an impeccable sausage, about everything, or everything and nothing'. They had popularity and longevity because they spoke to 'like-minded' readers who shared their sensibilities and covered 'familiar terrain'.[75] This description also fits Blyton, of course, and the vast quantities of correspondence which Blyton received from the readers of *Teacher's World* (which she references increasingly in her columns) suggest that they felt a rapport. What differentiates Blyton from her better-known contemporaries in the 1920s was that the circulation of a weekly like *Teacher's World* did not match that of a daily newspaper and also that she was a woman. This is significant. In 1927, an International Labour Association Survey estimated that there were only around 400 women journalists out of a total of 7000 in Britain.[76] Those who managed to gain a position in a national newspaper were generally restricted to the women's pages. The fact that Blyton was one of them is a frequently overlooked aspect of her early achievements.

MISS ENID BLYTON.

Fig. 3.1 Photo of Blyton aged twenty-six published as part of her article 'A Novel Map for Storytelling', *Teacher's World* (5 October 1923), 64

Another aspect of this activity, of course, especially in the context of Blyton's attempts to establish herself as an author, was the usefulness of 'From My Window' as a form of self-advertisement, something which by 1920 most authors felt obliged to involve themselves with if they wanted to become better known. A.A. Milne noted wearily that every successful writer necessarily 'surrendered some part of his privacy to others'. Their only choice, he added, was to decide how much and 'in what size lettering the WELCOME on our door mats shall be displayed'.[77] It was this need, as well, that Rose Macaulay was responding to in 1925 when she railed against having to pander to the 'eager, silly, gaping public'.[78] This 'culture of celebrity', as Patrick Collier has termed it, was widespread and encouraged by newspapers and magazines who would ask writers to supply 'tit bits' about themselves and ran illustrated features showing authors in their garden or seated at their desk at which they described their path to fame and their working habits.[79] In 1932 Virginia Woolf wondered if she, too, would become such a figure, 'a celebrated authoress', 'a lady in a tea gown, with a lap dog, a fountain pen' and 'a habit of writing her name with a flourish' across the photos of herself requested by fans.[80]

Like other publications, *Teacher's World* participated in this and it was something Blyton experienced first hand in October 1926 when she was sent to interview Mr. and Mrs. A.A. Milne and their famous son, Christopher Robin ('The latter just like the pictures by Ernest Shepard, except that he has much more hair', Blyton reported).[81] Blyton presented the young star with a copy of her *Book of Bunnies* (an event he recalled in later life).[82] She was also sent to interview Marion St John Webb (1888–1930), another novelist and poet who specialised in fairies and children. Long before Milne, Webb had become famous for nursery poetry and had scored a hit with *The Littlest One* (1918). But by 1926, it was a sign of Blyton's own standing that the issue of *Teacher's World* in which the interviews with the Milnes and Webb appeared (part of a feature on 'The Children's Poets') carried one with Blyton herself in which she too was billed as a writer whom 'children adore'. Photographed informally and posed alone by the pond at her new home, Elfin Cottage in Beckenham (snapshots were recommended as having more immediacy and authenticity than formal studio portraits), the feature was recognition on Blyton's part—and by *Teacher's World*, who were wont to claim Blyton as their 'discovery'—that there was an audience who wanted to know more about her. The article studiously avoids anything dark or controversial (one of its uses was as something to be read to Blyton's young admirers by their teachers), and it established a version of Blyton which would be repeated for the next forty years: much was made of the young author's sense of 'fun'. She was accessorised with pets and a garden, all of which were topped off by a focus on her work ethic: '[b]ehind all her child-like outlook on life there is a clever, active brain: a resolute will to be up and doing'. There was the idea also, as Blyton explains to the interviewer, 'H.A.', aka Hugh Alexander Pollock (her husband), that her writing was a vocation:

> 'Why must you work so hard', said I. 'You have a home, a husband, happiness, and peace. Why not rest from it all?'

> Miss Blyton laughed her happy laugh. 'Surely,' said she, 'the best sort of happiness comes in giving pleasure to others. So long as one child tells me that my work brings him pleasure, just so long I shall go on writing'.[83]

Annette Federico has made the point that '[e]stablishing taking ownership of images are part of the ongoing struggle to form an idea of self, to find some meaningful identity'.[84] Something of this process is apparent in Blyton's dealing with *Teacher's World*. From 1922 it proved to be a space which allowed Blyton—a young woman who, if we are to believe some of the reports of her, did not always feel secure—to set down who she was, who she intended to be and what she could do creatively. And as the interview cited above shows, by 1926 Blyton had also found the 'voice' that she would use to tell her own story.

Comparisons

Before considering some further examples of the ways in which Blyton sought to establish a writing career, it is interesting—given what we know about her background—to compare her origins and upbringing with those of some contemporaries amongst writers for children. How far were Blyton's lower-middle-class background and career experiences different? This question is significant because there is a tendency to present Blyton as a 'one-off' whose career was atypical, the result of 'genius' or a fluke in some way. In making some comparisons I have chosen six authors born (with one exception) within ten years of Blyton—and who rose to prominence at roughly the same time as she did. The writers included in the survey are thus: Alison Uttley, Richmal Crompton, W.E. Johns, Noel Streatfeild, Barbara Euphan Todd and Malcolm Saville.

Alison Uttley (1884–1976): The daughter of a Derbyshire farmer, Alison Uttley won a scholarship to Manchester University from where she graduated with a degree in Physics. She taught at Fulham Secondary School for Girls until her marriage in 1911. Her husband's suicide in 1930 meant that Uttley had to earn money to support herself and their son, which she did by writing as many as four stories a week. Her book, *The Squirrel, The Hare and the Little Grey Rabbit* (1929) was the first of more than a hundred titles that adopted the kind of anthropomorphism which had made Beatrix Potter famous. She prided herself on her professionalism and ability to keep to deadlines, but she could be demanding, snobbish and quarrelsome. Uttley's biographer, Dennis Judd, notes that despite considerable success and acclaim (not least for the historical novel, *A Traveller in Time* [1939]) she 'felt particular rivalry to certain women authors of children's books and she was to develop a positive dislike of Enid Blyton'.[85] I return to instances of this long-lasting dislike in later chapters.

Richmal Crompton (1890–1969): Born in Bury, Lancashire, Crompton was the daughter of a schoolteacher. After graduating from Royal Holloway College, she taught classics at Bromley High School for Girls (1917–1924). An attack of polio caused her to give up teaching whereupon she devoted her time to writing. From 1919 she published (anonymously) in magazines the stories featuring William Brown. As has been noted, the first books, *Just William* and *More William*, were published by George Newnes in 1922. William and his gang 'the Outlaws' occupy a carefully delineated middle-class milieu and are shown disrupting the social machinery of the grown-up world and the reader is encouraged to take their side. As a beginner in the publishing world, Crompton made the mistake of signing away all rights to the first stories, but in 1927 her income from writing was £2336, an enormous sum for the time. William also appeared on radio (from 1923) and film and the 300 stories about him which Crompton wrote until her death have never been out of print. One figure puts sales of the books at 96 million (1996).[86] The success of the books came partly because they were satires that spoke to adults as well as children. Crompton, who came to regard William as a weight around her neck, sought to gain credibility via a parallel career as author of fiction for adults, with some success beginning with *The Innermost Room* (1923). Crompton and Blyton were aware of each other. A character in *The Sea of Adventure* (1946) mentions William Brown and in 1947, Blyton withdrew a story, 'A Shock for William' from an anthology because she knew it 'is a little like another story coming out soon' (Mac, 18 May 1947). However, the women seem not to have met until the mid-1950s. A photo from 1957 shows Crompton looking cheerful, together with Blyton and Malcolm Saville at a performance of *Noddy in Toyland*.

'Captain' W.E. Johns (1893–1968): The son of a tailor, William Earl Johns was born in Bengeo, a village in Hertfordshire. He attended Hertford

Grammar School after which he was apprenticed to a surveyor; in 1912 he became a sanitary inspector. He enlisted in the Machine Gun Corps during the First World War (1914–1918) but transferred to the Royal Flying Corps where he obtained the rank of Flying Officer. He remained in service after the war but began to sell drawings and articles—usually of aviation-related subjects—to magazines, all signed by 'Flying Officer Johns'. It was while writing for *Popular Flying* that Johns introduced his most famous character, the airman James Bigglesworth (Biggles), who subsequently headlined ninety-five patriotic adventures, his popularity enhanced by serialisation in the *Eagle* and other comics. Johns created other characters in similar vein, including the commando, Gimlet (1943–1954), and a female equivalent of Biggles, Flight Officer 'Worrals of the WAAF' (1941–1950). He also ventured into science fiction. During the thirties and forties, Johns kept his profile (and income) high via weekly columns for the magazines *Modern Boy* and *My Gardener*. As with Blyton's output, it is difficult to put a figure on the total number but Johns wrote at least 160 books.[87] A letter from Blyton to 'Bill' dated 15 June 1946 gave him advice on the ins and outs of signing a deal with Marks and Spencer noting also that 'you & I were next to each other (once more) in popularity in a library poll'. 'They [Marks and Spencer] are after your name & they should pay well for it', she reminded him.[88]

Noel Streatfeild (1895–1986): Born in Frant, Sussex, where her father was a vicar, Streatfeild studied acting at the Royal Academy of Dramatic Art in 1919. In the mid-1920s, tired of touring, she decided to write and enrolled in a creative writing correspondence course of the kind described earlier in this chapter. She sold work to magazines; her first story, about a conjurer who turned his daughter into a rabbit (but forgot the spell for turning her back), earned her two guineas. Her first novel, *The Whicharts* (1931), was for adults and did not make much impression but, in 1936, her novel for children, *Ballet Shoes*, proved an enormous hit both critically and commercially; this was despite being told there was not much money in children's books. The focus in *Ballet Shoes* on children earning their own living reappears in *Tennis Shoes* (1937), *The Circus is Coming* (1938) and *White Boots* (1951).[89] Despite the comfortable settings of her novels (professional, middle-class), Streatfeild believed that authors for children needed to have suffered themselves in order to describe pain and anxiety accurately for their readers; people who had experienced childhood 'in a golden haze' made ineffective writers. 'I believe most writers for children, consciously or unconsciously write books that they themselves wanted when they were children but as "Victorians" they never got'.[90] Much respected, Streatfeild, like Blyton, was often asked for her opinions on items relating to books, children or women. She never married, claiming to write her novels while lying in bed, producing 1000 words a day by hand. Like several of her contemporaries, she thought little of Blyton. 'Hers are very simple stories. They are meant for the less intelligent public', Streatfeild explained publicly in 1951.[91]

Barbara Euphan Todd (?1897–1976) was the daughter of a vicar. She was educated "'very slightly'" at home and boarding school before working as a V.A.D. nurse during the War.[92] Afterwards she began contributing poems and stories to magazines, often in collaboration. Like Blyton, she was successful in capitalising on the fairy craze. *The 'Normous Saturday Fairy Book* was published in 1924. Her poetry collections *Hither and Thither* (1927) and *The Seventh Daughter* (1935) were likewise in the fashionable, lilting, whimsical style of A. A. Milne, in addition to being illustrated by Ernest Shepard, who also illustrated Milne's work. Her first novel, *Worzel Gummidge, or the Scarecrow of Scatterbrook Farm,* appeared in 1936 and the title character's anarchic behaviour and rudeness struck a chord with children brought up to value good manners and restraint. Between 1937 and 1963, Todd published nine more titles featuring her most famous character, interspersed with others: *Gertrude the Greedy Goose* (1939) *Mr. Blossom's Shop* (1954) and *The Boy with the Green Thumb* (1956). The first Worzel Gummidge title was well-regarded enough to be serialised on BBC Children's Hour after the Second World War and it was the first in the revolutionary Puffin paperback series launched by Penguin in 1941 under the direction of Eleanor Graham, which aimed to provide children with 'the best of the *new* classics of the new generation' and books which had lasting worth.[93] (Blyton's works were never included in the imprint.) Following marriage, aged fifty-two, to a retired naval officer, Todd lived in Berkshire until her husband's death in 1940. According to one critic, Todd 'reviewed children's books for *Punch*, identified as B.G.B., whence she began the campaign against Enid Blyton later associated with librarians'.[94]

Malcolm Saville (1901–1982): Saville was born in Hastings. On leaving Richmond Hill School, Richmond, in 1918, he worked in the stockroom for Oxford University Press. He would spend much of his working life in the book trade, including spells in the publicity department at Cassell & Company (from 1920) and from 1936 took on a similar role at George Newnes Ltd. In the 1930s, he began writing football reports at one pound per match. His first book, *Amateur Acting and Producing for Beginners* (1937), was published using the pseudonym D.J. Desmond. His first children's book was *Mystery at Witchend* (1943), the first of twenty titles in the so-called 'Lone Pine' series of adventures which featured recurring characters, 'written against an unmistakably English background' of Shropshire.[95] Other series followed, often featuring more spies and smugglers but, like Blyton, he also wrote non-fiction books encouraging children to explore the natural world. In addition to ninety books, he took on editing, notably *My Garden* (1946) and in 1954, *Sunny Stories*, after Blyton, whom he knew and admired, relinquished it. 'Enid Blyton knows exactly what she is doing' was his response to someone who suggested that Blyton's success was pure luck.[96] His adventure stories were admired enough to be adapted as serials for BBC radio's *Children's Hour* and in 1943 (before Blyton's 'Famous Five' club was begun), Saville started the Lone Pine Club for fans of the series.[97]

There is obviously variation in these six short biographies of popular children's authors working in early-mid-twentieth-century Britain. There are differences in social origins, education, productivity, and choice of lifestyle in adulthood. However, there are also similarities. With the exception of Malcolm Saville, all the authors began to get published in the period 1919–1930. Alison Uttley and Malcolm Saville were like Blyton in coming from the lower end of the middle class. W.E. Johns' parents were working-class, although his education helped elevate him. Post-war circumstances meant that all the authors needed to work; none had a private income sufficient to live on in the long-term; Blyton, Crompton and Uttley benefitted from Higher Education, which was also their route to becoming schoolteachers, an acceptable profession for middle-class women, although they relinquished these roles early on in their writing careers. In Blyton's, Johns' and Saville's cases, professional expertise proved a valuable entry point into regular writing work via specialisms: *Teacher's World* (Blyton), *Popular Flying* (Johns), sports reporting (Saville). Streatfeild, Todd and Crompton wrote without the distractions of children, something which was also true of Blyton in the 1920s. More speculatively, Streatfeild, like Blyton (reputedly), appears to have experienced childhood trauma for which writing provided a release. What is also apparent is that in these cases at least, these authors sidestepped—or did not have access to—the older model of public school followed by Oxford or Cambridge University. There is also, as others have pointed out, a sense of a matriarchy of children's literature taking shape.

Hugh Pollock

To return to the progress of Blyton's early career and her standing in the publishing industry in the 1920s, we end this chapter by adopting a more personal focus and thinking about a key influence: Blyton's first husband, Hugh Pollock. This involves a broader consideration of the barriers placed in front of Blyton's ambitions in the early 1920s: she was a young, lower-middle-class woman who worked as a teacher. We have seen how having this professional background helped her gain entry to the pages of *Teacher's World* but in other ways, it was of limited value. While the professional situation that Blyton had created for herself by 1924 was promising, she was also aware that despite all the democratic talk of authorship being a profession that anyone could enter, many of the old-fashioned ideas of how participants should proceed tended to prevail. Knowing the 'right' people—or if that was impossible, knowing someone else who knew them—was often still a 'thing'. John Baxendale describes the difficulties for outsiders of breaking into London's publishing scene: 'a small but intense world of over-lapping and sometimes contending circles based partly on aesthetic affinities, partly on self-interest, and sustained by magazines, newspapers and publishing houses, and an invisible hinterland of bookshops, libraries and readers'. It was a 'social and economic sub-system' which not only dictated what was published but by whom. The 'system' gave opportunities for freelancing to would-be writers 'provided they could negotiate its social and cultural networks'. Baxendale makes the point that the memoirs of writers who started out in the 1920s and 1930s—his example is the Bradford-born, J.B. Priestley—are invariably full of detail about making contacts not only in magazine offices but at dinners, pubs and parties.[98] But it was clearly easier for men to network than respectable women for whom loitering in bars and clubs (unless they were for women only) was no-go. Aspirant female writers *could* establish networks, of course. Catherine Clay has examined the supportive informal groupings established by some of the professional writers who were Blyton's contemporaries, including Vera Brittain, Winifred Holtby, Storm Jameson and Stella Benson. There are also the female writers—new or established—who congregated in and around the magazine *Time and Tide*, launched in May 1920 by the prominent suffragist Viscountess Rhonda, replete with an all-female board of directors; these writers included Cecily Hamilton, Elizabeth Robins, Eleanor Farjeon, Alice Meynell, Rebecca West, Ellen Wilkinson and Naomi Mitchison. Such networks were 'instrumental to women's writing careers in practical emotional and "inspirational" ways', but they are not something that Blyton invested much time in, nor were they part of her needs.[99] 'I always wanted to have to struggle for success, to get it without help, without "pulling wires"', she wrote defiantly in *The Story of My Life*, 'without hitching myself to somebody else's kind offers of help...' (*SML*, 73).

She had some help from women, of course, notably Phyllis Chase (who had useful contacts) and Hilda Russell-Cruise at *Teacher's World*. More often it was the case that those whom Blyton gathered around her were men, although again these—with the exceptions of W.E. Johns and Malcolm Saville with whom she occasionally corresponded—were not fellow writers but editors. By all accounts she was more than equal to sustaining these relationships; she was a lively, attractive young woman and her attractiveness was bolstered by the obvious competence with which she carried out her commissions and editors found it strategic to join hands with the young author. This was especially so when her column in *Teacher's World* became popular. Although Blyton continued the column alongside nature lessons, poems and stories, the work for *Teacher's World* was not enough to sustain her creatively and she took on the additional commissions she was offered. These included other teaching-related materials notably *Responsive Singing Games* (J. Saville, 1923; her second book), *Songs of Gladness* (with Alex Rowley; J. Saville & Co, 1924), *Sports and Games* (Birn Brothers, 1924) and *The Zoo Book* (Newnes, 1924). These were supplemented by enough stories and verses published across magazines to earn Blyton £300 from her writing during 1923 and £500 in 1924 (Stoney, 50; 66). These sums were roughly equivalent to the price of a new semi-detached house in the suburbs (depending on the suburb). Some of the subjects seem unexpected: *Motoring – A Book of Rhymes and Motors* and *All About Trains* were published by Birn in 1924, alongside more predictable titles for the same firm including *Peggy in Fairyland* (1924) *and Fairytales for the Little Ones* (1924). Blyton's diaries from this period and the workbook in which she carefully logged her commissions and their completion testify to her increased activity. On 3 January 1924, she notes that she went to London for a meeting with the firm of Nelson's: 'It's definitely decided I'm to do 36 books for them! To Birns. Gave me a cheque for £38.17s. Home at 3. Read. Bridge till bed'. On 10 January 1924, she went to London for further meetings with publishers: Birn Brothers, Cassell and Company, Evans Brothers, Davidsons. The picture that emerges is of someone who was consistently busy and whose work took in most of the children's specialisms as they then existed, much to the interest of editors.

It was after the meetings on 10 January 1924 that Blyton first mentions Hugh Pollock (1886–1971). He was a new(ish) book editor for the powerful firm of George Newnes Ltd. After finishing her business in town, she had caught the train back to Beckenham to find he had written 'a lovely letter' in which he 'asked if I'd collaborate with him' (D 10 January 1924). At this time Blyton saw her family only sporadically; her father had died suddenly of a heart attack on 17 July 1920. She 'lived in' as part of her teaching post with the Thomson family in Surbiton and at weekends stayed with her friend Mary Attenborough's family in Beckenham. As a young woman who (it is usually assumed) was romantically, as well as professionally inexperienced, she was susceptible to people taking an interest, particularly a suave editor who was also an ex-army Major with a Distinguished Service Order, whose other clients included Richmal Crompton, Edgar Wallace and Winston Churchill. Blyton confessed to her diary that she thought Pollock the same 'type' as the glamorous Prince of Wales (later Edward VIII) (D, 21 February 1924); they had the same dazzling blue eyes. 'I want him for mine', she wrote, and this ambition hardened, despite the fact that as she got to know him better, Pollock's less attractive qualities—an uneven temper and jealous nature—gradually revealed themselves, together with the fact that he was married already, albeit separated, and had two sons (D, 6 February 1924). For his part, Pollock, as well as being smitten, recognised Blyton's talent, and he offered opportunities and mentorship of the sort she needed, as well as romance to the young writer. Thus, an initial commission for a children's gift book swiftly developed into a succession of projects. By the time *The Enid Blyton Book of Fairies* and *The Zoo Book*, a survey of different animals (with photographs) were published in October 1924 Pollock had quietly divorced his existing wife, Marion, and married Blyton (in August 1924). The couple settled in a flat in Chelsea. The relationship which blossomed can plausibly be seen as an example of the type of '"desire" that converged with "work"', as noted by Catherine Clay in her study of 1920s women writerts, if only because as well as giving flowers, Pollock gave book contracts.[100] The *Enid Blyton Book of Bunnies* (1925), which deployed some of the pet names Blyton and Pollock used for each other, was also an attempt to tap into the demand for animal stories. Binkle and Flip are two baby rabbits who spend their time playing jokes on Wily Weasel, on Herbert Hedgehog (a policeman) and on other assorted inhabitants of Oak Tree Town. By the end of 1925, Blyton's yearly earnings from writing had risen to £1200.[101]

Not surprisingly, the contribution made by Hugh Pollock to Blyton's success has been the subject of debate. As noted in the previous chapter, it is striking how in *The Story of My Life* (and elsewhere), Blyton did not mention Pollock at all, let alone any influence he may have had. She did not need money desperately. Following her father's death, she had received a legacy of £500. It was not as much as he had given the two young children of his new family but it was a sizeable sum nonetheless. Blyton was also well-known to the extent that in 1924 *John o'London's Weekly* saw 'that it is almost superfluous to reintroduce her work to those who chose books for them [children]…she has advanced from success to success'.[102] Yet Blyton's detractors were prone to say that Pollock had 'made' her career.[103] Even friends like Phyllis Chase suggested that Pollock had given Blyton a 'leg up'. Marriage at least enabled Blyton to devote herself to writing full-time, having given up her teaching post. Pollock certainly encouraged Blyton, even suggesting that she learned to type: 'Worked all a.m. on typewriter, and got quicker at it', she recorded in her diary (D, 11 January 1927). In another entry: 'Worked all day till 4.30. Did 6000 words today, a record for me' (D, 25 October 1927). Pollock also seems to have acted as his wife's agent occasionally. Newnes published *The Radio Times* (the BBC had launched in 1922) and it was perhaps through these connections that he was able to negotiate for radio stations to take her work: Blyton's poem 'The Garden Party' was broadcast from the BBC's Plymouth transmitter on 24 May 1924, her story 'The Wizard's Magic Necklace' from Dundee on 26 May 1925 and 'The Rainbow Fairies' from Belfast on 23 May 1928. As 1920s literary couplings go, it was in the early years obviously more constructive than destructive. 'I am *glad* I married Hugh', Blyton wrote in August 1926, '& I wouldn't be unmarried for worlds. He is such a perfect dear' (D, 28 August 1926). To many observers, it seemed like 'an ideal partnership'.[104]

Pollock was also behind the plan hatched in 1926 for Blyton to edit Newnes' new weekly publication *Sunny Stories for Little Folks*. By this time most publishing houses had recognised that children (or their parents) had money to spend and that recurring publications could accrue loyal followings. Cosily titled publications for pre-school children already existed, including *Chicks' Own* (1920–1957) and later *Tiny Tots* (1927–1957). Slightly older readers had *Rainbow* (1914–1956), *Sunbeam* (1922–1940) and *Playbox* (1925–1955). The most prestigious publication was *Merry Go Round* (1923–1939), issued monthly by Basil Blackwell who, in imitation of the practice followed by magazines for grown-up readers, had sought to secure an advantage by enlisting a popular writer, Rose Fyleman, to serve as editor (or at least lend her name). In the case of *Sunny Stories*, it is not clear whether Newnes had already decided to launch a publication or whether it was always intended as a vehicle for Blyton; but as a new commercial venture, it proved remarkably successful. Moreover, Blyton became more than a figurehead and although the first 227 issues had 'edited by Enid Blyton' on the cover, she wrote the contents of all of them.[105] The result was more of a story paper than a comic and for two pence readers could buy (twice a month) two 'new' stories 'told by Enid Blyton' packaged together with bright illustrations. Unlike most magazines, the date of publication was not shown on the cover, a tactic intended to extend the shelf-life.

We will return to *Sunny Stories* in Chapter 4. For the moment it is worth noting several things about its contents because they seem to have set the tone for much of the next thirty years of Blyton's career. Firstly, that some of the work can seem second-hand or third-rate: in early issues, Blyton simply re-told familiar tales or 'classics' (Cinderella, Aladdin, Robin Hood, Gulliver's Adventures in the Land of Lilliput) or she adapted them, as in the stories she made out of Joel Chandler Harris's 'Brer Rabbit' series of folktales, set in the 'deep South' of the United States. But when she ran out of these, she made up her own stories, seemingly effortlessly. 'Yawnalot, the Bad Goblin' (April 1929), 'The Wizard and the Rubdubs' (May 1929), 'Klip-Klap and the Fireworks' (November 1929), 'Pickle-Puckle's Balloon' (February 1930) are just some of the titles in what seemed to be an endless supply.

The second thing which emerges about the fairy tales and re-hashed folk stories in *Sunny Stories* is how formulaic they are. This, though, was the point. Blyton deliberately uses what Ruth Robbins terms 'patterning'; that is to say,

> ...three wishes, three little pigs, three tasks or trials...the location of the story in the 'long-ago and far-away' imaginary spaces of no place and no specific time, and characters who are stereotypical (handsome princes, beautiful princesses, wicked wolves, ghastly hags and witches) rather than the individualized and fully realized or rounded figures that are supposed to inhabit realist writing.[106]

It was a structure Blyton stuck to, recognising that such familiarity helped readers who were taking the first steps towards reading on their own. The third aspect is that Blyton, whether she was writing a short story or a serial or a poem, believed young children to be 'really tender hearted' but also easily frightened. She often spoke of how as a girl she had been reduced to tears by Hans Christian Andersen's 'The Little Match Girl' (1845). This was not her intention for her own young readers: 'They could not possibly like reading about the poor little girl cast out by her parents to die in the cold'.[107] Finally, she wanted also to instil what she described as 'good' morals in her stories about animals and fairies, but not in a pious way. As a means of establishing a career, the combination seems to have worked. Blyton's association with *Sunny Stories* became the stuff of legend. It was the publication that along with *Teacher's World* promoted the Enid Blyton name most dramatically, at the same time as it showcased, alongside her other activities, her first phase of work. The success of the initial 250 issues of *Sunny Stories* (1926–1936), which roughly equates to 500 stories produced by Blyton, suggests that she was viewed as a safe pair of hands by parents (faced with the prospect of reading a bedtime story) as well as publishers.

Finally, five more general observations. First that Blyton's work as contrib-utor to magazines in the 1920s provided a good training ground in story-telling techniques—reader address, point of view, register—that she was to employ so successfully for the next forty years. Second, Blyton was determined to be wide-ranging in her scope from the beginning and disliked being pinned down as a type. Third, that Blyton's desire to speak to readers via an 'Enid Blyton' persona became a feature of her self-presentation early on and contributed to her popularity. A diary entry for 24 December 1927 records that she was receiving 500 letters a week from fans. Fourth, that looking at the sheer number of publications anxious to take Blyton's work, it is not surprising that her rapid progress can seem metonymic of the growth of children's literature itself during the decade. Fifth, that her work ethic was there from the beginning and helped install her in the minds of 1920s publishers as someone reliable who was to be reckoned with. She also, of course, needed to write for older children if her influence was to be maintained. As we shall see in the next chapter, Blyton's preoccupation with finding formats to do this becomes a recurrent one in the 1930s.

Notes

1. *Home for the Day: Enid Blyton*. Interview with Marjorie Anderson, BBC Light Programme 13 January 1963. https://www.bbc.co.uk/archive/home-for-the-day--enid-blyton/zvy6kmn. Accessed 1 March 2021.
2. Angela Smith, *The Second Battlefield. Women, Modernism and the First World War* (Manchester: Manchester University Press, 2000), 2.
3. Q.D. Leavis, *Fiction and the Reading Public* (1932; London: Bellow Publishing, 1978), 3.
4. Patrick Collier, *Modernism on Fleet Street* (Aldershot: Ashgate, 2006), 80.
5. Shafquat Towheed, Andrew Nash, and Claire Squires, 'Reading and Ownership', in *The Cambridge History of the Book in Britain, Volume 7: The Twentieth Century and Beyond*, eds. Andrew Nash, Claire Squires, and I.R. Willison (Cambridge: Cambridge University Press, 2019), 231–76 (232).
6. Unsigned Article, 'Children's Book Week in the United States', *The Times* (21 November 1921), 11.
7. Patrick Collier, *Modernism on Fleet Street*, 13.
8. Q.D. Leavis, *Fiction and the Reading Public*, 47.
9. Catherine Clay, Maria DiCenzo, Barbara Green, and Fiona Hackney, 'Introduction', in *Women's Periodicals and Print Culture in Britain 1918–1939: The Interwar Period*, eds. Catherine Clay, Maria DiCenzo, Barbara Green, and Fiona Hackney (Edinburgh: Edinburgh University Press, 2018), 1–9 (1).
10. D.J. Taylor, *The Prose Factory: Literary Life in England since 1918* (London: Chatto and Windus, 2016), 9.
11. Nicola Humble, *The Feminine Middlebrow Novel, 1920s to 1950s* (Oxford: Oxford University Press, 2001), 36.

12. 'RAB', 'To the Editor', *The New Statesman* (9 December 1922), 298.
13. Rebecca West, Notes on Novels', *The New Statesman* (2 December 1922), 270.
14. Mrs Champion de Crespigny, 'Literature', in J.A.R. Cairns (ed.), *Careers for Girls* (London: Hutchinson), 189; 194; 198.
15. Christopher Hilliard, *To Exercise Our Talents: The Democratization of Writing in Britain* (London: Harvard University Press, 2006), 8.
16. Unsigned Article, 'What Self-Reliance Will Do for You', *John o'London's Weekly* (7 June 1919), 264.
17. Advert, 'The Premier School of Journalism', *John o'London's Weekly* (10 January 1925), 567.
18. 'How I Write: Secrets of Authorship. By Famous Novelists', *John o'London's Weekly* (15 November 1924), 242.
19. Jessie Stephen, 'My Literary Career', *John O'London's Weekly* (14 February 1925), 723.
20. K.P. Hunt, 'My Literary Career', *John o'London's Weekly* (12 September 1925), 739.
21. Unsigned Article, 'A Guide to Short Story Writing', *Punch* 167 (July 1924), 122.
22. Michael Joseph, *Short Story Writing for Profit* (London: Hutchinson, 1922), 22.
23. Christopher Hilliard, *To Exercise Our Talents*, 68.
24. Unsigned Article, 'Free-lance War-Writing', *Nash's and Pall Mall Magazine* 55 (March 1915), ix.
25. Quoted in Christopher Hilliard, *To Exercise Our Talents*, 60.
26. The phrase 'make it new' refers to Ezra Pound's modernist call for change as well as being the title of his 1934 essay collection *Make It New* (London: Faber & Faber, 1934).
27. Enid Blyton, 'Sonnet', *Singers in the Crowd* (London: Noel James, 1921), 36.
28. Christopher Hilliard, *To Exercise Our Talents*, 223; 224.
29. Valerie Shaw, *The Short Story: A Critical Introduction* (London: Longman, 1983), 16.
30. Louise Heilgers, *How to Write Stories for Money* (1920), cited in Hilliard, *To Exercise Our Talents*, 73.
31. Unsigned Article, 'Hutchinson's Magazine', *The Bookman* 50:5 (January 1920), 348.
32. Unsigned Article, 'Puppet Pulls the Strings', *Books and Bookmen* (December 1957), 41.
33. Billie Melman, *Women and the Popular Imagination in the Twenties: Flappers and Nymphs* (Basingstoke: Macmillan, 1988), 111.
34. Christopher Hilliard, *To Exercise Our Talents*, 73.
35. [Enid Blyton], 'The Man She Trusted', *Home Weekly* (30 September 1922), 343–4 (344).
36. Christopher Hilliard, *To Exercise Our Talents*, 181.

37. Overall the evidence of these early magazine pieces reminds us that Blyton's aim was to produce work which was digestible and 'saleable' and she was partially successful, although the extent of this remains vague. This is despite the extensive work of Tony Summerfield whose *Enid Blyton: An Illustrated Bibliography Volume 1: 1922–1942* (Salisbury: Milford Books, 2002) has filled many gaps.

38. Peter Hunt, *Children's Literature an Illustrated History* (Oxford: Oxford University Press, 1995), 197.

39. Peter Hunt, Introduction, *Children's Literature: An Anthology* (Oxford: Basil Blackwell, 2001), xiii–xvi (xiii).

40. Unsigned Article, 'Children's Book Week', *The Times* (14 November 1922), 15.

41. Unsigned Article, 'Last Century Juveniles', *John o'London's Weekly* (6 December 1924), 379.

42. Unsigned Article, 'The Merry Muses: Verses for the Youngsters', *John o'London's Weekly* (5 December 1925), 395.

43. Unsigned Article, 'For Boys and Girls', *John o'London's Weekly* (6 December 1924), 390.

44. Eleanor Farejon, 'Child's Luck', *Time and Tide* (3 December 1926), 1107.

45. D. Billington, *Hints on Writing Juvenile Literature* (London: F Warne & Co, 1936), 13.

46. Ibid., 12.

47. 'Flopperty Castle', *Fairyland Tales* 4 (2 October 1922), 21–6; 'The Wizard's Necklace', *Fairyland Tales* 4 (9 October 1922), 21–6; 'Fanny in Fairyland', *Fairyland Tales* 4 (22 October 1922), 26.

48. 'A Wonderful Recovery', *The Leicester Advertiser* (4 November 1922), 18; 'Suppose', *The Leicester Advertiser* (4 November 1922), 20; 'Our Band', *The Leicester Advertiser* (4 November 1922), 21, 'Those Pigs!', *The Leicester Advertiser* (4 November 1922), 27.

49. Enid Blyton, 'The Enjoyment of Poetry', *The Voice of Youth*, 1.1 (Spring 1951), 4–7 (6).

50. Kimberley Reynolds, *Children's Literature: A Very Short Introduction* (Oxford: Oxford University Press, 2011), 96.

51. Lydia Miller Mackay, 'Books for Boys and Girls', *Time and Tide* (2 December 1921), 1156.

52. Philip Sidney, 'Fairy Lore', *John o'London's Weekly* (8 December 1923), 385.

53. Naomi Mitchison. 'What Do Children Want?', *Time and Tide* (7 December 1928), 1194.

54. Unsigned article, 'The Christmas Bookman', *The Bookman* 67 (December 1924), 182.

55. Lydia Miller Mackay, 'Wonder Tales', *Time and Tide* (3 December 1926), 1108.

56. Enid Blyton, 'The Enjoyment of Poetry', 6.

57. Lorna Lewis, 'Emil and Others', *Time and Tide* (5 December 1931), 1406.

58. Marjory Royce and Barbara E Todd, *The Very Good Walkers* (London: Methuen 1925), xii.

59. George Sampson, 'Poetry in Schools', *Teacher's World* (5 February 1923), 710.

60. 'Dominic', 'The Week's Causerie', *Teacher's World* (3 June 1923), 670.

61. D.J. Taylor, *The Prose Factory*, 86.

62. Enid Blyton, 'Suggestion and Auto-Suggestion', *Teacher's World I* (26 April 1922),180; 'Auto-Suggestion in the School: The Making of Merriden Major', *Teacher's World* (12 April 1922), 88; 122; 'A Fine Book', *Teacher's World* (18 August 1923), 942.

63. Cherry A. Hankin, ed. *Letters Between Katherine Mansfield and John Middleton Murray* (London: Virago, 1988), 204.

64. Virginia Woolf, 'Middlebrow' (1942), in *The Essays of Virginia Woolf*, ed. Stuart N. Clarke (London: The Hogarth Press, 2011), Vol. 6, Appendix II, 470–9.

65. Enid Blyton, 'Genius and Childhood', *Teacher's World* (4 July 1923), 691.

66. Quoted in Harry Hendrick, *Narcissistic Parenting. A History of Parenting Culture: 1920s to the Present* (Bristol: Policy Press, 2016), 56.

67. Susan Isaacs, *The Nursery Years* (London: George Routledge, 1929), 7; 9.

68. 'Romance', *Teacher's World* (29 August 1923), 1036.

69. 'Hassan', *Teacher's World* (14 November 1923), 395.

70. 'My Rock Pool', *Teacher's World* (22 August 1923), 974.

71. 'On Toys', *Teacher's World* (26 December 1923), 668.

72. 'Lord Mayor's Show', *Teacher's World* (21 November 1923), 439.

73. 'A Wonderful Remedy', *Teacher's World* (1 August 1923), 867; 'A London Miracle', *Teacher's World* (3 October 1923), 45.

74. 'A Confession about Adventures', *Teacher's World* (28 November 1923), 483.

75. D.J. Taylor, *The Prose Factory*, 87.

76. Adrian Bingham, *Family Newspapers? Sex, Private Life and the British Popular Press 1918–1978* (Oxford: Oxford University Press, 2009), 25.

77. A.A. Milne, *It's Too Late Now: The Autobiography of a Writer* (London: Methuen, 1939), 266.

78. Rose Macaulay, *Casual Commentary* (London: Methuen, 1925), 30.

79. Patrick Collier, *Modernism on Fleet Street*, 33.

80. Letter to Ethel Smyth 14 July 1932, in *The Letters of Virginia Woolf*, eds. Nigel Nicolson and Joanne Trautman. Vol. 5. 1932–1935 (New York: Harcourt Brace Jovanovich, 1979), 78.

81. Enid Blyton: 'The Children's Poets: A.A. Milne', *Teacher's World* (1 October 1926), 2.

82. Christopher Milne, who became a bookseller, recalls this in his diary for 24 August 1951: 'The other day came a letter from Enid Blyton saying she had heard we were opening a bookshop and enclosing her catalogue. It lists over 200 of her books....What a woman!

I wrote back to remind her that very many years ago she had presented me with a copy of *The Enid Blyton Book of Bunnies*, which in the end I almost knew by heart; and I asked if she would care to send a photograph of herself to go in our window. In reply I received three photographs, the latest version of her *Book of Bunnies*; two letters and a postcard'. Christopher Milne, *The Path Through the Trees* (London: Methuen, 1979), 187.

83. 'H.A'., 'The Children's Poets: Enid Blyton', *Teacher's World* (1 October 1926), 25.

84. Annette Federico, *Idol of Suburbia: Marie Corelli and Late Victorian Literary Culture* (London: University Press of Virginia, 2000), 50.

85. Dennis Judd, *Alison Uttley: The Life of a Country Child* (London: Joseph, 1986), 102.

86. Mary Cadogan, 'Richmal Crompton Lamburn', *New Dictionary of National Biography* (2004). https://doi.org/10.1093/refodnb/34386. Accessed 5 April 2021.

87. Peter Berresford Ellis & Jennifer Schofield, *By Jove, Biggles! The Life Story of Captain W.E. Johns* (Watford: Norman Wright, 2003).

88. Enid Blyton to W. E. Johns, 15 June 1949. http://www.wejohns.com/Blyton/. Accessed 1 March 2021.

89. Angela Bull, *Noel Streatfeild* (London: Collins 1984), 100; 252.

90. Noel Streatfeild, 'The Nesbit Influence', *Junior Bookshelf*, 22 (October 1958), 191.

91. Unsigned Article, 'Children's Book Forum', *W.H. Smith's Trade Circular* (25 August 1951), 11.

92. Wendy Pollard, 'Afterword', *Miss Ranskill Comes Home* (1946; London: New Persephone Books, 2003), 320.

93. Eleanor Graham, 'The Puffin Years' (1973), in Steve Hare, *Penguin Portrait* (Harmondsworth, 1995), 14.

94. Owen Dudley Edwards, *British Children's Fiction in the Second World War* (Edinburgh: Edinburgh University Press, 2007), 120. I am grateful to David Rudd for bringing this to my attention.

95. Unsigned Article 'Export consideration', *The Bookseller* (1 February 1945), 68.

96. Mark O'Hanlon, *Beyond the Lone Pine: A Biography of Malcolm Saville* (Worcester: M. O'Hanlon, 2001), 27.

97. Mike McGarry and Sally Walker, *Malcolm Saville. An Illustrated Bibliography* (Harpenden: Malcolm Saville Society, 2014), 65.

98. John Baxendale, *Priestley's England J. B. Priestley and English Culture* (Manchester: Manchester University Press, 2007), 10; 11.

99. Catherine Clay, *British Women Writers 1914–1945: Professional Work and Friendship* (Aldershot: Ashgate, 2006), 3.

100. Ibid., 3.

101. George Greenfield, *Enid Blyton* (Stroud: Sutton, 1998), xiv.

102. Enid Blyton, 'A Fairy Godmother', *John o'London's* (6 December 1924), 371.

103. Ida Pollock, *Starlight* (Hertford: Authors online, 2009), 25.

104. Blyton's gardener, Dick Hughes, quoted in *A Child-like Person*, dir. Roger Thompson, BBC Radio 4 (19 August 1975), 15.51. https://www.bbc.co.uk/archive/a-childlike-person/zvvt8xs. Accessed 14 March 2021.
105. Source: https://www.enidblytonsociety.co.uk/sunny-stories-for-little-folks.php.
106. Ruth Robbins, 'The Short Story and Genre Fiction', in Emma Liggins, Andrew Maunder, Ruth Robbins, *The British Short Story* (London: Palgrave, 2010), 193–208 (194).
107. Valerie Webster, 'Enid Blyton: She Was Banned Because of Noddy', *Reading Evening Post* (28 December 1966), 3.

Bibliography

Anderson, Benedict. 1983; 1991. *Imagined Communities: Reflections on the Origin and Spread of Nationalism*. London: Verso.

Baxendale, John. 2007. *Priestley's England: J. B. Priestley and English Culture*. Manchester: Manchester University Press.

Berresford, Peter, and Jennifer Schofield. 2003. *By Jove, Biggles!: The Life Story of Captain W.E. Johns*. Watford: Norman Wright.

Bingham, Adrian. 2009. *Family Newspapers? Sex, Private Life and the British Popular Press 1918–1978*. Oxford: Oxford University Press.

Bull, Angela. 1984. *Noel Streatfeild*. London: Collins.

Cadogan, Mary. 2004. 'Richmal Crompton Lamburn', *New Dictionary of National Biography*. https://doi.org/10.1093/refodnb/34386.

Cairns, J.A.R. Editor. 1928. *Careers for Girls*. London: Hutchinson.

Clay, Catherine. 2006. *British Women Writers 1914–1945: Professional Work and Friendship*. Aldershot: Ashgate.

Clay, Catherine, Maria DiCenzo, Barbara Green, and Fiona Hackney. Editors. 2018. *Women's Periodicals and Print Culture in Britain 1918–1939: The Interwar Period*. Edinburgh: Edinburgh University Press.

Collier, Patrick Collier. 2006. *Modernism on Fleet Street*. Aldershot: Ashgate.

Federico, Annette. 2000. *Idol of Suburbia: Marie Corelli and Late Victorian Literary Culture*. London: University Press of Virginia.

Hankin, Cherry A. Editor. 1988. *Letters Between Katherine Mansfield and John Middleton Murray*. London: Virago.

Hilliard, Christopher. 2006. *To Exercise Our Talents: The Democratization of Writing in Britain*. London: Harvard University Press.

Humble, Nicola. 2001. *The Feminine Middlebrow Novel, 1920s to 1950s*. Oxford: Oxford University Press.

Hunt, Peter. 1995. *Children's Literature: An Illustrated History*. Oxford: Oxford University Press.

————. Editor. 2001. *Children's Literature an Anthology.* Oxford: Basil Blackwell.

Isaacs, Susan. 1929. *The Nursery Years.* London: George Routledge.

Joseph, Michael. 1922. *Short Story Writing for Profit.* London: Hutchinson, 1922.

Judd, Dennis. 1986. *Alison Uttley: The Life of a Country Child.*

Leavis, Q.D. 1932; 1978. *Fiction and the Reading Public.* London: Bellow Publishing.

Liggins, Emma, Andrew Maunder, and Ruth Robbins. 2010. *The British Short Story.* London: Palgrave.

Macaulay, Rose. 1925. *Casual Commentary.* London: Methuen.

McGarry, Mike, and Sally Walker. 2014. *Malcolm Saville: An Illustrated Bibliography.* Harpenden: Malcolm Saville Society.

Melman, Billie. 1988. *Women and the Popular Imagination in the Twenties: Flappers and Nymphs.* Basingstoke: Macmillan, 1988.

Milne, A.A. Milne. 1939. *It's Too Late Now: The Autobiography of a Writer.* London: Methuen, 1939.

Nicolson, Nigel, and Joanne Trautman. Editors. 1979. *The Letters of Virginia Woolf.* New York: Harcourt Brace Jovanovich.

O'Hanlon, Mark. 2001. *Beyond the Lone Pine: A Biography of Malcolm Saville.* Worcester: M. O'Hanlon.

Pollock, Ida. 2009. *Starlight.* Hertford: Authors online.

Reynolds, Kimberley. 2011. *Children's Literature: A Very Short Introduction.* Oxford: Oxford University Press.

Royce, Marjory, and Barbara E. Todd. 1925. *The Very Good Walkers.* London: Methuen.

Shaw, Valerie Shaw. 1983. *The Short Story: A Critical Introduction.* London: Longman.

Smith, Angela Smith. 2000. *The Second Battlefield. Women, Modernism and the First World War.* Manchester: Manchester University Press.

Taylor, D.J. 2016. *The Prose Factory: Literary Life in England since 1918.* London: Chatto and Windus.

Towheed, Shafquat, Andrew Nash, and Claire Squires. 2019. 'Reading and Ownership.' In *The Cambridge History of the Book in Britain, Volume 7: The Twentieth Century and Beyond,* edited by Andrew Nash, Claire Squires and I.R. Willison, 231–76. Cambridge: Cambridge University Press.

Virginia Woolf. 2011. 'Middlebrow.' In *The Essays of Virginia Woolf,* edited by Stuart N. Clarke, Vol. 6, Appendix II, 470–9. London: The Hogarth Press.

4

Homes

Looking back in 1952 on her experiences, Blyton wrote that she had been 'lucky always to have had a full life: a life filled with people and things, with games and work, never-ending reading, nature-lore, music, theatres, and, later on, teaching, writing, getting married, bringing up my own children…caring for pets—and always, no matter what was happening, writing books, more books and yet more books' (*SML*, 106). This statement could be applied to almost any decade, but it is certainly an apt description of her life in the 1930s. Her marriage to Hugh Pollock had given her security. In August 1929 the couple had moved to 'Old Thatch', a picture-postcard, half-timbered cottage near the river Thames at Bourne End in Buckinghamshire. It was at Old Thatch that their daughter Gillian was born in July 1931 and Imogen in October 1935. The family lived there until 1938, at which point they moved to 'Green Hedges' in Beaconsfield, which would be Blyton's home for the rest of her life. For someone whose own childhood home had been unhappy, ownership of these places represented achievement and security. Blyton was no longer someone else's paying guest (as she had been at the Attenboroughs') or a paid servant in an employer's house (as at the Thompson's in Surbiton).

The shape that Blyton's life took in these different homes—her routines and relationships—is part of the focus of this chapter. Alongside it we will consider her developing career. As has been seen, she had become a successful writer, thanks in part to her work for *Teacher's World* and *Sunny Stories*, but she was still learning and carried with her a sense of optimism about the possibilities available to her. She knew she could expand her range. 'I can't

A. Maunder, *Enid Blyton*, Literary Lives,
https://doi.org/10.1007/978-3-030-76332-9_4

write only *one* kind of book', she later wrote. 'I have to write every kind of children's book there is!' (*SML*, 96). This sense of Blyton as a writer who in the late 1920s and 1930s was still experimenting with—or latching on to—different fictional sub-genres, is apparent in the texts examined in this chapter. These are the stories featuring the fox terrier, 'Bobs', and *The Secret Island* (1937). *The Secret Island* is an adventure story but it is also one of the first of Blyton's texts to offer a realist, equivocal, view of family life in which home can be a threatening environment. Childhood is not necessarily the place of innocence and wonderment presented in earlier works like *Child Whispers*. The focus on home—having one, escaping from one, establishing a new one—may have been a theme which struck a personal chord and it is certainly a recurrent feature in Blyton's works It is apparent, too, in the third case study discussed here—an examination of Blyton's circus stories beginning with *Mr Galliano's Circus* (serialised 8 April–30 September 1938) which shows her positioning herself again in another popular sub-genre.

Blyton's sense of herself as a commercial writer is also evident in her decision to serialise these works. Serial publication is most famously associated with Victorian novelists (Charles Dickens, Anthony Trollope and Wilkie Collins are notable examples) but it remained an accepted part of publishing practice in the 1920s and 1930s. W.E. Johns' Biggles stories appeared in this way as did more obviously 'grown up' novels such as Evelyn Waugh's *A Handful of Dust* (1934). Other contemporaries, for example, Noel Streatfeild, refused to have their stories 'chopped about' into serials on the grounds that it conflicted with the development of convincing characters.[1] Serialisation also placed structural demands on writers because of the need for action and cliff-hangers. Nonetheless, the shape of Blyton's career from the late 1930s onwards is that of a writer who always chose double publication (serial and book) if she could get it and she became skilled at 'chaptering', as she termed it, dividing up the story into chapters of fixed word counts to meet the requirements of the magazines in which it was due to appear (*D*, 24 November 1939). Meanwhile the value of *Sunny Stories* as a space to promote new work is evidenced by the fact that by the time Blyton gave up the editorship of the magazine in 1953, titles from most of her most popular series had been serialised in it, including: *The Naughtiest Girl in the School* (22 March 1940–30 August 1940), *Five Go off to Camp* (19 March–26 November 1948), *In the Fifth at Malory Towers* (25 November 1949–15 September 1950), and *Go Ahead Secret Seven* (17 October 1952–19 February 1953).

* * *

If we were able to ask young readers in the late 1920s and 1930s who 'Bobs' was, many of them would have been able to tell us instantly. He was one of Enid Blyton's pets, a black and white, smooth-haired fox terrier acquired in October 1926. Blyton began to feature Bobs (his name was a tribute to Field Marshal Roberts, one of Britain's most successful army commanders) in her 'From My Window' column in *Teacher's World* (from 10 November 1926). From here, his activities in Blyton's home—often mischievous, some-times serious (in May 1930, for example, he suffered burns after an accident with an electric heater [*TW*, 21 May 1930, 381])—were conveyed to readers with whom he was an instant favourite. Readers sent Bobs presents, including Easter eggs, and they were rewarded with photographs of him posed with and without his 'owner'.

By the time Blyton cast him as the centrepiece of the nineteenth issue of *Sunny Stories* in April 1927 (5–32), Bobs was thus a well-known and much-loved personality. In 'The Adventures of Bobs: The Story of a Dog', Bobs relates his adventures to the reader in the style of Anna Sewell's *Black Beauty*, which Blyton had read as a child. As in *Black Beauty*, the reader is invited to experience life from the perspective of a powerless animal who finds itself at the mercy of cruel humans. ('I am Sold' is the title of Chapter Two). In choosing a dog, Blyton was also perhaps trying to capture some of the senti-mental power of other famous animal stories, the touching one of Greyfriars Bobby, for example, a terrier who kept a loving watch by his owner's grave in Edinburgh in the 1860s.

Bobs describes a precarious existence which stems from the fact of being a dog. This is done in the first person and, like Sewell's equine narrator, Bobs has a trusting child-like vision of events. His adventures likewise follow a familiar pattern: ill-treatment by different 'owners' who, by virtue of being human, have power over helpless animals. Accordingly, Chapter Four, 'Stolen by the Gypsies' shows Bobs being knocked over the head and starved, while 'A Circus Dog' shows dogs being mistreated and one is killed by his trainer (a topical issue in 1927 when debates were taking place about the conditions under which performing animals were kept). Bobs then becomes a vagrant before finally being reunited with his original kindly 'master', Sandy, a young boy who has greater understanding of what animals need than the adults. Overall, Bobs is not quite as brutally treated as Black Beauty (Blyton was always mindful of her young audience), but the effect aimed at is similar. As Teresa Mangum notes, the talking animal story is a genre in which the abused animal 'serves as a voice of unmediated, hence honest, emotion; sensa-tion, often pain, forms its very language'.[2] The story's readers, meanwhile, learn lessons in animal welfare. One of Bobs' lowest moments comes when he is adopted as a lapdog and is petted and overfed, treatment which Blyton presents as another kind of cruelty. In contrast, the young owner, Sandy, is cast in heroic terms and Bobs knows that, with him as 'master', he can look forward to a life of companionship and mutual loyalty. Ultimately the affectiveness of 'The Adventures of Bobs' depends on what Heini Hediger has termed the 'assimilation tendency' whereby its readers, like its author, find it comforting to regard other animals as more or less like ourselves in terms of the range of emotions felt.[3] Inevitably, as with similar stories, some questions remain unanswered: who is Bobs dictating the story to and how do they understand each other? Does Bobs kill other animals? But for Blyton it was the soft-centred approach that worked. There were perhaps other considerations, too. It was the case that by the time Bobs appeared, anthropomorphic animals had become proven attractions in mass market publishing: Rupert Bear appeared in *The Daily Express* from 1920, *The Daily Sketch* introduced the public to Oojah, an elephant in 1921, while Pip (a dog) and Wilfred (a rabbit) had begun their adventures in *The Daily Mirror* in 1919. Jean de Brunhoff's *The Story of Babar*, published in France in 1931, was followed two years later by an English translation under the supervision of A. A. Milne. Faced with another pile of such books to review, Naomi Mitchison concluded that animals had become 'like film stars. They are so popular that publishers seem to think that anything about them is worth reading. Tell the world what an Aberdeen Terrier or Shirley Temple has for dinner and everybody will be happy'.[4] Animals *were* film stars, of course. Cinemagoers were lapping up the dozens of films starring 'thinking' canine action heroes: Rin-Tin-Tin in the 1920s, followed by Asta (another fox terrier) and Lassie in the 1930s and 1940s.[5]

Blyton had evidently stumbled on something with Bobs. The dog was so loved that publishers were willing to pay her to turn out more stories about him. By September 1929 Bobs had apparently learned to type and started to publish his own letters alongside Blyton's as *Teacher's World* gave the duo a weekly children's page. The pair would often write about the same topic from a different perspective, Bobs providing a sardonic running commentary on events in the Blyton household, including his relations with the other pets. He was fully aware of his own importance—at least in his own mind—and signed off with 'a loving wuff' (*TW*, 30 April 1930, 229). When in 1933 *Letters From Bobs* was published, it sold 10,000 copies in its first week; further collections followed in 1937 and 1941.[6] When the 'real' Bobs died on 26 November 1935, Blyton, out of a mixture of grief and pragmatism, made the '[p]oor old fellow' live on (D, 26 November 1935). Bobs' letters continued to appear, including in *Sunny Stories*. Meanwhile other Blyton pets began to

Fig. 4.1 Enid Blyton and Bobs (early 1930s)

write for the magazine, notably Bimbo, a Siamese cat (from June 1940) and Topsy, another fox terrier (from June 1942).[7]

Taken collectively, the voices of these animals cemented the appealing notion that pets derived pleasure from each other's company and that they were capable of feeling love and loyalty to their 'master'—or 'mistress', as Bobs referred to Blyton. In terms of her public image, there was clearly much to be gained by conveying the impression that animals, like children, loved Blyton, but it is also apparent that she in turn, loved them and genuinely shared the widespread belief—still prevalent today—that contact with animals offered connection to a special brand of goodness and that having a pet made one a better person.[8]

* * *

In trying to slice through the enormous quantity of fiction Blyton produced in the late 1920s and 1930s, a useful focal point is to consider as case studies some of the texts which appeared in *Sunny Stories* and later *Enid Blyton's Sunny Stories*. This was the name given to *Sunny Stories* after 15 January 1937, the point at which it was redesigned with 'all sorts of extra things', as Blyton explained in an introductory 'Letter from Old Thatch'. 'I am going to write your stories for you just as I have always done' but, as she explained, there would be competitions and puzzles, as well as prizes (quoted in Stoney, 113). One of the results was *The Secret Island*, serialised in *Enid Blyton's Sunny Stories* (24 September 1937–11 February 1938), a novel which has always held an important place amongst Blyton's 1930s works. While it was not Blyton's first attempt at an adventure story (she had published *The Wonderful Adventure* in 1927), it is one of the earliest stories in which ingredients familiar to readers of her better-known series were utilised for the first time. It was also a new type of story for *Sunny Stories* more generally. Up to this point, the magazine had mainly sought to feature goblins, pixies, fairies, brownies and talking animals who swarmed over its pages, giving it a rather 'feminine feel'—this at any rate was the feeling of one young reader, John Carey.[9] *The Secret Island* represented a shift towards a more robust form of storytelling. There are four independently minded, pre-teen children—Mike and Nora Arnold (twins), their sister Peggy, and a neighbour, Jack—who run away from cruel guardians and devise an alternative, safer, lifestyle on an island in the middle of a lake. 'And so it was. The little island seemed to float on the dark lake-waters. Trees grew on it, and a little hill rose in the middle of it. It was a mysterious island, lonely and beautiful. All the children stood and gazed...' (*SI*, 19). The island lures the children in with the promise of '[a]n adventure! A real proper adventure, almost like Robinson Crusoe...' (*SI*, 20).

The early reference to Daniel Defoe's famous castaway is Blyton's way of anchoring her story; thus it is to be her attempt at a 'robinsonade', a sub-genre of fiction derived from *Robinson Crusoe* (1719), which traditionally features young Europeans being shipwrecked on an isolated and seemingly uninhabited island where they are forced to make a new life. Traditionally in these narratives the island may be a paradise or a utopia, but it may also reveal hidden dangers: wild animals and sometimes cannibals.[10] Usually the emphasis is on the protagonists proving their physical and emotional toughness and if children, their maturity. When they are rescued they return to their old life 'better' people than when they left it. Johann David Wyss's *Swiss Family Robinson* (1812) was the most famous example of this kind of writing, in which the family find themselves stranded on a well-stocked island of exotic flora and fauna, but equally popular in Britain were Captain Frederick Marryat's *Masterman Ready* (1841–1842) and R.M. Ballantyne's *Coral Island* (1857). This last story in which a group of shipwrecked boys are left to fend for themselves was one of the texts referenced by Blyton in *The Story of My Life*. Growing up, Blyton would also have encountered the works of some of the period's famous writers for girls, for example those of Angela Brazil (1868–1947), Bessie Marchant (1862–1941) and also L.T. Meade (Elizabeth Thomasina Meade Smith (1844–1914)), whose *Four on an Island* was published in 1892. In Meade's novel, set off the coast of Brazil, the 'four'—two girls and two boys—are carried out to sea in a boat, land on a desert island, and manage, with the help of a conveniently discovered wreck, to live there for three months. For one reviewer, the success of Meade's novel was proof, if any were needed, that 'Crusoe stories have…a charm about them which is not readily worn out—what child has not fancied himself a Crusoe at some time or other?'.[11]

In writing *The Secret Island*, Blyton was again staking her claim to a genre with a long-established tradition whose popularity showed few signs of waning. The success of Arthur Ransome's *Swallows and Amazons* (1930) was further proof of the lure of islands, boats and lakes for city-dwelling children who were unlikely to experience them first hand. In July 1938, a new comic, *The Beano*, launched itself with a hair-raising serial titled 'The Shipwrecked Kidds', a breathlessly-told tale of brother and sister Cyril and Ethel Kidd (children of a millionaire), who with a cook's assistant and a sailor, escape on a raft. They find themselves stuck on an island somewhere near Africa, populated by serpents, giant crabs, gorillas, giant moles and fierce pygmy 'bird-men' who fly like bats, and they find home comforts by catching fish and making chips from yams.

Blyton's protagonists in *The Secret Island*—Jack, Peggy, Mike and Nora—do not travel as far: their 'secret island' is in Britain, not the South Seas; and they remain within striking distance of their former homes. This means that some of the frightening elements of making a home on a deserted island are removed by reason of geography. But it is worth noting as well that one reason why the island does not prompt feelings of fear is because the children's experiences on it are less traumatic than living with the relatives they run away from: a vicious aunt (Mike, Nora and Peggy) and a neglectful, bad-tempered grandfather (Jack). That the children escape from what was monstrous and appalling to a place of respite and safety also ensures that any disagreeable aspects to the children's new existence are rarely mentioned. In one sense they are castaways *before* they set off: they have been abandoned by their globetrotting aviator parents and tormented by their aunt. Compared to their previous lives, the work they are required to do on the island in order to survive does not seem arduous; it is neither soul destroying nor wearisome. The children lack luxuries, but Blyton's message is that material deprivations are better than what they had before. Nor do they suffer the disasters which might await real castaways—they do not go mad, starve or fall ill or experience hypothermia. Instead:

> They lay on their backs in the sand, looking up at the evening sky, listening to the crackle of the wood, and smelling a mixture of wood-smoke and honeysuckle…and the delicious smell of wild thyme crushed under their bodies. A reed-warbler sang a beautiful little song in the reeds below, and then another answered. (*SI*, 42–3)

They are shown leading a basic but comfortable life on an island which is not lashed by wind or rain but, unusually for Britain, is notable for its stable, mild climate, natural spring water and healthy vegetation including 'juicy green grass' for the cow which they manage to transport across at night in a rowing boat (*SI*, 73).

Given that *The Secret Island* is about the children's need to find a new home (the *Hull Daily Mail* described its theme as 'home building'[12]), the first task they set themselves is to construct one from scratch). Under the supervision of their slightly older, working-class mentor, Jack, they learn the old English art of willow-weaving, tying willow trees together, weaving branches and reeds in-between stakes to make walls:

> Everyone worked hard. The girls found it a rather nice job to stuff the soft heather and bracken into the cracks and make the house rain – and wind-proof. They were so happy in their job that they did not notice what a fine door Jack and Mike had made of woven willow twigs. (*SI*, 61)

As they do so, Blyton is quick to emphasise that this is a joyous time; there are no grumblers or dropouts. In building 'Willow House', there is a shared sense of community and of a mission and there are certainly no regrets about the homes left behind and none of the loneliness that attacks other castaways. A popular reading of Defoe's original Crusoe story argues that it operates as a 'fictional paradigm for creating society anew'.[13] Blyton shows the children doing just this, creating an independent world where there are no adults to spoil things. The island provides most of their material needs and they take pleasure in finding plants to eat, much as other (non-human) animals do. Eventually, the island provides more food than they need, prompting them to turn capitalist, making money by weaving baskets and filling them with wild strawberries and mushrooms which Jack sells in a market. The initial worry that they will be caught and dragged back to their families wears off and they settle down to a life of comfortable routine. There is a sense of a seasonal cycle which makes life on the island orderly. Only occasionally is this disrupted, such as when some noisy trippers arrive with their portable gramophone and seem likely to discover the children, until some bats send them squealing away (*SI*, 84). For the most part, adults, who are the cause of the children's problems, are left behind and the children establish an Edenic relationship with the natural world, working with it, rather than against it.

The Secret Island is thus different from what Mike, Peggy, Nora and Jack have experienced previously—and have suffered and hated—with the result that the story as it plays out becomes one where the children learn to care for the island, become proprietorial (as Crusoe does) and perceive it as their home. In turn, this makes it a kind of paradise which allows growth and happiness. However, if we examine the novel closely, it also becomes apparent that while the children restart to reinvent their lives, they do not escape entirely into new ways of thinking. They do not become 'wild children'; rather, there is an emphasis on washing and the Protestant work ethic. Likewise, the network of relationships is also more or less a replica of the one left behind and the children try out versions of adult behaviour patterns. While Jack and Mike play the roles of explorers and administrators, the girls, Peggy and Nora, perform what passes on the island for domesticity: they look after the hens, arrange the stores, keep the house tidy and, in Peggy's case, do the cooking and sewing. Meanwhile Peggy requests that the boys put shelves up in the cave, which will form their winter residence. The novel's approval of this behaviour might be yet another nod to *Robinson Crusoe,* a story which posits that knowing how to keep house and bake bread are vital survival skills. Like Crusoe, Peggy also makes a blanket out of rabbit skins. But the stronger echoes come from Wendy Darling's adventures in Neverland in J.M. Barrie's *Peter and Wendy* (1911), a work which Blyton greatly admired (in June 1937 she published a poem in *Punch,* 'J.M.B.', to mark Barrie's death).[14] As Christmas approaches, Jack plans to buy a new doll for Nora and a new sewing box for Peggy. The latter fusses over him when he leaves the island without a coat (in the same way that Wendy fusses over the 'Lost Boys'). When the children's parents finally return and visit the island it is her domestic skills that Peggy is most keen to show off, wanting her mother 'to see how nicely she could do things, even though they all lived in a cave!' (*SI,* 181). Peggy and Nora are having an adventure on the island, but their ambitions are carefully presented so as not to upset things too much. This includes obeying Jack without question.

The Secret Island is a text that collects together many of the different elements of Blyton's fiction. It testifies to an interest in adventurous children and offers a fantasy of childhood escape from adult control and the option to 'run wild' in the natural world (*SI,* 184). On the island, the children ostensibly end up living with less, but they are entirely happy with this and the novel ends with the prospect of returning in the school holidays: 'the summer days when they would go there once more, and live merrily and happily alone, in the hot sunshine...sleeping soundly on heathery beds' (*SI,* 190). At the same time the novel is as much about promoting middle-class value systems as it is about shaking them off and the children's life on the island does not mean these are disregarded. Finally, it is worth noting the ways in which adults are presented: as either cruel or absent. Missing parents are, of course,

Fig. 4.2 'Old Thatch'

useful plot devices in children's fiction because they allow children more independence than might ordinarily be the case. Mothers especially are noticeable by their propensity to be absent. Over the years, however, readers have also commented on the sheer amount of freedom Blyton's parents give their children and in *The Secret Island* Captain and Mrs Arnold are a case in point. They return from the dead, having been rescued from an island in the Pacific after a plane crash. One of the aspects of the story which prompts a raised eyebrow is the fact that, after having been separated from their children for two-and-half years, the first thing the couple intend to do is despatch them to boarding school. The parents' irresponsibility more generally and the fact they left their children in the hands of untrustworthy relatives is not touched upon. What Blyton seems to be encouraging is the idea that children need to be robust and that, in being sent away to boarding school, they *are* being rewarded with the promise of a world that is ordered and safe. The practical education provided by life on the island is valuable but so too is the world of books and Latin declensions.

* * *

Given the focus in *The Secret Island* on the importance of homes—
unpleasant ones, alternative ones—this is perhaps a good moment to consider
the reports of Blyton's own home life in the 1930s, both the image she created
for readers and the less comfortable accounts given by observers, which have
complicated the picture. As has been noted, in August 1929 Blyton and
Hugh Pollock moved to 'Old Thatch' near the River Thames at Bourne
End. It was there that their daughter Gillian was born in July 1931 and
Imogen in October 1935. Like Elfin Cottage, Old Thatch featured regularly
in Blyton's articles and stories in which daily life was embellished as something idyllic, harmonious and even magical. 'If ever you came to the gate of
old Thatch…you'd open the gate and creep in and see/That it's all just exactly
you "guessed it to be"' begins her poem 'Old Thatch'. The 'it' is that Blyton
and her family including Bobs (who had, in fact, been dead for two years)
live '[i]n friendship together…the year through' (*TW*, 25 August 1937, 17).
Andrew Motion has made the point that fictional houses 'create a universe
and reflect and confirm character'.[15] This was the role that 'Old Thatch'—a
real house and a fictionalised one—played. In fact, Blyton's diaries reveal a
sometimes-fraught environment: quarrels with servants and with Hugh who,
it has been claimed, resented his wife's friendship with Dorothy Richards,
who had been engaged as a nurse following the birth of Imogen and on whom
Blyton had come to rely for advice and companionship. Dorothy's presence
was also an offshoot of Blyton's determination that having a husband and
children could not be allowed to slow her down; that the dangers to creativity
presented by 'the pram in the hall', to use Cyril Connolly's famous phrase,
were to be avoided by the hiring of maids, cooks and nannies as needed
(Fig. 4.2).[16]

It is this prizing of order and routine that comes across in Blyton's diaries.
This excerpt is from 1935:

> 13 Jan: Did a/c & wrote letters. Hugh took pups to have tails cut.[17] The
> Wilcox's for tea and bridge. The Fishers for bridge at 8. Worked till lunch.
> 14 Jan: Worked till lunch. To Mrs Gilbert's for bridge. Read till bed.
> 15 Jan: Worked till lunch. Rested & read till tea. Wrote letters. To bridge at
> Wilcoxes while Hugh stayed at home and read.
> 16 Jan: Worked till lunch. Had bridge here. Read and wrote till bed.
> 17 Jan: Worked till lunch. To Mrs Gilbert's for bridge. To the Hopes at 8.30
> to bridge.
> 18 Jan: Worked till lunch. Rested till tea. Wrote letters. To Rialto Cinema to
> see The Barretts of Wimpole St.

The previous year Blyton had published at least eighteen books, including
Round the Year with Enid Blyton (four parts: 'Spring', 'Summer', 'Autumn'

and 'Winter'), *The Talking Teapot and other Tales*, *Brer Rabbit Retold*, *Happy Stories*, *The Enid Blyton Poetry Book*, *The Red Pixie Book*, *Stories from World History Retold*, *Ten-Minute Tales* and *Snowy Days*. In 1935, the year of the diaries, there would be twenty-nine, including *The Adventures of Bobs,* an enormous hit. Much of the work is formulaic (not necessarily a bad thing) but also trite and forgettable. As a commissioning editor for the BBC observed, it was the kind of stuff where 'the Pinky-winky-Doodle-doodle Dum-dumm type of name—and lots of pixies' ran unchecked but it was also well paid and helped fund a comfortable lifestyle.[18]

A corollary to this was that there were doubtless costs to be borne by Blyton's children who often seem not to have featured in their mother's plans except to the extent that they were available to be wheeled out for photo shoots or referenced in stories and articles for *Teacher's World* and thus embellish the public's sense of her as a child-friendly personality. ('Dear Boys and Girls, I have just read the story to Gillian and she has been out to her garden', was a typical example appearing in Blyton's weekly letter on 30 June 1937 [*TW*, 30 June 1937, 15]). It does seem the case that Blyton's commitment to her work meant that she saw less of Gillian and Imogen than readers of her columns were led to believe. When things were going well, she could be cheerful and enjoyed games, but she was also easily irritated, particularly by noise. Blyton's daughters began to know their mother was a busy and important/influential woman beloved by children all over the country but the younger daughter, Imogen, did not, by her own account, feel close to her. She recalled the confusing mixture of beatings and pocket money handed out by 'the woman with dark curly hair and brown eyes' who worked on a typewriter downstairs. It took Imogen a while to realise that this woman who saw her for prescribed periods after tea, 'who paid me just as she paid the staff', who was 'the absolute ruler of our household' and who answered letters from young fans 'with a pleasure and interest that she rarely showed with me', was 'also my mother' (Smallwood, 35; 36; 35). 'I was a little wary of her', Imogen recalled of the evenings playing Ludo or Dominoes, 'but she [Blyton] could make the game great fun and the hour, if a little tense, was certainly a release from the boredom of the nursery' (Smallwood, 31). In contrast, Blyton's relations appear to have been easiest with her elder daughter, Gillian, with whom she had been able to establish a closer bond before the demands of success got in the way.

By 1938 Blyton and Hugh felt confident enough about their financial position to move to a bigger house in Beaconsfield, 'Green Hedges' (Blyton's readers were invited to suggest names). Beaconsfield was a small, pretty town (population 4949 in 1931), twenty-three miles west of London and ten miles

Fig. 4.3 'Green Hedges'

north from Windsor.[19] There was an 'old-world' air to it but also good rail links to the capital as well as an 18-hole golf course (one of Blyton's passions was golf), and a well-known beauty spot, Burnham Beeches, nearby. The British Lion Film Corporation had also established studios there, something which prompted the town's expansion in the 1930s. The new home (Fig. 4.3), which cost £3000, was a mock-Tudor, eight-bedroomed house, on Penn Road, part of the 'new' town, set in three acres of grounds, containing a tennis court and a cottage (for the gardener). When she wanted to, Blyton could walk down to the local shops, only ten minutes away, as was the train station for trips to see her publishers. It was a large house to run and indoor and outdoor servants were employed; in 1939 there were two living-in: a house-maid, Mary Bale (Engres), and a cook, Gisela Pressburger.

Blyton enjoyed living at Green Hedges partly because it *was* big, and this suited her because the children could be kept from getting under her feet. Moreover, she quickly established a routine. She thought up stories for which she was handsomely paid but she also followed (apparently easily) the expected routines of the comfortably off housewife. She was more than equal to juggling these two lives. As Imogen explained, her mother was a 'cheerful' person:

She used to hum, and she used to do her flowers....[She] used to, each morning, go and talk to the cook, about...the menu for the day, and so on, and discuss the shopping. And then she would work right through the morning from 10.00 and then she would do a little bit of gardening or whatever she felt like doing in the afternoon and also work more. And in the evening, she used to do her fan mail which was huge, she used to read it all and started answering it.[20]

Blyton was not imprisoned at her typewriter or mailbag all the time. Her diaries, as demonstrated above, record her visiting other families and she was part of a bridge club along with other well-heeled women whom she occasionally hosted and sparred with. She was undoubtedly unusual amongst her neighbours in having a career of her own, but she also adopted their hobbies: cocktail parties, golf, tennis, trips to the cinema and to London for lunch and shopping at Dickens & Jones's in Regent Street. It was not a dull existence and there is no sense of Blyton being a dull person. Moreover, there is no sense of her being pestered either. Beaconsfield was used to having famous personalities reside in the town. Alison Uttley, author of the Little Grey Rabbit series of children's tales and the historical novel *A Traveller in Time* (1939) lived there, as did Angela Thirkell; the latter stayed with Dorothy Collins who had been secretary to G.K. Chesterton (another resident). Other inhabitants included James Garvin, editor of *The Observer*, and Lord John Reith, Director General of the BBC. There were also 'film people' who had been drawn to the town by the presence of the British Lion Film Corporation studios in Candlemas Lane: director Adrian Brunel and actresses Helen Misenor, Mary Riddle and Joyce Rollinson; the latter was a neighbour of Blyton's on Penn Road.

It is safe to assume that Blyton encountered some of these people, not least because she was sociable. However, relations between Blyton and some of the residents were not always friendly. Blyton and Alison Uttley (who lived at 'Thackers', a cottage on Ellwood Road) never really hit it off. Their first meeting at a lunch party in Beaconsfield, set up by well-meaning acquaintances who assumed that the two ladies, both successful authors, would have a lot in common, did not start well. Another guest, Katherine Wigglesworth, recorded how:

As they all moved into the dining room for lunch, Alison, doing her best to be pleasant, turned to Enid Blyton and said: 'I know the book you wrote about a horse, but what else have you written?' Enid Blyton drew herself up and replied frostily 'Smith's window is *full* of my books. You can see a few titles if you care to look'. As Alison later said, 'You see, Katherine, I had mixed her up with Enid Bagnold and *National Velvet*.'[21]

It is an interesting sidelight on Blyton—and on Uttley, of course, who was not as ignorant of Blyton's work as she made herself out to be and was threatened by the younger woman's success. Uttley, who crops up at regular intervals in the Blyton story, resented her new neighbour, finding her sales figures 'particularly galling'.[22] Blyton, meanwhile, seems to have ignored Uttley, although she probably would have liked to have written *National Velvet*.

* * *

As had been the case at 'Old Thatch', 'Green Hedges' became part of the Blyton brand. A poem published in August 1938 addressed the house with '[y]our leaded windows and cosy nooks,/Your sunny corners and smiling looks' and signalled the change of headquarters to readers of *Teacher's World* (*TW*, 24 August 1938, 9). Once established at the new house, Blyton quickly decided that she liked its veranda where she could get on with her work. It was here that George Greenfield recalled seeing her most often, sitting in a chair, a rectangular board on her knees on top of which rested 'an ancient manual typewriter that clanked like a threshing machine' as Blyton pummelled its keys.[23]

These glimpses are reminders of how by end of the 1930s Blyton had begun to take on so many commitments that she continually put herself under pressure, living on a treadmill of deadlines and commitments for almost the rest of her life. Other contemporaries—Noel Streatfeild, Arthur Ransome—were less inclined to publish all the time; they wanted work-free weekends and the time to enjoy the rewards. In 1934, the year in which Blyton's produced eighteen titles, W.E. Johns published two Biggles novels (a pattern he continued for the next twenty years). Despite a cruise to Madeira in October 1930 and some enforced rest in June 1931 and October 1935 when her children were born and later in the decade when Hugh was intermittently ill, Blyton always returned quickly to the high-pressure working which dominated her life. It is not easy to explain why. She could have earned enough to live comfortably as the editor of *Sunny Stories* while also publishing one book a year. Very few writers would have said 'yes' to magazines and newspapers so often. Blyton's own explanations tend to stress that she worked hard because she found the work easy. She had, she claimed, an imagination which could be 'tapped at any moment I like, for as long as I like...'. Her immense output was also 'the natural result of a love for all ages of children' linked to 'an absorbing interest in the things they love. The fact that it means ten times as much work is of no account, as all real enthusiasts know' (*CL*, 3). It was this, added to her sense of herself as having a vocation to help children, that led to her readiness to take on—and instigate—a continuous stream of projects. Continuing as a columnist in *Teacher's World*, she had the chance to be at the centre of a forum for the exchange of new ideas about pedagogy and child development; she could voice her own (very decided) Froebel-inspired views about classroom activities as well as indulging her passion for botany and nature studies. It also bestowed on her an aura of expertise and ensured doors in the world of educational publishing were kept open.

Another explanation of Blyton's readiness to work extra hours has been seen to lie in her upbringing. The compulsive-obsessive work ethic had been a way of escaping life with her uncongenial mother and achieving independence. Having established the habit of hard work and appreciating the plaudits, approval and sense of self-worth that came with success ('the trust and affection I get…is enough incentive to work a hundred times harder!') Blyton sought to maintain it (*CL*, 2). It has also been suggested that taking refuge in the world of children became a kind of retreat, a survival mechanism which allowed her to cope with the strains of the adult world. This of course is a diagnosis made of other writers for children who are often seen as 'damaged'—Rudyard Kipling, J.M. Barrie, Kenneth Grahame.

It is possible to see some of these ideas coalescing in one of the first works to be published from Green Hedges, *Mr Galliano's Circus* (serialised in *Sunny Stories*, 8 April–30 September 1938). They are present, too, in the other circus books which followed: *Hurrah for the Circus!* (*Sunny Stories*, 12 May–29 September 1939), *Circus Days Again* (serialised in *Sunny Stories*, 7 March 1941–29 August 1941) and *Come to the Circus* (*Sunny Stories*, 7 February 1947–5 March 1948). This last named continues the exploration of neglected children left to the mercies of callous relatives that Blyton had undertaken in *The Secret Island* (1938) and would continue in *Hollow Tree House* (1945). In 1940, writing as "Mary Pollock", Blyton also published *Three Boys and a Circus*. A longish short story, 'All About the Circus' in which Joan and Bobby encounter Galliano's circus and meet the showfolk, was published in 1939. A later story, 'A Circus Adventure', ran in *Sunny Stories* (21 Mar–2 May 1952) before being issued by Newnes in *Enid Blyton's Omnibus* (1952) with four other stories from the magazine. All featured return visits to popular series which had made their appearance in the magazine: *Adventures of The Wishing Chair*, *The Adventurous Four*, *The Naughtiest Girl in the School*, *The Enchanted Wood*.

One of the reasons Blyton was drawn to circus stories was because she held powerful memories of childhood visits and associated them with times when she was happy. 'I loved the circus so much…', she wrote. 'I do still, of course'. She recalled going behind the scenes to see the animals. Afterwards, lying in bed at night making up stories, 'many of the "night thoughts" that came to me were about the circus'. This allowed her to create 'a whole circus' in her imagination 'and so naturally, when I grew up and wanted to write, one of the things I found easy to do was to write books about circuses' (*SML*, 96–97).

While the topic may have been close to Blyton's heart, it was also the case that circus stories seemed to sell well. As *John o'London's* 1936 article, 'Under the Big Top', noted, the circus had become a 'most popular' subject 'of recent years'. There had been Hollywood films—Charlie Chaplin's *The Circus* (1928) and Walt Disney's *Bright Lights* (1928)—whose makers had been attracted by 'the teeming life and colour beneath and around the Big Top'. The celebrated painter Laura Knight had exhibited a series of paintings based on scenes from Bertram Mills' circus. Eleanor Smith's novel, *Red Wagon* (1930), which centred on the love between a circus owner and a lion tamer, had been a bestseller before being made into a film in 1933. In the popular imagination there was a widespread sense of the circus as a place of excitement and opportunity; 'the very air vibrates with courage, endurance, love, danger and death', as *John o'London's* pointed out, adding that '[a] rich field awaits the writer who explores the lives of the sideshow folk.…What a world of colour and romance lives in the great circus'. But where was the great circus novel going to come from? It needed someone like John Galsworthy, 'who could combine his sense of family history and changing fashion with the rich colourful descriptions of show life of a [J.B.] Priestley or a [A.P.] Herbert'.[24]

It is possible that Enid Blyton saw herself as someone suited to fill this role. Blyton's 'grown up' story, *The Caravan Goes On* (1932), was rejected unceremoniously by the agent A.P. Watt and was never published nor seen again. The circus featured, however, and Barbara Stoney has suggested that Blyton, never one to waste material, incorporated sections of the novel into *Mr Galliano's Circus* six years later (Stoney, 97). Blyton was certainly aware of the attractiveness of circus-based stories to audiences. Moreover, circuses were still a large part of the cultural landscape despite occasional voices speaking up about animal cruelty. A visit in 1935 by Princesses Elizabeth and Margaret to Bertram Mills' Circus had also caught the public's imagination: Laura Knight was commissioned to produce circus designs for a china dinner service while the London department store, Gamages, began holding Christmas circus shows in its children's department. Meanwhile there was a flurry of books, of which Howard Spring's *Sampson's Circus* (1936), James Hull's *The Stage-struck Seal* (1938) and Noel Streatfeild's *The Circus is Coming* (1938) were the best known. The last named is the story of two rather snobbish children, Peter and

Santa, who run away from the threat of being sent to live in an orphanage to find a new home with their Uncle Gus, a circus clown. The novel won the Carnegie Medal for Children's Book of the Year. It was hard for aspiring authors—or even established ones—*not* to get the messages, not the least of which, as John Masefield noted, was that 'to countless children…the circus is the greatest of all joys, and circus life the image of Paradise'. What was also true—Blyton, being an example—was that the attraction continued into adulthood. Gravitas and respectability were all very well, but who, Masefield argued, 'would not give a finger to be able to do a "jump-up," or somersault upon the back of a ring-horse, or hold a thousand people spellbound, like the clown in the red and white?'[25]

For Blyton, as for Masefield, part of the circus's appeal was that it represented an unconventional and alternative space and it offered the possibilities of escape and a new life—to adults as well as children. In *Mr Galliano's Circus*, published in 1938, a time when Britain was a land of dole queues (registered unemployment stood at nearly two million), the circus offers work for Jimmy Brown's carpenter father. Rather than being led astray, the circus is a place where, as members of the 'deserving poor', the Brown family re-establishes itself-worth albeit in a smaller space. The circus atmosphere, apart from occasional squabbles, is shown to be harmonious, with performers working together for the greater good—what real-life circus proprietor, Cyril Bertram Mills called 'the spirit of co-operation' necessary for success.[26] Although they inhabit a caravan rather than a house, Mrs Brown conscientiously follows familiar routines: polishing, dressmaking and rustling up delicious meals on a tiny stove. Jimmy, meanwhile, has the kind of affinity with animals that anticipates Philip Mannering in *The Island of Adventure* (1944). Meanwhile, a sequel, *Hurrah for the Circus!* (1939), introduces the idea of an actively rebellious girl, Lotta, who cuts her hair short in order to pass for a boy, which looks forward to the characterisation of George Kirrin in *Five on a Treasure Island* (1942). Lotta is irresponsible and slovenly but emerges as a sympathetic heroine: a 'clever, daring little girl' with 'a graceful little figure', whose trick of slipping under the horse she is riding and coming up the other side is the kind of feat Blyton's pony-riding readers could presumably only dream of doing (*HC*, 167). Some elements of circus life are skirted over. Lotta's circus performances are, after all, a form of child labour and child sexualisation. Instead Blyton shows the circus children enjoying a freer life than those of their counterparts living in suburbia who attend school. But there is also the sense that Blyton the Froebel teacher has an idea that for children the circus is an intellectually stimulating environment and place of practical learning.

In other ways, Blyton's circus novels conform to the idea that the genre afforded writers elbow room to construct thrilling plots involving exotic animals and larger-than-life personalities. They are places of colourful possibilities in a black and white world. It was perhaps no surprise that *Mr Galliano's Circus*, 'full of the vagabond spirit of circus life', as *The Book Window* reported, swiftly went into second edition (1939) and by November 1942 had reached its fifth.[27] Its successors, *Hurrah for the Circus!* and *Circus Days Again*, repeated the format and were equally popular. The sequels were a commercial decision. As Blyton explained in a letter to the publishing firm of Macmillan, 'this kind of book has a universal appeal' (Mac, 19 July 1943). But it is hard not to take away the impression that Blyton's passion for the circus was real and in the novels she asks her readers to share it. Often, as in *Hurrah for the Circus!*, the effect is of someone providing audio commentary, breathlessly, to a piece of silent film:

> Now come the caravans, the gay house on wheels, and how the children wish they could peep inside and see the circus-folk cooking their dinners! What fun it must be to live in a caravan.
>
> Now look at this glorious yellow caravan with gay curtains fluttering in the wind. Do you know who it belongs to? Of course, you do! It belongs to Jimmy, our old friend Jimmy, who lives there with his mother and father....
>
> And there is Jimmy, sitting on the steps at the back, and on his knee lies Lucky, his famous dog!
>
> We get a wag from Lucky, that clever little fox-terrier... (*HC*, 10).

Blyton would often explain that she 'saw' her characters moving across a cinema screen located in her own mind. The description here, which might also be called 'pictorialist' carries traces of this. The narrator is not completely omniscient with God-like knowledge of everything about the fictional world (the experience of living in a caravan, for example), rather she is more like an eagle-eyed observer noting the important points. The narrator immediately presents the reader with the main character—Jimmy and his dog, Lucky—who are placed in the contexts of family, home and work, aspects of life which are probably the most important ones for readers as well. At the same time, the narratorial voice also reveals an emotional interest in them and assumes that the reader's interest is likely to be the same. This sense of enrapturement in the narrator's manner is also that of an excited spectator and is repeated when the narrator describes the acts in the big top wherein the performers are brave and beautiful, dressed in glitter and spangles, and they perform effortlessly; offstage they are lively, generous and devoted to the monkeys, bears, parrots and seals with which they perform. There are hardly any merciless trainers, sickly performers or shabby, ill-treated animals—a topic of concern and legislation in the inter-war years. Indeed, Blyton, who was very anxious about cruelty to animals and had flagged it in *The Adventures of Bobs* does not address that here—nor the accompanying charge that the circus's magic is the result of living beings having to be imprisoned in cages. Instead she relies on a simplistic—albeit serviceable—anthropomorphism. "'Tigers hate doing tricks, and it's a shame to make them'", comments Jimmy in *Hurrah for the Circus!* (*HC*, 151). However, elsewhere he is permitted to play and box with the bears, who are also trained to play football and sit on stools. Their owner, Mr. Volla, explains that "'bears are the clowns of the animal world, you know. They are clumsy, and they know they're funny. They love it'" (*HC*, 148). The animals have personalities and the reader, meanwhile, is expected to buy into this vision.

As is often the case in Blyton's stories, the plots of her circus stories tend to hinge on an accident or disaster which badly disrupts the characters' lives. Because the community of the circus is a closed one plots can also involve the arrival of new people who upset things. The most striking example of this is the fascistic, moustachioed conjurer, Britomart, in the third Galliano book, *Circus Days Again* (1942). His taking command of the circus provides the opportunity for a variant on another of Blyton's favourite motifs: the abuse of power by a tyrannical adult. Britomart's name is presumably intended to evoke a cut-price department store where the profit motif tramples over the well-being of employees; 'the happiness of the people came second or not at all', as Blyton's narrator notes (*CDA*, 102). At the time of the book's appearance readers may also have been reminded of Adolf Hitler and Benito Mussolini, the dictators against whom Britain and her allies were fighting and who had risen to power by cunning sleights of hand, as well as brute force. Within moments of being appointed by the gullible Mr. Galliano, Britomart makes it clear he intends to be "'master'" (*CDA*, 99). He commandeers Galliano's caravan, locks up Sammy the chimpanzee, banishes Lotta to her caravan and reallocates the slots on the circus's bill to feature his favourites. He is recognised as an ingenious conjurer and organiser but also as a bully who begins to destroy Galliano's circus and its sense of collective identity. Blyton shows the unhappiness and resentment amongst the grease-paint and animal feed, something which prompts Lotta to ride horseback on an epic journey through the night, through Dorset and Devon to the Plymouth hotel, where Mr. and Mrs. Galliano are staying. There are times when Blyton rewards spontaneity and rule-breaking and this is one of them. Yet while accounts of trapeze artists and bareback horse riders offered visions of a world where girls were able to seize the reins, there is a suggestion—as there often is in Blyton's writing—that it is only with fatherly guidance (in this instance Mr. Galliano's return) that the circus will right itself and the circus folk can look forward to a better future. The exception is Britomart, who is told to leave, having not learnt that "'only one thing rules a camp, and that is kindness…!'" (CDA, 189). Traditional forms of entertainment were under threat in the 1930s and 1940s, but it is made clear that Blyton's circus doesn't need to change: it represents a model that remains intact. Despite the odds, it is constant and worthy of admiration. The display of community in Mr. Galliano's circus and the willingness of occupants like Lotta to undertake dangerous feats for the greater good also perhaps chimed with readers being exhorted in 1942 to think about doing the same.

Blyton's picture of 'circus-land' and her 'gay' excursions into circus life, as her contemporary critics termed it, met with general approval. As Mary Crosbie put it in 1939, the circus stories were examples of the author in 'her happiest vein'.[28] Meanwhile Circus Days Again was '[bright, unflagging and human, the tale goes with a swing'. 'Miss Blyton', Crosbie added, 'is as industrious as she is competent'.[29] These comments imply that, by this time, critics and readers knew what to expect from Blyton and where her strengths lay. They also suggest some of the expectations she was expected to meet; circus stories presented readers with an alternative lifestyle which, if not anarchic, was energetic and lively. Blyton's heroes run barefoot and play with exotic animals. Whatever happens, though, the carnivalesque atmosphere is never allowed to get out of hand. It might seem trivial but Jimmy's mother places great emphasis on brushing hair and cleaning teeth and the Blyton narrator is, as always, keen to point out the importance of doing so. Such things are markers of the sorts of civilised behaviour needing to be upheld amongst the displays of artistry and derring-do. 'I am', announced Blyton, '…a teacher and a guide (I hope) as well as an entertainer and bringer of pleasure' (CL, 2). By the end of the 1930s this, too, was part of the Blyton package and it was a mark of her skill that she managed it discreetly, not only on deserted islands but in the shadow of the big top. As we shall see in later chapters, Blyton's preoccupation with finding appropriate models for her readers to follow becomes a recurrent one in her works.

Notes

1. Noel Streatfeild, 'The Book and the Serial', The Author 68:3 (Spring 1958), 63–67 (64).
2. Teresa Mangum, 'Dog Years, Human Fears', in Representing Animals, ed. Nigel Rothfels (Bloomington: Indiana University Press, 2002). 35–47 (43).

3. Heini Hediger, 'The Clever Hans Phenomenon' (1981), in *The Routledge Handbook of Philosophy of Information*, ed. Luciano Floridi (London: Routledge, 2016), 295.

4. Naomi Mitchison, 'Animals Good and Bad', *Time and Tide* (5 December 1936), 1763.

5. Tess Cosslet, *Talking Animals in British Children's Fiction, 1786–1914* (London: Routledge, 2017); see also Deborah Deneholz Morse and Martin Danahay (eds.), *Victorian Animal Dreams* (Aldershot: Ashgate, 2007).

6. Brian Stewart and Tony Summerfield, *The Enid Blyton Dossier* (Penryn: Hawk, 1999), 86.

7. Blyton also continued to draw attention to mistreatment. The plot of 'Tibby's Adventures: The Story of a Cat's Life' (*Sunny Stories* 28) follows a similar trajectory to that of Bobs: the feline hero has a succession of owners before finding lasting happiness at Cherry Tree Farm. *Shadow the Sheepdog* (*Sunny Stories* 4 April 1941—27 March 1942) is likewise told partly from the point of view of the dog who encounters cruelty and danger but also security in the care of Johnny, his 'master' (*SSD*, 188).

8. See Katherine C. Grier, *Pets in America: A History* (Chapel Hill: University of North Carolina Press, 2006).

9. John Carey, *The Unexpected Professor* (London: Faber, 2014), 27.

10. Kevin Carpenter, *Desert Islands and Pirate Islands* (Frankfurt Peter Lang, 1984), 14.

11. Unsigned Article, 'Current Literature', *The Spectator* (5 November 1892), 626.

12. Unsigned Article, 'Children's Books', *The Hull Daily Mail* (10 December 1938), 4.

13. Lieve Spaas, 'Conclusion', in *Robinson Crusoe. Myths and Metamorphoses*, eds. Lieve Spaas and Brian Stimpson (Basingstoke: Macmillan, 1996), 320.

14. Unsigned Poem, 'J.M.B.', *Punch* (30 June 1937), 708. 'He dwelt in our world but his kindly eyes/saw more than we knew was there'.

15. Andrew Motion, 'Writing Houses: Dwelling on Dwellings', quoted in Phyllis Richardson, *House of Fiction* (London: Unbound, 2017), xii.

16. Cyril Connolly, *Enemies of Promise* (London: Routledge 1938), 153.

17. A reference to the process, now illegal but previously common practice, whereby a tail is partly or wholly removed for cosmetic reasons to fit the "look" of particular breeds. It was usually carried out without anaesthetic on puppies less than a week old.

18. Unsigned Article. '"Small beer" Blyton banned by BBC' (15 November 2009). http://news.bbc.co.uk/1/hi/uk/8361056.stm. Accessed: 8 March 2021.

19. Marjorie Lloyd, *Buckinghamshire: An Illustrated Review of the Holiday, Sporting and Industrial Facilities of the County* (London: E. J. Burrow & Co. 1937), 23.

20. Imogen Smallwood interviewed in Seven Stories, *The Blyton Legacy* (2013), 0.37–1.24. https://youtu.be/lTEjM2xLtTM. Accessed 3 March 2021.

21. Quoted in Dennis Judd, *Alison Uttley: The Life of a Country Child* (London: Michael Joseph, 1986), 168–9.

22. Dennis Judd, *Alison Uttley: The Life of a Country Child* (London: Michael Joseph 1986, 1884–1976), 102; 168.
23. George Greenfield, *A Smattering of Monsters* (1995; London: Warner, 1997), 115.
24. Francis Douglas, 'Under the Big Top: Circuses in Fact and Fiction', *John o'London's Weekly* (4 December 1936), 432–3.
25. John Masefield, 'Introduction', Edward Seago, *Circus Company* (New York: Putnam, 1933), xi.
26. Cyril Bertram Mills, *Bertram Mills Circus: Its Story* (London: Hutchinson, 1967), 57.
27. Unsigned Review, 'Mr Galliano's Circus', *The Book Window* 4 (December 1938), 125.
28. Mary Crosbie, 'Children's Books', *John o'London's Weekly* (8 December 1939), 317.
29. Mary Crosbie, 'Children's Books', *John o'London's Weekly* (18 December 1942), 109.

Bibliography

Carey, John. 2014. *The Unexpected Professor.* London: Faber.
Carpenter, Kevin. 1984. *Desert Islands and Pirate Islands.* Frankfurt: Peter Lang, 1984.
Connolly, Cyril. 1938. *Enemies of Promise.* London: Routledge.
Cosslet, Tess. 2017. *Talking Animals in British Children's Fiction, 1786–1914.* London: Routledge.
Floridi, Luciano. Editor. 2016. *The Routledge Handbook of Philosophy of Information.* London: Routledge
Greenfield, George. 1997. *A Smattering of Monsters.* London: Warner.
Grier, Katherine C. 2006. *Pets in America: A History.* Chapel Hill: University of North Carolina Press.
Judd, Dennis. 1986. *Alison Uttley: The Life of a Country Child*. London: Michael Joseph
Lloyd, Marjorie. 1937. *Buckinghamshire: An Illustrated Review of the Holiday, Sporting and Industrial Facilities of the County.* London: E. J. Burrow & Co.
Mangum, Teresa. 2002. 'Dog Years, Human Fears'. In *Representing Animals*, edited by Nigel Rothfels: 35–47. Bloomington: Indiana University Press.
Mills, Cyril Bertram. 1967. *Bertram Mills Circus: Its Story.* London: Hutchinson.
Morse, Deborah Deneholz, and Martin Danahay. Editors. 2007. *Victorian Animal Dreams.* Aldershot: Ashgate.
Richardson, Phyllis. 2017. *House of Fiction.* London: Unbound.
Seago, Edward. 1933. *Circus Company.* New York: Putnam.

Seven Stories. 2013. *The Blyton Legacy*, 0.37–1.24. https://youtu.be/lTEjM2xLtTM. Accessed 3 March 2021.

Spaas, Lieve, and Brian Stimpson. Editors. 1996. *Robinson Crusoe. Myths and Metamorphoses*. Basingstoke: Macmillan.

Stewart, Brian, and Tony Summerfield. 1999. *The Enid Blyton Dossier*. Penryn: Hawk.

Streatfeild, Noel. 1958. 'The Book and the Serial'. *The Author* 68(3): 63–67.

Unsigned Article. 2009. '"Small Beer" Blyton banned by BBC'. http://news.bbc.co.uk/1/hi/uk/8361056.stm. Accessed: 8 March 2021.

5

War-Time

For most of the 1930s, Enid Blyton, like many others, was a 'Chamberlai-nite', a supporter of Britain's policy of appeasing Adolf Hitler. Another war, at a time when the memories of 1914–1918 were still fresh, was horrible to contemplate. In early October 1938, Blyton wrote passionately to the Conservative Prime Minister, Neville Chamberlain, after he appeared to have achieved 'peace in our time' on signing the Munich Treaty with Germany, France and Italy. In her letter Blyton also enclosed a poem she had composed for this man of the moment: 'Neville Chamberlain' celebrates 'a statesman rare/Who champions all the lands at peace, a source/Of brilliant common-sense beyond compare'.[1] Chamberlain's triumph was short-lived, of course. Britain declared war on Germany on Sunday 4 September at 11am. Blyton, as was her wont, accepted the perils of the country in a matter of fact way. 'Chamberlain spoke at 11.15', she noted in her diary. 'We made blackout blinds & painted windows black all day. I did my a/cs in a.m. the King spoke at 6'.

Although life in war-time Beaconsfield is not the kind of experience discussed in accounts of the conflict—it lacks the visceral and dramatic details captured in accounts of the London blitz—the upheaval and sense of alarm made itself felt in the lives of those who were there. The Wilton Park estate in Beaconsfield was requisitioned by the government as a (supposedly secret) interrogation centre for Nazis and sympathisers. The Town Hall and Police Station were protected with sandbags and a hospital for sailors of the Free French navy was opened. London firms moved into the town. There were

A. Maunder, *Enid Blyton*, Literary Lives, https://doi.org/10.1007/978-3-030-76332-9_5

also fears of invasion, especially after Belgium and Holland were overrun by the German *Blitzkrieg* in spring 1940. Townsfolk started to discuss what *they* would do, with their fears heightened by the fact that Chequers, the Prime Minister's country residence, was close by. Alison Uttley imagined the worst: 'If the Germans come marching through here, I shall have to fly', she confided to her diary in May 1940, '...on my cycle perhaps, and I can't ride more than 2 miles'. She added 'I wonder if one ought to hide one's silver, or what one ought to do....I feel rather lost'.[2] In the summer *The Buckinghamshire Advertiser* reminded its readers that now that the 'aerial war' had developed, church bells would remain permanently silent only 'to be used in case of invasion of parachutists'.[3] The invasion never came but German air raids began, the effects of which *did* reach Beaconsfield, as Blyton recorded in her diary on 16 October 1940: 'A very noisy evening with planes, guns and bombs'. 15 November 1940: 'Had to spend night in shelter with kids & Nanny as bombs fell near us'.

In the meantime, there was plenty for people to do. There was the matter of protecting the security of the town. This was, of course, what the Local Defence Volunteers (the Home Guard) were tasked with. When the scheme was announced on Tuesday 14 May 1940, Hugh Pollock, who wanted an army job, immediately signed up. He was put in charge of recruiting the local platoon, whose duties included manning the machine-gun posts and tree trunks which protected the entrances to the town. 'Many men', as Blyton recorded in her diary on 21 May, arrived at Green Hedges to enquire about joining up, and it is a sign of her allegiance to Hugh that she was proud of him and his military activities.

For Blyton in her role as a housewife, the prospects were less obviously exciting: 28 May 1940: 'Delivered things for Hugh. Saw about new ration cards etc., so was busy all am. To Christine's to bridge in the afternoon. Hugh out with L.D.C. tonight, so I wrote & read till bed'. Both *The Buckinghamshire Advertiser* and *The Buckinghamshire Examiner* announced a flood of civic directives, speeches, recruitment events, fund-raisers, sewing circles, flag days, first-aid classes, bazaars—all of which Blyton dutifully attended. In the daytime she waited in line at shops, carried a gas mask and—possibly with an element of play-acting—"made do" and mended. In November 1940 she had to appear at a tribunal with her maid, Mary Bale, in order to have the latter accepted as a 'friendly alien'. The alternative was for Mary, who was Austrian, to be interned. Meanwhile Green Hedges, as Blyton's diaries record—and as Bobs reported to his readers—was like every other house in having to follow official advice: tape was stuck across its windows to stop the glass shattering in the event of bombing and food was rationed for its occupants from January 1940. In the meantime, Blyton and her friends tried to retain a semblance of normality and, in a small gesture of defiance, the bridge parties continued: Tuesday 13 August 1940: 'Worked till lunch. To club at Mrs. Zobel's. Air-raid siren in middle so the wardens had to go. We who were left played on. Read and knitted till bed'. When Hugh Pollock's promotion led to his being stationed at an army training camp in the autumn of 1940, Blyton's card-playing friends and the social life they provided became increasingly important.

What this narrative omits, of course, is the impact of the war on Blyton's writing life. How did she align her career within the difficulties and limitations thrown up by the conflict? 'I am quite determined to do my part', she wrote (Mac, 19 July 1943). But what did this mean? British writers had engaged with their country's wars before but most people agreed that the Second World War was different: the threat seemed closer and more immediate. As Juliet Gardiner notes:

> shortages, privations, restrictions, regulations – as well as destruction, loss, injury and death – all impacted on the civilian population....To use a time-worn phrase, civilians were in the front line of war; the Home Front became another battle front – one on which, as Churchill recognised, the war could equally be lost if morale cracked and production ground to a halt.[4]

This was partly the message given by King George VI in his Christmas 1940 radio broadcast to Britain and the Empire, a speech which, according to Blyton's diaries, she and her family listened to. The King reminded his people that '[i]n the last great war the flower of our youth was destroyed, and the rest of the people saw but little of the battle. This time we are all in the front lines and in danger together'. The population also faced a new technology of weaponry: bombs dropped by the Luftwaffe, including 'parachute mines', which floated to wherever the wind happened to take them. By the end of 1940 German air raids had killed 13,596 people and injured another 18,378. 'We are slowly choking England to death' boasted Hitler's Minister of Propaganda, Joseph Goebbels, as he explained that he expected Britain's surrender very soon.[5]

It was frightening, exhausting and gruelling and people looked for distraction and amusement from the country's cultural industries: cinema, radio, music and books. The message of the war-time government, as announced by Duff Cooper, Head of the Ministry of Information in 1940, was that books represented freedom. They were 'part of the cause for which we fight' and symbol of 'the great heritage of civilised communication'.[6] The

Nazi rulers 'hate books', was the message relayed by Cooper's successor, Brendan Bracken, in a 1941 article, 'Books: our best export'. He urged British publishers to use the written word to boost support for the country's cause, particularly in America where 'good British books' were helping President Roosevelt garner support for the United States' joining the allied cause.[7] This followed an earlier call by *The Bookseller* magazine for authors to pick up their pens and go on the offensive. As William Cederwell points out, there was 'a need, even a desire for uplifting imagery and optimistic propaganda'. The 'best' new writing would exhibit a patriotic appeal which would align with—or awaken—a reader's sense of national identity and appreciation of the country's traditions and her present cause. Britain would be shown to be 'strong and united' with a sense of 'togetherness', and emphasis would be placed on 'the importance of collective effort and resilience' in the face of evil.[8]

The story of British writing during the war is partly bound up with how firmly those like Blyton, who were doing the writing, were prepared to embrace these directives. Some, like Graham Greene and E.M. Delafield, author of the bestselling *Diary of a Provincial Lady* (1939), were signed up by the Ministry of Information. Agatha Christie volunteered in a pharmacy, as she had done in the First World War while continuing to publish two novels a year. Noel Streatfeild was a fire watcher and wrote bulletins for the Women's Voluntary Service while receiving requests 'asking me to write a fairy story for children in connection with war weapons week'. Others thought writing should be a reserved occupation, to be used, as Cyril Connolly put it, 'to interpret the war world so that cultural unity is re-established and war effort emotionally co-ordinated'. Not every writer was expected to turn propagandist, of course. The Ministry of Information told Siegfried Sassoon that 'authors can best serve by continuing their ordinary work, and addressing the public, through the channels that are open to them'.[9]

Just how far a writer specialising in works for children was expected to write about the war was another question. 'What shall we tell our children?', asked Willa Muir, writing in *The Listener* in 1940: 'The War is not confirmed to the fighting forces: it has long ago reached the Home Front. So, we can't keep our children out of war, much as we should like to'.[10] Initially this was Blyton's stance. Her task, as she saw it, was to become a reassuring voice to the nation's children. It is difficult to quantify all the channels through which she communicated—300+ weekly children's pages and letters in *Teacher's World* and *Sunny Stories*—and various fund-raising initiatives. But like the makers of propaganda films such as *London Can Take It* (1940), which celebrated the defiant spirit of 'ordinary' people getting to grips with air-raids and their after-math, Blyton adopted a breezy, up-beat tone. Judy Giles and Tim Middleton have written of the emergence in 1930s literature onwards of a type of 'brisk' English woman—one who possessed 'robust common sense'.[11] Blyton, along with the famous Mrs. Miniver, the eponymous heroine of Jan Struther's bestselling 1939 novel (later a film)—epitomised her. This at least was the impression Blyton conveyed to the readers of *Teacher's World*: 'The war is making all our lives different and until things shake down a little, we will put up with them cheerfully' (quoted in Stoney, 125). Her columns became an expression of what Bruce McConachie has termed the hegemonic 'we', a kind of 'common ground strategy' whereby audiences identify with the actions of certain characters on the basis of certain 'taken-for-granted values'.[12] Tradi-tional expressions of duty, stoicism, helpfulness and self-sacrifice were what was needed.

Blyton adopted a similar stance in *Enid Blyton's Sunny Stories*. The maga-zine, which now had the tag line, 'The Best Children's Weekly', already had a large audience, but by the beginning of 1940 sales had risen to 59,000 per issue.[13] It is safe to assume that it was passed around from child to child, making its actual readership much higher. All the contents continued to be written by Blyton, who also began each issue with a short letter. Once again, the effect was to make her a familiar, reassuring voice for children, in much the same way that the 'Forces Sweetheart', Vera Lynn, became one for soldiers and their families on BBC radio's *Sincerely Yours* (1941–1942). The maga-zine's title obviously set the tone but Blyton's own voice—or what passed for it—built on this and reached out: 'I like to think I am with you in that way, when you are waiting underground for the all-clear to go…', she wrote in December 1940. She knew that some of her readers were amongst the thou-sands of people who spent their nights sheltering in London's tube stations or in damp air-raid shelters, facing possible death (by the end of 1941 5626 children *had* been killed in air raids).[14] 'I only wish I could come myself and tell you stories - that would be fun for you, and fun for me, too!' (quoted in Stoney, 125). In September 1940 she did visit a shelter and wrote approv-ingly of the brave way the children behaved (*TW* 4 September 1940, 24). She encouraged readers to write to her, assuring them that 'every single one of your letters gets to me, and is read and enjoyed by me!' (*SS* 181, 1). In issue 174 of *Sunny Stories*, she published a 'prayer poem' sent in by a reader, Marion King (aged nine): 'O Lord, above those clouds so high,/Where no airplane can roam,/Please look after my soldier Dad/and bring him safely home' (*SS*, 174, 2). Blyton hoped that readers, '[i]f you have a Daddy in France', would be inspired to post the poem out to him (1). In her weekly page for *Teacher's*

World she spoke to those who were part of the 700,000 who, by April 1940, had been evacuated into the care of strangers in the countryside and were often homesick.[15] It was, Blyton, told them, part of a great adventure and a chance to explore the wonderful British countryside. Meanwhile, teachers, experiencing their own shortages and disruptions in classrooms, told her that her chatty weekly letters and light-hearted short stories (examples include 'The Tiresome Twins', 'Poor Dicky Duck!' and 'Mr. Tantrum and the Fog' [*SS*, 7 November 1941]) filled gaps and made the situation a little more bearable. In *Sunny Stories* these were accompanied by longer 'to be continued' stories *The Secret of Spiggy Holes* (from October 6, 1939), *The Naughtiest Girl in the School* (from 22 March 1940) and *Circus Days Again* (from 7 March 1941) which, by unfolding over many weeks, were intended to give readers the comforting sense of meeting up with old friends, as well as filling their need for spaces to escape to.

The war posed various challenges to authors wanting to write about it. Partly these were artistic—confusion about what aspect of it to choose—but they were also ideological. As has been mentioned, there were frameworks within which writers were expected to operate, and these applied to those who wrote for children as well as those seeking a grown-up audience. *The Adventurous Four*, drafted while the 'Battle of Britain' was taking place in the summer of 1940 and serialised in *Sunny Stories* between 6 September 1940 and 28 February 1941, was not Blyton's sole attempt to dramatise the wartime situation but it is very obviously a topical thriller, part of a whole raft of propagandist or consciousness-raising narratives on offer and part of the first wave of stories which tried to suggest to children what was at stake in the fight against Nazism. 1941 also saw the publication of Noel Streatfeild's *The Children of Primrose Lane*, a tale of a group of children who discover a spy living in an empty house, and Mary Treadgold's *We Couldn't Leave Dinah*, set in the Channel Islands, in which a group of children encounter the local resistance movement (Dinah is a pony). Similar themes later cropped up in Malcolm Saville's *Mystery at Witchend* (1943) in which children foil German spies intent on blowing up a reservoir, while in Norman Dale's *Secret Service* (1943), two evacuees track a German prisoner and enable the sinking of a U-boat.

In *The Adventurous Four* the three pre-teen children (Tom and his twin sisters Jill and Mary) have been evacuated with their mother to a village on the North West coast of Scotland while their father is in the RAF. There are boats and planes and Germans. The children are friends with an older Scottish boy, Andy. He, we are told, 'knew everything about the sea, boats, and fishing' and 'could mimic any sea-bird, and could call the wild gulls to him by crying to them' (*AF*, 8). Andy works for his father, a fisherman. He is allowed to take the children sailing to Little Island. After surviving a storm, they arrive on the island which was once home to crofters but is now abandoned. The children set up camp in an out-building and forage for wild potatoes, runner beans and bilberries—provisions that, along with fish caught from the sea, ensure they do not go hungry. The novel's ideological thrust includes the idea that these British children are well-brought up and inherently civilised; there is no Lord of the Flies-type descent into anarchy. Instead their behaviour replicates that of the protagonists of *The Secret Island* published two years earlier: the children domesticate—or colonise—the space; the boys renovate the ruined shack while the girls cook dinner and wash up. They make beds using wild heather for mattresses (a favourite Blyton staple) and even put up shelving. Tidiness and order are paramount. They enjoy themselves by discovering and taking cans of tinned food from stores mysteriously hidden in a cave, sensibly picking the most useful items. Gradually, however, it dawns on the children that they are not alone. They discover German seaplanes and submarines using the island as a base prior to attacking the British fleet.

It is at this point that *The Adventurous Four* takes on new dimensions, emerging as a tale not simply of sailing and bivouacking, but of fighting back and overcoming evil; in this case, Nazi invaders: 'the foe of half the world'. They are represented, as the children know, by '[t]he sign of the crooked cross...painted on each wing' of their planes (*AF*, 67). War-time writers often struggled to represent the 'Hun' or the 'Jerries', as they were nicknamed. Blyton chooses to cast them as stupid and ruthless but, in a typically Blytonian touch, 'the enemy', as the narrator refers to them, also drop litter. They throw away cigarette packets on the unspoilt, Edenic island (a symbol for Britain perhaps), which quickly begins to echo to the 'thud' of their 'footfall' (*AF*, 111; 181). The remainder of the story focuses on the children's attempts to get back to the mainland in order to alert the authorities. When their own boat is confiscated by the invaders the children build a raft on which the two boys sail for the mainland: 'I don't care how much danger we're in', said Tom, and he didn't. 'All I know is that we've *got* to go and tell our people at home about this submarine base. It's got to be cleared away' (*AF*, 81). On route they are rescued by a British seaplane containing Tom's father, with whom they return to the island to save the girls. This discovery, that the commander of the seaplane is his father, contains what Blyton presumably intended as a very powerful (and heartfelt) description of what it might be like to be reunited with a parent: '"DADDY! Oh DADDY! It's YOU!"' (It is difficult not to notice, too, the link with the phrase's forerunner in Edith Nesbit's *The Railway Children* [1906] and its climatic scene of the children's father returning.) 'The grave-faced man stared at Tom as if he couldn't believe his eyes. Then he took the boy into his arms and gave him such a bear-like hug that Tom felt as if his bones would break!' (*AF*, 169). As well as depicting a war-time world where children and parents do 'meet again', as Vera Lynn would have it, the novel's patriotic—and occasionally bombastic—aesthetic also encourages its readers to believe that the Germans and their swastikered planes are '"no match for our pilots!"', who finish the novel by bombing them (*AF*, 188). Readers already know, of course, that they are also no match for the preternaturally intrepid British children whose pluck is never in doubt.

As an illustration of Blyton's writerly interests, *The Adventurous Four* is familiar in many ways. Readers who come to it after reading the better-known Famous Five series, for example, will recognise the importance placed on physical activity and the outdoors, the challenges and opportunities posed by the absence of parents, the overcoming of threats to 'civilised' [British] patterns of behaviour, the bravery of 'go-ahead' children, who win the day. There is a strong and familiar focus on action as events unfold in easy-to-follow, linear fashion. In the children's pupil–tutor relationship with the fisher-boy Andy, there is also an example of what Beverley Skeggs has termed 'propertising'. This is the process whereby young middle-class characters, who are usually on holiday, 'plunder what is attractive and desirable about the cultures of less prestigious groups', usually working-class people whom they befriend: circus-folk, gypsies, fishermen.[16] Thus Andy teaches the children things they are not taught at school: how to fish, to recognise the region's bird-life, 'to row strongly, and to climb the rocky cliffs like cats' (*AF*, 8). He expands the children's world—for free. Just what the middle-class children give back remains vague. Is it their companionship? Social polish? Good manners? Or is it nothing at all? Or is what Blyton depicts meant to be an idealised friendship between classes of the kind that would be necessary if Britain was to come through the war successfully?

Where *The Adventurous Four* is *unfamiliar*—at least as insofar as fits the mould of Blyton's adventure stories—is not only in the way it picks up the war-time government's propaganda agenda (including the need to be vigilant against invaders) but also how it conveys a sense of unease and an awareness of the personal qualities needed to resist the enemy. In the introduction to her anthology of war-time stories, *Wave Me Goodbye* (1988), Anne Boston also makes the point that part of the importance of such texts lies in the ways in which they tell something about 'the special circumstances of war-time', the way the war was imagined, and 'the territory of feelings, emotions and attitudes' it produced.[17] Given the fears about invasion in 1940 and

1941, it is not surprising that *The Adventurous Four* gives us a rather double-edged view of war-time Britain. The country is a stronghold of civilisation but also a place which has become vulnerable to attack. Blyton, a writer who usually writes her adventure stories in a naturalistic mode, conveys this in an unusually melodramatic way. As Elaine Hadley has pointed out, melodrama has long been the kind of 'behavioural and expressive model' wheeled out at moments of crisis in Britain's history.[18] The Second World War was no exception: in newspapers of the time events were often represented in terms of good versus evil, civilisation versus savagery. In a radio broadcast made on 11 September 1940, Winston Churchill described Hitler's bombing of London as an attempt 'by this wicked man…to try to break our famous island race by a process of indiscriminate slaughter and destruction'.[19] As German forces invaded Luxemburg and Belgium these small, vulnerable countries were often said to have been despoiled, rather like an old-fashioned stage heroine being preyed on by a voracious aristocrat. Melodrama thus offered a workable narrative structure and moral pattern: a stirring struggle between good and evil, constructed around ordinary men or women coping with highly pressurised situations while showing the hero and his (or her) solid 'British' values emerging triumphant.

One of the things Blyton does in *The Adventurous Four* is to re-choreograph for children some of these longstanding melodramatic conventions to fit the demands of the moment. One instance occurs when Andy and Tom observe the German vessels from their vantage point on the cliff: 'The boys lay looking down on the water. Some of the submarines lay like great crocodiles, humped out of the water. One or two were moving out of the harbour, their periscopes showing. It was a curiously silent place' (*AF*, 80). The 'nest' of submarines waiting to strike—or feed—on British ships appears monstrous and was a keynote of Britain's propaganda machine. But their appearance is also a striking example of Blyton's ability to 'bridge' the generation gap so that childish ways of looking at the world are 'endorsed', a skill noted by Barbara Wall in *The Narrator's Voice. The Dilemma of Children's Literature* (1991). As she explains: 'The narrator briefly recounts an action and then slides imperceptibly into the thoughts of the character, so that it appears as though the narrator is commenting on the action in the voice of the child character'. Wall describes the technique as kind of '*free indirect discourse*' in which the narrator speaks but with the character's words—or the sort of words and images they 'might have used'. The effect, as Wall sees it, is to allow 'children's thoughts, language and syntax [to] dominate the narrative'; it is the child reader rather than the adult one who Blyton keeps in in view at all times.[20]

Another thing which we might take away from *The Adventurous Four* is the way in which Blyton suggests that the physical threats to the children are very real. It is not simply that their plan to alert the authorities is hazardous, not least because it necessitates the boys attempting to sail across the Atlantic on a flimsy raft. There is further danger in the fact that the girls agree to stay behind. They agree to do so without '"any fuss"' and '"for the sake of our country"' but in agreeing they take on the risk of being raped, the possibility of which one of them at least, seems aware (*AF*, 155; 156). The fear that this might happen is seen to place more strain on Andy who 'longed desperately for some grown-up who could take command and tell him what would be the best thing to do. But there was no grown-up. This was something he had to decide himself – and he must decide well, because the two girls were in his care' (*AF*, 94).

None of this sounds like the work of a novelist accused—as Blyton often is—of being twee or safe. Her protagonists are continually plunged into situations where their seeming lack of power is brought to the fore. When the Germans discover the children, the plot encourages readers to believe that the soldiers will keep them indefinitely. Certainly, no-one on the mainland knows where they are. Tom is taken prisoner but, readers are told, 'would not cry. He would not show the men how frightened and worried he was....No – he was British...' (*AF*, 104; 139). Blyton is also messaging her readers at a time when, as William Cederwell points out, '[t]he expectation to think and behave in a certain way, to present a certain front' was 'one of the many exhortations and instructions that pervaded everyday life', alongside the wearing of gas masks and exhortations to 'make do and mend' or 'Beat the Invader'.[21] Occasionally the mask slips, not least when British planes bomb the island and the children risk being killed by friendly fire. One of the girls, Mary, begins to cry, realising that the war is no longer a game but a place where death is a real possibility.

The Adventurous Four represents Britain's children at their best. Buoyed up by this, Blyton (adopting the pseudonym Mary Pollock) attempted a similar thing with *The Children of Kidillin* (1941). This is a less exciting text than *The Adventurous Four*, but equally excitable, taking its cue from the widespread belief that war-time Britain was full of Nazi spies, something which the popular press encouraged as a way of 'keeping people on their toes'.[22] One reason why Hitler's armies had been able to sweep so easily across Europe was because they had (allegedly) been helped by sympathisers on the inside, a so-called 'Fifth Column' working against their own nation's interest. The country was encouraged to look out for people behaving suspiciously, or who were oddly accented, or who took photographs of places of strategic importance and talked in a defeatist way.

Graham Greene's 1940 short story, 'The Lieutenant Died Last' (subsequently filmed as *Went the Day Well?* [1942]), which shows English villagers valiantly battling against an invasion of German parachutists who have been helped by British traitors, is possibly the best-known fictional response to these fears. *The Children of Kidillin* envisions a similar scenario from the point of view of children. Four cousins, Scottish siblings Sandy and Jeanie, and an English brother and sister, Tom and Sheila (evacuated from London), live on the west coast of Scotland. They demonstrate the level of alertness required by the British public when they discover that two men, one of whom, 'a fat man', pretends to be dumb in order to disguise his guttural German accent, are camping out in an abandoned cottage on the cliffs along with 'Nigger', a black dog, whose fierceness mirrors the brutality of his owners (*CK*, 15). (I discuss some of the implications of the dog's naming in Chapter 6.) The local police accept the men's story that they have left London to escape air-raids and are doing no harm, but the children remain suspicious. '"I wonder if we've hit on something peculiar!"' says Tom. '"Perhaps those two men are spies!"' (*CK*, 18). The peculiarity is revealed when the children peer through the cottage window and spot a 'strange-looking machine, that had knobs and handles, valves and levers on it' (*CK*, 12). This '"queer"' device turns out to be a wireless transmitter which the cunning and efficient two men use to signal German submarines about the whereabouts of British ships— which the submarines then torpedo. Worried by the children's interest, the two men transfer their sabotage operation underground to a maze of underground caves linked by tunnels and a rushing 'black' river (*CK*, 68). This emphasis on subterranean spaces seems a neat symbolic representation of the unfathomable and of things hidden. It has rich potential and other novelists might have taken the time to develop it. Blyton, however, flattens it. Instead, the story pivots on how her characters behave and the daring actions they undertake for the sake of their country. Blyton invokes the cult of the 'manly' boy by showing Tom and Sandy swimming through a freezing underground river to re-locate the wireless, scare off the spies (by pretending to be ghosts) before alerting the police. Like many spy or invasion stories, the narrative goal of *The Children of Kidillin* is to remove the destabilising characters so that the spies ('"wretches"' [*CK*, 80]) are arrested and led away to prison and, although it is not mentioned, to possible execution. The message is a simple one. By careful vigilance, Blyton suggests, even children—who are shut out from the main sources of war-time action—can do their bit.

* * *

The relationship between patriotism, propaganda and other forms of war-time discourse thus represents one of the entry points into a discussion of Blyton's war-time activity and the ideological framework within which she was expected—or chose—to operate. It is not too far-fetched to see her work as part of what another war-time propagandist, J.B. Priestley, in his BBC 'Postscripts' broadcasts (1940–1941), termed the 'collective effort'.[23] But in studying Blyton it is clear that the war made itself felt not simply through her writing but in a more dispersed way via the war-time publishing industry of which she was part. What happened was that Blyton, like every other author, had to negotiate an industry having to adjust to more than just the blackout: paper rationing (imposed in March 1940), the conscription of skilled staff into the armed forces or other war work, the imposition of an Excess Profits Tax, the shortage of equipment and the closure of bookbinders' workshops posed severe challenges. 'As you know', editor, Roland Heath, told Blyton in 1941, 'production costs are now much higher than they were before the war' (Mac, 13 March 1941). Then there was the bombing. In one air-raid on 29 December 1940—a night which became known as the Second Fire of London—several publishers and book distributors had their premises destroyed and over six million books were lost.[24] This was not an isolated incident. The following year the destruction of a binder's workshop resulted in the loss of Methuen's entire stock of Blyton storybooks (*Ten-Minute Tales, Fifteen-Minute Tales, Twenty-Minute Tales*) and the best-selling 'Babar the Elephant' stories. Also destroyed were the firm's stocks of Winnie-the-Pooh stories, prompting A.A. Milne to remark caustically that no-one should be surprised at such raids since 'Hitler's dislike of education is well-known'.[25] One observer, Lorna Lewis, took heart from the fact that while London's publishing district looked horrible, a mass of 'twisted iron work and broken skeleton brick walls', the industry would continue. After all, 'though bombs may destroy bricks, they don't destroy books and the creating of books'.[26] It is a sign of the difficulties that the publication of books fell rapidly. In 1939 14,904 books had been published; by 1945 the number had dropped to 6747. The figures for children's books tell a similar story: 951 new titles in 1939 to 397 titles in 1941, before recovering to 676 titles in 1945.[27]

The flip side of this was, as Juliet Gardiner points out, that the war 'created an unprecedented demand for something to read'.[28] Spending on books rose accordingly: from £9 million in 1939 to £23 million in 1945.[29] What Blyton and others registered was that the demand extended to children as well. 'I was at Methuen's and at Newnes yesterday', Blyton told Roland Heath in December 1941, 'and was glad to hear how amazingly well children's books are doing' (Mac, 6 December 1941). Earlier, A.L. Rowse, writing in *Country*

Life, had noted the same, predicting that 'whatever we learn to do without, it is not likely that the demand for children's books will cease. Children evacuated, or travelling across the seas, children in air raid shelters, children sick or in hospital, all want books for all childish ages....sometimes only something quite new will charm his attention'.[30]

Given all this, how did Blyton try to manage her career during the war, and how did she take advantage of the opportunities which came her way? First, already being popular helped. Faced with paper rationing (typically 37½ % of pre-war usage)—one choice for publishers was how to use it. Despite the brave talk about the value of books, publishers could not support all the authors on their lists. Some would have to go out of print. An example of this kind of decision made came in July 1940, when *The Bookseller* reported that Basil Blackwell would be cutting back their children's section to publish just three new books 'all by successful authors'. These were Enid Blyton's *The Secret of Spiggy Holes* (a sequel to *The Secret Island*), Mary Baker's *Lady Arabella's Birthday Party*, and Geoffrey Trease's *Cue for Treason*, an adventure story set at the time of the Spanish Armada.[31] A similar thing happened at Newnes. Blyton's books were kept in, along with Richmal Crompton's 'William' stories. As the firm's marketing manager reported, these were authors who achieved 'great' sales 'without publicity'; 'they just gobble up their paper quota!'[32] Meanwhile other authors began to feel neglected. In May 1941, Alison Uttley, who by this time had developed a hatred of Blyton, describes dispatching Katherine Wigglesworth to the Beaconsfield branch of W.H. Smith's. Here she spoke to the manager, 'trying to get him to stock my books...he refused. No demand! "Now if it was Miss Enid Blyton's books! They sell marvellously. Do you know her? She is a charming woman. Here is her photograph". Mrs. Wig, "She looks rather harassed", – as she looks at the awful picture of a vulgar curled woman'.[33]

A corollary of this was that other publishers also began to include Blyton amongst those writers they judged reliable and not 'difficult'. According to John Attenborough of Hodder and Stoughton, one of the firms damaged by the December 1940 bombing, his company 'devoted most of its paper quota to new book publication for those authors who could deliver new typescripts without fuss'. 'It was in these circumstances', he adds, 'that several authors attained great sale and popularity'.[34] For Hodder, these were often writers of popular fiction like Patricia Wentworth, whose detective stories were just the kind of satisfying Agatha Christie-eque fare people wanted. But Hodder also published children's books and by 1940 they were anxious to expand their lists. They took on Captain W.E. Johns when Biggles's previous publisher, Oxford University Press, decided that the stories were too 'low brow'. Hodder published *Biggles Sweeps the Desert* (1942) which, after eighteen months, accrued impressive sales of 39,933. The second book in John's newer series, *Worrals Flies Again,* featuring Flying Officer Joan 'Worrals' Worralson (1942) sold 29,688 copies in its first year.[35] In 1941, Hodder approached Blyton as well who submitted *Five on a Treasure Island* to them. Published the following year the novel achieved even better sales than those of W.E. Johns'. By April 1943, 50,261 copies had been sold, bringing Hodder a profit of £7682 and earning Blyton (who was on her usual royalty of 10% on the first 5000 copies sold and 12½% thereafter) £1506. By April 1944 the next book, *Five Go Adventuring Again*, published in July 1943, had sold 51,821, earning Blyton a royalty of £1510. In 1942 Hodder also published in *The Enid Blyton Happy Story Book* (compiled from short stories published in *Sunny Stories* in the 1930s). Priced at five shillings, it sold 48,258 copies in its first year, bringing Blyton an initial royalty of £1237. *Enid Blyton's Merry Story Book* followed in 1943, selling 44,466 copies by April 1944, earning Blyton £1158.[36]

Alongside this, Blyton also benefitted from Hodder's creation in 1940 of new imprints, including the Brockhampton Press, set up with the intention of specialising in children's books. The government had permitted the launch of a new firm on the understanding that it would not lay claim to Hodder's paper ration. Instead, the Press was expected to find innovative ways of working and did so by acquiring paper off-cuts discarded by magazine printers, which was then pulped. The quality of the paper was said to resemble toilet paper but, in 1942 was deemed good enough for Blyton's 'Mary Mouse' booklets—anthropomorphic stories about a mouse who is exiled from her mouse hole and gets a job as a maid in the home of Sailor Sam and the doll family, wherein she is able to indulge a passion for cleaning. The premise was uninspiring but when Brockhampton printed the one-shilling booklets in batches of 200,000 a time, replete with inexpensive two-tone colour illustrations by Olive Openshaw. they quickly sold out. The series would go on to sell 4.5 million copies for Brockhampton.[37] The fact that they were cheaply made ensured a low price (one shilling) but it also meant that few copies survived because they quickly disintegrated.

Another way in which Blyton managed to continue to publish large numbers of books was 'to spread her wares that much wider', as George Greenfield recalled, by which he meant she sought to add to the (already large) number of publishers she did business with.[38] In addition to Hodder, there were William Collins, Pitkin, Werner Laurie and Odhams. She also continued to publish extensively with Newnes. Between 1939 and 1945 the firm published at least twenty-five titles under Blyton's own name including *Naughty Amelia Jane* (1939); *The Naughtiest Girl in the School* (1940), *The Adventures of Mr Pinkwhistle* (1941); *Shadow, the Sheep-Dog* (1942). Blyton also deployed her 'Mary Pollock' pseudonym when even she became worried about flooding the market. *The Secret of Cliff Castle* (1943), *Smuggler Ben* (1943), *The Adventures of Scamp* (1943), *Mischief at St Rollo's* (1943) were all published under this name. Blyton's diaries convey something of these efforts. Wednesday 17 January 1940: 'Up to town by [the] 8.50. To Derry and Toms shopping. Lunched with Sir R. Evans, Allen & Noel Evans till 3 and fixed up book [*Enid Blyton's Book of the Year*]...saw Calkin of *Country Life*'. Later that year, *Country Life* published *The Children of Cherry Tree Farm*, followed in 1942 *by The Children of Willow Farm*. In 1940, another firm, J. Coker, published *The Talking Teapot and Other Tales*, *The Strange Tale of Mr Wumble* and *Brer Rabbit Retold*. Meanwhile Methuen, who before the war had only sporadic dealings with Blyton, took on much more of her work: *The O'Sullivan Twins* (the first of the St. Clare's series) appeared in 1942, and *The Mystery of the Burnt Cottage* (the first of the 'Find-Outers' books) in 1943. Staff at Methuen recalled Blyton as 'a model author...always on time...beautiful type-scripts...never argued about terms'.[39] In 1944 Blyton also secured contracts with *The Sunday Graphic* and *The Sunday Mail.* In 1945, Lutterworth Press brought out *The Caravan Family*, the first of Blyton's so-called 'family' stories (examples of these are discussed in Chapters 8 and 9).

The most satisfying of these new relationships but also the most curious (at least on the surface) was with Macmillan and Company. They were the most prestigious firm Blyton worked with; its staff included the future Conservative Prime Minister, Harold Macmillan, and its 'house' authors had included Henry James, Rudyard Kipling, W.B. Yeats, Rebecca West, Winston Churchill, Hugh Walpole, Edith Sitwell and an assortment of archbishops (a testament to the high ideals and strong Christian principles of its Victorian founders). Macmillan had not published contemporary children's fiction for many years until Blyton approached them in 1940. Her works, she informed them, had 'sold by the hundred thousands' (Mac, 30 October 1940). The firm was unsure at first, but Blyton seemed a good bet, a former school teacher whose stories offered an unimpeachable moral tone but made profits. The firm dipped its toe in the water by publishing three *Enid Blyton Readers*, anthologies of short stories which had already appeared in *Sunny Stories* in the 1930s. Blyton meanwhile suggested ways to do it, as well as how to reach the biggest audience. Other publishers, she explained:

...like to produce my books for the general juvenile public first and then run them for the educational market afterwards...Methuen's, for instance, published my 'Five-Minute tales', 'Ten-Minute tales', 'Fifteen Minute Tales' etc. at 3/6 first for the general public and then at 1/6 for the educational market. The book was exactly the same except for the jacket, and the series did very well in both markets. Blackwell's did this too – general public price 5/-, school edition 2/-. Evans Bros. of course, produce my books for the educational market only...

I now await your comments and hope that we may be at the beginning of a profitable venture for both of us! (Mac, 9 February 1941)

'I am', she added, 'quite prepared to do any children's books you like for Macmillan's, and you know that I would be proud to do them for you. You haven't many children's titles and it would be lovely if I could give you some best-sellers' (Mac, 19 July 1943).

Macmillan took the hint. *The Enid Blyton Readers,* priced at one shilling, were published in 1942 with illustrations by the distinguished watercolourist Eileen Soper (see Chapter 6). The selection was then whittled down and a handful of the stories were gathered together again and published in an anthology, *I'll Tell You a Story,* also illustrated by Soper, which sold at a still-affordable four shillings and sixpence. The book looked attractive: 'like a good pre-war book', Blyton noted. 'I feel very proud of it...I hope you'll let me do some more books for you soon!' (Mac, 19 December 1942). *I'll Tell You A Story* appeared in the shops in time for Christmas in December 1942. On Boxing Day Blyton reported how it had 'gone like hot cakes' (Mac, 26 December 1942). The first run of 25,000 copies quickly sold out. Meanwhile, she was filled with enthusiasm for her new publishers who had also, by way of a Christmas present, sent her their new edition of Leo Tolstoy's *War and Peace.* Blyton was delighted: 'I'm as busy as I can be, but it will always be a temptation to put aside other work to do books [for you]' (Mac, 19 December 1942).

It was for this reason that in 1943 Macmillan sought to deploy Blyton's credentials as a teacher and amateur botanist and arranged for her to work with Lionel John 'Jack' Brimble, editor of the scientific magazine *Nature* (which Macmillan published). Their plan was to publish thirty *Nature Readers* (1945–1946) which, as Blyton explained, were about 'things children should know & love knowing' (Mac, 10 March 1943). Blyton would write a story about the daily life of an animal—Bushy, the forgetful Squirrel, is one of two stories comprising *Reader No.2.* These were then illustrated in colour (again by Eileen Soper) and fact-checked by Jack Brimble. The Readers were put in seasonal order to help teachers, particularly (as Blyton explained) 'the more stupid type...some of them know very little about Nature' (Mac, 1 June

1943). It helped that additional rations of paper for the venture were available via the Moberly Paper pool—administrated for the duration of the war by the Publishers Association—which would sometimes supply extra paper for projects held to serve the national interest; if they were 'educational' for example. Blyton took pains with the work which she found 'necessarily slower than *ordinary* creative work, as it has to be so factually accurate'. Writing the short stories she found it difficult to get the same 'impetus' as when she worked on 'a complete book' (Mac, 20 August 1943). Nonetheless, Brimble was impressed. Blyton was 'Bomber Command, the Eighth Army & the Navy' rolled into one (Mac, 3 March 1943).

It was not simply about the money. Blyton appreciated the way in which Macmillan treated her. They made her feel an important person and they showed the same appreciation of her work as they did towards that of other more-obviously distinguished authors on their lists, Edith Sitwell, for example, or Rebecca West. It helped that she was much easier to deal with. She, in turn, liked writing to them and telling them what she had been up to:

> You know that I shall not mind any comment or criticism....I was on a Brain's Trust on Monday night & I did enjoy it – the first I have been on! I wasn't at all nervous & discovered two things – that I could get hold of the audience & that I had a carrying voice - it really was great fun. Of course, it was only a local affair for Wings for Victory Week, but it was amusing. (Mac, 26 May 1943)

Blyton's letters convey a sense of a cheerful, self-effacing woman, with a business-like attitude and obvious grasp of the production process as well as an appreciation of the kudos of being a Macmillan author. She could be a stickler for detail and the firm would joke to her about 'the grindstone that…you are rather keeping us up to' (Mac, 31 January 1944). But, as other publishers also found, Blyton was conscientious and punctual; she was willing to cut or extend stories as required; she did not ask for an advance and was never greedy about royalties (ten or twelve per cent), not least because she wanted children to be able to afford her books.

* * *

What is striking about the creative projects pursued by Blyton in the early-mid 1940s is that the war as a subject or setting featured less and less. Here again we can see the impact on Blyton's thinking of booksellers and readers who increasingly told her that they wanted to escape the conflict. There was the argument that people needed what the Archbishop of Canterbury, echoing Churchill, termed the 'mental rest' provided by books and maga-zines, the provision of which was 'a social service'.[40] By 1943 Blyton had begun to refuse such commissions altogether:

> ...do you mind if I don't write a book bringing in the war? I say this for two reasons – one is that the war inevitably dates a book, and after the war is over few people will want to read about it – certainly we shall want our children to forget it! Another reason is that there are still a great many people who definitely will not buy a book about the war for their children – they prefer stories that take the children's minds away from it, and this is quite right. (Mac, 19 July 1943)

It is a revealing glimpse into Blyton's professional mind, what she would do and what she would not, as well as into the creative direction in which she had decided to head. It explains titles like *Five on a Treasure Island* (1942) and *The Twins at St Clare's* (1942), both of which Blyton quickly developed into series, in which the war was never mentioned or at least not directly. It was part of wider trend amongst writers for children for stories 'remote from war or war conditions', as Lorna Lewis noted in 1942. 'In most of them delicious pre-rationing meals are described; tables groan with cakes iced and otherwise; sandwiches, treacle and jam (two kinds), even with cream; sweets unlimited may be bought at any shop'.[41]

This sounds familiar to anyone who has read any of the Famous Five stories—or indeed wished they were partaking of one of the midnight feasts in the school stories—and Blyton's appreciation of the power of hunger is something discussed more specifically in Chapter 6. But there were other creative directions, too. For example, when seen in this context, Blyton's deci-sion in March 1942 to serialise another fantasy story, *The Magic Faraway Tree* (6 March 1942–29 January 1943) made perfect sense. She had introduced the magic tree—up which siblings Jo, Bessie and Fanny climb in order to explore the different lands at the top—in earlier wish-fulfilment stories, notably *The Enchanted Wood* (serialised in *Sunny Stories* October 1938–May 1939). The earlier book., Lorna Lewis reported approvingly in *Time and Tide*, was 'a gay story' ('gay'—implying a harmless jollity—was a favourite adjective of unimaginative reviewers of children's books during the 1920s and 1930s).[42] In *The Magic Faraway Tree*, Blyton thus sought to recapture something of this for war-time. As the book's title implies, the tree takes centre stage: a 'simply enormous' oak which also (wonderfully) produces apples and plums (MFT 9). It stands in a 'dark, thick wood...not far from the bottom of the garden' (MFT 8). In fairy tales woods are invariably sinister places—think of Snow White, Hansel and Gretel, Little Red Riding Hood or even the Wild

Wood of *The Wind in the Willows*. In her own story, however, Blyton seems to have abandoned the possibilities inherent in her initial description to focus on the Faraway Tree which, apart from its trunk having been converted into apartments (lived in by an assortment of quaint but benign folk) and being an entry point to adventure, comes to be seen as being like other trees children might climb in search of a safe familiar space. The main difference, of course, is that the Faraway Tree is simultaneously the point at which 'real' time stops and through which the children explore alternative worlds. (In this regard, it is rather like the wardrobe in a later space slip story, C.S. Lewis's *The Lion, the Witch and the Wardrobe* [1950]).

It is sometimes said that the appeal of fantasy stories for young readers is that the characters' adventures amongst strange peoples who act by unfamiliar rules are metaphors for the experience of childhood itself. As V. Glasgow Koste puts it, adults may find themselves 'strangers in a strange land...but a child is most poignantly so, passionately trying to...fathom contradictions of behaviour and motive; to challenge or adapt to the ways of the world'.[43] The most famous example is Dorothy Gale in *The Wizard of Oz*, the film version of which was released in 1939. But Blyton's interest in fantasy went back further—to Beckenham in the early 1900s and her life as a child closeted in her tiny bedroom away from her annoying mother. Fantasy fiction offers an escape from real life and its rules and Blyton's childhood coincided with the moment at which E. Nesbit, J.M. Barrie and Kenneth Graeme achieved enormous popularity. Nesbit's *Five Children and It* (1902), the first volume in the trilogy of novels featuring the middle-class Barnstable children, their meeting with the Psammead, a 'sand-fairy', and the granting of a wish each day, was a hugely influential text for Blyton's generation. The same is true of Nesbit's *The Phoenix and the Carpet* (1904) and *The Story of the Amulet* (1906). In these loosely structured adventures, children shake off the adults who control their lives and move effortlessly between the Edwardian suburbs and alternative worlds—places of quests, dreams and escape. Impressionable young readers like Blyton were fed stories which asked them to believe in apparently real, self-contained alternative worlds where impossible things happened.

One of the criticisms made of Blyton's fantasy stories is that they fail to live up to these earlier examples; hers are simplistic and possess no deep meaning. According to Colin Manlove, stories like *The Enchanted Wood* and *The Magic Faraway Tree* are proof of how, by the end of the 1930s, children's fantasy literature was no longer an opportunity 'to reflect on an area of human experience' but was 'more to amuse the 'kiddies'.[44] But, perhaps in depression-ridden or war-time Britain, where people were struggling to be cheerful, this was the point. Peter Hunt gives a less antagonistic explanation for Blyton's success suggesting that such stories were a way of showcasing for readers 'the joy of invention and discovery, the wonder at variety and ingenuity'. Fantasy was a 'simplifying activity—with simple acts and resolutions' in a complicated world. Expansiveness, 'freshness' and 'freedom' were on offer, in stark contrast to the attempts by parents to instil 'discipline' and routine.[45] As in the earlier *Adventures of the Wishing Chair* (1937) and *The Enchanted Wood*, there is occasional danger. The children's experience of 'The Old Woman who lived in a Shoe' sees them confronted with adult violence and anger directed towards powerless people and it is tempting to read these and similar encounters with malevolent witches and giants as being allegorical in some way: mirrors of real-life, power-crazed dictators who destroy lives via a single spell or command. For the most part, though, danger, when it does come tends to be a result of the children behaving recklessly—for example taking a potion which makes them so big that they can't fit through the hole in the cloud leading to the Faraway Tree and home. Elsewhere the emphasis is, as Manlove complains, very much on cheeriness and *pleasure*: the three children whom the reader assumes are experiencing the privations of war-time rationing (introduced in January 1940), acquire the use of a magic jug which dispenses treacle or cream as required; they visit the Land of Do as You Please where Jo drives a train and Fanny rides an elephant; in the Land of Magic Medicines they buy a tonic for their mother who is ill (dosing her with the medicine prompts an instantaneous recovery). The children's adventures are a form of escape from the chores and anxieties of the Home Front: digging, sewing, ironing—nods to the collective spirit required of children in war-time Britain but wearisome. Their father is absent, and their hard-working mother holds things together. The world has become shabbier and dimmer. Being allowed to visit the Faraway Tree is a reward as well as an escape, and brings joy, something which was in short supply. Tantalisingly, as the narrator explains in the final chapter: 'the magic Faraway Tree is *still there*' and waiting to be visited by any child lucky enough to stumble across it (*MFT*, 184).

Elsewhere Blyton sought to cater for older children via a new series: 'The Five Find-Outers'. Published by Methuen, this began with *The Mystery of the Burnt Cottage* in 1943 and continued with *The Mystery of the Disappearing Cat* in 1944. In look and feel these are war-time books. The copy of the latter title which is open in front of me was originally a present (it is inscribed 'To Roger. From Auntie Maggie & Uncle Bill'). It has some evocative illustrations by J. Abbey—but in black and white. It also contains a note assuring the authorities that the publishers have had it 'produced in complete conformity with the authorized economy standards' (*MDC*, iv). In other respects, however, the new 'Find-Outers' books were comfortingly *pre-war*, deliberately recalling the 'Golden Age' detective stories of the 1920s and 1930s: country villages inhabited by people who value their respectability, places where politeness is prized and afternoon tea looms large. Blyton, an aficionado of the genre which had made the likes of Agatha Christie, Freeman Wills Crofts and Dorothy L. Sayers famous, felt that she too, 'must try my hand at detective stories', but ones 'where the children themselves are the detectives'.[46] She would claim the genre with its puzzles and clues for them:

> Soon after tea Mrs Hilton came back. She went straight to the children, looking rather worried.
>
> 'Children,' she said, 'what do you think has happened? That lovely prize-cat, called Dark Queen, has disappeared!... And the dreadful thing is – Luke may have stolen her!'
>
> ....The children stared at Mrs Hilton, feeling upset and puzzled. Fatty took command of the whole affair, and spoke politely to Mrs Hilton.
>
> 'Luke is a very good friend of ours...and if he is in trouble, we must help him....Could you please give us the whole story? This looks like something the Five Find-Outers can tackle again.' (*MDC*, 39)

So begins the puzzle in *The Mystery of the Disappearing Cat*. For readers of detective stories the story's ingredients are familiar ones: a closed circle of suspects and a Home Counties village, Peterswood (possibly modelled on Bourne End), which turns out to be a place where a surprisingly large number of secrets lie repressed beneath the surface gentility. A pedigree Siamese cat has been taken from its cage. The nice, but illiterate, apprentice gardener, Luke, is, for Mr. Goon (known as 'Clear-Orf'), the dim village policeman assigned to the case, the prime suspect. It is left to the team of young amateur detectives, in this case 'The Find-Outers' (Larry, Daisy, Pip, Bets and Frederick ('Fatty'), to work their way through the facts (which may be clues) and uncover the truth. The crime is old-fashioned, and the identity of the real culprit seems predictable (the bullying gardener, Mr. Tupping). Yet seventy-five years after its first appearance, the appeal of this and the other books in 'The Find-Outer' series is not hard to explain, especially for war-time audiences. The war brought fragmentation, confusion and uncertainty about the future. In contrast, the detective story is a form of story-telling with a strong narrative drive which works towards a tidy ending and which tends to be comfortingly certain in its answers—a trait Blyton believed that children liked.

In some ways the detective story seems an odd genre for someone like Blyton to choose—a writer who, as we have seen, claimed that she produced her best results when she did not plan her work and had no idea how the story would turn out. Advice for would-be Agatha Christies given in writing manuals of the 1940s was always that, unlike colleagues working on other subjects, he or she needed to work backwards rather than forwards, that the ending and the explanation shaped the rest of the story. How much planning Blyton did is unclear but her Find-Outers' novels *are* very Christie-like. Christie, too, was someone who wrote seemingly simple stories, seemed to have little obvious talent for writing stylish prose or to have much aware-ness of what her critics called 'the real world'. Like Blyton, her stories are told mostly via dialogue and populated by 'flat' characters whose flatness is designed to keep the reader's focus on the central puzzle. *The Mysterious Affair at Styles* (1920) had introduced Hercule Poirot, the fussy Belgian detective with a mania for order. Blyton, too, creates a dominant, eccentric, sleuth, in this case 'Fatty', the analytical (and occasionally pompous) boy who is a master of disguise. Fatty works with a group of less-intelligent assistants and potential Captain Hastings (Poirot's regular companion) or Dr. Watsons. As well as being able to disguise himself as a 'grown-up' whenever he wants, Fatty is like Poirot or Sherlock Holmes in being able to "read" the crime scene and draw conclusions based on what he sees; as a task of interpretation it rarely seems for him to be much of a challenge, despite his youth. It is Fatty who deduces, for example, that it is the little baker, Mr. Twit, who by wearing oversize shoes has avoided being caught for the thefts in *The Mystery of the Invisible Thief* (1950); or that in *The Mystery of Tally-Ho Cottage* (1954) the missing art thieves, far from having skipped the country, are hiding in plain sight disguised as a lower-class married couple, betraying themselves by the strangely kind way in which they treat a previously neglected poodle—"'the game's up'" is all that one of them can say after being unmasked (*MTC*, 168). It is thus through Fatty that Blyton encourages her readers to believe that the world is legible if they only learn how.

In contrast, Bets and the other 'Find-Outers' are more obviously 'normal' (a favourite Blyton distinguisher). They are in thrall to the kind of behaviour expected by their parents (notably Pip and Bets, whose mother Mrs. Hilton is a stickler for good manners). They are also less skilful readers, less exhibition-istic than their plump leader and presented as more conventional in the way they detect things. They use readily available methods—chat, observation, logic, decoding—to solve puzzles and reach resolutions, perhaps allowing readers to feel these are things that they too could do. (Much is made of using oranges as invisible ink.) In *The Mystery of the Disappearing Cat*, they painstakingly piece together forensic clues: the smell of turpentine, dirty boots, a whistle. They also interview suspects—often surreptitiously. In *The*

Mystery of the Spiteful Letters (1946), the children show their skills in surveillance, stalking out bus routes and shadowing suspects as well as examining postmarks and postal routes. Bets is also encouraged to 'prattle' to people on the basis that, because she is a little girl, they will drop their guard and tell her things. There *is* occasionally danger (in *The Mystery of the Secret Room* [1945] Fatty is beaten up by the villains) but for the most part this tends to get diluted, or 'euphemised', as Stephen Knight has noted of Golden Age detective fiction. Like Christie, Blyton manages to create a world where, to quote Knight, 'the game-like features' of the story 'are forceful enough to dilute the real strength of the threats that are played with'—an accomplishment trickier than might be supposed.[47]

All this could seem ridiculous, of course, as could the proliferation of crime in a single village during the school holidays or the direct line the children seem to have to the police inspector, who treats them with complete seriousness. But in the war years when readers turned to reading for entertainment, none of this seemed to matter. '[F]unny as well as exciting' was *Time and Tide's* verdict on *The Mystery of the Secret Room* (1945).[48] The solving of an exciting mystery, topped by the meting out of poetic justice, gave colour to drab war-time—and post-war—lives. Readers got to share in the 'game' and to share the intellectual satisfaction and sense of a job well done when the culprit's identity was revealed. Blyton offered situations in which children's intelligence and voice were taken as seriously as those of Holmes and Poirot. It was an appealing and comforting prospect and readers came back for more. There were eventually fifteen books petering out with *The Mystery of Banshee Towers* in 1961, as well as short stories, 'Just a Spot of Bother' (1957) and 'The Five Find-Outers and Dog Tackle the Mystery Sneak Thief' (1961), and in 1958 a card game tie-in (cards featuring PC Goon counted against players).

* * *

In the next chapter we consider further examples of Blyton's war-time output. What should be clear, for the moment, however, is that these years were a period of concentrated production: 25 titles in 1940; 12 in 1941; 25 in 1942; 22 in 1943. This is a vast amount of work requiring sustained periods of time to complete it. Blyton's exceptional success with the public may have been due to the reduction in competition. Noel Carrington, writing in *The Bookseller* in January 1942, put it pithily: 'Where there is not much choice parents take what they can get and children are glad of anything new...'.[49] But as we have seen in this chapter, it was Blyton, more than contemporaries such as Alison Uttley, who mostly retained her pre-war ways of doing business, who enhanced her reputation farthest during the war years. There is her use of *Enid Blyton's Sunny Stories*, the switching between publishers and their faith in her, the continuation of links with education (despite the fact that she had not taught for at least fifteen years), the maintenance of friendly relations with booksellers and the willingness to take on new projects. When the blackout meant that parents kept their offspring at home, Blyton accommodated them, becoming as Crompton Mackenzie put it in 1943, 'almost a necessity in homes where there are...children'.[50]

Notes

1. Enid Blyton, 'Neville Chamberlain', MS Papers of Neville Chamberlain, University of Birmingham Library Series 1: Gifts received after the Munich crisis. Correspondence 1938–39. Letters 134–192 No. 13/7/154. Gale document number GALE/SC5109133809.
2. Dennis Judd (ed.), *The Private Diaries of Alison Uttley* (Barnsley Pen and Sword, 2009), 89.
3. Unsigned Article, 'Notes by the Way', *The Buckinghamshire Advertiser* (31 August 1940), 4.
4. Juliet Gardiner, 'Introduction', in *These Wonderful Rumours: A Young Schoolteacher's Wartime Diaries, 1939–1945*, ed. May Smith (London: Virago, 2010), vii.
5. Erik Larson, *The Splendid and the Vile: A Saga of Churchill, Family and Defiance during the Blitz* (London: Collins, 2020), 328; 334; 398.
6. Unsigned Article, 'Books Are Part of the Cause for Which We Fight', *The Bookseller* (18 July 1940), 1.
7. Unsigned Article, 'Books: Our Best Export', *The Bookseller* (23 October 1941), 1.
8. William Cederwell, *Reading London in Wartime: Blitz, the People and Propaganda in 1940s Literature* (London: Routledge, 2017), 3.
9. Juliet Gardiner, *Wartime Britain 1939–1945* (London: Headline, 2004), 416; 424.
10. Willa Muir, 'What Shall We Tell Our Children', *The Listener* (14 March 1940), 17.
11. Judy Giles and Tim Middleton (eds.), *Writing Englishness: An Introductory Sourcebook* (London: Routledge, 1995), 7.
12. Bruce A. McConachie, 'Using the Concept of Cultural Hegemony to Write Theatre History', in *Interpreting the Theatrical Past: Essays in the Historiography of Performance*, eds. Thomas Postlewait and Bruce A. McConachie (Iowa City: University of Iowa Press, 1989), 14; 47.
13. From 10 April 1942 the magazine was published fortnightly. From 19 June 19, its title reverted to *Sunny Stories*.
14. Erik Larsson, *The Splendid and the Vile*, 484.

15. Unsigned Article, 'Children in Wartime', *John O'London's Weekly* (12 April 1940), 53–54.
16. Beverley Skeggs, *Class, Self, Culture* (London: Routledge, 2003), 175.
17. Anne Boston, 'Introduction', *Wave Me Goodbye* (Harmondsworth: Penguin, 1989), 12.
18. Elaine Hadley, *Melodramatic Tactics: Theatricalized Dissent in the English Marketplace, 1800–1885* (Stanford: Stanford University Press, 1995), 3–4.
19. Larsson, *The Splendid and the Vile*, 223.
20. Barbara Wall, *The Narrator's Voice. The Dilemma of Children's Literature* (Basingstoke: Macmillan, 1991), 191; 192.
21. William Cederwell, *Reading London in Wartime*, 23.
22. Anthony Aldgate and Jeffrey Richards, *Britain Can Take It* (Oxford: Basil Blackwell, 1986), 97.
23. Eric Sevareid (ed.), *All England Listened. The War-time Broadcasts of J.B. Priestley* (New York: Chilmark Press, 1967), 57.
24. William Cederwell, *Reading London in Wartime*, 1.
25. Maureen Duffy, *A Thousand Conspicuous Chances. A History of the Methuen List, 1889–1989* (London: Methuen, 1989), 118, 123.
26. Lorna Lewis, 'For Boys and Girls', *Time and Tide* (6 September 1941), 760–1.
27. Unsigned Article, 'Book Production in the War Years', *The Bookseller* (8 March 1945), 180–1.
28. Juliet Gardiner, *Wartime Britain*, 416.
29. William Cederwell, *Reading London in Wartime*, 8.
30. A.L. Rowse, 'Pleasures of the Mind', *Country Life* (20 July 1940), 52.
31. Unsigned Article, 'Autumn Books for 1940', *The Bookseller* (18 July 1940), 53.
32. R.S. Lyons, 'Newnes' Children's Books Now', *The Bookseller* (4 December 1941), 501.
33. Dennis Judd (ed.), *The Private Diaries of Alison Uttley*, 96.
34. John Attenborough, *A Living Memory: Hodder and Stoughton Publishers 1868–1975* (London: Hodder and Stoughton, 1975), 141.
35. Royalties Ledger: 'Juveniles', London Metropolitan Archives/Hodder and Stoughton Archives, M 16,312.
36. Ibid.
37. John Attenborough, *A Living Memory*, 143.
38. George Greenfield, *Enid Blyton* (Stroud Sutton, 1998), 28.
39. Maureen Duffy, *A Thousand Conspicuous Chances*, 105.
40. Unsigned Article, 'The Love of Good Books by the Archbishop of Canterbury, Dr Temple', *John O'London's Weekly* (18 June 1943), 764.
41. Lorna Lewis, 'Books for Boys and Girls', *Time and Tide* (11 March 1942), 252.
42. Lorna Lewis, 'Summer Holiday Reading', *Time and Tide* (8 July 1939), 924.
43. V. Glasgow Koste, 'Mere Giants: The Child Protagonist in Drama for Intergenerational Audiences', *Children's Literature Association Quarterly* 12:1 (Spring 1987), 33–5 (33).

44. Colin Manlove, *From Alice to Harry Potter: Children's Fantasy in England* (Rochester: Lisa Loucks Christenson Publishing, 2003), 54.
45. Peter Hunt, *Children's Literature. An Anthology* (Oxford: Basil Blackwell, 2001), 4.
46. Enid Blyton, 'Why I Write so Many Stories', *Evening Express* (27 September 1952), 5.
47. Stephen Knight, *Form and Ideology in Crime Fiction* (Basingstoke: Macmillan, 1980), 127.
48. Bloomfield, 'The Rising Generation', *Time and Tide* (8 December 1945), 1038.
49. Unsigned Article, 'A Year of Puffin Books', *The Bookseller* (29 January 1942), 72.
50. Compton Mackenzie, 'Compton Mackenzie Chooses Gift Books Children Will Love', *Daily Mail* (11 December 1943), 2.

Bibliography

Aldgate, Anthony, and Jeffrey Richards. 1986. *Britain Can Take It*. Oxford: Basil Blackwell.

Attenborough, John. 1975. *A Living Memory: Hodder and Stoughton Publishers 1868–1975*. London: Hodder and Stoughton.

Boston, Anne. 1989. *Wave Me Goodbye*. Harmondsworth: Penguin.

Cederwell, William. 2017. *Reading London in Wartime: Blitz, the People and Propaganda in 1940s Literature*. London: Routledge.

Duffy, Maureen. 1989. *A Thousand Conspicuous Chances: A History of the Methuen List, 1889–1989*. London: Methuen.

Gardiner, Juliet. 2004. *Wartime Britain 1939–1945*. London: Headline.

Giles, Judy, and Tim Middleton. Editors. 1995. *Writing Englishness: An Introductory Sourcebook*. London: Routledge.

Hadley, Elaine. 1995. *Melodramatic Tactics: Theatricalized Dissent in the English Marketplace, 1800–1885*. Stanford: Stanford University Press.

Hunt, Peter. 2001. *Children's Literature an Anthology*. Oxford: Basil Blackwell.

Judd, Dennis. Editor. 2009. *The Private Diaries of Alison Uttley*. Barnsley: Pen and Sword.

Knight, Stephen. 1980. *Form and Ideology in Crime Fiction*. Basingstoke: Macmillan.

Koste, V. Glasgow. 1987. 'Mere Giants: The Child Protagonist in Drama for Intergenerational Audiences'. *Children's Literature Association Quarterly* 12(1): 33–5.

Larson, Erik. 2020. *The Splendid and the Vile: A Saga of Churchill, Family and Defiance during the Blitz*. London: Collins.

Manlove, Colin. 2003. *From Alice to Harry Potter: Children's Fantasy in England*: 54. Rochester: Lisa Loucks Christenson Publishing.

McConachie, Bruce A. 1989. 'Using the Concept of Cultural Hegemony to Write Theatre History'. In *Interpreting the Theatrical Past, in Interpreting the Theatrical Past: Essays in the Historiography of Performance*, edited by Thomas Postlewait and Bruce A. McConachie: 37–58. Iowa City: University of Iowa Press.

Sevareid, Eric. Editor. 1967. *All England Listened. The War-time Broadcasts of J.B. Priestley*. New York: Chilmark Press.

Skeggs, Beverley. 2003. *Class, Self, Culture*. London: Routledge.

Smith, May. 2010. *These Wonderful Rumours: A Young Schoolteacher's Wartime Diaries, 1939–1945*. London: Virago.

Wall, Barbara. 1991. *The Narrator's Voice. The Dilemma of Children's Literature*. Basingstoke: Macmillan.

6

Adventure

I was amused to see that the excellent book-shop here had one of its windows devoted to Enid Blyton books. I went in & made myself known to the manager, who was overcome with delight as it appears that the children of Swanage are one & all my fans, and he cannot get a quarter of my books that he wants....

I have promised to go to his shop for an hour next week & autograph any books the children bring, which will be rather amusing – I am afraid his shop will be crowded out.

(Enid Blyton to Roland Heath, Mac, 20 August 1943)

If the war years represent a watershed in Blyton's career, it was partly because they coincided with her emergence as a writer of what could loosely be termed adventure fictions. In this chapter we will examine some of the most successful. These books, many of which became series—The Famous Five (Hodder and Stoughton; 1942–1963), the Adventure series (Macmillan; 1943–1961), the Barney Series (Collins; 1949–1959), the Secret Seven series (Brockhampton Press; 1949–1963)—can also be taken as representative of Blyton's tendency to adapt and mix up adult sub-genres for a child audience. The Famous Five novels are mystery or detective stories involving the bringing to light of criminal activities while selling a seductive vision of child-power set against an idyllic backdrop of rural England. The Adventure series follows a similar pattern, but Blyton increasingly makes use of some of the features of the adventure romance or 'imperial romance', taking her insular

© The Author(s), under exclusive license to Springer Nature
Switzerland AG 2021
A. Maunder, *Enid Blyton*, Literary Lives,
https://doi.org/10.1007/978-3-030-76332-9_6

English characters abroad to increasingly exotic locations. The Secret Seven series with its clues, puzzles and shadowing of suspects, is, like the Find-Outers series, based on a format adopted by crime writers during the so-called 'Golden Age' of British detective fiction (roughly 1918–1945). In so far as she shows the children's skills in surveillance and the power of the group, Blyton also perhaps draws on the example of Erich Kästner's *Emil and the Detectives* (1929), while extending Emil's 'boys only' gang, to include girls. Blyton's use of the forms of the detective story and thriller in which a group of children (usually two boys and two girls) solve a crime or uncover a sinister activity is also the central thread of other novels, including *The Rockingdown Mystery* (1949) and its sequels. As is always the case with Blyton, these series are also part of a much larger body of work in which ingredients from various sub-genres are mixed up and recalibrated for children: *The Secret of Spiggy Holes* (1940) revisits the protagonists of *The Secret Island* (1938) involving them in the discovery of a foreign prince being held captive; *The Treasure Hunters* (1940) shows children using maps to find the lost jewels hidden on their grandparents' estate before a shady businessman beats them to it. *The Boy Next Door* (1944) shows children thwarting kidnappers of their friend, a wealthy American boy, by hiding him on a secret houseboat. Two of Blyton's final works, *The Adventure of the Strange Ruby* (1960), in which children rescue a pair of kidnapped twins who have inherited the jewel of the title (which is supposedly cursed), and *The Mystery That Never Was* (1961) in which children and their dog investigate flashing lights coming from a burnt-out house, follow a similar pattern albeit with a good deal less flair than the earlier works.

In writing about Blyton's creative development, I have avoided using the terms 'originator' or 'innovator' because it is doubtful whether she was either of these things. Her adventure fiction is no exception. (This is even though during the war—and afterwards—Blyton became increasingly identified with this genre.) From the beginning, she drew on the formulaic forms of genre fiction—adventure and spy stories featuring robberies and kidnappings which had long been a feature of magazines for children, such as the *Boys' Own* Paper (1879–1967) and the *Girls' Own Paper* (1880–1956). More directly, there was, as we saw in Chapter 4, the inescapable example of Arthur Ransome, who had helped revitalise this kind of writing with two bestsellers—*Swallows and Amazons* (1930) and its sequel, *Swallowdale* (1931). Between 1930 and 1947, Ransome published twelve stories about the Walker and Blackett children; in 1945, his sales stood at 560,000.[1] It was Ransome whom Geoffrey Trease, writing of the world of mid-century writing for children, judged '[t]he outstanding literary landmark of this period'. As Trease explained, it was Ransome who, being tired of the school story 'cried "What about the holidays?" and flung open the door upon a fresh view'. In what was possibly a dig at Blyton, whom he did not rate highly, Trease also noted that the quality of Ransome's novels 'shames those prolific yarn-spinners who present their public with a litter of several books per season'.[2] Ransome himself claimed to hate children but realised that he had been given a key to knowing what they wanted. '[T]he reason my brats like my books', he explained, 'is that they are all something that happens today and MIGHT happen to themselves given only some quite small modification in their circumstances, such as a different mother, or a reformed father, or living a bit nearer a lake, or something like that'.[3] His most famous protagonists—John, Susan, Titty and Roger—were clearly not 'wishy-washy' and the 'Ransome virtues'—teamwork, hardiness, 'decency', independence—were much imitated and it was difficult to escape Ransom's shadow. This was the point made by V.S. Pritchett when, in 1936, he reviewed a large pile of such stories, including such (now forgotten) titles as *Coconut Island* by Robert Gibbings and *Henry Against the Gang* by T.H. Johansen. As Pritchett reported, most of them were set against a 'background of easy homes, sudden journeys to coral reefs…pleasing dinghies on the Solent'. Ideologically, it was 'jolly, well-fed, healthy, sporting middle-class stuff', with a 'solid suburban fence', but which also pandered to children's 'momentous egotism' and fostered a sense of youthful superiority, making readers feel important. It seemed an irresistible mixture. 'The most humdrum boy hits upon a plot against the Empire, stumbles upon secret planes, over-hears significant conversations at every street corner, solves a mystery which has baffled the police for years, is always on holiday, and adults…are not bored with him but indeed defer'.[4]

It is easy to recognise in these descriptions the ingredients of Blyton's adventure stories. It was a tone set by her early story, *The Wonderful Adventure* (1927), a formulaic tale of boats, picnics and the search for treasure, the spirit of which is apparent in its chapter titles: 'The Secret Passage', 'The Hidden Room', 'The Old Sea-Caves', 'The Smuggler's Cave'. By the time she began to publish adventure stories more consistently in the late 1930s, she could not fail to be aware that this was a crowded field, nor that Ransome ('Children's Author No. 1' as a reviewer in *The Spectator* described him), had set new stan-dards.[5] Blyton was very conscious of Ransome, even as she began to outsell him in the 1940s. On one occasion she hinted that she believed he had copied from her, noting that the forthcoming *Great Northern* (1947) was 'awfully like' her own forthcoming *The Sea of Adventure* (1948), including the use of a puffin as comic relief. 'I hope it isn't (for his sake!)', she wrote. But equally she was worried that people would think that she had stolen from him (Mac, 26 August 1947). She was keen to differentiate them. While Ransome's style and hers were 'not', she espoused 'very different', his novels were 'for rather older children than I usually write for' and, as 'a general rule I think I get on more quickly with my tales – I mean, I put more action and drama into my full-length stories for children – his are more leisurely…'. A good deal of the negative criticism of Blyton, then and since, has hinged on the idea that the Famous Five stories are best classified as 'sub Ransome'. This argument is not something Blyton would have countenanced. She believed that the 'best type' of adventure stories were those 'told in a simple, direct style', that is say, hers (Mac, 14 July 1943). For his part, Ransome believed it a 'melancholy fact that children are omnivorous. They will like almost anything. They cannot distinguish between originals and imitations', i.e. Blyton's. 'All alike are new to them'.[6]

Blyton's other recorded comments on 'typical adventure stories', as she termed them, tend to follow a similar pattern (Mac, 19 July 1943). '[G]ood, sound books, written in straightforward language with live characters in a first-rate story', and 'decent in every way', was what she put forward as recipes for success in an interview in 1949.[7] Inevitably Blyton's terminology appears dated but her use of the term 'live' suggests a desire to achieve the illusion of spontaneity—as if she were telling the story in the classroom to a circle of children. She explained (somewhat disingenuously) that despite her stories being plot driven, she rarely worked details out before starting:

> You see, when I begin to write a book, I only have a hazy idea as to how it will develop – I don't plan my books or make any kind of syllabus or synopsis beforehand, except, of course, in the case of educational books, which are quite different. The creative mind usually works in a queer way, often in a haze or a mist, out of which come the characters, the incidents, the dialogue, and even the names of the characters themselves! This probably seems quite mad to you, but it's the only way I can work with any success and does bring a spontaneity and fertility of imagination into my books, which children enjoy. (Mac, 19 July 1943)

Blyton's emphasis on allowing a story to 'grow and develop' and of characters appearing fully developed before her seemed curious to some but it was clearly a method with which she felt comfortable and confident, and which resulted in a good many critical plaudits. Thus in 1948, *The Birmingham Daily Post* made the following comments on her story of camping and gun-running, *The Sea of Adventure*:

A third story of home life which has the quality I have tried to suggest - skilful packing with small and comfortable likelihoods so that you slide into the unlikely as easily as you go to bed is Miss Enid Blyton's The Sea of Adventure....Energy and invention are Miss Blyton's great assets and they show no sign of failing. Her improbabilities are so deftly administered that you take them unthinkingly.[8]

The idea of Blyton as a kind of literary mesmerist able to convince readers to accept the most implausible events made sense, as did the more prosaic explanation that she was at least a 'skilled' technician or 'craftsman', adept at working within the confines of the genre, mixing up ingredients sufficiently to make things appear fresh, usually by providing different settings and situations, but invariably, as *The Scotsman* noted, of *Five Get into Trouble* (1949), 'creating characters with whom young readers find it easy to identify themselves, and in evolving situations the drama of which directly appeals to them'.[9] True to form, she also showed 'the inevitable triumph of Right and Fair Play', as *Teacher's World* noted.[10] In interviews Blyton explained that she sought to do this not in a didactic or pious way and we discuss her sense of mission in Chapter 8. However, one way of reading Blyton's adventure stories is to say that, rather like training manuals, they teach young readers—and their parents—how to behave. In some cases, particularly texts written during the war, this is pronounced. Thus, as the aviator, Captain Arnold, announces in *The Secret of Killimooin* (1943): "'[W]e want boys and girls of spirit and courage, who can stand on their feet and are not afraid of what may happen to them. We want them to grow up adventurous and strong, of some real use in the world! So we must not say no when a chance comes along to help them to be plucky and independent'" (*SK*, 12). As was seen in the previous chapter, one context for Blyton's texts is the extent to which they suggested that the kind of 'English' behaviours on display were important given how Britain was being besieged by the forces of totalitarianism and Nazism. In the young middle-class adventurers, Blyton shows proper conduct; in the criminals and foreigners they encounter, unmanly and un-English conduct.

This ideological dimension is also apparent when Blyton moves the settings of her stories abroad. *The Secret Mountain*, published in 1941 as a sequel to *The Secret Island*, takes 'Africa' for its setting and subject, which leads (inevitably) to fears of being "'eaten by wild animals, or taken prisoner by savages'" (*SM*, 16). Later when the 'white and worried' children—Jack, Nora, Mike, Peggy and Paul—encounter the spear-wielding tribe of sun worshippers who speak in 'high-pitched, shrill voices' (and whose propensity for human sacrifice seems likely to be demonstrated via Paul), they only narrowly

escape (*SM*, 123). The novel is littered with images of primitive unpre-
dictability; the sun people 'jabber and shout' when Captain Arnold fires his
gun (*SM*, 172). The point has often been made that what these novels also
do is remind us of another dimension to Blyton's writing: that the non-British
people who stray into the pages of her stories are often liable to be portrayed
in racist terms either as crass vulgarians (usually Americans), violent thugs or
simple children of nature—a sign that Blyton's ideas of representation were
set in narrow grooves, ones which she could not—or would not—try to get
out of. Some of these strains, together with Blyton's contrastingly modern
interest in gender identities, are played out in the Famous Five series. Here
the idea of Blyton as a writer whose novels are essentially a celebration of
Englishness is given added heft by the presence of Eileen Soper's illustrations.

The Famous Five

> I am so glad you like 'Five on a Treasure Island' – it is the kind of story that any
> child likes, English or otherwise! Surprisingly enough grown-ups have enjoyed
> it too, judging by many letters I have received!
>
>   (Enid Blyton to Roland Heath, Mac, 26 July 1943)

Five on a Treasure Island: An Adventure Story for Boys and Girls (1942) is
a more confident text than Blyton's earlier adventure stories, *The Secret of
Spiggy Holes* (1940) and *The Adventurous Four* (1941); it is the first of
Blyton's works to feature the siblings Julian, Dick and Anne, their cousin
Georgina ('George') and her dog, Timmy, and it marks her full transition
into the mode of middle-class adventure writing which she never abandoned.
The series stretched over twenty-one titles, eventuating in *Five are Together
Again* (1963), and having several offshoots: short stories, card games, annuals
(*The Famous Five Big Book* [1964]) and a stage play produced in London's
West End (1955–1956; 1956–1957). I discuss this adaptation in Chapter 11.
Several of the titles were serialised; the first instalment of *Five Go off to Camp*
appeared in *Sunny Stories* on 19 March 1948 and, when *Enid Blyton's Maga-
zine* was launched in 1953, other titles appeared there as well. As shown in
Fig. 6.1 which, by way of example, shows sales of the first nine titles in 1951,
the books sold consistently well over many years. It seemed to prove, as Paul
Hodder-Williams of Hodder and Stoughton noted, that Blyton was an author
for whom the market 'renews itself every 4 or 5 years'.[11]

It is impossible to summarise all the commentary which the series has
provoked, although some important sources are listed in the bibliography.

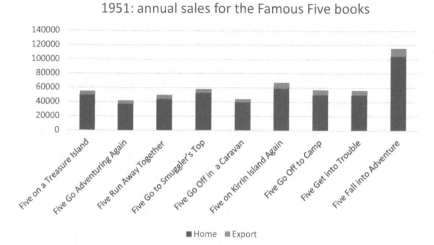

Fig. 6.1 Sales figures in 1000s (*Source* London Metropolitan Archives/Hodder and Stoughton Archives, M. 16327)

However, if we take the first and most successful book, *Five on a Treasure Island*, as a starting point, two things are worth noting. First, that unlike *The Adventurous Four*, published the previous year, there is no explicit trace of external world events. This includes the war, although as David Rudd has argued there may be a case for seeing the crooks who appear as metonymic of German invaders.[12] Secondly, just as the outcome of the earlier text has much to do with the way in which a working-class boy finds himself conscripted as leader, much of the impact of *Five on a Treasure Island* comes from Blyton's decision to give most attention to another outsider: Georgina/George, the girl who identifies as a boy.

Most critics of the Famous Five series come sooner or later to George. In the novel's second chapter, entitled 'The Strange Cousin', an initial conversation between George and her cousin, Anne, who has arrived with her older brothers, Julian and Dick, to stay at Kirrin Cottage, helps establish some of the tensions involved:

'I'm George,' said the girl. 'I shall only answer if you call me George. I hate being a girl. I won't be. I don't like doing the things that girls do. I like doing the things that boys do. I can climb better than any boy, and swim faster too....You're to call me George. Then I'll speak to you. But I shan't if you don't'. (*FTI*, 19)

Anne, who is much more conventional, appears not to be used to this kind of assertiveness in girls, nor has she met any who seek to rebel against constraints in the way her cousin does. So, she warns her: "'You're not very polite…You won't find that my brothers take much notice of you if you act as if you know everything. They're *real* boys, not pretend boys like you'" (*FTI*, 20).

Anne is exactly the passive, obedient, open-hearted and cautious girl of the mid-twentieth-century feminine ideal. In particular, she hero-worships Julian (or 'Ju') as she is taught to—and understands him. Julian is the male ideal: the public-school prefect, initially younger but more confident than Andy in *The Adventurous Four*, for example—in his willingness to lead the group in the absence of adults. He is the traditional 'good' boy as described by George Orwell in 'Boys' Weeklies', his 1940 essay on school stories: 'good in the clean-living Englishman tradition—they keep in hard training, wash behind their ears, never hit below the belt, etc'.[13] Julian is set to be, like Blyton, a member of the comfortably off professional elite—energetic and organised, a figure through which Blyton can make a very clear statement about the positive value of such people. In fictional terms, he is the younger cousin to W.E. Johns' man of action, Biggles, rather than Richmal Crompton's equally ageless but anarchic William Brown. An intelligent and confident boy, who prides himself on his good manners, Julian seems to his relatives to be a suitable figure to whom to entrust the erratic behaviour of George, as well as his more obviously pliable younger brother and sister.

Where Julian operates within a cultural framework centred around masculinity and leadership that he and Anne—and presumably most of Blyton's 1940s readers—both understand and were taught to respect, George is not so easily slotted in. This was presumably one of the reasons that she appears to have been popular with readers who in their own lives were expected to conform to expectations. Partly these are to do with gender. As part of the scene setting, the children go to the beach where they 'bathe':

> …the boys found that George was a much better swimmer than they were. She was very strong and very fast, and she could swim under water, too, holding her breath for ages.
> 'You're jolly good,' said Julian, admiringly. 'It's a pity Anne isn't a bit better. Anne, you'll have to practise your swimming strokes hard, or you'll never be able to swim out as far as we do'. (*FTI*, 36)

Ideas of what readers 'like' about a character are obviously partly dependent on the time and place in which they live. Much of what readers have liked about George is that she represents a challenge to the usual power relationships between boys and girls in fiction and the patronising stance of male characters like Julian. Detractors would say, of course, that what we are presented with is (at best) two-dimensional, a cliché of a tomboy.

Few have been more damning than Wallace Hildick who cited George as the supreme example of the Five's 'nasty, snobby, cruel selfishness…petulant, childish viciousness'.[14] From her first jarring appearance, it is George's behaviour—her willingness to set her dog, Timmy, on other children, for example—which is the real source of disquiet in the novels, not the pushing at the boundaries of gender. It is for this reason, too, that Blyton's depiction of her heroine follows a definite pattern, from rebellion and anti-social behaviour with attendant physical violence, to the emergence of a dual existence which hovers between boarding school and the outdoors and finally to fear of adult life. "'I don't want to grow up'" George thinks in *Five Go to Billycock Hill* (1957). "'There can't be anything nicer in the world than this – being with the others, having fun with them'" (*FBH*, 46).

When *Five on a Treasure Island* appeared in September 1942, it was well received. '[Robert Louis] Stevenson would have enjoyed reading of these brave children and their 'Treasure Island', gushed the *Liverpool Daily Post*.[15] As Christmas approached, relatives who were not normally book buyers were encouraged to see Blyton's books and annuals as 'safe' presents. Thus, *The Daily Mirror*, noting the war-time shortage of toys, recommended the novel alongside David Severn's *Rick Afire* (another series novel), about two evacuees who reap the benefit of country living. It was clear to some reviewers that Blyton, as she was often inclined to do, was simply taking in hand a well-established sub-genre. As *Country Life* noted, her new novel was 'an oft told story of dungeons and ingots and hair-breadth escapes', but this did not seem to matter.[16] Meanwhile, Blyton waxed lyrical about the novel's 'enormous success' and realised she had hit upon a rich seam (Mac, 19 July 1943).

Looking back at *Five on a Treasure Island* as it appeared in 1942 and the immediate sequels—*Five Go Adventuring Again* (1943), *Five Run Away Together* (1944), *Five Go to Smuggler's Top* (1945)—it is easy to see why the books were appealing. For parents, the premise was unobjectionable: in keeping with the traditions of the genre, Blyton presents a world of healthy outdoor activities—some of the rituals of which are explained in detail—in which children are generally polite and right always prevails over wrong. For children she offers fantasies of independence whereby children escape irritating adults and go off on their own. The Five (including the preternaturally intuitive dog, Timmy) are always happy to do so, seemingly having, as Nicholas Tucker has observed, 'virtually no psychological or emotional needs for their mother or father'.[17] (Nor are they required to clean their teeth or eat vegetables). But thanks to their parents' money and connections they *do* have access to interesting places—castles, farms, islands, skiing lodges, lighthouses—wherein they enact what might best be described as fantasies of homemaking. They also have the use of equipment, such as boats, tents, ropes, sledges, ponies and bikes.

Thus, by the time the later books appeared, readers knew what they were getting. Anne's wish, plaintively expressed in *Five Go Off in a Caravan* (1946), to have "'a nice ordinary, peaceful holiday'" is never fulfilled (*FC*, 82). Instead the children encounter mysterious lights signalling from towers, something which Blyton was fond of deploying, along with dungeons, shipwrecks, underwater caves, secret panels and catacombs. The later books follow the pattern set down by *Five on a Treasure Island* to the extent that these discoveries mean that the Five always encounter criminal activity: the theft of top-secret scientific papers (*Five Go Adventuring Again*), the kidnap and imprisonment of a young child (*Five Run Away Together*), kidnap, secret scientific plans and smuggling (*Five Go to Smuggler's Top*). In *Five Go Off in a Caravan*, which doubles as a circus story, it is the proceeds of the burglaries carried out by the circus's acrobat and his sidekick, the clown, which they stumble across. The loot is stored underground in the maze of tunnels, streams and "'ENORMOUS'" caves, some of them 'bigger than six dance halls', over which the Five have inadvertently parked their vans (*FC*, 157). Later, these are the caves in which the children are hunted down by the villains, imprisoned and shot at.

The sense of things hidden underground is also a reminder that, in keeping with the detection element of the stories, the task facing the children often involves a form of excavation; they discover secrets beneath the landscape or in the sea (the submerged ship which is raised to the surface in a storm in *Five on a Treasure Island*) or, more specifically in *Five Go Off in a Caravan*, in the grounds beneath their temporary home, the same pretty caravan in which Anne naturally enjoys playing house. A Freudian critic might say that the series shows a tendency to play on Sigmund Freud's sense of the uncanny (*das unheimliche*), that set of frightening experiences installed within, or rising in supposedly safe (familiar) environments.[18]

Some of the scenarios are genuinely nasty, notably the kidnapping, from her parents' garden, of the little girl, Jennifer Armstrong, in *Five Run Away Together*: a plotline which owes something to Agatha Christie's *Murder on the Orient Express* (the kidnapped children have the same surname), itself based on the Lindbergh baby kidnapping of 1932. Others hint at nastiness: the abuse of the circus boy, Nobby, in *Five Go Off in a Caravan*, or the way in *Five Go Adventuring Again* that the duplicitous tutor, Mr. Roland, appears to take a fancy to Anne and attempts to groom her in order to get her onside. Martin Heidegger describes the *unheimliche* as 'that which casts us out of the "homely", that is, the customary, secure' and civilised world and this is what always happens and what readers expect.[19] Yet because this is Enid Blyton telling the story, the effects are only temporary; there is simply no time to get too scared, depressed or introspective. The children—even the young kidnap victim, locked up alone in a pitch-black, underground dungeon—bounce back unscathed from their traumatic, near-death experiences. In *Five Go Off in a Caravan*, the children are repeatedly threatened with violence by the working-class villains, but their responses (apart from Anne's, who cries) are to become more angry, inventive and courageous until the responsible adults (represented by the police) arrive to take over. The relish with which the villains are handed over and the stolen property returned to its rightful owners forms a comforting resolution.

Like all of Blyton's adventure series, the Famous Five books can thus be inserted into different interpretative frames. They are examples of children's literature as wish-fulfilment, offering activity and danger (experienced vicariously). Summarising the initial appeal to readers during the war, Cyril Garbett in 'Reading War-time' (1945) suggested that such stories offered children 'a way of escape', they were 'the "magic casements" through which they [children] can gaze on a world more beautiful and orderly than that in which they are now living'.[20] The series also (like others in the Blyton collection) played a role in offering readers a sense of belonging or the opportunity not to be the outcast 'other'. Lonely children could share in the adventures of a group that did interesting things. With the Famous Five series the sense of identification readers felt with the characters—George especially—was encouraged by the creation of the Famous Five club in September 1952.[21]

There were other attractions, too. The stories offered readers a vision of power which was put in the hands of protagonists who were vaguely like themselves, or whom they might aspire to be. Not everyone appreciated the sentiments. Anthony West, writing of adventure stories more generally, announced his boredom with the examples he was forced to read in a review for *The New Statesman*, populated by '[h]orrid little goody-goodies' who never got older and whose resolute lack of interest in sex struck him as unnatural and even creepy: 'How odd that this arid stuff should be considered healthier than the romantic sort of book which makes a child long for its maturity...one might as well bind their feet in the Chinese fashion'.[22] Others expressed weariness at the identikit characters, 'the same kind of children' whose role during the breaks from their private school was to 'wear shorts and swarm up ropes efficiently'.[23] Much was made, too, of the series' obsession with food, 'delicious meals' which '"jolly decent"' children 'guzzle daily...', as Frances Bird noted in 1948.[24] The fact that space is also devoted to the preparing of food, as well as washing up afterwards, has led to the suggestion that Blyton the teacher sought to offer her readers displays of civilised values which are also part of the 'rehearsals for adult life' as Kimberly Reynolds puts it.[25] The ease with which the delicious food is acquired was another part of the appeal of course, linked as it is with the idea of the countryside as a hygienic place of generous hospitality and cross-class—even feudal—co-operation. Locals are pleased to meet the well-spoken children and load them up effortlessly with produce at knockdown prices, or at no cost at all: "'It'll be a pleasure to see your bonny faces at my door!'" a farmer's wife tells Julian, "'That'll be part of my payment, see? I can tell you're well-brought-up children, by your nice manners and ways. You'll not be doing any damage or foolishness on the farm, *I* know'" (*FC*, 73). Bacon, eggs, freshly baked rolls, milk, butter, cream, raspberries, potted meat sandwiches, plums, cake are shown as there for the taking, and in quantities which would be unthinkable for most children in the war years unless they were royal or had unlimited access to the black-market.

The indomitably good-natured countryfolk are a feature of the series. They are part of what we might call the Blytonian landscape, but they also contribute to the sense that alongside the kidnappings and buried treasure, what Blyton, like many war-time writers, was seeking to encourage was a distinctive view of England and of Englishness and did so by casting the country and its heritage in rural terms. David Trotter has made the point that the formation of a national heritage which is always 'a fiction' becomes a matter of hand-picking key images to appeal to the needs of the moment. Unsurprisingly, in the years 1939–1945 this 'subsoil' of signifying systems, which was used to remind people what was at stake, included a pastoral version of the English landscape and the histories and traditions which lay within it.[26] As was seen in the previous chapter, the sense of an island under attack was one of the images used by Winston Churchill in his broadcasts. It was something taken up as well in the 1939 hit 'There'll Always Be an England', popularised by 'forces sweetheart', Vera Lynn: 'There'll always be an England/While there's a country lane,/Wherever there's a cottage small/Beside a field of grain'. And whether the English population truly believed this or not, they were certainly believed to be susceptible to it. In 1941, George Orwell, writing as a film critic, suggested that the English 'derive their patriotism from a passionate love of the English soil', despite not knowing 'the difference between a turnip and a broccoli if they saw them growing in a field'.[27]

Blyton's Famous Five novels are full of images lifted from the same recipe. She evokes a peaceful, pre-war idyll: 'a red-roofed building, with moss-covered barns, stood glowing in the evening sun. Hens clucked about it, and a dog or two watched them from a gateway' (*FC*, 34). And in *Five Run Away Together* (1944): 'It was gorgeous to…see how blue the sea was, and how lovely Kirrin Island looked at the entrance of the bay' (*FRT*, 16). 'They could see right down the steep hillside to the lake. It lay spread out, flat and smooth, like an enchanted mirror… "Isn't it blue?" said Anne, staring. "Bluer even than the sky"' (*FC*, 73–4). Blyton's detractors would argue that her single simile descriptions remain at the level of the picture postcard, betraying an ignorance of what the countryside is actually 'like'. As a tourist, she sees only strong outlines and bright colours; she offers crude word-painting without shadow, an offering which is inadequate for developing the vocabulary of young readers. But as a 1940s project, it makes sense: Blyton wanted her readers—whether reading the story themselves or having it read to them—to be able to visualise the scene and to share her characters' delight. Peter Hunt has pointed out that such idealisation was already a familiar ingredient of the holiday adventure genre's 'sense of place'.[28] But as part of the 'people's war' of 1939–1945 it had added impetus. Moreover, as one of the stories Britain told itself it was clearly powerful, not simply for readers at home but for those living in the country's colonies. The playwright Ronald Harwood (1934–2020), growing up in South Africa in the 1940s, recalled being 'drawn to books which fed my hunger for Englishness, defined by me then and now, as an ideal of gentleness, culture, countryside and justice. Enid Blyton, more than any other writer…fulfilled much of that definition, those longings for England…in her Favourite Five stories'. He remembered the 'green hillsides' which existed in the books alongside the 'gentle justice' meted out by its protagonists, all part of a world which would come to be criticised as a 'sugary, middle-class idyll' but to him was one of which he longed to be a part.[29] Britain's vision of itself—a mixture of imagination and authenticity—is familiar in films of the period, but its presence in Blyton's work suggests how widespread the process was and how seriously it was taken. Blyton, like other children's writers, used her work to reinforce the sense of what it meant to be English—with England standing in as proxy for Britain—and, in the case of the Famous Five, the children became symbolic figures.

Eileen Soper

The notion that Enid Blyton's Famous Five stories could function as a source of Englishness in answer to a nation in crisis—that they presented a purer, prettier, self-sustaining and ordered world (everything that war-time Britain was not)—was helped by the novels' illustrations which supported—or complemented—Blyton's writing. These were by Eileen Soper (1905–1990), a Hertfordshire-based artist famed for her depictions of animals, plants, landscapes and children. Soper gained recognition as a teenage prodigy when she became the youngest ever exhibitor at Royal Academy Summer Exhibition in 1921 and the next two decades established her reputation. In 1940, she was part of a distinguished group of British artists invited by the American organisation, the Pilgrims' Trust, to paint watercolours depicting England's countryside. The purpose was, as the art critic Herbert Read put it, to show the United States, whom Britain wanted as an ally, 'exactly what we are fighting for – a green pleasant land, a landscape whose features have been moulded in liberty, whose very winding lanes and irregular building is an expression of national character. We are defending our very possession of these memorials....'.[30] In terms of the Famous Five, David Wootton suggests that Soper was chosen by Blyton and her publishers Hodder and Stoughton 'in the knowledge that her visual types would ideally match Blyton's texts'. Her illustrations would act as a gateway into the stories themselves.

What Byton admired about Soper's work was her ability to depict children in action: playing at the beach, swimming, diving, riding or rowing. Soper's clean, spare, style allowed her to depict groups of characters at decisive moments (Fig. 6.2) without making the space look cluttered. The novels' covers often carry these kinds of images as a way of tempting the reader to pick up the book and find out more. But the illustrations do other work, too. For example, the frontispiece for *Five on a Treasure Island* shows Julian, Dick and Anne, and their parents having a picnic, their figures dwarfed against an expanse of rolling countryside and hills while a road, empty of traffic, stretches into the distance. Soper's illustrations are reminiscent of the images used in adverts in the 1930s by organisations like the Ramblers' Association which sought to entice people back to the countryside, far away from arterial roads and new housing developments. Soper presents the Five against backdrops of open spaces, mountains, picnics, boating and fresh air.

Blyton rarely describes her characters' physical appearances in detail, but the illustrations help the readers here as well, suggesting handsome, upright, fine-featured children, strong and active, untouched by malnutrition or tuberculosis. Soper's clean lines and uncluttered compositions also work to convey a sense of childhood innocence, capable of prompting a powerful emotional response. Lillian Rea, writing in 1929, noted of Soper's drawings that 'they appeal to the heart as well as the eye, smooth out twisted nerves and revive one's earliest most treasured memories when the heart was young and life a dream of grown-up days that should be full of the delight of childhood'.[31] It is not too much of a stretch of the imagination to think that this

Fig. 6.2 Eileen Soper's cover for *Five Go Adventuring Again*. The cover is from 1951 when those of the first ten books in the series were re-designed. Blyton's trademark signature with two lines beneath the name was now being used

is part of the achievement of the Famous Five illustrations as well. Looking at the images now, Soper's figures in their collared shirts and baggy shorts appear as historical curiosities from a distant past. But even in the 1940s they appeared that way to some people and conveyed a world of unspoilt child-hood happiness in more innocent times. The texts showed a world that had disappeared—if only temporarily—one where children *could* go on holiday and knew that there would be good weather, ices, cakes and ginger beer for tea.

Blyton appreciated Soper's work and her ability to catch the 'spirit of the stories', but in personal terms the relationship was a curious and distant one (Mac, 23 May 1941). Soper referred to her drawings for Blyton as 'hack work' and she resented Blyton's tendency to interfere. She would certainly have resented her biographer, David Wootton's, description of her as 'an indis-pensable member of the Blyton stable'.[32] That this was Blyton's attitude is evident in her letters. 'I have always found her [Soper] accurate and depend-able—in fact excellent in every way', she explained to a publisher, a comment which has undertones of an employer releasing a housemaid with a testimonial as to her good character.[33] Soper's job, as Blyton saw it, was to serve her and her work. At other times, as for example when she wrote directly to Soper, she could be very generous: 'I have praised your illustrations, end-papers & jackets most fulsomely to Hodder & have said how lucky it was that we hit on you at the beginning for this series because a good artist really does help to "make" the series'.[34] Eileen Soper continued to provide illustrations for the Famous Five novels, as well as for at least seventy other Blyton publications including *The Secret of Killimooin* (1943), *Secret of the Old Mill* (1948), and assorted *Enid Blyton Readers* and *Story Books*. One reason she became important was, as Blyton notes above, due to the large number of illustrations she had to provide for each volume: a full-colour, wrap-around dust-jacket, including a spine that could be spotted and identified across a shop floor. 'All my books have these now', Blyton explained in 1949, 'it's part of the E.B. tradition!' (Mac, 30 June 1949). Then there would be two drawings for end papers, a frontispiece (acting, along with the cover, as an entry into the story) and up to thirty additional drawings in black and white. Despite her dismissal of this work, it is evident that Soper slowly came to value her role in the process. It is an indication of her personal investment that, in February 1960, she was furious when the publishers of *Princess Magazine* (which was due to serialise the eighteenth story, *Five on Finniston Farm*), commissioned additional illustrations from a staff artist, Eric Parker. As Soper put it: 'It has been pleasantly agreed between myself, Miss Blyton, and her various publishers that I would continue to do this as they wished to retain the combination of my work and the text, and in any case another artist would have to imitate the long established characters so closely as to become involved in plagiarism'.[35] It is a telling comment, not simply for its reminder of how important continuity was in the success of Blyton's series works but for its highlighting the way in which words and illustrations worked *together* to produce meaning.

The Adventure Series

It has been seen how one of the strategies Blyton adopted during the war was to seek out new publishers, one of which was the prestigious firm of Macmillan. As part of her dealings with them Blyton negotiated a contract for an adventure novel. Initially Macmillan wanted her to write one based on a plot of their own design. This featured two teenagers, an older girl and a younger boy, returning from the United States to do war work in Britain via the Atlantic (a perilous crossing, given the threat of being torpedoed by German submarines). Once in London, the girl would get a job at the Admiralty, during which time she would meet an American pilot (on leave after being wounded on a bombing raid over Germany). He would take the girl and her brother under his wing (Memorandum: 'Enid Blyton: a book to launch her in America', Mac, 16 July 1943).

The thinking behind the story seemed logical. The United States had entered the war in December 1941 on the side of the Allies and Macmillan envisaged that a transatlantic theme would be a way of 'cementing the bond between [the] USA and Britain' as well as a way of establishing Blyton in America (Memorandum, Mac, 16 July 1943). Blyton's reaction was lukewarm. It was not only that she was uncomfortable writing anything which smacked of romance. It was also that, by 1943, as we saw in the previous chapter, her attitude to using the war as the basis for stories had changed to one of reluctance. However, she was, she explained, quite ready to prioritise a 'special book for here and America' and persuaded Macmillan that 'the "Five on a Treasure island" type of story would be the best for what we have in mind' (Mac, 17 August 1943):

> You must not worry about the book being too English or having references to our own flora and fauna. I am used to writing adventure, circus and ordinary stories that have no local atmosphere at all, because most of my publishers do a big trade with my books in Australia, New Zealand, South Africa and so on, and I have learnt to depend, in those books, on character and incident and not at all on references to nature....So, you do not need to worry about that.
>
> I am sending you two typical adventure stories, one written for Hodders, the other for Newnes. Both were best-sellers....I think if you could take time to skip through one, you would see that there would need to be very little altered in books such as these, in order to be read with understanding by American children. I hope you won't be bored by them! They are the type that modern children adore – plenty of excitement, easily read, simple in language, and with characters very like themselves and their friends. In fact, they contain the fundamental elements of storytelling for children, which are more or less the same all over the world, and even in any era! (Mac, 19 July 1943)

Two months later, on 21 September 1943, Blyton delivered the manuscript of *The Island of Adventure* (1944). To make it appear less parochial she had, as promised, removed references to British locations. She explained that the novel 'is not set in any definite district' and she was confident that its story 'can equally well happen in either Britain or the USA. There are copper mines in the tale, but these are found in either hemisphere. Also, the bird specifically mentioned, the Great Auk (now extinct) had a very wide range, and was found off the coasts of N. America as well as off the coasts of northern Britain'. Some elements would need amending—money values, the name given for the telephone—and she wondered whether Kiki the parrot could be made to use an American expression instead of shouting God Save the King (Memorandum, Mac, 21 September 1943).

The plot of *The Island of Adventure* follows the formula Blyton had already established for herself. Siblings Jack and Lucy-Ann, and Philip and Dinah, together with Jack's talking parrot, Kiki (see above) are the central characters and they are as independently minded, if not quite as obviously privileged, as the protagonists of the Famous Five novels. Philip is obsessed with collecting small animals and, rather like Jimmy Brown in the Galliano's Circus series, has an otherworldly power over them. Dinah is hot tempered; Lucy mild and loyal; Jack is an ornithologist. Philip and Dinah's widowed mother is absent for most of the story; the other pair of siblings, Jack and Lucy-Ann, are orphans whose parents have been killed in a plane crash. The trauma of this event is not explored (like the war, it occurs offstage). As always, the interest lies in the experiences of the child characters with each other (and, to a lesser extent, with the adults supposedly looking after them) and then with the string of suspicious goings-on in the immediate vicinity of Craggy Tops, where they are sent to stay with their cash-strapped Aunt Polly and Uncle Jocelyn. The house is old, 'built of great grey stones…massive and ugly' (*IA*, 37). It stands overlooking some cliffs and faces out on to the Isle of Gloom '[w]here rocks cast shadows' and 'deep black patches lay on the sea' (*IA*, 95). The children are taught to sail by Bill Smugs (a policeman posing as an ornithologist). Using their new skills, they visit the Isle of Gloom and notice traces of copper in the rocks. They discover men apparently working in secret in the derelict copper mines and believe that Bill is the men's contact. In fact, when Philip and Jack are captured, they realise that the men are using the mine as a base to make counterfeit money, Bill is a secret agent and it is Jo-Jo, the apparently unintelligent black handyman employed by Aunt Polly, who is the accomplice:

'We just want to say a fond good-bye to you,' said Jo-Jo, his black face gleaming in the lamp-light. 'We've finished up our business here…we're flooding the mines….It will hide our machines, and all traces of our work. I am afraid it will hide you too.'

'You're not going to leave us here, surely,' said Bill. 'Leave me, if you like - but take these boys up with you.'

'We don't want any of you,' said Jo-Jo, still in the same horribly polite tones. 'You would be in the way.'

'You couldn't be as cruel as that!' cried Bill. 'Why, they're only children.'

'I have my orders,' said Jo-Jo. He did not seem at all the same stupid, half-crazy fellow that the boys knew before – he was a different Jo-Jo altogether, and not at all a pleasant one. (*IA*, 303–4)

This is familiar melodramatic stuff, supplied in magazine serials and on cinema screens all over the world. The boys are on the side of good while Jo-Jo, who has replaced the Nazi invaders of the earlier war-time novels, is on the side of bad. The fact that he is prepared to leave the children to drown—something which appals Bill, the upright white man—is the typical behaviour of the criminal mastermind as he appears in exciting thrillers of the 1930s, such as those featuring the gentleman adventurer Bulldog Drummond. It is also the case, of course, that in depicting Jo-Jo in the way she does, Blyton is also making a racist statement: black people are naturally savage in this way, so Blyton's thinking goes, and lack the elements of moral restraint that characterise white people. Blyton constructs Jo-Jo as "other", a man with 'powerful arms swinging by his sides' who rolls his eyes 'in a peculiar way', before revealing himself as a ruthless criminal who has a cruel and alien punishment lined up (*IA*, 32; 59). Jo-Jo's 'darkness' turns out to be a moral darkness equated with the ability to behave in horrible ways. He is thus a threatening presence—a fantasy stereotype of the black man as thug—as well as being a vehicle for the inscription of anxieties about black people more generally. Moreover, in an example of what postcolonial critics might call 'reverse colonisation', Jo-Jo has invaded Craggy Tops and its land, which he intends to exploit; he understands the children and their aunt and uncle better than they do themselves; and, as a coloniser, he has no interest in the morality of what he is doing. In this respect he might be said to be rather like the Nazis, but also, of course, like the British whose colonial ambitions had brought them an Empire.

It is also true of course that much of Jo-Jo's way of behaving turns out to be play-acting. When he warns about spirits on the '"bad"' island he seems to adopt deliberately the pose of one of the spear-wielding 'savages' or 'exotic primitives' popularised in British adventure films in the 1930s (*IA*, 32). The actors employed in these roles had to perform appearing dazzled by, or threatening towards, the European characters in a way that perpetuated long-held essentialist beliefs about what it meant to be black as opposed to being white. (Presenting native peoples in this way was a historical justification for subjecting them to colonisation.) This was the fate of the period's most celebrated black actor, Paul Robeson, who, in the 1935 film *Sanders of the River* (1935), played a chieftain, a character partly 'civilised' (evident by his perfect English) but nonetheless 'naturally' prone to deviousness. Blyton, too, links Jo-Jo with a performance in which everyone is tricked. Jo-Jo, as he gradually reveals, is as good an actor as Paul Robeson, and is no more superstitious than the children themselves. In turn, their sense of him as a 'half-crazy' black man is shown to be as far removed from reality as Jack's delusion that Great Auks (long extinct) are alive and well on the island (*IA*, 51).

These facts do not exclude or repress *The Island of Adventure*'s racist dimensions or the idea that Jo-Jo is a prop used by Blyton to reinforce the children's bravery. However, in 1944, the novel's racism was not something which prompted overt criticism, at least in the magazines and journals which might have been expected to review it. This was a time when another hero of the 1940s, Wing Commander Guy Gibson (1918–1944), who led the Dambusters air raid in 1943, could be photographed with his black dog called Nigger and few people would bat an eyelid. (As we have seen, Blyton uses the same name for the German spies' fierce dog in *The Children of Kidillin*.) Yet, as Caroline Bressey has pointed out, by the 1940s the word 'Nigger' *was* recognised as offensive. In 1940 the League of Coloured Peoples (established 1931) which was concerned about the crude representation of black people in literature, media and film complained to the BBC when one of the station's announcers used the word on air. The BBC understood the offence and issued a formal apology.[36] Yet the fact that powerful people like Blyton could carry on using the word clearly says much about race and representation in the Britain in which they lived. As far as Macmillan was concerned, they had no worries about how the character of Jo-Jo would be received by readers. When the North American office suggested that the novel would go down especially well in the Southern States, a box of Blyton books was despatched to schools in Alabama.[37]

Blyton was proud of *The Island of Adventure* ('a real thriller'), and was appreciative of Stuart Tresilian (1891–1974), another 'tip-top artist' Macmillan had commissioned to illustrate the book (Mac, 21 September 1943). 'Aren't they absolutely first-rate!' she wrote to the firm about the illustrations. 'I think they are magnificent & Mr Tresilian has made the book twice as good with his interpretation of the characters, especially the parrot! I hope you will tell him how delighted I am' (Mac, 14 June 1944). She was also confident about the novel's chances: 'I have one of my "hunches"', she explained '& feel we are at the beginning of a Big Thing...' (Mac, 14 July 1944). Macmillan clearly thought so too, and in a letter clearly designed to flatter, Roland Heath explained to Blyton that they had chosen to manufacture the book 'in what we call our Kipling size' (Mac, 4 October 1943). Fifty years earlier the firm had published some of Rudyard Kipling's books for children: *The Jungle Book* (1894), *Captain's Courageous* (1897) and the

Just So Stories (1902). Blyton, they implied (very gratifyingly), was his natural successor. Other considerations were also at work. *The Island of Adventure* was designed for older children and one of the ways in which it and the sequels differ from The Famous Five novels is in their word length. The Famous Five books ran to between 40,000 and 50,000 words. *The Island of Adventure* was close to 63,000 words, 'long for a children's book' explained Blyton, 'but then Arthur Ransome's are long too. His are 8/6 so they need to be long! (Mac, 21 September 1943). In a bid to undercut Ransome, and sway cash-conscious Christmas shoppers, *The Island of Adventure* was priced at 7/6. While the sales figures did not reach the level of the Famous Five, *The Island of Adventure* did well, selling 6801 copies in its first two years and a film company quickly expressed an interest in buying the film rights. Not surprisingly, this sounded 'too good to be [true]', to Blyton, '& the handsome way in which you say they [the rights] "will, of course, be entirely mine" is most gratifying – makes me feel that I have a cheque for £50,000 coming *any* moment from Hollywood!' (Mac, 5 October 1943). The film did not get off the ground, but the book sold steadily and added to the royalties Blyton was already accruing. By October 1945 she had earned £11,548 from her Macmillan publications, equivalent to roughly £496,564 in 2021 values.

There would be eight novels in the Adventure series, all aimed at the upper-age range of Blyton's audience; that is to say, children between the ages of twelve and fourteen. What is perhaps most striking about the series is that Blyton, inspired perhaps by the Kipling comparison, began to shift the action away into locations overseas. Thus the series takes in the Scottish Highlands and Islands (*The Castle of Adventure* [1946] and *The Sea of Adventure* [1948]) but also post-war Austria and art treasures stolen by the Nazis (*The Valley of Adventure* [1947]), Wales (*The Mountain of Adventure* [1949]) the Greek Islands (*The Ship of Adventure* [1950]) and Tauri-Hessia, an invented Balkan kingdom (*The Circus of Adventure* [1952]). George Greenfield noted that Blyton was someone whose 'attitudes and beliefs were moulded in the golden years before the Great War, when the sun did not set on the British Empire and Britannia in fact ruled the waves'.[38] As part of this legacy, it is possible to see her constructing a junior version of the adventure romances of her youth—or 'imperial romances', as they were sometimes termed—a sub-genre popularised to varying degrees at the end of the nineteenth century by the likes of Robert Louis Stevenson and H. Rider Haggard, and, in Blyton's own day, by W.E. Johns in his 'Biggles' series: *Biggles in Borneo* (1943) and *Biggles Hunts Big Game* (1948). This was a kind of writing in which, as Stevenson explained, the interest lay in 'clean-open air adventure'.[39] Deirdre

David notes the form's emphasis on 'tropes of travel and hazardous adventure' but also a tendency to employ race as a 'glamorous or demonic marker'. The plots invariably tended to deal with adventurous Britishers coping with violent situations often involving hordes of 'savages' or 'non-white' people more generally, events invariably described in similar terms: 'them' and 'us'.[40]

These ideas are played out in *The River of Adventure* (1955), by which time Blyton had shifted her interest to somewhere in the vicinity of what was regarded at the time as Britain's 'informal Empire' in the Middle East.[41] The setting is 'some way from the borders of Syria' wherein the four children, plus Bill Smugs and Mrs. Mannering (who has become Mrs. Smugs), travel down river—rather like protagonists in a Joseph Conrad story—in search of the mysterious Raya Uma, on behalf of the British Government (*RA*, 33). When the parents are kidnapped, the children, plus Oola, the young boy they rescue from an abusive snake-charmer 'master', go in search of them, discovering an underground temple full of treasures in the meantime. Here Blyton introduces examples of ostentatiously brave behaviour on the part of the girls as well as the boys, who escape from underground caverns whilst battling a 'gigantic underground waterfall', 'an *enormous* cataract' which almost smashes the children's boat into the rocks (*RA*, 186). Readers of imperial romances had been brought up to expect a sense of menace in their stories. It was a genre in which, as Richard Ruppel has noted, the landscape 'is nearly always an antagonist', standing for aspects of a region which have been resistant to the colonial invasion.[42] At the same time, the way characters meet the challenge is at least as important as the events themselves. '"Fun this, isn't it?" said the indomitable Jack, looking round at the little company' (*RA*, 190). Blyton's children maintain stiff upper lips helping to bolster the consoling myth that the English deserve to win through, even though the non-British villains threaten to overwhelm them.

The River of Adventure, then, can be read as another text contributing to the constitution of white subjectivity, and Blyton asks us to accept the middle-class British children as suitable figures to whom to entrust the deeds of derring-do embedded within it. There was perhaps a sense of urgency or nostalgia in all this. By the time Blyton began writing the story in January 1955, it had become increasingly obvious that Britain was well advanced along what Winston Churchill's Private Secretary, Anthony Browne, termed her 'transition from being a really great world power downwards'. As Peter Hennessey has explained, it was part of a 'long retreat' from the days when Britain ruled two-thirds of the world and celebrated the fact with events such as the British Empire Exhibition which, as we saw in Chapter 3, had inspired Blyton in the 1920s. There were shifts in attitude as heads of government in other countries became openly resentful of the patronising ways in which they were treated. In 1955, the Egyptian leader Colonel Gamal Abdel Nasser was left fuming after a meeting in Cairo with the British Foreign Secretary, Anthony Eden. Feeling as if Eden 'was talking to a junior official who could not be expected to understand international politics', Nasser was angry not least at the lavish hospitality displayed by British officials, which attempted to make it look 'as if we were beggars and they princes'.[43] The Suez Crisis, in which Britain was humiliated on the world stage and its policy towards Egypt exposed as morally bankrupt, emerged the following year.

Without wishing to project too much onto a novelist whose attitudes towards race and whose (powerful) role in disseminating stereotypical images and racist propaganda would make her appear not only out of touch but noxious, there are occasions where Blyton's novels, too, can be seen to be part of this psychodrama. There are moments when she, too, finally seems willing to expose the fault lines and contradictions embedded in the ideologies of race and colonialism. Thus, in *The River of Adventure*, the 'queer' atmosphere which the British protagonists encounter is dependent (as in other Blyton stories) on the gap between what seems to be and what is: the fact that the mysterious and much-talked about Sinny-town is actually a gigantic film set—a cine town—a place of illusion. Elsewhere, amidst its excitements, there is a sense that this final novel in the series might also be read as a parody of the British abroad and Blyton makes clear the children's intrinsic sense of superiority. Soon after arriving, the children are taken on a trip down the River of Abench under the care of a local guide, Tala:

'What's this river called, Tala?' asked Philip.
'It is called the River of Abencha', answered Tala, his eyes on the water ahead.
'I say, you others!' called Philip. 'He says this river's called the River of Adventure – sounds exciting, doesn't it?'
'Abencha, Abencha,' repeated Tala, but Philip thought he was trying to say 'Adventure' and not pronouncing it correctly. (*RA*, 44)

Blyton is not really interested in Tala as much more than a comic stereotype (no change there). Nonetheless, part of the sense of disturbance in *The River of Adventure* amid its raging rivers, hair-breath escapes, kidnappings and poisonous snakes, comes from Blyton allowing readers to see her protagonists' white privilege. Our attentions are drawn to what Richard Ruppel notes is a 'persistent imperialist idea' in adventure fictions, namely 'that the whites know more about the colonial world than do the people who were born and raised there'.[44] There is, then, something double-edged in Blyton's final treatment of the British overseas in this last novel in the Adventure series. Her characters are not troubled; their confidence is neither crumbling nor defeated, but they encounter forces they do not understand, people they offend and powers they have less control over. How far this stance is deliberate or conscious on Blyton's part is a moot point—it's not clear whether we will ever know.

The 'Barney' mysteries and The Secret Seven

Eagerness on the part of her readers to experience adventures and to solve mysteries was also catered for in the 'Barney' novels published by Collins between 1949 and 1959. Collins had published Agatha Christie's novels since 1926 and was the leading publisher of detective fiction at this time (other authors on their list included Ngaio Marsh and Freeman Wills Crofts). Blyton was thus in good company and was an obvious fit for the firm's Junior Mystery Series. In *The Rockingdown Mystery* (1949) Blyton introduced Barney—the teenager with 'brilliant, wide-set blue eyes' and 'corn-coloured hair' (always a positive look in her world) whose origins are part of the mystery: he 'had a slight American twang, and yet … sounded foreign - Spanish - Italian - what could it be? Nor did he look English, for all his blue eyes and fair hair' (*RoM*, 42–3). Five further titles followed: *The Rilloby Fair Mystery* (1950), *The Ring o'Bells Mystery* (1951), *The Rubadub Mystery* (1952), *The Rat-a-Tat Mystery* (1956) and *The Ragamuffin Mystery* (1959). The first four stories follow similar themes, drawing contrasts between the lives of three comfortably off children, Roger, Diana and Snubby, and their holiday adventures—and Barney's hand-to-mouth existence, sleeping rough, scraping a living in whatever short-term jobs he can pick up in fairgrounds and elsewhere. The characterisation is better conceived than Blyton is given credit for. Barney is tormented and serious whereas Snubby (and his dog Loopy) is a lively comedic chatterbox in the mould of Richmal Crompton's William Brown, constantly flouting the rules. But Blyton is very sympathetic to her irrepressible joker (who like Barney is also a homeless orphan) and admires his curiosity and zest for life in the face of the disapproval shown by pompous adults.

One of the things that elevates the stories is that Blyton devotes a good deal of space to evoking Barney's loneliness and isolation, and his sense of loss and emptiness as he tramps round the country in search of the father he has never known and may never meet: 'What a strange life he must lead' muses Diana, struck by Barney's bleak lifestyle, 'wandering about' (RoM, 70).

This lifestyle is the catalyst for the events of *The Rockingdown Mystery* when, dossing down at the deserted Rockingdown House, Barney discovers a secret passage, underground stream and caves in which smugglers are at work. Men are busy, winching crates of smuggled goods (revolvers, silk, silver bars) along the stream and repacking them. Barney is caught, imprisoned and despatches his pet monkey, Miranda, to get help.

If a series like the Famous Five represents one tradition of the mystery story (the action adventure) and the Find-Outers' another (the Golden Age puzzle), the Barney mysteries are yet another turn of the wheel. Blyton was always adamant that her stories would eschew murder and violence—she had, as she was always pointing out, a 'horror' of them.[45] As she explained to one interviewer, 'I am careful to see that the crime is never sordid or frightening....There are never any ghosts either'.[46] Nonetheless, Blyton makes an exception to her own rule, drawing on several lines of influence, not least models offered by earlier 'creepy' stories. In her description of Rockingdown Hall, Blyton uses many of the conventions of what is recognised as Gothic writing: 'weird' deserted mansions, secret passages, noises in the night ('a queer whining, half-screeching sound' [*RoM*, 145]). '"I feel as if somebody is going to jump out and grab me all the time!" said Diana with a shiver' (*RoM*, 113). Emotions are heightened. Sleeping at the house with its 'miserable dark rooms' stuffed full of old furniture and abandoned toys (the remnants of a child who died long ago), Barney feels as if he has been incarcerated or buried alive; in the abandoned ballroom 'the mirrors gave back a dozen reflections of his dim, shadowy figure and made him feel uncomfortable' (*RoM*, 87). It is a stretch perhaps, but in the novel, which followed it, *The Rilloby Fair Mystery*, Blyton seems to be channelling Edgar Allen Poe, the 'parent' of the detective story whose locked-room mystery, 'The Murders in the Rue Morgue', was published in 1841. Save for the fact that Blyton eschews the brutal murder, the ingredients are recognisable. A theft takes place from a locked building; the culprit is an ape who climbs the outside walls, breaks in through a window and leaves the same way.[47]

Other things to note include the fact that, whereas in other Gothic tales the sinister is kept at a safe distance by being in an exotic location far away, Blyton's mysteries describe threats appearing in locations we assume to be safe: idyllic English villages or seaside resorts, making the events more uncanny. In *The Rockingdown Mystery*, Barney discovers the smugglers working in the caves beneath the house are '"evidently foreigners"' (*RoM*, 224). Yet when the children subsequently discover that the mastermind is a local farmer, their initial reaction is one of disbelief and shock that the criminality is real and taking possession of this rural community. It is not

London's East End but the country house which is the site of gangland activities.

As well as nods in the direction of the Gothic and the thriller as literary modes, the Barney mysteries are also notable for Blyton's immersion in—and affection for—English popular culture: fairs, circuses, inns and the seaside recur frequently, as they do in other series. These settings can make Blyton's stories seem like museum pieces but in the early 1950s she was striking a topical note. In the war years there was a notion of the British seaside (like the countryside) as something worth fighting for, a lively world of 'Pierrots and piers, ham-and-egg teas, palmists, automatic machines and crowded, sweating promenades', as J.B. Priestley explained in one of his celebrated BBC radio broadcasts.[48] Blyton, whose reach was as great as Priestley's and who had the same popular—or commonplace—touch, was doing something similar, notably in *The Rubadub Mystery* (1952). Rubadub, the seaside resort where the children stay for their summer holidays, is loud and full of visitors; the old gabled inn where the children stay is a nod to a past which is being elbowed out by fairgrounds, slot machines and the jukebox, 'a machine that played tunes if you put money into it – loud blaring tunes that never seemed to stop!' (*RuM*, 60). It is a place of excess and the anarchic Snubby embraces not only the town's liberating atmosphere but its entertainment, winning a talent competition on the pier thanks to a devastating impersonation of the ukulele-playing comedian, George Formby. Meanwhile Barney lands a job with the conjurer, Mr. Marvel, who is performing at the town's theatre for the summer season. He claims to know Barney's long-lost father (whom Barney is desperate to meet) but, at the end of the story, is revealed to have another existence as a spy who uses his on-stage patter to convey messages to his accomplices in the audience. Meanwhile, his claims to know Barney's father are as illusory as the sleights of hand by which he magics up vegetables from behind Snubby's ears. The book was published in 1952 and it is hard not to think that along with her focus on spies and sabotage Blyton had in mind the flight of the British diplomats and communist agents Donald Maclean and Guy Burgess to the Soviet Union in May 1951, stories of whose treachery had rocked the British public (traitors and secrets also feature in *The Mystery of the Strange Bundle* [1952]). The notion of the seaside as a place of skulduggery is not a new one, of course—films such as *The Brighton Strangler* (1945) and *Brighton Rock* (1948) led the way in establishing a rather double-edged view of such places as not only strongholds of English popular culture but also as places which can be dangerous.

To some of Blyton's young readers in 1952 such allusions would have been incidental to the familiar Blyton ingredients. The prospect of a perfect holiday experience 'full of sunshine and walks and reading' is delayed thanks to criminal complications (*RuM*, 47). Rubadub is a seaside town but it is also a testing ground for submarines, which leaves it vulnerable to attack from hostile powers. There is signalling at night and few people are who they seem to be. Meanwhile the rambling old inn where the children stay is revealed as 'a perfect hot-bed of extraordinary happenings!' (*RuM*, 195). As in other series, the book celebrates its middle-class children as heroes and there is still evidence of traditional class structures, something which the war had not managed to remove. Dinah's observation about the rest of the clientele at the Fair ('"a pretty rough lot, some of them"') shows that she is, like all Blyton's heroines, part of a group committed to the preservation of good manners at the very least (*RuM*, 60). If the Famous Five stories are generally understood to be the most iconic of Blyton's adventure series, the early Barney stories at least match them in their liveliness and the scope of their plots and, as with the figure of George, Blyton's characterisation of Barney succeeds in being at once recognisably formulaic while generating a variety of questions and possessing a complex emotional hinterland.

Other Blytonian adventurers and sleuths—and these could be duplicated at length—include Robin, Betty and Lucy, who foil a kidnapping in *The Boy Next Door* (1944), Pat and Tessa, who do something similar in *The Adventure of the Strange Ruby* (1960) and the characters from *The Secret Seven* (1949–1963). The latter were an enormous success and, after their initial appearance in *Secret of the Old Mill* (published in 1948 and not seen as part of the series proper), featured in fifteen full-length adventures, plus supplementary short stories—not all of them terribly well-characterised but nonetheless appealing enough to provoke strong loyalties in Blyton's readers. Blyton created the Secret Seven as a way of capturing the pre-Famous Five age group. Some of the stories thus appeared as illustrated strips in comics like *Micky Mouse Weekly*, as well as in Blyton's own magazine and although the vocabulary was simpler, the content was familiar. Summarising the series' appeal, Christine Hall and Martin Coles note that 'Blyton offers children an enticing invitation in a realistic setting…a chance to behave with independence in the world she creates, to be part of a special small club which makes its own decisions, and with that group to take part in an exciting adventure'.[49] Whether such independence was unusual or not—and those who lived in the 1950s such as Jacqueline Wilson have made the point that people were 'a different breed', who allowed their children to go off on their own 'in a way that seems inconceivable to parents nowadays'—it was part of the Blyton package.[50] She creates a clearly demarcated world in which middle-class children from well-off families in a 1950s English village are given their own shed as HQ for their weekly meetings, replete with password and badges and a large 'S.S.' painted on the shed door. By asking seemingly innocuous questions about local mysteries, tracking clues, some of which are red-herrings, and indulging in some daring stunts, they discover more than the police. This is notably so in *Good Work Secret Seven* (1954) in which the Seven unmask a gang of car thieves with a ruse which, because it is Bonfire Night, involves one of the boys—it is usually the boys who do the dangerous activities—disguising himself as a 'Guy' and being placed outside a café as a way of keeping watch on the thieves. The success of this trick depends on the thieves not noticing the boy (Peter) breathing.

As with the Famous Five, a contemporary reader approaching the Seven stories can easily find their central characters grating—or 'obnoxious', as a reviewer for *Good Old Secret Seven* put it in 1961.[51] Following the pattern set with Julian in the Famous Five series, there is an emphasis on hierarchy— boys are in charge, just as in the adult world the children's fathers who 'know what to do' are the source of ultimate power (*TCSS*, 97). The group's leader, Peter, can appear dictatorial and pompous, as he does in *Three Cheers Secret Seven* (1956): "'Nothing is too far-fetched to examine'" he tells his admiring audience, who think the little tyrant "'like a first-class detective'" (*TCSS*, 70; 73). "'[I]f you've got something better to do than to belong to the Secret Seven and attend the meetings, well do it! We can easily get somebody instead of you'" is his response to his sister Janet's announcement that she would quite like to read a book (*TCSS*, 1). Elsewhere the group's collective attempt to prevent anyone else from joining their ranks—notably Jack's 'clever' and confident sister Susie—come across as petty and misogynistic (*TCSS*, 17). There is disquiet on their part that Susie does things that are supposed to be the preserve of boys—such as climbing walls and fishing—and, in *Three Cheers Secret Seven*, she is the possessor of a splendid mechanical toy aeroplane which requires them to be polite to her if they want to fly it. There is even an air of Cosa Nostra, as the Mafiosi would put it, about the relationships on show. In *Shock for Secret Seven*, Jack himself is expelled from the group and it is not until he has solved the mystery, namely that the person stealing pet dogs (a heinous crime in the Blyton universe), is the village postman, wearing oversize boots (a repeat of the tactic deployed by the criminal in *The Mystery of the Invisible Thief*) that Jack is allowed readmittance. The reader, meanwhile, is encouraged to accept the incarceration of the postman as inevitable and right:

'Where is Postie now?' asked Janet.
    'In a prison-cell,' said her father grimly, 'and he deserves to be well punished. Dog-stealing is a wicked thing – a cruel thing.' (*SSS*, 117)

All these images are of well-considered rules and boundaries which, despite the upset of crime, ensure that life preserves its routines.

* * *

Although the various adventure series discussed in this chapter helped establish Blyton's reputation, there is also a case for arguing that they helped unravel it. For a time, her name was 'surety' for 'gripping quality', *The Scotsman* noted in 1945.[52] The appearance of a new title was also 'an event in the children's world', as *The Western Morning News* put it in 1946.[53] Moreover, many of the stories are accomplished pieces of work: they demonstrate Blyton's mastery of a distinctively lucid prose style; they offer scope for reader-identification; the early texts are works born out of crisis (World War Two) and respond to war-time anxieties; they are didactic but not overly so, and offer reassurance and appealing visions of what might be. Throughout the war years and in the drab post-war years that followed, magazines, publishers and readers continued to hoover up adventure stories like a powerful vacuum cleaner. 'They [children] want excitement', wrote Naomi Michison, 'vicarious danger…identification with some hero, the feeling of importance and otherness'.[54] Blyton delivered this and the fact that she wrote stories so quickly meant that readers never had to wait very long for the next one: there was always one more to read. In a country like Britain where people expected to wait for almost everything, Blyton offered instant gratification.

The downside of this was that, by apparently reproducing the same thing—which is of course what we expect of genre fiction: it is formulaic and uses the same ingredients again and again—Blyton pleased readers but not critics. Blyton's adventure stories started to be judged second-rate; examples of hack work by a woman who was increasingly careless about what she wrote. Blyton's adventure stories *are* clearly written with an eye to what she thought her readers wanted, which was familiar characters doing familiar things. Geoffrey Trease's review of *The Rilloby Fair Mystery* (1950) was particularly damning:

> We can almost see Enid Blyton cooking up The Rilloby Fair Mystery…stirring in the wholesome if rather tasteless child characters, adding one pompous old gentleman, one lovable spaniel, one dignified cat, one jolly fair and one mysterious burglary, and serving it up in an attractive way which puts no strain on the mental digestion and affords little exercise for the imaginative teeth….Is it really true that most children want only the mixture as before?

Trease went on to ask: 'What would happen if Miss Blyton someday stemmed the flow of her immense output and used her knack of storytelling on fresher

material, about which she had given herself more time to think and feel?'[55]
It is hard not to think this a valid question.

Notes

1. Hugh Brogan, *The Life of Arthur Ransome* (London: Jonathan Cape, 1984), 412.
2. Geoffrey Trease, *Tales out of School* (1948; London: Heinemann, 1949), 161; 162.
3. Arthur Ransome to Margaret Renold, 24 January 1938, quoted in Hugh Brogan, *The Life of Arthur Ransome*, 391.
4. V.S. Pritchett, 'The Middle-Class Child', *The New Statesman* (5 December 1936), 931–2.
5. Quoted in Hugh Brogan, *The Life of Arthur Ransome*, 112.
6. Arthur Ransome, Diary 23 October 1944, in Brogan, ibid., 403.
7. Enid Blyton, 'If I Were a Bookseller', *W.H. Smith's Trade Circular* (9 April 1949), 30.
8. Unsigned Article, 'Books for Children', *Birmingham Daily Post* (5 December 1948), 2.
9. Unsigned Article, 'Children's Books', *The Scotsman* (8 December 1949), 5.
10. Unsigned Article, 'New Books: The Circus of Adventure', *Teachers' World and Schoolmistress* 83 (5 November 1952), 465.
11. Paul Hodder Williams to Ewart Wharmby, 3 December 1971. London Metropolitan Archives/Hodder and Stoughton archives, M.16352A.
12. David Rudd, *Enid Blyton and the Mystery of Children's Literature* (London: Palgrave Macmillan, 2000), 89.
13. George Orwell, 'Boys' Weeklies', in *Inside the Whale and Other Essays* (1940). https://www.orwell.ru/library/essays/boys/english/e_boys. Accessed 4 March 2021.
14. Wallace Hildick, *Children and Fiction* (London: Evans, 1970), 86.
15. Unsigned Article, 'Children's Books', *Liverpool Daily Post* (12 December 1942), 2.
16. Unsigned Article. 'Some Gift Books for Adults and Children', *Country Life* (20 November 1942), 1001.
17. Nicholas Tucker, 'Missing Parents in the Family Story', *New Review of Children's Literature and Librarianship* 11:2 (2005), 189–93 (190).
18. See also David Rudd, 'Digging Up the Family Plot: Secrets, Mystery and the Blytonesque', in *Mystery in Children's Literature: From the Rational to the Supernatural*, eds. Adrienne E. Gavin and Christopher Routledge (London: Palgrave, 2001), 82–99.

19. Martin Heidegger, *History of the Concept of Time*, quoted in Julian Wolfreys, *Victorian Hauntings: Spectrality, Gothic, the Uncanny and Literature* (London: Palgrave, 2001), 150.

20. Cyril Garbett, *Reading in War-Time* (Oxford: Oxford University Press, 1945), 3.

21. Membership of the club was advertised on the flyleaves of the Famous Five novels. Members were sent a printed letter from Blyton and a badge. In her letter Blyton explained that 'the reason for starting the Club was this: everywhere I go I meet boys and girls who are already my friends because they are friends of the Famous Five.... The great pity is that I can't recognise you, and you don't recognise each other.... If all our members wear their badges we shall know each other at once.... I shall come up to you and speak to you, so look out for me! ... that is the first purpose of the Famous Five Club, to recognise each other and show friendliness everywhere. The second purpose is to help children who are not nearly as fortunate as you are'. Blyton explained that the membership fees went to the Children's Convalescent Home in Beaconsfield. The club continued after Blyton's death. Membership in March 1970 stood at 201,416. London Metropolitan Archives/Hodder and Stoughton Archives, M 16,353.

22. Anthony West, 'Coloured and Plain', *The New Statesman* (9 December 1939), 840.

23. Frances Bird, 'Children's Books', *The New Statesman and Nation* (13 December 1947), 474.

24. Frances Bird, 'Books for Older Children', *The New Statesman and Nation* (4 December 1948), 501–2.

25. Kimberley Reynolds, 'Changing Families in Children's Fiction', in *The Cambridge Companion to Children's Literature*, eds. M.O. Grenby and Andrea Immel (Cambridge University Press, 2009), 193–204 (204).

26. David Trotter, *The English Novel in History, 1895–1920* (London: Routledge, 1994), 144; 154.

27. George Orwell, 'The Young Mr. Pitt', *Time and Tide* (3 May 1941), quoted in Anthony Aldgate and Jeffrey Richards, *Britain Can Take It* (Oxford: Basil Blackwell, 1986), 140.

28. Peter Hunt, *An Introduction to Children's Literature* (Oxford: Oxford University Press, 1994), 122.

29. Ronald Harwood, in *The Pleasures of Reading*, ed. Antonia Fraser (1992; London: Bloomsbury, 2015), 128–35 (128–129).

30. David Wootton, *The Art of George and Eileen Soper* (London: Chris Beetles, 1995), 26.

31. Lillian Rea, in Wootton, 62.

32. Ibid., 50.

33. Ibid., 26.

34. Ibid., 67.

35. Ibid., 68.

36. Caroline Bressey, 'It's Only Political Correctness—Race and Racism in British History', in *New Geographies of Race and Racism*, eds. Claire Dwyer and Caroline Bressey (Aldershot: Ashgate, 2008), 29–41 (31).

37. Despite publishers' attempts to 'modernise' Blyton's novels in the 1970s, updating the currency and the expressions ('queer') it was not until the 1980s that the use of Nigger was removed from all the texts. It is present in the 1983 Armada edition of *The Children of Kidillin*.

38. George Greenfield, *A Smattering of Monsters* (1995; London: Warner, 1997), 113.

39. Robert Louis Stevenson, 'Gossip About Romance', *Memories and Portraits*, in *The Works of Robert Louis Stevenson* (New York: Charles Scriber's Sons, 1922), XII, 188–9.

40. Deirdre David, 'Empire, Race and the Victorian Novel', in *A Companion to the Victorian Novel*, eds. Patrick Brantlinger and William Thesing (Oxford: Blackwell, 2002), 84–100 (96).

41. Peter Hennessey, *Having It So Good: Britain in the Fifties* (2006; London: Penguin, 2007), 270.

42. Richard Ruppel, '*The Lagoon* and the Popular Exotic Tradition', in *Contexts for Conrad*, eds. Keith Carabine, Owen Knowles, and Wieslaw Krajia (New York: Columbia University Press, 1993), 177–87 (178).

43. Peter Hennessy, *Having It So Good*, 270; 279; 309.

44. Richard Ruppel '*The Lagoon* and the Popular Exotic Tradition', 180.

45. Enid Blyton, 'No Violence Please', *W.H. Smith's Trade Circular* (4 March 1950), 9–10.

46. Peter, Hawley, 'Enid Blyton's Twenty Books a Year', *The Reading Lamp* 1 (July 1947), 15.

47. Anita Bensoussane draws this parallel in her articles on the Barney series, available on the Enid Blyton Society website. https://www.enidblytonsociety.co.uk/book-details.php?id=176&title=The+Rilloby+Fair+Mystery. Accessed 21 June 2021.

48. Eric Sevareid, ed., *All England Listened: The War-Time Broadcasts of J.B. Priestley* (New York: Chilmark Press, 1967), 57.

49. Christine Hall and Martin Coles, *Children's Reading Choices* (London: Routledge, 1999), 52.

50. Jacqueline Wilson, 'Preface', Eleanor Graham, *The Children Who Lived in a Barn* (1938; London: Persephone Books, 2001), viii–x.

51. Unsigned Article, 'New Books for Children', *The Times of India* (17 December 1961), 11.

52. Unsigned Article, 'For Younger Readers', *The Scotsman* (22 November 1945), 7.

53. Unsigned Article, 'Books of Today', *Western Morning News* (13 February 1946), 2.

54. Naomi Mitchison, 'Alternatives to Comics', *The New Statesman* (18 December 1954), 836–7.

55. Geoffrey Trease, 'Best Books for Boys', *John o'London's Weekly* (7 July 1950), 425.

Bibliography

Aldgate, Anthony, and Jeffrey Richards. 1986. *Britain Can Take It*. Oxford: Basil Blackwell.

Blyton, Enid. 1950. 'No Violence Please'. *W.H. Smith's Trade Circular* (4 March): 9–10.

Bressey, Caroline. 2008. 'It's Only Political Correctness—Race and Racism in British History'. In *New Geographies of Race and Racism*, edited by Claire Dwyer and Caroline Bressey, 29–41. Aldershot: Ashgate.

Brogan, Hugh. 1984. *The Life of Arthur Ransome*. London: Jonathan Cape.

David, Deirdre. 2002. 'Empire, Race and the Victorian Novel'. In *A Companion to the Victorian Novel*, edited by Patrick Brantlinger and William Thesing, 84–100. Oxford: Blackwell.

Garbett, Cyril. 1945. *Reading in War-Time*. Oxford: Oxford University Press.

Greenfield, George. 1997. *A Smattering of Monsters*. London: Warner.

———. 1998. *Enid Blyton*. Stroud: Sutton.

Hall, Christine, and Martin Coles. 1999. *Children's Reading Choices*. London: Routledge.

Harwood, Ronald. 2015. *The Pleasures of Reading*, edited by Antonia Fraser, 128–35. London: Bloomsbury.

Hawley, Peter. 1947. 'Enid Blyton's Twenty Books a Year'. *The Reading Lamp* 1 (July): 12–15.

Hennessey, Peter. 2007. *Having It So Good: Britain in the Fifties*. Penguin.

Hildick, Wallace. 1970. *Children and Fiction*. London: Evans.

Hunt, Peter. 1994. *An Introduction to Children's Literature*. Oxford: Oxford University Press.

Orwell, George. 1940. *Inside the Whale and Other Essays*. https://www.orwell.ru/library/essays/boys/english/e_boys. Accessed 4 March 2021.

Reynolds, Kimberley. 2009. 'Changing Families in Children's Fiction'. In *The Cambridge Companion to Children's Literature*, edited by M.O. Grenby and Andrea Immel, 193–204. Cambridge University Press.

Rudd, David. 2000. *Enid Blyton and the Mystery of Children's Literature*. London: Palgrave.

———. 2001. 'Digging Up the Family Plot: Secrets, Mystery and the Blytonesque'. In *Mystery in Children's Literature: From the Rational to the Supernatural*, edited by Adrienne E. Gavin and Christopher Routledge, 82–99. London: Palgrave.

Ruppel, Richard. 1993. 'The Lagoon and the Popular Exotic Tradition'. Contexts for Conrad, edited by Keith Carabine, Owen Knowles, and Wieslaw Krajia, 177–87. New York: Columbia University Press.

Sevareid, Eric. Editor. 1967. All England Listened: The War-Time Broadcasts of J.B. Priestley. New York: Chilmark Press.

Stevenson, Robert Louis. 1922. Memories and Portraits. The Works of Robert Louis Stevenson, XII, 188–9. New York: Charles Scriber's Sons.

Trease, Geoffrey. 1949. Tales Out of School. London: Heinemann.

Trotter, David. 1994. The English Novel in History, 1895–1920. Abingdon: Taylor & Francis.

Tucker, Nicholas. 2005. 'Missing Parents in the Family Story'. New Review of Children's Literature and Librarianship 11:2 (2005): 189–93.

Wilson, Jacqueline. 2001. 'Preface: Eleanor Graham'. The Children Who Lived in a Barn, i–x. London: Persephone Books.

Wolfreys, Julian. 2001. Victorian Hauntings: Spectrality, Gothic, the Uncanny and Literature. London: Palgrave.

Wootton, David. 1995. The Art of George and Eileen Soper. London: Chris Beetles.

7

Austerity and Kenneth Darrell Waters

In 1945 the Second World War ended. On 8 May, Britain and her allies accepted Germany's surrender and on 15 August, the surrender of Japan was announced following the bombing of Hiroshima and Nagasaki. The 8 May 'Victory in Europe Day' was a national holiday. In Beaconsfield, as in towns and villages up and down the country, there were street parties and bonfires lit in celebration, replete with effigies of Hitler, Goebbels and others sitting on top. After six years it was a moment to savour. 'I don't feel as if I'm living in days when magnificent history is made, and neither do you, I expect', Blyton remarked to the readers of her children's page in *Teacher's World*, 'but nevertheless we are, and in years to come people will envy those of us who lived to-day to see the downfall of so much that is terrible, and to welcome peace and goodness into the world once more'. In a letter on the same page, Bobs explained he would be wearing 'a red, white and blue bow on my collar today because I'm a VE-Day dog' (*TW*, 16 May 1945, 15).

The cessation of hostilities was not the only momentous event. In May 1945, within weeks of VE Day, a Labour government under Clement Attlee displaced the Conservatives led by the war-time Prime Minister Winston Churchill, a man idolised by Blyton (amongst millions of others). It was a move against 'the old gang', 'Colonel Blimp' and 'similar die-hard types', toffs who were out of touch and represented a pre-war Britain mired by class deference, 'privilege' and inequality.[1] The country's mood was for change and the new government, with its slogan 'Let's Face the Future', set about implementing an ambitious socialist programme including the nationalisation of

© The Author(s), under exclusive license to Springer Nature
Switzerland AG 2021
A. Maunder, *Enid Blyton*, Literary Lives,
https://doi.org/10.1007/978-3-030-76332-9_7

major industries, the creation of the National Health Service (1948) and the provision of free secondary education for all children up to the age of fifteen.

However, despite the prospect of a 'brave new world', Britain in the immediate post-war years was for many people a grim and challenging environment, as Tony Rennell describes:

> The country was beset by the gloom of winning a war heroically and then having to settle for a peacetime that was drab, impoverished and anything but glorious.
>
> The fighting spirit that had kept the country battling on from 1939 to 1945 was all but gone two years later, drained away for most people via a lack of everything: food, adequate housing, money and prospects.
>
> The only things in abundance were rationing coupons....A newcomer to London was appalled at 'public buildings filthy and pitted with shrapnel scars running with pigeon dung. Bus tickets and torn newspapers blew down the streets: whole suburbs of private houses were peeling, cracking, their windows unwashed, their steps upswept, their gardens untended.' He thought London 'a decaying, decrepit, sagging, rotten city'.[2]

The feeling of euphoria that the war was over was also tempered by the realisation that Britain was in debt (£3.5 billion), with ruined cities and infrastructure. During the war over 200,000 houses had been destroyed by bombing—the resulting shortage being one of the starting points of Blyton's 1945 novel, *The Caravan Family*. Government restrictions remained, as did belt-tightening and rationing (which did not end until 1954). In February 1946, Alison Uttley was one of many people for whom complaining about the 'awful' state of affairs under the new government was a frequent pastime: '...most depressing...strikes, depressions....England is on the down grade, lost'.[3] Things did not improve. Winter 1947 was the coldest on record and there were power cuts and more food shortages.

The impression of Blyton which emerges at this time is similarly that of a woman with a traditional—or narrow—outlook not quite in step with the post-war world. Some of her letters from this time, sent to Macmillan & Co., show her evolving a distinctive style of correspondence in which her business-like manner is punctuated with personal snapshots of family life but also snobbish digs at the Labour government and the regime's representatives. Her targets included new kinds of ministers, such as Emmanuel ('Manny') Shinwell (1884–1986), the son of Jewish immigrants who was Minister of Fuel and Power, Ernest Bevin (1881–1951), former Secretary of the Transport and General Workers Union and war-time Minister for Labour, who was the Foreign Secretary, and George Tomlinson (1890–1952), a former cotton weaver and union representative who was Minister for Education. In 1948 Blyton was a guest at one of the big London concerts run by Robert Mayer (1879–1985), a German-born businessman and philanthropist, who sought to promote music education to children. Afterwards she complained that:

> Sir Robert sat Mr Tomlinson & his wife next to me. What a very extraordinary thing to choose a man for Minister of Education who cannot speak English properly & keeps on retrieving his H's! I saw children winking at one another when he got up & spoke. I suppose, however, one does not need education, or a knowledge of its needs to be its minister! His wife told me that 'Mr T' (as she called him) believed that a knowledge of music made a man a better citizen. I replied gravely that it might even make men better ministers, & after that she eyed me very doubtfully! However, he left at half-time to go to a football match. (Mac, 24 January 1948)

Blyton's apparent incompatibility with the people now running the country is not altogether surprising. She could be very snobbish. It also chimes with an observation made by David Kynaston in his *A World to Build: Austerity Britain 1945–1948*, namely, that it was 'the middle-class that *felt* a relatively greater sense of deprivation during these austerity years' and that within a couple of years 'it had become almost axiomatic that it was the middle-class that had taken the biggest hit'.[4] In spring 1947, there was widespread furore when Shinwell announced that his party 'did not care "a tinker's cuss" for any class other than the organised workers of this country'.[5] This 'sense of somehow being muscled out of the picture by the working class' went down badly amongst those who had enjoyed the privileges of money and rank before the war. 'I just hate this cold weather & everything that is associated with Shinwell', wrote Blyton in February 1947. 'We shall all be living on the poverty line soon, even successful publishers & authors' (Mac, 14 February 1947). Elsewhere Evelyn Waugh complained of how '[t]he Socialists are piling up repressive measures', while the celebrated travel writer, H.V. Morton, told a friend that England had become a society where 'things moved steadily towards Communism' and 'everything that can be done is being done to pamper the masses and to plunder anyone with capital or initiative'.[6] Blyton, who earned rather more than Waugh or Morton, felt particularly victimised, although it is difficult to imagine how she could not have felt well off. The war years had seen her achieving increased professional success; by the end of it she appeared to be 'illimitable', as one observer noted.[7] *Five Go Off in a Caravan*, published by Hodder and Stoughton in November 1946, sold 40,146 copies in its first five months and by April 1947, had earned her an initial royalty of £1361; she was already earning similar royalties each year from the continuing sales of other titles in the same series.[8] In the year October 1946–October 1947, she earned £5976 in royalties from Macmillan; the following year, to October 1948, she earned £6433 from the same company.[9] Back in her large house in Beaconsfield, daily life followed familiar routines. Her meals were agreed with the cook and were served in the dining room brought from the kitchen by the maid. Blyton replied to her voluminous correspondence, read *The Times* and did the crossword. She played golf, listened to the wireless and went to the cinema. Every few months she would go on holiday—the Grosvenor Hotel, Swanage was a favourite—where she would play bridge as well as tennis and more golf. It was while staying at the Grosvenor in September 1947 that Blyton discovered that Ernest Bevin was a fellow guest. Somehow, Blyton could not help but notice that when the hotel requested his ration book it was 'quite untouched—not a point, not a week's meat, sugar eggs, tea, etc., had been marked!' To Blyton it was obvious that Bevin, a portly man, 'just gets as much as he wants of everything without being rationed. How wild the public would be if they found out that Labour Ministers break the law so flagrantly!' (Mac, 6 September 1947). For this Churchill-loving Conservative it was all too much and made her long for the days when the elderly war-leader would be back in power. In the meantime, she still knew what her public wanted, and she could supply it, but there was also the shock of receiving a large tax bill, the result of several years under-payment.

Meanwhile, back in Beaconsfield things had changed in other ways, too. Like many other marriages, Blyton's marriage to Hugh Pollock had not survived the war and the couple had divorced in December 1942. The previous year had seen the arrival into Blyton's life of Kenneth Darrell Waters (1892–1967), whom she would marry in October 1943. The relationship between Blyton and Pollock remained an extremely bitter one; Blyton refused him permission to see their daughters and she has been implicated in putting her ex-husband out of his job when Newnes terminated Pollock's contract with them (a dismissal which was illegal according to a government rule that returning solders be allowed to return to their old employment after the war). There was little further contact between the couple and, after June 1942, when Pollock was posted to the United States, their children did not see him again; Pollock was not invited to his elder daughter's wedding in 1957.

In contrast, Kenneth Darrell Waters was the person who would have the most influence over Blyton for the remainder of her life. He was a surgeon at St. Stephen's Hospital in Fulham, west London. Like Blyton, when they first met he was married but the couple began meeting in a London flat on a regular basis and Waters was a regular visitor to Green Hedges through

1942 and 1943. He became known to Blyton's daughters as 'Uncle Kenneth' and, in newspaper interviews, the impression was generally given that he was their biological father (Hugh Pollock having been removed from the equation). The situation in which Blyton found herself or created—living out a romantic dream—was not unheard of during the war and plenty of other women whose husbands were away on service (sometimes for several years) also pursued clandestine extra-marital relationships. The risk was, of course, greater for Blyton because of her public profile; the audience of *Sunny Stories* and their parents had been trained to like and approve of her but she and Waters were careful enough for their relationship to be known only by a few people, including Blyton's friend Dorothy Richards, whose discretion could be relied upon. Unpleasant scenes were mostly avoided; initially Waters was kept out of the way when Hugh Pollock returned on leave from his army base in Dorking. When Waters' wife stormed down to Beaconsfield to confront Blyton, the wife was informed that it was not the famous authoress but her friend Dorothy who was having the affair. What Dorothy Richards' reaction was to this is not known, but she was upset by the divorce from Hugh (Stoney, 139). To Blyton there were more important things to consider, notably her own good name. The 1940s were less-forgiving times and, while the media offered women a range of messages about their wartime roles in and out of the home, being unfaithful was not one of them. For Enid Blyton to be exposed as an adulteress could have destroyed everything she had worked for. The same protective attitude towards the Blyton name—and also to protect their mother's reputation in the eyes of his daughters—meant that when Hugh discovered the affair and wanted a divorce, he agreed that Blyton could divorce him, rather than the other way around. The legal system at the time gave only four grounds ('matrimonial offences') for divorce—adultery, cruelty, incurable insanity and desertion—and each 'offence' had to be proved via witnesses giving evidence in court. Hugh, who by 1943 had begun a relationship with a young author, Ida Crowe (whom he later married), agreed that it would be shown that it was he, rather than his famous wife, who had been unfaithful. Couples were not supposed to collude in staging evidence but the Pollocks' decision to do this was not unusual. Divorcees were not permitted to re-marry in church so, when Blyton and Waters were married on 20 October 1943, it was at Westminster Office, with the event recorded by a discreet two-line notice on the 'Births, Marriages & Deaths' page of *The Times*.

It has been difficult for writers to characterise Blyton's new marriage. There are few letters. In most accounts of the couple, Waters has not received a very good press. Imogen Smallwood, required to accept him as her new father,

Fig. 7.1 Enid Blyton and Kenneth Darrell Waters, early 1950s

described him as 'small and very athletic…with an impatient temperament that was always threatening to break through his courteous manner' (Small-wood, 61). Elsewhere he comes across as a dreary, humourless and ignorant man, someone who was not as clever as he thought he was and liked involving his wife in deals designed to enrich them but which only ended up creating more work for her. Blyton's agent, George Greenfield, described Waters as 'one of the most stupid and philistine men I have met', whose most striking feature was his voice: a 'bleating falsetto'.[10] Waters also liked his own way but in this he was not so different from many other men of his generation or since then. At the same time, he was proud of his new wife's achievements, was protective of her and liked the good things that marriage to a woman of wealth brought him (Fig. 7.1).

The dynamics of Darrell Waters' role in Blyton's life is something we return to in later chapters. For her part it seems safe to say that Blyton did not like being on her own and, in common with other women of her age, had been trained to cherish the status of being married—and of being the wife of a respected surgeon. Waters often sounds a disastrous choice for a creative person. There were several observers like George Greenfield who thought that the hard-working author needed to be rescued from her husband and his cronies, and like Blyton's younger daughter, held a good many negative memories of him, long after the marriage had proved to be workable.

In 1942–1943 the repercussions of Blyton's divorce and re-marriage were obviously felt by those closely involved but there was success in keeping the details from the general public. However, it is likely that people in Beaconsfield knew something of what went on and gossiped—perhaps disapprovingly—while they queued up at the shops with their ration cards. It made a change from hearing about the war. It seems fitting that this chapter concludes as it began by returning to Beaconsfield in wartime, with a sighting of the recently divorced Blyton going about her daily activities in her role as housewife. It was there on 21 April 1943 that Alison Uttley saw her hated rival being served at the fish shop:

> At Wilkinson's I was watching a woman ogling [the fishmonger], her false teeth, her red lips, her head on one side as she gazed up close to him, – suddenly he turned to me and to my surprise introduced her, Enid Blyton! The Blyton, photographed and boastful![11]

Such comments reveal Uttley's maliciousness, but they also offer a sense of the varied dimensions of Blyton's life during this time: the surface image of commonplace housewife, the down-to-earth celebrity with no 'side' to her, the flirtation with the tradesman. For Alison Uttley, a woman who was always very much on her dignity, such behaviour was unutterably vulgar; as her diary entries suggest, she herself adopted a rather seemlier—and highhanded—attitude to shopkeepers, which they resented, on one occasion accusing her of pulling rank and jumping a queue. But behind this, there is in Uttley's sighting of Blyton something more ambiguous—a knowledge perhaps of Blyton's extra-marital affair with Kenneth Waters or at least of her divorce, however discreetly this was handled, and of Blyton's other existence, not as a monogamous wife but as a woman wearing garish lipstick seeking out male attention. These war-time Blytons exist alongside one of her other incarnations as best-selling author, someone in demand to comfort the nation's children, open garden fetes and other fund-raisers, a publicityseeking celebrity of usurping ubiquity whose books, views and name were rarely out of the papers. It was a hard act to carry off but she managed it.

Notes

1. Paul Addison, *The Road to 1945: British Politics and the Second World War* (1975; London: Quartet, 1977), 14–15.
2. Tony Rennell, 'Britain 1947: Poverty, Queues, Rationing—And Resilience', *Daily Mail* (20 November 2007), 24.
3. Dennis Judd (ed.), *The Private Diaries of Alison Uttley* (Barnsley Pen and Sword, 2009), 134.
4. David Kynaston, *A World to Build: Austerity Britain 1945–48* (2007: London: Bloomsbury, 2008), 260.
5. Ibid., 262.
6. Ibid., 260–1.
7. Unsigned Article, 'Newsbriefs: More from Enid Blyton', *W.H. Smith's Trade Circular* (28 February 1948), 9.
8. Juveniles Ledger, London Metropolitan Archives/Hodder and Stoughton Archives, M 16,327.
9. John Basden (Darrell Waters Ltd) to the Macmillan Company Secretary, 16 April 1952, The Archives of Macmillan and Company, British Library Add Ms. 89,262/1/8.
10. George Greenfield, *A Smattering of Monsters* (1995; London: Warner, 1997), 120; 119.
11. Dennis Judd (ed.), *The Private Diaries of Alison Uttley*, 109.

Bibliography

Addison, Paul. 1975; 1977. *The Road to 1945: British Politics and the Second World War.* London: Quartet.

Greenfield, George. 1995; 1997. *A Smattering of Monsters.* London: Warner.

Judd, Dennis. Editor. 2009. *The Private Diaries of Alison Uttley.* Barnsley: Pen and Sword.

Kynaston, David. 2007; 2008. *A World to Build: Austerity Britain 1945–48.* London: Bloomsbury

Rennell, Tony. 2007. 'Britain 1947: Poverty, Queues, Rationing—And Resilience'. *Daily Mail* (20 November), 24.

8

Blyton the Missionary

It is inaccurate to discuss the Blyton of the post-war years as a fossil; she was still relatively young after all (age fifty in 1947). She still possessed enormous energy and an unshakeable belief in her gifts as communicator and was one of the most visible writers. With the resounding success of her books, her presence was also much in demand at discussions to do with education, childcare and what she vaguely termed 'moral welfare'. Following the publication of *The Six Bad Boys* in 1951, a book designed for grown-ups as well as children, she wrote to Roland Heath: 'If I don't look out I shall be switching over to the adults entirely & neglecting my friends the children!…That book I wrote on Juvenile Delinquency (in story form for both children and adults) is causing quite a stir – but is involving me in all kinds of Marriage Guidance councils…N.S.P.C.A. affairs & goodness knows what' (Mac, 22 October 1951). One of the things that the post-war period brought with it was a broadening of Blyton's writing to incorporate a very deliberate sense of herself as someone with a mission and she increasingly announced herself in this way. 'I am a writer for children, and into my books I pack moral and ethical teaching' she wrote in *The Sunday Times*, 'the children must get it somewhere!….But I sometimes feel I am just a voice crying in the wilderness'.[1]

Blyton was not really on her own. The idea that writers for children *would* impart some kind of lesson—'a philosophy of life', as David Garnett put it—was commonplace.[2] W.E. Johns, writing in 1949, was in no doubt that 'today more than ever' young minds needed to be trained. Such training (which, he pointed out, could be picked up from the Biggles books) included ideas

© The Author(s), under exclusive license to Springer Nature Switzerland AG 2021
A. Maunder, *Enid Blyton*, Literary Lives,
https://doi.org/10.1007/978-3-030-76332-9_8

of 'sportsmanship according to the British idea', as well as 'teamwork' and 'loyalty', both to Queen and country but also to parents and other forms of 'rightful authority....I hold the view', Johns explained, 'that every normal boy is born with an inherent love of manly courage, straight dealing and fair play. If in later life he slips, it is due to an unfortunate environment'. He added that '[t]he brain of a boy is flexible. It can be twisted in any direction'.[3] This was also broadly the view of the romantic novelist and author of (by then) fifty books, Barbara Cartland. Canvassed in 1951 by *W.H. Smith's Trade Circular* for her view as to what made the best reading for children—girls as well as boys—she explained how:

> Nothing is worse than an obviously 'goody-goody' story but a book which glorifies the wrong standards and idealises lawlessness or anti-social behaviour can do irretrievable harm.
>
> Children love adventure, excitement and suspense – don't we all? - and they identity themselves closely with the experiences and personalities of the characters in their favourite books.
>
> There rests…a grave responsibility on those who write for the young. Early impressions form the foundation stones of future development….
>
> What virtues do we want in our children? I ask for courage, self-confidence…kindness of heart and patriotism….These qualities all lie dormant within us all to be awakened in many different ways….and in this changing, difficult and uncertain world we need pioneers, adventurers, idealists and above all individualists.[4]

In 1951 it would have been hard not to think of Blyton at this point—and people did. Her characters *were* 'adventurers' of the kind described by Cartland, but they were *not*, as Donald Mackenzie noted, 'mere feat-machines'. Instead, they were 'live and real, springing from a convincing background, natural and normal young humans whom any parents would be glad to see their children emulate'.[5] Mackenzie possibly had in mind the Famous Five series, although by this stage other Blyton titles would have fitted equally well, a reminder that, in a sense, Blyton had long been a writer with teacherly—or missionary—tendencies. As we saw in Chapter 4, 'The Story of Bobs' (1927) exposes cruelty to animals and Blyton used the pages of *Teacher's World* to encourage children to engage in charitable fund-raising. And, as we have seen in earlier novels like *The Secret Island* (1938), she is keen to draw attention to cruelty against children, or to counsel against cheating, as in school stories like *Mischief at St. Rollo's* (1940). Yet in these instances the point is made more indirectly. In the years following 1945 she became more explicit in her wish to help children 'see things in the right way', as she put it. 'I want them to grow up into good, decent grown-ups. I want them to be kind and loving and generous'. It could sound, she admitted, 'very pious'.[6]

The present chapter aims to chart this sea change in Blyton's perspective and to describe the main arenas in which she articulated her ideas in the late 1940s and 1950s, suggesting some of the impacts they had on her writing. There are several important strands here: the publication of her novel-with-a-purpose, *The Six Bad Boys* (mentioned above); her crusade against 'trashy' comics; her forays into religious writing, and the launch in 1953 of *Enid Blyton's Magazine*, following Blyton's exasperated resignation as editor of *Sunny Stories*. These activities caused Blyton to mix with different sets of people: social workers, clergymen, magistrates, librarians, psychiatrists. Some of these, notably Sir Basil Henriques, a philanthropist and juvenile court magistrate, had an effect on her writing and its subject matter. These people were often dedicated professionals who took Blyton seriously. In 1950, she was asked to deliver the annual Hannah Hyam lecture (named after the Jewish campaigner and philanthropist) to social workers, youth club leaders and policewomen: 'an honour, I know, but I feel very scared. It's the Police Women who frighten me the most – what *can* I say to interest them?' (Mac, 11 January 1950). They were also frequently people who shared her belief that the world was changing too fast; the 'progressive phase' through which Britain was now going under the Labour government was moving swiftly and the country was going to the dogs.[7]

The Six Bad Boys

One of the things used to undermine the Labour government's achievements and which is directly relevant to the work produced by Blyton—*The Six Bad Boys* in particular—was the idea that Britain was witnessing an increase in crime. In 1945, 478,349 indictable offenses were recorded, mostly for larceny and breaking and entering, a figure which was almost 70% up on that recorded in 1938. In particular, as Peter Hennessey has explained, offences committed by pre-teens and teenagers ('juvenile delinquents') were heavily publicised. This 'led to the sensation that standards and civil culture generally were declining in ways that spoke volumes about the national fibre'.[8] During the war there had been a dramatic rise in offences committed by people in the 8–17 age group and, although crime levels fell between 1945 and 1950, fears about 'delinquents' were well into their stride by the time the war ended. Such activities seemingly signalled a new culture of selfishness and violence, an American-influenced dystopia of teenage gangs carrying out daily thefts, muggings and beatings-up. Writing in the aftermath of the so-called 'Cleft Chin Murder' of 1944, in which G.I. Karl Hulten and his teenage British girlfriend, Elizabeth Jones, went on a spree of robbery and killing in London, George Orwell discerned a new kind of 'meaningless' violence taking hold, set against 'the anonymous life of dance-halls and the false values of the American film'. The fact that such viciousness was what newspaper readers seemed to want to read about was proof of how British society had been changed by 'the brutalising effects of war'.[9] It was a theme taken up in Britain in 'serious' films like *The Blue Lamp* (1950) and *I Believe in You* (1952), the latter showing the work of well-intentioned—and well-spoken—probation officers and their teenage charges.

Not surprisingly, underage crime also became, as *John o'London's Weekly* noted in an article on 'The Bad Child' in 1952, the one subject on which everyone is 'ready to express an opinion' and 'is always sure of a large audience…'.[10] Letters and articles in newspapers and magazines sought to explain the problem: the war-time blackout, 'the dislocation of home life', the 'disruption of school life' during the war, 'mental defectiveness' were variously cited.[11] One of those most widely listened to was the psychiatrist, John Bowlby. His study of teenage criminals, *Forty-four Juvenile Thieves* (1946), pushed the idea that this was a family problem, something which was grist to the mill for those worried about women's post-war place. The country's education system also came in for scrutiny and questions were asked about whose fault it was: 'The school thinks that the home should guide the child to some bright conception of life's meaning; the bewildered home hands this duty to the school and the total result is that the average child often grows up with no clear teaching of any science or art in joyous efficient living'.[12] James Chuter Ede, Home Secretary (1945–1951), blamed working mothers 'leaving their children to roam the streets' for the increase in juvenile crime and he urged them to think carefully before leaving their children and going out to work.[13] 'MOTHER WANTS THE COSH BOYS FLOGGED', was a headline in *The Daily Herald* in 1952, and the paper quoted an interviewee explaining how 'as a mother I dread to think what state of society my children will live in when they grow up. Day after day we read of cosh attacks, cruelty to animals and other vicious crimes committed mostly by young people'.[14] During the trial in December 1952 of Christopher Craig (aged sixteen) and Derek Bentley (aged nineteen), who had been caught breaking into a warehouse, at which point Craig had shot a policeman with Bentley reputedly shouting '"Let him have it"', it emerged that Craig, a boy of limited intelligence, as was Bentley, had only ever read—or had read to him—Enid Blyton stories. Despite not having fired the shot, Bentley was hanged at London's

Wandsworth Prison amidst public petitions for clemency, while Craig, who was legally under age, was imprisoned. There was no suggestion that Blyton's work had corrupted anyone (or was anything but morally sound).

However, as Blyton's career progressed into the 1950s, she became more and more identified in the minds of the reading public as someone worth listening to on these topics. Her ability to capture the public mood is apparent in an execrable poem, 'The Little Thug', published in *The Sunday Times* (20 April 1952, 4). An un-named narrator addresses the 'thug' of the title as he appears before the magistrate's bench:

> So you had a gang, and you swore and spat,
> But you're not yet thirteen years old?
> Poor little sallow, undersized brat,
> You strutted so brave and bold.
> You robbed, you struck, and you ran away,
> And now you stand here alone... (1–6)

The 'thug' is voiceless; the summary of his life to date is read out by the omniscient narrator—whether s/he is acting for the prosecution, the defence or the social services is not clear—but as the poem progresses it is clear that the charges should really be laid at the door of the child's parents. The drunkard father is often absent and the 'bitter-mouthed mother' is at least in the courtroom but thanks to her apparently selfish desire to have a job, has abnegated her proper responsibilities, which include making her child's tea. In any case, she wants nothing more to do with her rudderless young son. The poem, which seems quite socialistic—almost Blakean in tone—ends by stressing the need to help 'our poor little brother'—a 'bent' twig who needs straightening—but the litany of question marks suggests that there is no single solution. The message seems to be that better parenting would be a start (the boy's mother is mentioned three times) and that Britain's education or legal systems are not at fault.

The idea of children 'going wrong' was also, as we have said, the subject of *The Six Bad Boys*, published with a good deal of fanfare in 1951. Described by *Books of the Month* as being 'a story that no child will want to put down', the novel relates what happens when two middle-class boys—Bob Kent (aged ten) and Tom Berkeley (aged twelve) 'stumble' into a gang calling itself 'the Four Terrors' (*SBB*, 101).[15] Its other members—Len, Jack, Patrick and Fred—are aged between eight and fifteen and are working-class, already mired in a life of mischief and petty crime; their headquarters is not a cosy garden shed of the kind given to the Secret Seven but the cellar of 'a terrace of half-ruined old houses', a relic of war-time bombing but a location full of symbolism, too, especially given the gang's destructive tendencies (*SBB*, 98).

Some of what the gang gets up to might be described as youthful mischief, but Blyton was also intent on addressing more serious issues. Len and Fred steal from their harassed mother who is unable to control them; their father has left. Patrick has no mother, only a father who beats him. Jack has both parents but lives with them and five siblings in two 'dirty and smelly and untidy' rooms, an indictment of his mother's approach to her domestic duties but also, perhaps, of the post-war housing shortage. As the narrator explains: 'It was no wonder the boy went to find happiness somewhere else—and to him the little hidey-hole down in the cellar was heaven' (*SBB*, 100). Likewise, Bob Kent's problems are bequeathed to him by his widowed, vain, 'hard-faced' mother who fits the description of what 1950s newspapers termed the 'cuckoo' mother (*SBB*, 151). She was the kind of woman featured in a 1950 article, 'Bomb-site playgrounds for children left by working mothers'—that is, a mother 'who neglects her children for a good time'.[16] It was a theme Blyton liked to take up and was in evidence in a much-reported speech that she delivered at the opening of the Mothercraft Exhibition in London in November 1949. There had been a huge increase in the number of married women who had been tempted back to paid employment (from 16% in 1931 to 40% in 1951). Blyton spoke witheringly of such women and described the Labour Government's encouragement of them as 'one of the most disastrous things at the present time'. It was a question of priorities:

> [W]hat is it going to profit the nation if we gain dollars – or even the whole world – but lose the souls of our young children?
> …It is when the mothers of the nation begin to fail in their duty to their children that religion disappears, moral standards fall and the nation begins to go down.
> Mothercraft is not just learning how to bath the baby or to feed him correctly. It is something much more than that. It is watching over his mind and soul as well.[17]

By criticising working mothers Blyton was accused of being out of touch and laid herself open to charges of hypocrisy. Yet it was not the first time she had endorsed the essentialist models of femininity current at the time, in order to elaborate on the strengths and duties of the 'gentler sex'—nor would it be the last. In *The Six Bad Boys*, Bob's mother enjoys her job at a beauty salon but finds her son a '"a bother"' who prevents her from working more, a fact that she does not bother to disguise (*SBB*, 42). As she explains: "I'd like to earn good money and have something to spend on better clothes and go to a dance at times, and to the cinema more often. But I can't because I've got you to see to'" (*SBB*, 42). Gradually she starts staying out late, leaving Bob on his own, compensating him with money. When, in frustration, he smashes up one of the cold meals she has left out for him, Mrs. Kent, who maintains that Bob "'has always been a difficult boy'", responds by locking him out altogether and leaving his tea in the garden shed (*SBB*, 151).

It thus becomes inevitable (according to Blyton's logic) that, as Bob wanders the streets, he meets the gang in their cellar and is invited to join. In return he ingratiates himself by stealing items from his mother's house to furnish the cellar, which comes to be recognised by the boys as a 'the cosiest, finest place in the whole kingdom', a substitute home (*SBB*, 111). When, in the story's other middle-class home, Tom Berkeley's father leaves (the result of Mrs. Berkeley's nagging), he, too, joins the gang as a way of escaping his 'tearful, complaining, angry mother' (*SBB*, 89). These plot lines join up when the two boys get into trouble by sneaking (without paying) into an 'Adults Only' film, an act of rebellion for which they are caned. In what is presumably an attempt to galvanise those adult readers who have missed the point that society's problems would be solved if mothers embraced—or at least accepted—their all-encompassing legacy of home-making, family and duty, Blyton's own opinions are voiced by Bob and Tom's neighbours, Mr. and Mrs. Mackenzie. They are represented as a balanced, decent couple who manage their own 'serene' family home in ways that seem straight out of one of the parenting manuals of the time (*SBB*, 152). "'I'd like to knock their heads together'", said Mrs. Mackenzie, digging her needle into her sewing as if she were digging it into Mrs. Berkeley. "'Thinking of themselves all the time, while their boy is running wild'"....Mrs Mackenzie could have said a lot of [other] things about Mrs Berkeley and her behaviour but she didn't' (*SBB*, 120; 128).

Blyton's righteous disapproval of working mothers and wives was not shared by everyone in 1951. "'A LOT of nonsense is spoken and written about the working mothers who neglect their homes and children'", announced an Epping magistrate at the annual conference of the Magistrates' Association in 1950, telling the conference that she was one of these "'dreadful'" women "'gadding about'".[18] This was also the feeling of the young Labour Member of Parliament, Barbara Castle, who pointed out that '[t]hose who moralise about the beauty of work in the home usually have in their minds an ideal picture remote from reality'. As she pointed out, being stuck at home could be tedious and unfulfilling: 'The sink cannot chat to you…there is nothing to break the monotony as you struggle with the relentless pile of washing up'.[19] It was a modern take on the issue, but one that

Blyton and many others found hard to get their heads round. For them the working mother served as a bogeyman—or woman—central to explanations for juvenile delinquency and thus deserved to be called out and shamed. In December 1950, as Blyton was writing *The Six Bad Boys*, Basil Henriques, the Chairman of the East London Juvenile Courts, was reported as lecturing a working mother whose son had been playing truant from school and who claimed she had to go to work to earn them '"the necessities of life"'. '"A mother's love is more important than television sets"' he told her.[20] Blyton and Henriques seemed to be kindred spirits, and Henriques valued Blyton's novel enough to provide a foreword in which he informed readers that: 'The description of the workings of the minds of Bob and Tom is, in my opinion, absolutely brilliant. It shows *why* the broken home causes children to go wrong, and the gradual deterioration of both boys is told in a manner which I have never seen surpassed....Indeed, old and young alike will be deeply grateful to Enid Blyton....' (*SBB*, 'Foreword', 7–8).

This type of endorsement was obviously gratifying. It also chimed with a good deal that Enid Blyton saw herself as standing for at this moment: she was an expert in child psychology, an advocate for the importance of family life, a teacher of moral lessons. In *The Six Bad Boys* it is the two middle-class boys 'deterioration' from misbehaving at school, to sneaking into the cinema without paying, to joining a gang, to robbing a tobacconist and keeping the money from a wallet found in the street, that forms the central narrative around which the story's plot is woven. The novel's moral aesthetic encourages us to believe that, once they have begun to engage in rebellion and petty theft, Bob's and Tom's collapse into a life of full-blown criminality is inevitable—unless they can be saved by responsible adults. Both are shown to be partly driven by anger at their betrayal—as they and, indeed Blyton, see it—by their parents who are poor role models and who deserve the rebukes they receive. The boys are adrift. For the boys' families, the mystery of the items going missing from their homes—the bits of furniture, carpet, food and toys that are put in the gang's hideout—becomes wrapped up in the mystery of their conduct. In effect, the boys also go missing—by means of their absences, their entanglement with their working-class counterparts, and the new personalities they try on; Tom, in particular, seems influenced by the '"tough guy"' actors he has seen on the cinema screen (*SBB*, 146). Tom is a rather unengaging character unlike Bob, whose situation is powerfully and movingly brought to life. Isolated and lonely, Bob moves in and out of different identities in the story—dutiful son, kindly substitute brother, well-meaning friend, class clown, delinquent—while being someone who needs saving, and restoring to the fold of a '"nice"' family (*SBB*, 162).

It is the boys' capture by the police, following their robbing a newsagent and the preparations for their appearance at the Juvenile Magistrates' Court, which propels the second half of the plot. The novel's didactic element is unsurprisingly more evident in this section. The chapter, 'At the Juvenile Court', is deliberately reminiscent of the journalistic "special assignment" in that it describes everything: the layout, the procedures, the roles of each individual—magistrate, policeman, ('kindly') probation officer, victim, teacher, defendants and their parents (*SBB*, 164). The extent to which the parents' failings are examined but also harshly criticised by the magistrate is a case of Blyton's handing out some poetic justice but, as we have said, her representations also owe much to the popular views of the time and anxieties about the breakdown of family life following the war. The anti-social behaviour of the 'bad child', thus labelled by Dr. Josephine MacAlister Brew in 1952, was not simply the result of over-crowded homes or classrooms, but '[t]he inability of many parents to provide the happy and secure home influence'.[21] Blyton gives her readers not unredeemable thugs but boys who, when asked, have strong feelings about the type of family they want. What they would like are tidiness, decency and discipline—if they can only get it. At the end of the novel, Tom, Patrick and Fred are—to nobody's surprise in 1952—sent away to approved schools; they have shown themselves to need more training, or taming, than conventional establishments can provide, and Tom, at least, is reconciled to his fate. Bob, as the most sympathetic of the boys, is fostered by the Mackenzie family, and rewarded with a '"*real proper* mother"' after his own mother declares she wants nothing more to do with him (*SBB*, 170). '"I've been saved"' he realises, as he reflects on these arrangements which seem to him to be a dream come true, and to the reader are a ringing endorsement of the middle classes as the backbone of British society—their well-regulated homes being more necessary than ever (*SBB*, 168).

The combination of Blyton's ability to tell a good story inoffensively and the topicality of her subject matter meant that, when it appeared in 1951, *The Six Bad Boys* proved very popular. It was published by Lutterworth Press, a firm that had initially (in the late eighteenth century) traded as the Religious Tract Society and was still publishing improving literature, as well as respectable magazines for the young, notably *The Girl's Own Paper* (1880–1956). It had already published *Hollow Tree House* (1945) and *The Family at Red-Roofs* (1945), and they would publish twenty-two of Blyton's novels (the last was *The Hidey Hole* [1964]). In 1952, Blyton and her husband were invited to serve on the Board of the firm's magazine division, presumably as a token of appreciation for her contribution to their profits and for the kudos which the Blyton name brought. Blyton's correspondence shows her writing excitedly about the new novel "causing quite a stir", its big launch party ('I enjoyed myself greatly'), and the flood of invitations for speaking engagements arriving off the back of it. As she told Roland Heath, one of the public appearances she had taken on involved delivering another lecture to an audience of social workers and policewomen. She was unsure of what to say:

> Will it do if I outline some of the main causes of J. Delinquency & quote various cases, both from the Courts, & also from our Children's Home here in Beaconsfield, which I help to run? We have, at this Home (for under-fives) the first results of bad homes, in mental & physical deficiency – at the Courts we see the final childhood results. I could also say this is why I felt I had to write the book & give a rough outline of it. I hope people won't think I'm trying to boost the book – but I certainly would like to boost the idea that bad homes are very costly to the nation! Anyway, the book has caught on all right, thank goodness – the first print was 50,000 (last Sat fortnight) & we are reprinting at top speed to get another large edition out before Christmas! I believe Chuter Ede [the Home Secretary] has read the book, but I don't know what he thinks of it!
> ....Now I am up to my eyes in work – it's dreadful. I keep trying to catch up with my letters & can't....We've booked a table at the Savoy for Friday, to celebrate a Tory victory...warm wishes in spite of your roping me in for Moral Welfare. (Mac, 22 October 1951)

Alongside a desire to see the back of the Labour government (the reference above is to the general election of 1951 which saw Winston Churchill's Conservatives returned to power), Blyton's other bugbear during the late 1940s and early 1950s was the issue of comics. The idea had emerged that children were being indoctrinated by the brutishness, violence and promiscuity that featured in publications imported from the United States (originally brought to Britain by GIs in the Second World War and later as ballast on ships). These had now spawned a host of British imitations. Titles such as *Crime Detective*, *Crimes by Women*, *Eerie* and *Superman*, produced on cheap paper aimed at the mass market, horrified many adults who, as *The Times Educational Supplement* noted, feared their 'effects on the morals and manners of English children' and worried that they might even provoke children into 'copycat' crimes.[22] In June 1951 the case of Alan Poole, a borstal escapee who shot a policeman, hit the headlines. When caught, he was found to have large numbers of such comics and his case was held up, like that of Craig and Bentley, as indicative of the collapse of pre-war standards as well as encouraging the idea of a link between reading and violence.

Chuter Ede declared himself 'certain' that comics 'get the child into an atmosphere where proper development becomes difficult', causing him or her 'to worship the wrong kind of hero'.[23] This was Blyton's fear, too. She introduces it in *The Six Bad Boys*, in which one of the ways the gang passes its time is in their communal reading of trashy 'everlasting comics' (*SBB*, 7). Earlier the topic had also formed the subject of a talk she gave to social workers in March 1950. She recounted how someone had sent her two 'pernicious' and 'wickedly corrupting' American comics, one of which (*Big Shot*) she was horrified to see had 'British Edition' emblazoned on the cover and, at a price of only sixpence, promised 'Sensational value'. How, Blyton asked, was it possible that such works now 'retailed in the British Empire'? Sounding rather like Mary Whitehouse, the famously conservative leader of the National Viewers' and Listeners' Association, who took up similar issues in the 1960s, Blyton explained:

> Both of them glorify gangsterism and violence, the moral standards are very low, they are incredibly vulgar. This is, of course, merely the thin end of the wedge. If they became popular in this country, they would corrupt our children's minds quickly and absolutely. On the front should be printed in large letters, the name of the *real* publishers – SATAN & CO., Unlimited.

Blyton refused to be caught up in projects which smacked of anything so horrible and reminded her audience that *her* young heroes and heroines—Julian, George, Fatty, Philip and the others—did not have to be on first-name terms with gangsters, thieves and hitmen. 'This is unfortunately, an age of violence', Blyton announced, 'but let us at least keep it from the children when we can'.[24] This was also her message when, on 4 April 1953, she appeared as a panel member on the BBC's *Now's Your Chance*, a popular radio programme that debated issues of the day in front of a live audience. Other guests were the Reverend Marcus Morris (founder of the *Eagle* comic), Sydney Pemberton (publisher and book distributor), Leonard Millar (of the Arnold Book Company which specialised in comics, including British reprints of *Marvel* comic-books) and Dr. Michael Lewis (an educationalist). In the discussion of 'depraved' comics that followed, Blyton, the only woman on the panel, predictably came out on the side of what an observer described patronisingly as 'all things nice', telling the audience that she 'never put anything frightening in her books, and if she included anything the slightest bit questionable she got thousands of letters from parents saying "'Miss Blyton, how could you?'" Blyton was equally firm about the even more dangerous influence of the cinema, noting that 'there was a great deal of difference between reading a book and seeing these same horrible things being put into pictures by men who surely must have depraved minds'.[25]

Blyton's appearance on the programme cemented her reputation as a figure of unimpeachable respectability, but her views were not out of step with other commentators: 'If we continue to feed impressionable young minds on savagery and sex, vice and violence need we be surprised when they try to emulate what they have seen on the screen or read?', asked T. Buchanan Hooper in 1953.[26] This was also the view of Malcolm Saville who warned that 'civilisation' would most likely 'go under and our own country fall, without a revival of Christian principles, which should be taught and practised first in the home'. It was for this reason that he sought 'to emphasize…[in his books] the value and significance of true family life'.[27]

Seen in this company, Blyton's own stance does not seem so outlandish and it explains some of her other publishing ventures at this time. These included the large-scale religious projects she undertook with Macmillan, notably the series of *Enid Blyton's Bible Stories—Old Testament* (1949) and *New Testament* (1953). She had already published *The Children's Life of Christ* (Methuen, 1943) and *Tales from the Bible* (Methuen, 1944) and followed these up with *The Greatest Book in the World* (British and Foreign Bible Society, 1954) and *A Story Book of Jesus* (Macmillan, 1956). Unlike Malcolm Saville, Blyton was not a practicing Christian, but the post-war mood of confusion and deterioration seemed to her—and religiously inclined publishers like Macmillan—to require a counter assertion of stability, peace and optimism. They thus sought to supply audiences with a tried and tested—and comforting—philosophy, albeit one packaged so that Blyton's name took top billing. The potential for hubris was considerable and the project raised hackles. As she had done in the early issues of *Sunny Stories* in the 1920s, Blyton retold familiar biblical tales and parables. Some reviewers thought her 'interpretations', as they were labelled, on the level of the suburban housewife: 'superficial', 'undisciplined', 'long-winded' and 'inaccurate' was theologian David Christie Murray's, verdict on *A Story Book of Jesus*. There was, he reported, nothing 'remarkable except the price'—a hefty eighteen shillings and sixpence. Moreover, Blyton and her publishers had overstepped the mark by blurring the lines between material taken from the New Testament and that written by Blyton. As Murray explained: 'The chapter "When Jesus was a child" is not a Bible story and should not be called one'.[28]

Enid Blyton's Magazine

The other large-scale project with which Blyton (naturally enough) became associated was *Enid Blyton's Magazine* which launched on 18 March 1953. Whether by accident or design, this was just prior to her radio appearance on *Now's Your Chance* during which she reminded listeners that she was particularly attuned to the impact of comics on the young having spent twenty-seven years running the much-loved *Sunny Stories* but she was now casting this off in favour of a new publication. In arriving at this decision Blyton had been influenced by what seems to have been a deteriorating relationship with Newnes who (understandably enough) refused to let her advertise works from her other publishers in *Sunny Stories*. Another reason was that she was still ambitious and had felt stifled. The new magazine would be bigger and, in adverts, she explained that the magazine would serve the public in at least four ways. It would be:

- a competitor to American-style magazines in which comic-strips had ousted 'proper reading'
- a place where 'backwards' readers would improve their skills
- a space where children's imaginations would be stimulated
- a space in which 'decent values of life' and 'worthwhile activities' were on display.

When *Enid Blyton's Magazine* was announced, *W.H. Smith's Trade News* described it (with some exaggeration perhaps) as '[o]ne of the biggest post-war ventures of the magazine world', led by 'the book trade's greatest single asset'.[29] The second part of this description may have been true. It was at least partly in recognition of this that the magazine's publishers, Evans Brothers, the firm that had published *Teacher's World*, granted Blyton 'complete control' (Mac, 14 January 1953). It was an 'unusual arrangement', as Noel Evans noted nervously, but one which the firm seemingly felt powerless to prevent.[30] A huge (and expensive) marketing campaign was launched. Blyton, meanwhile, declared herself a woman on a crusade: 'I have long wanted a magazine that could be my headquarters', she told reporters and she reiterated her intention to 'challenge…the frightening "American-style" comics and gangster films'.[31] A new company was set up—the E.B. Magazine Co. Ltd, the initials of which had the happy advantage of standing for both author and publisher; inevitably Kenneth Waters was one of the five directors. Privately Blyton expressed nervousness. 'I do need to be brave & energetic', she told Macmillan, '…but it's very <u>interesting</u> & finance reaches high planes!' (Mac, 21 January 1953). It is not clear whether Blyton invested any of her own money into the venture—probably not; 'the power of my name', as she put it, was enough (Mac, 21 January 1954). This was also the feeling of *W.H Smith Trade News*, which reminded readers that 'Miss Blyton has managed to establish in the minds of all parents the knowledge that her name on any book or product does guarantee the very high standards for which she is famous'.[32] A good name is, to use Pierre Bourdieu's phrase, a kind of 'symbolic capital' with its own value.[33] Blyton knew that she was trusted by parents but also that she sold better than any competitor. She felt great satisfaction as she contemplated the 250,000 initial print runs proposed. This was, she reported, 100,000 more than *Sunny Stories*. 'I expect we shall soon shoot up' (Mac, 21 January 1953). In fact, circulation figures tended to remain around this mark: 231,876 in 1954 before dropping to 200,000 in 1956. Priced initially at fourpence and aimed at a younger audience than other, bigger-selling publications for children—*School Friend* (932,000 in 1953), *Eagle* (750,000 in 1953) or *Girl* (500,000 in 1953)—*Enid Blyton's Magazine* presented itself as being for both pre-teen boys and girls.[34] It was these children into whose heads Blyton wanted to put 'ideas' and she was confident she could do so. She would, as she explained to them, be their 'storyteller' and their 'guide' (*EBM*, 2 September 1953, 3).

It is beyond the scope of this chapter to provide a detailed analysis of the six years'-worth of magazine issues—162 in total—produced fortnightly between March 1953 and September 1959—or to draw any solid conclusions about all the pressures it placed on Blyton. What *is* true is that, like *Sunny Stories* in the previous decades, *Enid Blyton's Magazine* enabled Blyton to obtain for herself a psychological presence in Britain that was hard to shake off. That Blyton again took on the challenge of writing and overseeing her enterprise was clearly part of it. A magazine is usually a space for competing as well as complementary voices and points of view. But the fact that Blyton wrote all the content allowed her to do what even the most watchful editors often struggle to do with a magazine. This is to reduce the contents of a magazine to a homogenous whole, or, as Margaret Beetham puts it, create 'a dominant discourse from which to read'. Discourse is here understood as something shaping social and personal relations and offering readers ways of both understanding the world and behaving in it. Beetham argues, of magazines generally, that there is a tendency to present 'real life' in a particular way, to close off 'alternative readings', a position that is maintained consistently across and between different issues.[35] Something of this was, of course, hinted at in Blyton's comments to the press and it was apparent, too, in her regular letter to readers which opened every issue.

On the one hand the magazine promised to be expansive, as Blyton explained: 'My new magazine is for every child in the kingdom, or anywhere else in the world, who loves stories and fun and competitions, for every child who has ever met me or written to me, for every child who has ever had his or her head buried in one of my books' (*EBM*, 18 March 1953, 3). On the other hand, while the magazine expected to gain entrance to lots of different kinds of homes, there is a very clear sense that it enveloped readers in a very specific set of ideologies. A feeling of community and team spirit existed alongside a set of civilising exhortations: respect for one's elders, patriotism, tradition, honesty, kindness, charity and politeness were constantly emphasised. These social virtues (which the protagonists of *The Six Bad Boys* were obviously lacking) were the catchphrases that promoted social stability in 1950s Britain and often *Enid Blyton's Magazine* devoted large parts of an issue to conveying specific messages about such values.

This is apparent in the first six issues (18 March–27 May 1953), which carried instalments of Blyton's 'The Story of Our Queen', the book version of which was not yet available and eagerly awaited (in February pre-orders stood at 110,000).[36] The magazine's readers were thus being rewarded with a sneak preview. Unsurprisingly, amidst Coronation fever and, given the editor's belief in the monarchy as a source of strength, the magazine did not disguise its admiration for the young Queen Elizabeth: both as a glamorous symbol of a new age and as a figure of continuity and tradition. 'She belongs to us, she is ours - and we are hers to command', explained Blyton ('The Story of our Queen', *EBM*, 27 May 1953, 7). It was not all glitter, however. Blyton reminded her readers that the Queen was in the unenviable role of a hard-working mother who rarely had time to see her two young children; readers were invited to pray for her, 'because you will want to help our Queen' ('Green Hedges', *EBM*, 15 April 1953, 2–3). In a neat bit of marketing, one of the prizes offered in the magazine's competition was the chance on 2 June to watch the coronation—'one of the most solemn, important and glorious days in our history'—up close, or at least part of it, in a specially constructed viewing stand on the processional route ('Green Hedges', *EBM*, 13 May 1953, 2).

The idea that the Blyton brand was one which aimed to dictate a reading position and embrace or confirm readers in a particular world view is, of course, one which has been voiced many times—both by Blyton's admirers and her detractors. As noted above, what is interesting about *Enid Blyton's Magazine* is the way in which Blyton's words, as they appeared in its pages, can be read as creating a particularly powerful 'comradeship' of readers. Committed to speaking to thousands of children from roughly six years old up to the age of about twelve, who were healthier than their predecessors a decade before but who—Blyton thought—needed the capable guidance she could give, the magazine set out quite deliberately to appeal to a post-war generation looking for an identity. Other comics—most notably the *Eagle*—did this too, of course. Blyton, however, was particularly good at talking to her readers, saying what she felt without any sense that it had been carefully crafted. In tones that seem authentic, she chatted about the letters she had received from them, or their occasional face-to-face encounters. In June 1953 she reports that readers' letters arrive at the rate of 1000 per day ('Green Hedges', *EBM*, 24 June 1953, 3). At the same time, she publicised her other ventures. Blyton's stage adaptations are discussed in Chapter 11 but one of the things she talked about regularly were the film and theatre productions of her works. In her editorial for 24 October 1956, she explains that she had been down to Dorset to see part of the Famous Five film being made by the Children's Film Foundation: 'How you would have loved watching it!' she tells them. She then gives details of the forthcoming London productions of *Noddy in Toyland* (its third appearance in the West End) and *Famous Five Adventure* (its second) and describes her involvement in the casting of the child actors: 'Soon there will be rehearsals, and the children will learn their parts well, just as you learn yours in your school play - and Timmy the dog will learn his! He loves acting as much as the children of course'. In describing the canine actor, Blyton's tendency to anthropomorphise had clearly not faded. In the same letter she congratulates children who have sent letters telling her the number of books they own. A boy from New Zealand who has 395 is the winner, although they are all made to feel like winners, of course. 'I am keeping all your cards out of interest', Blyton tells them, 'so that I can show them to anyone who says that children do not read nowadays! Little do they know what bookworms you are!' ('Green Hedges', 2–3). In all these letters, adults are never addressed; the magazine is not a space for them, rather it is a space where children form part of a collective of like-minded people for whom the act of reading—and reading books by Enid Blyton— is offered as an important aspect of their lives. What is also noticeable is that, as well as casting herself as a children's defender against ignorant adults, Blyton's support for the act of reading, rather than, for example, football or playing the piano, seems designed to inject confidence into those who are perhaps not very good at either. In her magazine, she suggests that being bookish is something to be admired; reading is joyful and the pleasure it brings is one of the things that should unite her readers.

A large part of the story of *Enid Blyton's Magazine* thus involves Blyton's apparently successful attempt to create a sense of community in which she tries to instil in the magazine's readers her own version of a post-war consensus. As she had done in *Sunny Stories*, Blyton attempts to foster a sense of identification between herself and her readers by using words like 'we' and 'our'; for example, 'our magazine'. Elsewhere there is a sense that the effect aimed for seems to be something equivalent to the modern 'global village'. This is Blyton on 18 March 1953, telling her readers about the publication of the magazine's first annual, by which time she had begun her pursuit of children in the newly established British Commonwealth:

> It is going out all over the world – to Australia and New Zealand and South Africa, to Singapore, Ceylon, Malay, India – to every place where there are English-speaking children. So, I am going to take this chance of holding out a friendly hand to all those overseas readers of mine. They have our magazine, they love the same stories as we do, they belong to us and are our friends. I like to think of so many children in different corners of the world reading this letter – we do have fun together, don't we? What a truly enormous family I have! (9)

As a demonstration of how Blyton brought her 'self' to her public in the early 1950s, this passage is revealing. The tone is self-congratulatory, but this is tempered with a sense of disbelief that she cannot quite believe her good fortune in having so many friendships. She is appreciative of her readers' loyalty and makes it clear that she values them. She also encourages them to recognise themselves as part of something bigger. As subscribers to *Enid Blyton's Magazine* its British readers are part of an assemblage of boys and girls everywhere, children much like themselves. We might say, of course, that there is still a feeling that overseas readers ('they') are 'others', just as they were in the days of the Empire, but what does seem to be genuine is Blyton's commitment to the idea of a fellowship of readers—*her* readers— brought together as a totality in a single place (the magazine). They share allegiances to Enid Blyton (first and foremost) and to each other, and as becomes apparent, to particular social values. Indeed, while the 'Enid Blyton' who appears in *Enid Blyton's Magazine* treats members of her audience as equals and friends, she was also, as we have seen, very aware of her power as a teacher—or an 'influencer' (as we might call it nowadays) who valorises certain ways of behaving for these pre-teens. Daniel Cook has argued that childhood is not just a 'life stage' but 'a cultural category', a 'set of discourses that seeks both to define childhood and to articulate the behaviours, activities and values that should be associated with it'.[37] Every issue of *Enid Blyton's Magazine* contains evidence of this idea—we could even say it was part of its reason for existing. Respect for parental authority is important, but so, too, is the idea that children themselves have responsibilities and even agency.

Part of this idea is apparent in the magazine's expectation that readers will exercise good sense and have regard for others. 'PLEASE remember your pets on Bonfire night', was a recurrent exhortation ('Green Hedges', *EBM*, 24 October 1956, 3). It was usually accompanied by a grim anecdote. In October 1956, Blyton told of a friend's cat running away and returning with its paws shredded by burns ('and it could not walk again for weeks' ['Green Hedges', *EBM*, 24 October 1956, 3]). This need to care for animals was one of the ways in which real-world experiences made themselves felt in the magazine, not least because it was the basis of the oldest of the three charitable clubs co-ordinated under its auspices. This was the Busy Bees movement, established in 1929 by Maria Dickin, the founder of the People's Dispensary for Sick Animals, with a view to encouraging children to care for their pets responsibly. When Dickin died in 1951, Blyton took over as 'Queen Bee', reputedly accruing 20,000 new members in her first year, for whom, she announced in March 1953, '[o]ur new magazine will…be a meeting place' ('Green Hedges', *EBM*, 8 March 1953, 3). Busy Bee members wore a membership badge as 'a symbol of service' and they were encouraged to write in, detailing how they had raised money to support the club's projects, one of which was a mobile veterinary practice. The magazine also hosted the Famous Five Club (established in 1952), membership of which totalled 30,000 by December 1953 and helped raise funds for Beaconsfield's Children's Home. On 16 September 1953, Blyton announced a new club, the Sunbeams, the intention of which was to raise money for the blind. By the end of the year membership stood at 2800 (*EBM*, 23 December 1953, 45–6).

Primarily the clubs presented a way for the magazine's readers to become part of a larger project, part of a vision to create a generation of responsible citizens of the future. As we have seen, there was an urgency about this in the moral discourse surrounding the family which dominated post-war society, especially given the fears about what children would become in the vortex of the post-war world. But it was also the case, of course, that children bought the magazine to escape the world and to read Blyton's work, particularly her fiction. From the beginning, the proportion given over to stories and serials was considerable. The magazine's by-line promised not simply 'the best stories for all children' but exclusive access to them. 'You will not', Blyton told her readers, 'find stories about the Famous Five, Pinkwhistle, the Secret Seven…and the rest in any other magazine but this one' ('Green Hedges', *EBM*, 1 April 1953, 2). This may have been a dig at Newnes, which continued to bring out *Sunny Stories*—and as Blyton saw it—had been slow to alert its readers that she was no longer involved. The first issue of her new magazine (18 March 1953) thus included the first instalment of *Five Go Down to the Sea*, which ran for nineteen issues until 25 November. In September, as the serial neared its end, Hodder and Stoughton published the complete story in volume form and readers of the magazine were offered the 'opportunity' to reserve an advance copy (7/6) at their local bookshop. The magazine's lead serial was supplemented by shorter, self-contained tales: 'You Can't Trick Brer Rabbit', 'Tinkle-Tinkle', 'Jingle-Jing!', 'Noddy' and 'The Adventures of Josie, Click and Bun'. These were directed towards a younger age group and one of Blyton's expectations was that older readers would be 'kind' towards their younger siblings and read these tales to them, instilling in them a love of stories and, particularly, those by Enid Blyton ('Green Hedges', *EBM*, 2 September 1953, 3). Towards the end of each serialisation Blyton's own voice would rise to the surface as she told them about the next one: 'I asked you last time to let me know what serial you all wanted next—and postcards have been coming in by the hundred about it!', she writes in the 25 November 1953 issue as *Five Go Down to the Sea* drew to a close (2). The answer was 'another adventure story' (followed by one about animals), and *Good Work Secret Seven!* began serialisation two weeks later. The impression Blyton was trying to give, of course, was not that she had a filing cabinet full of ones she had prepared earlier, but rather that she framed their production in terms of her close relationship with readers and stressed the authenticity of what she wrote.

Whether the magazine's fiction was its chief attraction or not (it probably was), it is apparent from looking at the contents of individual issues that Blyton's readers experienced the longer novels in a way that was different from those who read them in book form. Like *Sunny Stories*, the new magazine's reliance on regular demand, with readers needing to be stimulated in one issue to purchase the next, meant that an exciting 'to be continued' story was an important component. Instalments would often end on cliff-hangers, or at least would point towards the story's continuation: 'Next time-A Dreadful Shock', is how the instalment of *Five Go to Billycock Hill* ends on 24 October 1956 (32). *Secret Seven Mystery*, about the search for a runaway, Elizabeth Sonning, follows a similar pattern with readers being offered the prospect of answers: 'Next time-Mostly about Elizabeth' (16). It is also the case that while we think of the Secret Seven and Famous Five stories as having their own textual identities and messages when they appeared alongside one another within the covers of the magazine, they were also to be understood in terms of these inner relations. The 24 October instalment of *Five Go to Billycock Hill* shows the boys, Julian and Dick, gallantly venturing out into the rain so that the girls, Anne and Georg(ina), don't have to (26–32). A previous instalment (26 September) features an uncharacteristic outburst from Anne about the selfish use of portable radios in public places. Some readers would have connected this modelling of behaviours to earlier titles featuring the Five, and to Blyton's moral centre which is to be found deep in the deep English countryside as experienced by the middle-classes and compliant locals; it's even possible that fans with very good memories would have connected Anne's outburst to a similar one in *Five on Kirrin Island Again* (1947). But in autumn 1956 it was also part and parcel of the ideological outlook *Enid Blyton's Magazine* was seeking to foster. In the 24 October issue, the short story 'The Firework Club' shows the son of a cash-strapped family unselfishly using the money he has earned from odd-jobs to buy his hard-working mother a pair of nylon stockings, rather than continue to contribute to the firework club he has joined—a reminder that not all children have the opportunity to participate in the forthcoming bonfire night (4–12). 'Keep Out' is a cautionary tale about respecting the countryside and keeping out of farmers' fields (18–22). In another story, 'A Smart Piece of Work', two 'latch key' boys, whose parents are at work when the boys finish school, exhibit intelligence and bravery in catching a burglar who has broken into their empty house (35–40). Chapter 2 of *Secret Seven Mystery* shows the seven on the trail of a missing schoolgirl (14–16). The fact that all the stories are situated in middle-and lower middle-class England suggests that this setting was a factor in imagining the presumed readership for the magazine. But what is also significant is that these stories were part of the wider discourse of the magazine as a whole. Most of the literary items have as their concern questions of social responsibility and behaviour. The magazine's fictional content represented Blyton's commitment to safe entertainment, but it was also a means of educating readers, providing them with a moral location as they struggled, as Blyton saw it, to keep their bearings in a changing world. One of the things that emerges is that, despite liking adventurous plucky children, willing to take risks, she also liked those who were willing to toe the line. In 1947, George Orwell had written approvingly of 'the gentle-mannered, undemonstrative, law-abiding English' and 'the orderly behaviour of English crowds, the lack of pushing and quarrelling, the willingness to form queues'.[38] Throughout the 1950s Blyton sought to continue to school her readers in the same conformities. There may have been some youthful rebellion in the decade, against the restrictions imposed by the older generation, but the evidence of *Enid Blyton's Magazine* is that this was at least one space where this was not the case.

A final thing to note about *Enid Blyton's Magazine* is that, like all magazines, it was a double commodity. The different elements of the magazine—the stories, the warm welcome letters, the clubs, readers' letters, the competitions—worked to construct an ideal audience that readers wanted to be part of and for which they came back for more. But what is also apparent is that while the magazine's publishers, Evans Brothers, sold their merchandise (Enid Blyton) to consumers (readers), they also, with Blyton's endorsement, 'sold' the readers to advertisers. It was not, perhaps, surprising. Prime Minister Harold Macmillan's complacent declaration of July 1957, that the British population, eagerly buying up cars and television sets, had 'never had it so good' did not apply to everyone, but the economic situation in the mid-1950s certainly induced a *feeling* of affluence.[39] And, although an upward trajectory may not have been the universal lot of every reader's family, it was trend that was increasingly implicit in *Enid Blyton's Magazine*. The 24 October 1956 issue is a case in point. Interspersed with the stories were adverts not simply for books published by Evans (John Pudney's *Friday Adventure*; Kathleen Mackenzie's *Three of a Kind*, Lorna Hill's *Roseanna Joins the Wells*) or endorsed by Blyton (*Oldham's Encyclopaedia*) but wigwams, cowboy outfits, prams, stamps ('bumper' packets), records (Jerry Lewis, Eddie Cantor, Tweetie Pie, Bugs Bunny), 'Sculptorcraft' kits (to make models of 'Little Noddy'), puppets, California syrup of figs ('when every child gets moody'), correspondence courses (to help one secure a place at grammar school). Part way through the issue's instalment of *Five Go to Billycock Hill*, readers were confronted with an advertisement for Famous Five windcheaters and sweaters made by J. &. R. Baker (Leicester). Meanwhile fans of Noddy ('now on ITV') could buy a Noddy puppet, seemingly identical to the one they saw bouncing about on screen each week (Noddy had been televised in September 1955). Although some of the adverts were presumably aimed at parents (the syrup of figs is an obvious example) most of them constructed children as consumers in their own right and offered them a world of exciting (but harmless) things to think about spending money on. By buying them, readers could be part of another imagined community comprised of other children enjoying and wearing similar things.

What ultimately makes *Enid Blyton's Magazine* relevant to the story of Blyton's career, is the way in which it sheds light on another way in which 1950s readers encountered her and her work. *Enid Blyton's Magazine* exhibited a determination to explain things simply and pragmatically, to stimulate reading but also observation and fellow-feeling, and to offer rules for living. If the protagonists of *The Six Bad Boys* were the fictional embodiments of the post-war fascination with the delinquent, then the children who populated *Enid Blyton's Magazine* were their counterparts. When Blyton signed off on 9 September 1959, readers of the final serial, *Bonfire Night for the Secret Seven*, were (as usual) left in little doubt that crime did not pay, no matter how cunning the criminal's plan—in this instance seeking to evade capture by disguising himself as the guy on top of a bonfire. They knew, too, that responsible pet owners kept their animals indoors on 5 November (a repeat of the message of 1956). The magazine dominated much of Blyton's life, and it was important to her not least because it was a way of articulating what childhood was in a rapidly changing world—a world in which she did not always feel entirely at ease.

****

As with other voices of the 1940s and 1950s, Enid Blyton's response to social problems can sometimes seem heavy-handed and unimaginative. There are also occasions when she seems to be jumping on a band-wagon—seizing on a topic of the day, arriving at a simple solution, and deploying the results in her next story. This could be said to be the case with *The Six Bad Boys*, where there is little evidence of Blyton's continuing interest in juvenile delinquency once the book was published and the round of accompanying public talks completed. On the other hand, she saw *Enid Blyton's Magazine* as a counterweight to modern juvenile behaviour as seen in the real world. In Blyton's personal opposition to working mothers and their bad effect on the home, and in her support for campaigns related to animal welfare and child cruelty, there was a good deal of long-term energy expended, not only in her fiction but in her charitable activities. Throughout the 1950s, the proceeds of The Famous Five Club were sent to the Children's Convalescent Home in Beaconsfield. This funded a special ward called 'The Famous Five Ward' (with Noddy wallpaper) and included children paid for by the profits from selling badges and by gifts from members. The fate of the nation's children, is 'one of my great interests', she told Macmillan, 'little mal-nutrition babies, abandoned children, children who are the victims of parental cruelty, & the like…I cadge for them! I'm not really a very good beggar, but I feel I can be a little more eloquent than usual when I have 30 small & most unfortunate children to beg for' (Mac, 25 November 1951). Perhaps Blyton's decision to embark on social missions via her writing was not so cynical as some of her detractors would have us believe.

Notes

1. Enid Blyton, 'Letter to the Editor: The Roots of Crime', *The Sunday Times* (10 June 1951), 4.
2. David Garnett, 'Books in General', *The New Statesman* (5 December 1936), 896.
3. W.E. Johns, 'What the Modern Boy Expects of His Hero, Biggles', *W.H Smith's Trade Circular* (20 August 1949), 15.
4. Barbara Cartland, 'Buying Books for Children', *W.H. Smith's Trade Circular* (25 August 1951), 27; 31.
5. Donald Mackenzie, 'Pot Boilers? No!', *W.H. Smith's Trade Circular* (2 December 1950), 13.
6. *Home for the Day—Enid Blyton*, BBC Radio (13 January 1963). https://www.bbc.co.uk/archive/home-for-the-day--enid-blyton/zvy6kmn. Accessed 8 March 2021.
7. Peter Hennessey, *Never Again: Britain 1945–1951* (2005; London: Penguin, 2006), 454.
8. Peter Hennessey, *Having It so Good: Britain in the Fifties* (2006; London: Penguin, 2007), 445.
9. George Orwell, 'Decline of the English Murder', in *Decline of the English Murder and Other Essays* (Harmondsworth: Penguin, 1986), 9–13 (9; 13; 12; 13).
10. Josephine MacAlister Brew, 'The Bad Child', *John o'London's Weekly* (9 May 1952), 1–2.
11. M.E. Bathurst, 'Juvenile Delinquency in Britain during the War', *Journal of Criminal Law and Criminology* 34:4 (1944), 291–302.
12. McEwan Lawson, 'Those Annoying Adolescents', *John o'London's Weekly* (8 February 1946), 190.
13. Unsigned Article, 'These Working Mothers', *Daily Worker* (6 December 1950), 2.
14. Unsigned Article. 'Mother Wants the Cosh Boys Flogged', *Daily Herald* (7 October 1952), 4.
15. Unsigned Article, 'Six Bad Boys', *Books of Month* (December 1951), 4.
16. Unsigned Article 'Bomb-Site Playgrounds', *The Birmingham Daily Gazette* (22 June 1950), 7.
17. Unsigned Article, 'Let Mothers Stay at Home—Enid Blyton', *Daily Mail* (24 November 1949), 3.
18. Unsigned Article, 'Working Mothers', *Leicester Daily Mercury* (21 October 1950), 6.
19. Barbara Castle, 'Women's Work: Men's Views on It and Women's', *John o'London's Weekly* (16 May 1952), 1–2 (2).
20. 'Unsigned Article, These Working Mothers', 2.
21. Josephine MacAlister Brew, 'The Bad Child', 2.

22. *The Times Literary Supplement* (19 February 1952), quoted in Martin Barker, *A Haunt of Fears: The Strange History of the British Horror Comics Campaign* (London: Pluto, 1984), 45.

23. Ibid., 41.

24. Enid Blyton, 'No Violence Please', *W.H. Smith's Trade Circular* (4 March 1950), 9–10 (9).

25. Unsigned Article, 'Comics Analysed by BBC Team', *W. H. Smith's Trade News* (4 April 1953), 7. Blyton was not against all comics. A letter of 1951 suggests that 'Tintin' by Hergé (Georges Remi) was passable. 'Thank you for sending the Belgian comics. I was most astonished! I supposed I <u>had</u> heard of them but I had completely forgotten….The comic is quite well produced…that adventure series certainly goes places' (Mac, 27 June 1951). It is not clear which titles she was reading. Fifty years later the racism and animal cruelty on display in *Tintin in the Congo* (1931), for example, would lead to attempts to ban the story.

26. Unsigned Article, 'News Briefs and Comment: Comics "Savagery"', *W.H. Smith's Trade News* (28 March 1953), 4.

27. Quoted by Blyton in 'No Violence Please', 9.

28. David Christie-Murray, 'Religion in Story', *The Times Literary Supplement* (11 May 1956), 288.

29. Unsigned Article, 'Enid Blyton's Magazine', *W.H. Smith's Trade News* (14 February 1953), 4.

30. Noel Evans, 'The Birth of Enid Blyton's Magazine', *W.H. Smith's Trade News* (7 March 1953), 33.

31. Unsigned Article, 'Enid Blyton's Magazine', *W.H. Smith's Trade News* (14 February 1953), 4.

32. David White, 'But Give Parents a Guide', *W.H. Smith's Trade News* (18 April 1953), 18.

33. Pierre Bourdieu, 'The Forms of Capital', in *Handbook of Theory and Research for the Sociology of Education*, ed. J. Richardson (Westport: Greenwood Press, 1986), 241–58 (249).

34. George H. Pumphrey, 'Children's Periodicals—Some Disturbing Developments', *Junior Bookshelf* 24(4) (October 1959), 194–201 (196).

35. Margaret Beetham, 'Open and Closed: The Periodical as Publishing Genre', *Victorian Periodicals Review* 22(3) (Fall 1989), 96–100 (96).

36. Unsigned Article, 'Book Gossip: Royal Blyton', *W.H. Smith's Trade News* (7 February 1953), 9.

37. Daniel Cook, 'Interrogating Symbolic Childhood', in *Symbolic Childhood*, ed. Daniel Cook (New York: Peter Lang, 2002), 1–14.

38. George Orwell, *English People* (London: Collins, 1947), 11–12.

39. Dominic Sandbrook, *Never Had It so Good: A History of Britain from Suez to the Beatles* (2005; London: Abacus, 2006), 80.

Bibliography

Barker, Martin. 1984. A *Haunt of Fears: The Strange History of the British Horror Comics Campaign*. London: Pluto.

Beetham, Margaret. 1989. 'Open and Closed: The Periodical as Publishing Genre'. *Victorian Periodicals Review* 22(3): 96–100.

Bourdieu, Pierre. 1986. 'The Forms of Capital'. In *Handbook of Theory and Research for the Sociology of Education*, edited by J. Richardson: 241–58. Westport: Greenwood Press.

Cook, Daniel. Editor. 2002. *Symbolic Childhood*. New York: Peter Lang.

Hennessey, Peter. 2005; 2006. *Never Again: Britain 1945–1951*. London: Penguin.

———. 2006; 2007. *Having It so Good: Britain in the Fifties*. London: Penguin.

Home for the Day—Enid Blyton. 1963. BBC Radio (13 January). https://www.bbc.co.uk/archive/home-for-the-day--enid-blyton/zvy6kmn. Accessed 8 March 2021.

Orwell, George. 1946; 1986. *Decline of the English Murder and Other Essays*. Harmondsworth: Penguin.

———. 1947. *English People*. London: Collins.

Pumphrey, George H. 1949. 'Children's Periodicals—Some Disturbing Developments'. *Junior Bookshelf* 24(4): 194–201.

Sandbrook, Dominic. 2005; 2006. *Never Had It so Good: A History of Britain from Suez to the Beatles*. London: Abacus.

9

Blyton and Gender

The previous chapter looked at the ways in which Blyton sought to encourage particular patterns of behaviour in her readers and her idea of herself as a moral guide. Blyton acquired a reputation as someone willing to write, lecture and give her views on post-war society, particularly regarding the topics of children and the family. Here we will consider further how Blyton's texts exhibit these interests, in particular the ways in which they engaged with the roles of girls and women and their place in post-war society. Contemporary reviewers often approved of the way in which she dealt with this topical question, alongside what the journalist and campaigner Vera Brittain described as 'women's attitude to themselves'.[1] In 1943, *The Observer*, in its review of *Five Go Adventuring Again*, singled out the depiction of George—'a grossly misunderstood little girl'—as evidence of Blyton's willingness to challenge gender stereotypes.[2] The girls in *The Island of Adventure*, were, as a reviewer for *Birmingham Daily Post* noted approvingly in 1944, 'active', not passive, 'bringing a coining gang to its deserts'.[3] The observation that Blyton's adventuresome young females 'think nothing of exposing the plots of desperate men and hunting down resourceful criminals', was a frequent one and, although they often had brothers for protection, they were not playing with dolls or tea-sets.[4] In 1947, the writer of a long review for the *Coventry Herald* said something similar about *The Twins at St. Clare's*, describing it as the story of 'two remarkable girls…who overcame prejudices of their own making…and rose triumphant over many difficulties'. Although the book was set in the familiar atmosphere of the boarding school with

© The Author(s), under exclusive license to Springer Nature
Switzerland AG 2021
A. Maunder, *Enid Blyton*, Literary Lives,
https://doi.org/10.1007/978-3-030-76332-9_9

its 'peculiarities of matches, midnight parties [and] tricks', it was written with a stress on the necessity for 'hard work' and achievement and readers could see for themselves how much progress had been made in giving the girls opportunities.[5] Blyton deals with the position of girls—and women—to varying degrees throughout her writing: their roles and assigned place in society, the choices they make, the pressure on them to act in a certain way, their rebellion (or not) against conventional standards of behaviour, their relations with brothers, fathers and husbands and the paternalistic—sometimes patronising—attitudes exhibited by these male relatives towards them. This chapter will focus on some of Blyton's works from the 1940s and early 1950s, the years during which she was at her most productive and influential. These are the boarding school stories set at St. Clare's (1941–1945) and Malory Towers (1946–1951), and the family stories *House-at-the-Corner* (1947), *Six Cousins at Mistletoe Farm* (1948) and its sequel, *Six Cousins Again* (1950).

In many ways, Blyton would, of course, seem a likely person to urge a more forward-looking and sympathetic understanding of female experience. She was part of a generation of independently minded young women who had benefitted from increased freedoms in the years following the First World War. In her day-to-day life she was energetic and organised, forging two satisfying careers—as teacher and writer—the latter involving many public activities. She was a passionate advocate of education for girls, sent both her daughters to an expensive school (Benenden) and was pleased when they both went to university. Yet she could also be contradictory in her views on female roles and responsibilities, both in what she said and what she did. We saw something of her tendency to criticise working mothers in the previous chapter and she attempted to avoid charges of hypocrisy by presenting herself as a woman who—despite her personal success of '300 books unaided by secretary or typist'—always 'found time to run her Beaconsfield (Bucks.) home for her surgeon-husband and two daughters'. This insight into Blyton's life was part of a 1947 magazine profile which explained that, while she was happy to be referred to as 'a capable businesswoman', she was essentially a gentle soul who found editors and publishers '"terrifying"'.[6] In another interview Blyton explained that she worked only part-time on her publishing projects ('usually Tuesday, Wednesday and Friday'). The remainder of the time was spent with other Beaconsfield housewives queuing up at the shops, sewing and arranging the family's food.[7] Presenting oneself in this way was not unusual. It was one of the pretences you adopted if you were a woman in the public eye in 1950s—whether film star, sportswoman, politician or bestselling author. Elsewhere Blyton's comments are, as in other areas, those of a woman of her time and class. Her advice to a correspondent to get a nanny because 'they do enable mother to have time to spare for husband & friends' (and could also be 'someone to do the donkey work') seems to come straight out of the advice page of a women's magazine, not least in that the demands of the husband should be prioritised over those of the children (Mac, 21 January 1953). As we shall see, Blyton's novels likewise tend to conclude with an apparent endorsement of conventional (gender-based) standards of behaviour: the idealisation of good mothers, the authority of the father/husband and the importance of regular meals.

Some critics have suggested that in her depiction of the varied relations which exist between fathers and mothers, or husband and wives, or her presentation of different kinds of family and home life more generally, Blyton was meditating on her relationships with figures in her own life. As we saw in Chapter 2, much has been made of Blyton's childhood unhappiness at home and her dysfunctional relationship with her mother—based on rumours of Theresa Blyton's uncongenial attitude towards writerly pursuits and her impatience with her ambitious daughter. The (apparently) narrow-minded Theresa who sought to hold her daughter back might be seen as an example of what Barbara Creed has called the 'monstrous feminine', a figure which can (like many of Blyton's ogres, witches and cruel female guardians) be situated in relation to what Julia Kristeva has famously termed 'abjection', that which threatens life.[8] From Enid Blyton's perspective her (malevolent) mother was a starting point for understanding what she herself did or did not want out of

Fig. 9.1 Blyton and her daughters, Gillian (left) and Imogen, late 1940s (private collection)

life but so, too, it has been claimed was Blyton's lively but irresponsible father Thomas's leaving the family home. It was an event said to have formed the basis for the scenes of marital breakdown depicted in *The Six Bad Boys*. In the young Enid Blyton's embattled psychology, as it is seen, these events left behind a feeling of 'father hunger', to use Margo D. Maine's phrase, which she then needed to have filled by dominating older men: Hugh Pollock, then Kenneth Darrell Waters. This kind of theorising can seem quite a good 'fit' where Blyton is concerned, as can the concept whereby the deserted daughter (now prone to narcissism) searches for other sources of self-esteem and male approval.[9] How far such speculations can be taken is obviously a matter of debate, but it is certainly true that when taken together, Blyton's relationships with her husbands, Pollock (married 1924; divorced 1943) and surgeon, Waters (married 1943), gave her the opportunity to experience some of the ways men patronise women. This seems to have been particularly so in the case of Waters, a 'domestic despot', according to George Greenfield, who at business lunches would, with his associates, 'talk across Enid and in a sense down to her, treating her almost like a favourite niece who was still feeling her way in a man's world'.[10] This was despite his knowing nothing about the publishing industry in which his wife was such an important and capable player. In 1950, Waters, a surgeon, offered the public his own idiosyncratic interpretation—or diagnosis—of his wife. She was someone who combined 'two types of personality seldom, if ever, united in one person – the imaginative dreamer, and the utterly normal and practical woman'. She was also, he was pleased to report, 'a wonderful wife and mother' whose 'enormous literary enterprises don't interfere in the least with the peace and happiness of our home. She has quite abnormal vitality, which she conserves by an incredible efficiency'.[11] Blyton seems to have tolerated or even appreciated Waters' complacency, although there are moments in her writing, from her 'From My Window' column in *Teacher's World* in the 1920s through to her later novels, which suggest that she was aware of the slights women faced on a daily basis: '"Where there's a master I don't take no notice of what the missus says"', is one of the homespun pieces of wisdom proffered by the old poacher Twigg to his protégé Roderick in *Six Cousins Again* (*SCA*, 137). At the very least it is an acknowledgement on Blyton's part of the way in which attitudes towards women are passed down between men from generation to generation.

But a biographical explanation of Blyton's work should not mean we should dehistoricise it. Her representations of girls and women and their experiences may have been personal to her or the people she knew but they are also derived from wider contemporary contexts. The middle decades of the twentieth century saw great upheavals in women's lives, the implications of which have been the subjects of important scholarship by (amongst others) Penny Tinkler, Penny Summerfield and Helen McCarthy.[12] The continuation after the Second World War of debates and questions about woman's role in the modern world—whether the figure of the housewife, presiding over 'homes fit for heroes', was the proper reference point for post-war femininities—occupied a good deal of newspaper space. The returning serviceman was warned by one 'expert' in 1945 that his wife had probably 'managed pretty well during his absence' and had been left with 'a pleasant feeling of independence and self-confidence'. But he was also reassured that roles would adjust to their pre-war state and he could expect 'to resume his rightful place as the breadwinner of the household'.[13] Even apparent progressives like the veteran Labour politician Margaret Bondfield and eugenicist Eva Hubback were counselling in 1945 that, for the good of the nation, 'domestic work in a modern home will be a career for educated woman'. It was, as Gertrude Williams put it in *Women and Work* (1945), her 'real business of life'.[14] The response of many people in the post-war period was thus to try and rein women in, prevent them from deviating from existing moral codes and seek to contain them within a prelapsarian framework, one which sustained established masculine identity. So strong were these expectations that the years between 1945 and 1960 have frequently been seen as going backwards, at least as far as the expectations placed on women were concerned. Thanks to washing machines and hoovers, their home lives were sometimes easier, but this was at the cost of accepting that men were in charge.

Not everyone thought like this, of course. In 1952, the sociologist Richard Titmuss sounded an increasingly popular note when he suggested that the British woman was in a 'new situation' and was looking for a new kind of 'emotionally satisfying and independent life'.[15] And, as readers of mid-twentieth-century fiction, we do not have to travel very far to realise how writers remained preoccupied with an idea of woman 'in flux', as Rosamond Lehmann put it: the emancipated woman who rejected marriage and motherhood for a career, or the middle-class woman living a life of stultifying boredom at home. "'It's particularly difficult to be a woman just at present'" the heroine of her novel *The Echoing Grove* (1953) realises. "'One feels so transitional'".[16] So while Blyton's own personal relationships can be useful in shedding light on her fiction, it is worth thinking, too, about the ways in which her works, no matter that they were aimed at children, inevitably draw on and engage with some of these other prevailing character types and anxieties, as well as with other discourses of the 1940s and 1950s—about womanhood, about careers for women, about femininity and the feminine—which formed part of the wider uncertainty about post-war identities. It is striking, for example, how in texts like *The Secret Island* and *The Six Bad Boys*, Blyton adopts a conservative-gendered stance, with the result that there is an emphasis on the importance of girls and women becoming responsible housekeepers and carers. These markers of an ideal conventional femininity also form an important touchstone for the protagonists in *Hollow Tree House* (1945) in which runaways Peter and Susan, helped by their friend Angela, set up a cosy home in the trunk of a tree. In the children's Aunt Margaret, who is also their guardian, Blyton creates a vindictive figure devoid of kindness. Because this is the Blyton universe of right/wrong there is little examination of why Aunt Margaret is as vicious as she is—her role is simply to 'be'—but she might also be read as an example of a woman for whom the post-war domestic dream has long since died; lumbered with a husband who cannot keep a job and forced to scrimp, save and embrace domestic drudgery, hers is not an enviable life. This was partly the point behind the young Labour M.P. Barbara Castle's article, 'Women's Work' (1952), in which, keen to help women to return to work, she suggested that '[t]he nagging wife is usually a bored and frustrated one: a neurotic woman is one who has not enough outlets for her natural abilities…'.[17] Thus, while Blyton, a writer for children, does not offer an explicitly feminist critique of her society in the way that, for example, more highly regarded women writers of the 1940s and 1950s such as Elizabeth Taylor or Rebecca West might do, it is difficult to read her work without noticing that she is interested, at least some of the time, in the underside of domesticity, in the darker workings within the family unit and in the restrictions faced by her female characters, women as well girls.

School Stories: St. Clare's and Malory Towers

The generic formula of the boarding school story—lots of female bonding and hockey matches—in which pupils learn to respect rules and the importance of being a team player—recurs with variations at various points in Blyton's career. *Mischief at St. Rollo's* (1940), published under the pseudonym of Mary Pollock, is set at a coeducational boarding school, as is *The Naughtiest Girl in the School* (1940). The latter is run by two female principals and there is a strong emphasis on pupil power, including a school council and the pooling of extra pocket money for the greater good. Like most of the schools featured in Blyton's work, it is the kind of place sensible children appreciate. Elizabeth, the 'naughtiest girl in the school', is fairly quickly brought to recognise the truth behind her governess's words of encouragement: '"Most children simply *love* school. It's great fun. You play games, you go for walks, all together, you have the most lovely lessons, and you will make such a lot of friends"' (*NGS*, 10–11).

By the time that Blyton came to write school stories regularly in the 1940s, she was following in the popular footsteps of Angela Brazil (from 1906), Elinor Brent-Dyer (from 1925) and Dorita Fairlie Bruce (from 1921)— the latter's total sales had reached 500,000 by the end of the 1940s. Frank Richards' comic tales about greedy Bessie Bunter (sister of Billy) of Cliff House School, were other examples of how school stories became an integral part of comics and magazines, in this case *The School Friend* (1919–1940). It was a well-trodden path. As early as 1926, a reviewer for *The Times Literary Supplement* wrote wearily about the flood of stories about boarding schools, which 'flow out from the various publishing houses every year…impossible stories, ridiculous adventures…girls exactly like each other…and schools that one cannot believe ever existed'.[19] Although by the 1940s the genre's popularity had declined, it still enjoyed wide appeal. As Declan Kiberd has noted, the attraction for many readers was the boarding school's promise of a 'dream life' and 'a fantasy of an existence in a more cushioned section of the community' than they themselves lived in.[20] In 1960, this was also the view of one of the new generation of children's writers, Wallace Hildick, who suggested that boarding school stories offered readers 'the glamour and fascination of the unobtainable', while for writers they offered an attractive stating point: 'a small closed community with sharply set bounds and firmly fixed rules – the sort of compact world within a world that any reasonably competent author…find[s] easy to manipulate'. Working within this setting the writer could risk experimentation, safe in the knowledge that there was 'little danger of the plot-lines straying very far' for 'even the plainest, flattest, flimsiest set of characters…soon take on a plausible appearance of life when caught up in the currents of boarding school routine'.[21]

The St. Clare's Series (six titles; 1941–1945) emerged out of this basic pattern. The opening chapters deal, in a brisk, (middle-class) way, with the trauma of leaving home. At the train station parents *and* children keep their emotions in check. On arrival at the school there is the need for acclimatisation and initiation. The other pupils (from similarly comfortably off family backgrounds) include an array of 'types': the reliable best-friend whose stolid attractions are contrasted with livelier pupils—spoilt rich girls, vulgar nouveau riche arrivistes, practical jokers, sporting legends, exotic foreigners. These are complemented by assorted (usually) spinster teachers—mixtures of fairness, despotism, kindliness, sarcasm and eccentricity, but all exemplars of the ethics of middle-class self-improvement: hard-work, honesty, commitment and fair play. Combined with the promotion of these qualities are plots which mix fun with personal crises (not getting selected for the lacrosse First XI or struggling to pass a music exam), with the challenges of living away from home in a communal environment, with its possibilities for comradeship but also claustrophobia. It is an ordered world where head girls and prefects are given power and act as role models and enforcers of the school rules. What disruption there is comes when girls who do not 'fit in' threaten to disrupt the school's values and a kind of collective policing kicks in—sometimes in ways that can seem quaint or even snobbish. Thus, in *The Twins at St. Clare's*, Sheila, a new girl from a family whose wealth is recent and self-made, is criticised for not washing properly (the implication is that this is a clue as to her family's working-class origins). She is later castigated by another pupil for faulty grammar: "'Haven't you learnt by now that decent people don't say "'Didn't ought to"'! My goodness, you talk about your servants, and your Rolls-Royce cars, your horse and your lake and goodness knows what - and then you talk like the daughter of the dustman!'" (*TStC*, 147). As an exchange, it comes across as unattractively snobbish but, to Blyton's devoted readers (some of whom were undoubtedly the daughters of dustmen) who were brought up to believe in the importance of class distinctions, such pompousness did not seem to matter. Other girls at St. Clare's—and later Malory Towers—are policed in a similar way. Sometimes St. Clare's does admit defeat and recalcitrant girls are asked to leave but there is never any suggestion that the school itself needs to alter its way of doing things.

One of the benefits of the school story, which Blyton was able to exploit, was the way in which each volume could begin with a new term. New pupils arrived at the school in every book, 'each of whom brings something fresh to the life of hard work, exciting experiences, school-girl tricks [and], happy days' gushed the *Coventry Herald*.[22] These ingredients are on display in *Claudine at St. Clare's*, the fifth book in the series, published in 1944. Twins, Pat and Isabel O'Sullivan are now in the fourth form (Blyton seems to have decided to omit a book dealing with the third). They return to St. Clare's and, from their form room, gaze out at 'miles of beautiful country. It was country they knew well now, and loved very much. Down below, in the school grounds, were the tennis-courts, the games fields, and the big swimming-pool...the school gardens too, and the big kitchen garden full of fresh vegetables' (*CStC*, 2). It is a return to the familiar in an uncertain world, but there are outside 'threats' in the shape of some new girls: Angela Favorleigh and Pauline Bingham-Jones (both labelled "'disgusting snob[s]'"), Eileen Patterson (daughter of the 'thin and sour-looking' new matron)—and therefore a 'charity' student (*CStC*, 5; 48), and Claudine (niece of Mam'zelle, the school's eccentric French mistress). As the volume's title suggests, it is

Claudine—Blyton's nod to internationalism—who dominates the story. Her 'un-English ways', which include an open dislike of sport (she tricks Matron into giving her extra sewing so as to avoid games), and her readiness to cheat openly at her schoolwork, come across as at odds with those of her school-mates and refreshingly so, although that may not have been the intention in 1944. This is not least because one of the striking things about this novel— although not perhaps surprising given its appearance in war-time—is the space given over to myths about national identity, team spirit and fair play. In one scene, Miss Theobald, the 'wise' headmistress, explains the meaning of 'honour' to the flippant Claudine:

> 'You speak lightly of it, even mockingly – but I think, Claudine, in your heart of hearts you see it for the good and fine thing it really is. When you go back to France, Claudine, take one thing with you – the English sense of honour'.
> Claudine looked solemn. She was very much moved. (*CStC*, 118)

In other ways the story is business as usual. There are questions to answer and mysteries to solve: someone is stealing money from Matron's room. Who? Why does Eileen's brother visit her secretly? Where are Pauline's parents? Why do they never visit her? The solving of these puzzles is inevitable—nothing is secret for long in the confines of the boarding school, as Pauline finds out when she is unmasked as the daughter of plain Mr. and Mrs. Jones, who are definitely not of the 'top drawer'. Pupils can never pretend to be something other than they are: the truth will always out. This emphasis on honesty is an important lesson, but Blyton also uses storylines involving Pauline and Angela to make comments on social snobbery as well as showing how catty teenage girls can be. Angela, in particular, is unpleasant and 'spiteful' (*CStC*, 39). Her surface appeal—blonde beauty, moneyed background and conspicuous consumption—prompt admiration from a few (weak-minded) girls but her arrogance and readiness to blackmail Eileen cause disquiet and disgust in the others. Angela's father has sent her to St. Clare's to be moulded into a more responsible, sober type of modern womanhood, but on Parents' Day (another ritual) it becomes evident that the biggest obstacle to all this is Angela's glamorous mother, of whom the hapless Angela is a miniature version. One of the terrors of school (then as now) is to have parents who do not pass muster or who make a 'show' of themselves, and Mrs. Favorleigh is one of them. Her mean-spirited comments about the school and its pupils are duly punished and in a way that hurts her most. Claudine, after hearing her aunt ('Mam'zelle') mocked, overcomes her fear of the water and executes a fall into the swimming pool and, in the process, soaks Mrs. Favorleigh in her *haute couture* outfit. In the world of the story this is rough justice at its exemplary best: physically uncomfortable and personally humiliating. But it is also a prime example of how mothers, like the school's teachers, are shown to act as examples of future possibilities. Great store is set on having a mother who is also a role model: kindness, competence (social *and* domestic), good sense and generosity are the most admired qualities. Although separated from them, their mothers' influence on the St. Clare's pupils is always acknowledged. For all that it is a model of good educational practice, St. Clare's can only do so much.

The St. Clare's series ends abruptly with *Fifth Formers of St. Clare's* (1945) and the O'Sullivan twins being made joint Head Girl, the pinnacle of achievement. It is testimony to their ability to carry what their headmistress describes as 'the weight of leadership and responsibility on their shoulders' (*FFStC*, 160). It is not clear why Blyton did not carry on the series. She may have intended to but became overwhelmed by other projects. Or it may have been a backlash in the face of the changing political and social landscape after 1945. Complaints about the genre's narrow social range did crop up. In 1949, Naomi Lewis lamented the fact that she had not come across a single recent school story set in a state or a progressive school. She confessed herself weary of fictional public-school children, 'bouncing and undistinguished', their tuck-shops, feasts and careless parents 'making the flimsiest of arrangements for their family's welfare' before flying off abroad.[23] This was also a criticism made by Geoffrey Trease in his important study *Tales Out of School* (1949), which argued that children's literature should be a serious subject for study. Writing specifically of Blyton, his view was that the school stories were entertaining but 'they can hardly be said to go far in depicting reality, stimulating the imagination or educating the emotions'. He continued:

Their style, drained of all difficulty until it achieves a kind of aesthetic anaemia, is the outstanding example of …[the] trend towards semi-basic.…The exclamation-marks which often splash across the page like raindrops, suggest the kindergarten teacher telling the story 'with expression'.

At the same time, Trease admitted, he was fighting a losing battle:

The idea of boarding-school – the escape from at least parental authority, and the companionship of the dormitory fascinates millions of English children who realise that they have not the slightest chance of experiencing the reality and are thankful, with the rational part of their minds that they have not.[24]

Yet, any negative reactions against the genre proved slow to take hold. As far as authors were concerned, it was partly pragmatism. Secondary modern schools were day schools and did not offer the same creative opportunities. Children were in lessons most of the time and went home at 3.30. It was harder to generate plots. When Trease demonstrated it *was* possible to write about day pupils in his own 'Bannerdale' series (1949–1956) he remained one of the exceptions.

The six books in Blyton's Malory Towers series (1946–1951) made, if anything, a greater impression than St. Clare's in their idealisation of school life. As Trease was aware, their lack of 'reality' did not matter. In fact, like the earlier series, the atmosphere of the Malory Towers books is best described as '*un*real' (deliberately so) and the novels again presented readers with what Jeffrey Richards terms an 'alternative universe' to the drab world of post-war Britain.[25] Far away in Cornwall, Malory Towers appears to be as firmly sealed off from world events and working-class contagion as was St. Clare's. The first glimpse of the school is of a vaguely fortress-like building. However, it is far from being a grim prison and its classrooms are not those of the urban, brick-built secondary-modern. Instead it is a place of beauty, standing 'high up and overlooking the cliff. Down below was the blue Cornish sea, as blue as cornflowers today, the waves tipped with snowy white' (*IFMT*, 7).

Beginning with *First Term at Malory Towers* (1946) and ending with *Last Term at Malory Towers* (1951), the stories take in the boarding school career of Darrell Rivers, who is twelve when the series begins and eighteen—and Head Girl—when it finishes. What is striking about her journey is that it is by no means as frivolous as Geoffrey Trease would have us believe. Alongside the focus on sport—tennis, lacrosse, swimming—Blyton follows a familiar pattern of the school as a place of opportunity and self-discovery (in this she was no different from Elinor Brent-Dyer [1894–1969], Dorita Fairlie Bruce [1885–1970] and many others). There is also—and this is apparent in Blyton's work more generally, of course—a kind of idealisation of child-hood on display. There is never any trace of sexual feeling, an attempt perhaps to combat fears of 'teenage precocity', which the popularity of home-grown, blonde, 'busty' film starlets like Diana Dors and Christine Norden seemed to signal in the late 1940s.[26] Alarm bells do sound in *Third Year at Malory Towers* (1948) with the arrival of a new pupil, Zerelda Brass, with her 'glinting hair the colour of brass, arranged in a big roll on the top of her head, with curls cascading over her shoulders....She looked like somebody out of the films' (*TYMT*, 4). By wearing lipstick and powder Zerelda looks 'really grown-up' and the other girls are slightly awestruck (at first) (*TYMT*, 6). She is pleased with the effect she has, thinking she looks like 'Lossie Laxton, the film-star she admired most of all' (*TFMT*, 24).

The school is also shown as a place full of tension: there is thieving and bullying (*In Second Form at Malory Towers* [1947]), physical assault (*Upper Fourth at Malory Towers* [1949]) and spiteful anonymous letters (*In the Fifth at Malory Towers* [1950]). Thus, the pupils do not always behave well. In *First Term at Malory Towers*, Darrell's classmate, Sally Hope, an only child, is consumed with first-born jealousy (as psychologists would diagnose it) when her mother has a second baby, a girl. Sally views being packed off to Malory Towers as proof she is no longer wanted. The idea that siblings might not get on with each other is apparent too, in *In the Fifth at Malory Towers*, where two sisters, Moira and Bridget, exhibit an unalloyed mutual hatred that is never resolved.

Alongside this, and save for the obvious fact that there are no men to mess things up, the school is also presented as a microcosm of the outside world; the different—often awkward—personalities Darrell encounters amongst her fellow pupils—Sally, Catherine, Moira, Maureen, Alicia, Daphne, Irene, Belinda, Mary Lou, Clarissa, Gwendoline, June, Felicity, Connie, Ruth Wilhelmina (Bill, the 'tomboy'), all with their seemingly old-fashioned 1930s names—suggest not simply a selection of people for different readers to find identification with, but a societal and psychological cross-section with whom Darrell must learn to work and coexist. In this sense, education is not just about doing well in the School Certificate but about sociality (pupils rarely spend time on their own), social duty, and becoming a functioning member of society—at least insofar as the school's teachers define it. Gradually the pupils recognise this as well, as this extract from the penultimate volume, *In the Fifth at Malory Towers* makes explicit. The speaker is Darrell:

> 'I suppose any good boarding-school does the same things—makes you stand on your own feet, rubs off your corners, teaches you common-sense, makes you accept responsibility.'
> 'It depends on the person!' said Sally, with a laugh. 'It doesn't seem to have taught dear Gwendoline Mary much.'
> 'Well, I suppose there must be exceptions'. (*IFMT*, 100)

One of the things that emerges in Malory Towers—the later volumes in particular—is the recognition (on display here) that post-school life might involve more than domesticity. The series is full of nods to what women are and are supposed to be. The need for "'women the world can lean on'" is a mantra (*IFMT*, 20). In contrast, physical beauty is shown to be of little importance; the girls are 'pleasant looking' or occasionally 'pretty' but their looks have no currency—yet. There is a sense, meanwhile, that consciously or not, Blyton's depictions of the older pupils' discussions about what to 'do' mirrors the sorts of discussions taking place in the outside world and urged by more obviously feminist contemporaries like Vera Brittain and Barbara Castle, who pleaded with parents not to restrict their daughters' opportunities. In 1952, Castle wrote of 'the social revolution which has taken place [since the war]' and warned that the emerging generation of young women 'will never go back to the old ways'.[27] Inside Malory Towers, Darrell Rivers and her friends are looking to turn their backs—at least temporarily—on the traditional paths available to women; Darrell is not (for the moment), going to be like her mother.

In turn, it is hard not to notice that the ambition of the most unpopular girl in the school, Gwendoline Mary Lacey, to attend a '"very, very select"' Swiss finishing school, is viewed as a silly investment: '"Dad"', she reports, '"said it was too expensive and…all nonsense, and I ought to get a job – a *job*"' (LTMT 37; 10). Gwendoline will end up like her mother, a clingy, selfish woman for whom fluffy femininity has been an effective weapon but has also meant she has contributed very little to the world. In contrast, Blyton presents the other girls' ambitions for university education and careers as impeccable and attractive—certainly more attractive than Gwendoline's wish to spend her life being helpless, decorative—and lazy. '"Why aren't there any nice *feminine* girls here"', she asks, '"ones who like to talk and read quietly, and not always go pounding about the lacrosse field or splash in that horrible pool!"' (*UFMT*, 40).

One of the reasons why Gwendoline is always represented as antithetical to Darrell and her friends is because she is a bastion of out-moded, genteel female values in which her mother's training has worked almost too well: idle, helpless, '"beastly and selfish"' with 'a silly, weak face', she is the embodiment of self-interest (*LTMT*, 39; 41). At the same time, it is her scheming and her egocentricity which make her the series' most interesting character, though this may not have been Blyton's intention. While the other girls discuss university, art school or running their own businesses, Gwendoline wants to put herself outside the possibility of direct action, refusing her father's request that she get a job and treating him cruelly in the process. '"I'm *glad* I've made him miserable – it'll teach him a lesson!"', she says of her long-suffering parent and she is triumphantly pleased by this demonstration of her power (*LTMT*, 41). In turn, Gwendoline is uncomprehending of her classmates' legitimate ambitions, unable to believe anything other than that a middle-class woman should be ornamental and that her husband or father should provide for her. As the series' anti-heroine, she negotiates and embraces a set of ideologies that are simultaneously constructs and very real for her; her desire for a place at a Swiss finishing school is driven by them and the teachings of Malory Towers have little effect. It is in this sense that the school stories can be read as a powerful attack on the subject positions available to middle-class girls for much of the twentieth century. But, as the series draws to a close, it is also very clear that, as far as Gwendoline is concerned "'a terrible lesson'" is around the corner and "'[s]omewhere in her life, punishment is awaiting'" (*LTMT*, 42). At the end of *Last Term at Malory Towers* Gwendoline receives the news that her father has had a stroke and that her role is to look after him and her weak mother, at the same time as living a 'dull and humdrum life' working in an office (*LTMT*, 147).

In looking at these examples it seems clear that at some level, Blyton was persuaded by contemporary feminist arguments about the need for women to be given the same educational, political and social opportunities as men. Their role, as explained to them in *Last Term at Malory Towers* is to "'go out into the [post-war] world'" equipped with "'eager minds, kind hearts and a will to help'" (*LTMT*, 21). Being a woman is not a problem. But there *is* a sense, as Mavis Reimer points out, that 'what was wanted of girls' was still 'quite different from what was wanted of boys'.[28] The exhortations on the Malory Towers pupils to be "'good, sound women'", able to make themselves "'kind…and trustable'", suggests a different trajectory than that which might be set out for men (*LTMT*, 21). The girls are encouraged to look forward to a life beyond school and to putting into practice what they have been taught but, while the overall thrust is forward-looking, it is also the case that here, as in other novels, Blyton herself cannot think too far ahead. As we saw in the previous chapter, she was a stickler for tradition, and this may have been one reason why boarding schools with their sensitivities to issues of order and hierarchy appealed as settings. In both the Malory Towers and the St. Clare's series the schools are spaces which work to encourage particular ideas about what is 'normal' and also the consequences of deviating from prescribed codes of conduct for women. It is for this reason that one of the things that Malory Towers seeks to do is contain what might be termed feminine excess. The girls are never allowed to be too eccentric or ambitious. This is a point made in *Last Term at Malory Towers* where the fate of arrogant new pupil Amanda, who is training to compete in the 1952 Olympics, is to have the muscles of her leg torn on rocks when she takes an illegal swim. It is hubris, a punishment not only for her conceit but her unwillingness to be part of the community. This kind of moral story was a favourite of Blyton's. In 1951, readers might perhaps have spotted that Amanda's fate is a reworking of a storyline from *Third Year at Malory Towers* (1948), in which Mavis, a talented but spoiled new girl, obsessed with the thought of becoming an opera singer, disobeys school rules to take part in a talent contest in the belief that this is a sure-fire way of becoming famous. She misses the last bus home and is found collapsed at the side of the road; she survives but loses her precious voice. "'I've lost it – perhaps forever!'" she realises. "'I've been an idiot'" (*TYMT*, 140). It is when characters dream too big and too early and try to seize fame and fortune prematurely that they are most vulnerable and, it is suggested, most irresponsible. Whether intended or not, there is a strong contrast with the kind of precocious career girl celebrated in contemporaneous novels by Noel Streatfeild, notably *Curtain Up* (1946) and *The Painted Garden* (1949), in which performing in public, even in Hollywood, is presented as a viable option and a sign of self-reliance. In contrast, and bursting with energetic potential though they may be, the aspirations of Blyton's obsessive schoolgirls Amanda, Mavis and would-be film star, Zerelda, don't come to very much at all.

Family Stories

Alongside the publication of the Malory Towers stories, Blyton was also developing a collection of family novels for Lutterworth, including *The Family at Red-Roofs* (1945), *The Put- 'Em-Rights* (1946) and *House-at-the-Corner* (1947). Blyton explained that in writing these stories she aimed to give 'a small replica of life' and 'a novel in miniature for childhood', which took as its basis not thrilling adventures but 'the play of one character on another'. There would be 'fun' but above all 'the importance of family life – the "one for all and all for one" idea should be stressed'.[29]

The most ambitious of these books was *House-at-the-Corner* and, while it is little known, there are good reasons for revisiting it, not least for the way in which it embodies some of the main concerns of Blyton's postwar works more generally, particularly as they relate to female characters. Like other family stories, the novel's concerns are played out against a series of life-changing challenges—financial, moral and medical—encountered by an apparently model family. The opening chapter sets the scene. The Farrell family comprise a surgeon father, a lazy stay-at-home-mother and five contrasting children: clever, beautiful Pam, irresponsible Mike, kindly, put-upon Lizzie and the nature-obsessed twins, David and Delia. They look to have perfect lives in 'an old rambling house, big and lovely, moss growing here and there on its old red tiles. Round it spread a garden as rambling as the house itself, full of flowers' (HC, 8). However, what Blyton is also concerned to emphasise is the disjunction between appearance and reality, the most striking suggestion being that cruelty and neglect are as much part of the fabric of middle-class life as anywhere else. The novel shows Blyton at her best. It is gripping and insightful, tautly plotted but also multi-layered. Thematically it covers a range of topics and strands of late 1940s debate, each of which was a concern to the public: the 'best' type of education for children, careers for girls, motherhood and housecraft as woman's true vocation, social responsibility and lack of discipline in the young that, if not checked, could lead to delinquency. The novel's central premise is the importance of 'united' families and Blyton (writing perhaps from personal experience) places a good deal of emphasis on getting along and repairing quarrels before they fester irrevocably (*HC*, 51).

The novel begins with the arrival at the family's home of their eccentric Great Aunt Grace and her talking parrot, Sukie (both unwelcome guests). Aunt Grace knows she is tolerated, not loved, by her relatives but imposes herself on them anyway because the alternative for an elderly unmarried woman is worse. "'I'm afraid'", she confesses, "'of living alone….I've made a lot of mistakes in my life, and I remember them when I'm alone. I'm a lonely old woman, and I want life and friends around me – yes, even if people don't want me, I still want to be with them!'" (*HC*, 11). Her closest relationship is with Lizzie who, like her, exists on the fringes of the family: a "'[n]ice child – but very plain'", her teeth imprisoned by disfiguring braces and her 'gawky' appearance topped off with "'ugly glasses'" (*HC*, 13; 9; 117). As is often the case in Blyton's stories, one of the family's servants, in this case, the gardener's plain-speaking wife, Mrs. Frost, is one of the few people shrewd enough to see how things really stand; like Aunt Grace, she recognises Lizzie's worth and that, "'for all their handsome ways and smarty talk'", Lizzie is better than her "'spoilt'" siblings with their social polish. "'I've no time for them'" she says (*HC*, 20).

The novel's interest in the choices open to teenage girls as they approach adulthood—what they want (or think they want), and the kinds of behaviour they exhibit while trying to obtain it—is played out most strikingly in the character of Pam, who is seventeen, 'vain' and "'stuck-up'" (both damning Blyton pejoratives) (*HC*, 7). She is the character in the story who stands out as most representative of modern young womanhood—or at least what Blyton disliked about it. In common with everyone else, Pam admires her own golden hair and long eyelashes and, allied with her academic prowess, is counting on them being the passport to a comfortable life. Hers is, as the narrator reminds readers, a blinkered vison: 'She didn't see the hard little mouth that spoilt her pretty face, nor the frown-lines that told of bad temper. She only saw a very pretty face, clever and attractive' (*HC*, 16). As Pam explains to an admiring friend, she expects to "'take a fine job somewhere, and make a lot of money'", and then (using her beauty as a commodity) "'I shall marry a very rich man, and have poor old Lizzie to stay with me...'" (*HC*, 16–7). It is no surprise to anyone, least of all Pam herself, when she is cast as the beautiful princess in the school play, the showiest role, which will give her ample opportunity to bask in the audience's admiration. As an actress she is stiff and wooden and, as the narrator explains, this is because she is too full of self-love and, being devoid of empathy, is unable to imagine herself in anyone else's shoes. Her younger sister, Delia, recognises that Pam "'doesn't really *belong* to the family'" and this is because she has already removed herself from it, in her mind at least, because they are not polished enough for her (*HC*, 49). Pam's egotism reaches its peak in her displays of viciousness to her hard-working father who thinks her "'hard and wilful'" (*HC*, 40). Punishment arrives—as it always does is in Blyton's stories—when her father is critically injured in a car crash and, like the karma which overtakes Gwendoline Lacey in *Last Term at Malory Towers*, Pam is forced to reconsider, shame-facedly, her own conduct towards him. This is topped off by public humiliation when she fails to win the university scholarship everyone has been expecting. In this sense Pam's story is an act of confronting and paying the price for laziness and self-absorption. She has "'no character'" as one of her teachers observes (in a kind of unofficial school report). "'She would crack like a brittle stick if anything happened to her'" (*HC*, 35).

In addition to exposing a void at the heart of the family, *House-at-the-Corner* also taps into other issues relating to women's roles as these made themselves felt in post-war Britain. Blyton surveys the choices and restrictions on women and offers numerous representations of, and reflections on female behaviour. Readers are made aware, for example, of the different paths middle-class school-leavers might take once they have left the Sixth Form. In a long conversation between Pam and her seemingly timid friend, Joan, the latter explains:

'I want to be the centre of a home, like women used to be in the old days.'
    Pam stared at her. 'Whatever do you mean?' she said. 'The centre of a home! Why, girls are trying to get out of being in their homes now. Even married women take jobs outside their homes!'
    'Yes, I know all that,' said Joan, in an obstinate voice. 'But when I look at my mother and see how happy she is in her own home, and how we all love to be there, and when I see all the things she knows how to do so well, I just want to be like her, that's all....'

...Pam was astonished. 'You're mad,' she said at last. 'Fancy wanting to get *back* into your home when we girls have got the chance to get *out* of it. Everyone knows that housework and cooking are drudgery.' (*HC*, 31–2)

For once, Joan stands up to Pam. She explains herself as '"new-fashioned"', someone who envisages her life quite differently from what people might expect. '"I don't want to rush away from my home as girls have been doing for years – I want to be the centre of it, the star of it, making it lovely..."' (HC 33). Picturing herself as a kind of 1950s domestic goddess, Joan sees such a life as creative, privileged and empowering. Her aim is to '"learn how to run what all families long for and very few get – a really good home!"' (*HC*, 33). This is not presented as masochistic self-repression in the name of duty, which is often said to be typical of the grey 1950s, but an assertion of a way of life and of '"always having something different to do all the year round, not the same old routine of a musty little office"' (*HC*, 33). Meanwhile she sees, presciently, what is in store for Pam who, in employing an army of staff to do the cooking and cleaning, will become '"only half a woman..."' (*HC*, 34). Cooking, dusting and cleaning the cooker, these are the tasks which make up '"real women's work..."' (*HC*, 181). The fact that Blyton was writing this from her own fully staffed house is worth noting.

Comparison of Pam Farrell with other protagonists—those of the St. Clare's and Malory Towers series, for example—suggests that Blyton intended to do three main things when she focused specifically on female characters. First, to make a spectacle of femininity, whether of the sturdy, sensible variety (Darrell Rivers in *Malory Towers*/Anne in the Famous Five series) or in the form of the spoilt brat type (Gwendoline Lacey in *Malory Towers*/Angela Favorleigh in the St. Clare's series); second, to examine some of the social conventions under which women lived; third, to suggest that her female characters might have other desires beyond acting as assistant to their brothers or husbands. But there is also the suggestion that the trajectories of career and domesticity were not parallel lines which never meet. Instead there is recognition that, at some point in their futures, most young women would be forced to choose and that the 'proper' woman would commit herself to marriage, running a home and becoming a mother. In *House-at-the-Corner*, it is this which Pam is unwilling to countenance: '"Mess around the house! That was just what she didn't intend to do.... She would save her brains for better things"' (*HC*, 75–6). Whereas her friend Joan operates within a cultural framework that she both understands and ultimately wants to serve, Pamela is not so easily persuaded: it takes the shock of her father's car crash, invalidism and the family's resulting loss of income to shock and shame her out of her plans. She determines to '"learn all the things...a woman ought to know, the real things, the things that matter in every home, and I'll do them well"" (*HC*, 194). As she does so, readers are in no doubt (partly because they are told it several times) that she is "'all the better for knowing what every woman ought to know...'" (*HC*, 198).

Pam is the character that contributes most obviously and noisily to the novel's sense of disturbance, but she is not the only one. Others include Greta, the Austrian maid, taking refuge in a foreign country, whose guarded comments—"'I am alone, and my family is dead. It is a good thing to have a family, I tell you. I have none'"—hint at experiences in Nazi-controlled Europe worse than anything Blyton's 1940s readers could imagine (*HC*, 55); Mrs. Farrell, who accepts her comfortable domestic role complacently and idly, with the result that when disaster comes, she is ill-equipped to deal with it. As she explains pathetically: "'I'm not *very* good at facing up to trouble....I've always had people to do it for me....They've always tackled trouble for me'" (*HC*, 164). It is Mrs. Farrell's preferences for some of her children and her lack of involvement in the lives of others that provide the starting point for many of the novel's debates, one of which stems from their ideas about children's training (Pam has never been properly disciplined or even "'spanked'" as a child [*HC*, 78]). Alongside her preference for Pam, Mrs. Farrell favours the ostensibly charming Tony. She does not realise that their handsome surface is precisely that—a surface—and that underneath lurks cruelty and self-absorption, traits exhibited most obviously in these elder siblings' treatment of Lizzie, whom they despise. There is a strong sense of disturbance in the well-kept rooms of *House-at-the-Corner* and to a degree that is unusual in Blyton. It is one which is intensified by the bleak vision of family life which she presents: the home for some children, she suggests, is not a place of safety but neglect and bullying.

Not surprisingly, in its exposé of the failings at the heart of the English home and the attention given to a favourite child, *House-at-the-Corner* can seem an unusually pessimistic text. Its positive values lie partly in the enthusiasm exhibited by the nature-loving, ten-year-old twins, David and Delia and in the practical wisdom exhibited by Aunt Grace and her encouragement of the neglected middle child, Lizzie, whose story is the novel's second transformative narrative. It is made clear that the family's tendency to use the diminutive 'Lizzie', rather than her full name, 'Elizabeth', is not indicative of affection but the lack of importance they ascribe to her; it is perhaps more of a servant's name. In part she is her own worst enemy: "'there's not enough *go* in you'", her aunt tells her (*HC*, 11). Lizzie is a doormat and her passive acceptance of her role as her elder siblings' servant and punchbag is hard to shake off.

What saves Lizzie is her passion for writing. She writes stories in secret, knowing the family will mock her ambition, but is discovered by Aunt Grace who thinks the work '"amazingly good. Interesting – and simple – and really amusing"' (*HC*, 61). She counsels Lizzie to pursue her vocation: '"Those of us who have gifts"' she tells her—and there is a sense of Blyton's own voice breaking through here—'"are the lucky ones – if we use them properly. You certainly have a gift. You must go on and on. You will give many people great pleasure"' (*HC*, 62). Although Lizzie thinks that, if she had a story printed, she would '"die of happiness!"', she eventually sends one to *The Quiet Magazine* (*HC*, 62). It is rejected and when her siblings, as she feared, mock her presumption, she flies into a rage and tears up the typescript. However, eventually she types it out again with her aunt's reprimand ringing in her ears: '"If you've not got a character strong enough to stand a defeat or disappointment now and again, you're not fit to be a great writer"' (*HC*, 69–70). Lizzie posts the freshly typed story again—wishing it good luck 'when the letter goes "plop" into the pillar box' (*HC*, 80). This time a paper not only accepts the story but syndicates it to other magazines. This, leads to Lizzie being commissioned for a series of similar tales. As disaster strikes and the family loses its income, it is Lizzie who Blyton reconfigures as the family wage-earner, whose dedication to the craft of writing proves not only enjoyable but profitable as well. 'She had not attempted grown-up stories. She felt she didn't know enough to do that. But she could write stories for children. She knew exactly how to tell those, because for many years she had told Delia and David stories when they were in bed' (*HC*, 60). The idea that Lizzie is a version of the young Enid Blyton is perhaps one reason that the novel's heroine is imagined so strongly from within and why *House-on-the-Corner* is such a notable depiction of this particular teenage life.

This leads to another possibility, which is that in writing the novel what Blyton also wanted to do was write her own version of Louisa M. Alcott's *Little Women* (1868), a book for which she held a passion as a girl. She read it, she recalled, 'again and again' (*SML*, 48). Famously, the novel interrogates the expectations placed on the four March sisters by family and society. These include the notion that there is a domestic ideal that young women should aspire to, or at least train themselves to endure. But the novel also raises the ideas that some of them might have other aspirations, which in the case of the tomboy, Josephine ('Jo'), include wanting to become a writer. One of the reasons why the book endured was that it struck a chord: many girls were enthralled by, and identified with, Jo's ambitions and the obstacles put in her way, as well as her dislike of housework. The young Enid Blyton was one of them. Those who knew her made the point that she also did not fit into the patterns of behaviour expected of an Edwardian girl. Hanly Blyton recalled of his sister how 'at no time was she a normal child. A normal child was brought up docile and had to pay attention to what the mother and father said. But if she disagreed with anything she would always argue...particularly with my mother'.[30] Given what we know of Blyton's home life as a rebellious teenager with an absent father (his absence was another similarity to the March sisters) and her ambitions to get published, it is no surprise that the middle-aged Blyton should recall *Little Women* so fondly and seek to pay tribute to it. Jo March, accessible and very 'alive' in her similar battles, became an icon for single-minded readers like Blyton who shared her aspirations and were presumably disappointed when Alcott married her vital heroine off to the much-older Professor Bhaer.

This was not something Blyton allowed to happen to her own heroine. Instead, it is via Lizzie, rather than Pam, that Blyton hints at the possibilities for advancement and self-fulfilment outside the home, although she makes it clear that Lizzie's stories are published anonymously and that her actions are dictated by her passion for writing and subsequently by a desire to save the family from financial ruin, rather than by a desire for adulation. More importantly, writing brings self-worth, exemplified in a scene where the heroine, having had a succession of stories published, contemplates herself in the mirror:

> She took off her glasses and the wire from her front teeth. She pushed back her heavy dark hair and looked at herself in the glass. Her cheeks shone because she was happy over her story. Her cheeks were red. She looked quite different already, she thought – not pretty, like Pam, but not plain or homely anymore.
> 'That's *Elizabeth* in the mirror now,' she said to herself. 'I can always be Elizabeth when I want to. And I shan't tell anyone, then nobody can laugh and spoil it all!'. (*HC*, 30)

This spectacle of the heroine's feelings and her subsequent epiphany comes near the beginning of the novel. It contributes to the sense that while *House-at-the-Corner* can be seen as a liberating mediation on female subjectivity and selfhood, Blyton is also prone to resolve some issues conventionally. Being attractive matters. Lizzie's removal of her glasses seems akin to scenes favoured in Hollywood films of the 1940s and 1950s, where the hero removes the glasses of the (apparently) 'plain' heroine and discovers she has been beautiful all along. Of course, Lizzie's success is also intended to carry another, more liberating message—character and brains are what is important—and this element of the novel, like many of Blyton's stories, is escapist, offering young girls the possibilities of autonomy. But Blyton is also a realist and knows what matters to young women. As a young woman lacking the commodity of beauty, Lizzie is virtually invisible to everyone around her; most of them are indifferent to her and her voice can only be heard second-hand.

* * *

In writing her family stories, part of Blyton's interest was often, she explained, in the parents. 'I must say', she wrote, 'that, being (I hope) a good parent myself, I heave a sigh of relief when writing a Family story if I find the parents acting as I myself would act'.[31] All the texts discussed in this chapter present the reader with different kinds of parents, some intended to be admirable and others who are clearly failing—at least as Blyton saw it. However, some of the most striking representations come in *Six Cousins at Mistletoe Farm* (1948) and its sequel, *Six Cousins Again* (1950). On the one hand, these novels show Blyton keen to celebrate rural life and she again exploits a traditional fund of images of the English countryside by which to do so (leafy lanes, blue skies, open fields, rambling old farmhouses). In 1948, food-producing farmers were widely regarded as heroic figures after their efforts during the war and, in *Six Cousins at Mistletoe Farm*, the farming couple, Peter and Linnie Longfield, are presented in this vein, hard-working custodians of the land whose lives are fraught with difficulties. On the other hand, like *House-at-the-Corner*, these novels take the construction of the feminine (and also the masculine) as central concerns, particularly as this relates to the figure of the mother. Blyton's interest is again on the way in which some women fail to live up to their responsibilities and, the persuasive ways in which she presents this, embodies much of what she and others writing in the 1940s argued about the importance of 'mothercraft'.

The first novel, *Six Cousins at Mistletoe Farm* (dedicated to Blyton's younger daughter, Imogen, aged twelve, 'who chose and described all the horses in this book' [SC, 5]), follows a pattern familiar to Blyton's readers. Children who are strangers to one another are brought together by family circumstances and forced to mix. The fifteen-year-old twins, Jack and Jane, and eleven-year-old Susan are vexed when their spoilt town cousins, Cyril (sixteen), Melisande (fourteen) and Roderick (eleven), are billeted on the farm after their (uninsured) home has burnt down. Cyril and Melisande are judged '"[a]wful snobs – turning up their noses at everything..."' (SC, 15). Cyril, in particular,—who judges the farm and his cousins '"primitive"' (SC, 42)—is set up as in need of fixing; he is over-fond of poetry and music in a superior kind of way and wears his hair too long, a 'pretty, girlish boy, too plump, and with rather a stupid look on his pale face' (SC, 27). His sandals, beige corduroy velvet trousers, yellow shirt and floppy tie give him a "'namby-pamby'" air (*SC*, 50). Meanwhile, Melisande is 'vain' and prissy and Roderick is his "'[m]other's own boy!'" (*SC*, 84). As has been seen, Blyton is always interested in the possibilities of transformation and it is no surprise that the predictable part of the narrative is about how—out of the tensions and through being forced to muck in on the farm, which is presented as a kind of boot-camp—the six children help shape each other for the better. Melisande becomes stronger while Jane becomes less tomboyish and more conventionally feminine, especially when she realises a boy she is romantically inclined towards does not see her as attractive. Another improvement is the way the 'languid' Cyril transforms from a 'cissy' into a model young Englishman, 'sturdy and hard as nails' (*SC*, 49; 183). He begins to 'delight in his strength' and his skills at football and gains people's respect as a result (*SC*, 182). Although she is unlikely to have read it, Blyton's representations of the children seem to embody much of what her contemporary, Simone de Beauvoir, noted in *The Second Sex* (1949), about gender being cultural rather than something biological: 'one is not born a woman, one becomes one'. As Ruth Robbins notes, the reason why this remark has come to be seen as important is that it highlights the fact that 'the ideas about male and female roles which any given society may have come to regard as natural are not really so'.[32] In *Six Cousins* the boundaries at issue are the distinctions between boys and girls, the separate spheres of their existence and what needs to happen when either sex seems to question the construction of gender.

If Jane's acquisition of femininity and Cyril's acquisition of masculinity throws the focus onto social expectations as a major factor in defining identity, so too does the attention Blyton gives to the issue of maternity via their respective mothers. In contrast to the model mother, Linnie the farmer's wife, who is sensible, balanced and unselfish and whose pleasure comes from seeing the farm survive and her family flourish, Rose is the absent mother who is presented as weak and egotistical. This is hinted at when the reader learns that the reason why the town cousins need to be sent to Mistletoe Farm is that the house fire has caused Rose to collapse from nervous prostration, an act which is presented as being entirely in character. She is reported as being someone who "'always retires to bed when anything happens to hurt her family'", a display which is given short shrift by her relatives on the farm (*SC*, 14). These judgements pave the way for Rose's sole visit to see her children. Rose, whose appearance is 'like a beautiful china doll', arrives at the farm fussily dressed as if for a garden-party wherein she totters reluctantly round on her high heels unable to disguise her distaste at the dirt and the smells (*SC*, 94). For her children, however, it proves a transformative moment. Prior to their arrival at the farm they had been proud of their elegant mother, failing to notice how she 'fussed…pouted…simpered' or that she 'never looked very deep into anyone or anything' (*SC*, 16). In the environment of Mistletoe Farm she is out of place and has the air of a horrid germ bent on contagion, undoing the good work that has been achieved in making her children into better people. Over tea, she shames Melisande, pointing out that she has become unrecognisable, "*fat* - quite coarse-looking". That Melisande *has* put on weight—and grown—thanks to the farm's diet of manual labour and hearty food—is confirmed when she splits her best dress (*SC*, 87). Nor does Rose think much of the rest of the family. "'But he's so *dumb*, isn't he! So silent" she says of Jack (*SC*, 89). This may be true, but it is also the case that in these exchanges Blyton's point is that, while Rose's brittle, bitchy, conversation might pass muster at a cocktail party, the farm, a happy place, has no room for it. As the visit progresses, Roderick, who has always been his mother's 'pet', is 'shocked to find he was very bored' (*SC*, 90). Cyril is similarly disillusioned as he realises that 'a pretty mother with a fund of light conversation was amusing for a little while, but now that he had got so used to being on the go all the time, he found it difficult to sit in the darkened room indoors, and converse lightly and amiably with someone who treated him like a small and delightful boy' (*SC*, 93). Rose, as they all realise, does not belong to the world of Mistletoe Farm on which life is 'real' and 'earnest' (*SC*, 89).

Rose is acute enough to pick up on the differences that staying at Mistletoe Farm has wrought on her cossetted children: the farm is the antidote to her influence. Sensing rejection she storms off, lashing out proprietorially as she goes: "'I'm not wanted here – not even by my own children. I can see that. They're different. You've changed them", she tells Linnie (*SC*, 100). It is in this way that the narrative moves inexorably towards the children's re-education and the novel's imposition of a familiar Blytonian discourse of mothering, which is voiced by Linnie in this case: "'They've changed themselves", she tells Rose. "'They were spoilt, Rose. Now they're not" (*SC*, 100). At the same time, in the presentation of fashionably dressed Rose, readers are led to see something of the weakness of the doctrine that allows women a solely decorative function. As Linnie (again) puts it: "'[t]he wife should also be a responsible woman, Rose. And you are not. You won't take up your responsibilities. You don't help at all" (*SC*, 36). The novel suggests that such behaviour is unwomanly, depriving children and husband of support and guidance. The novel's examination of types of womanhood is summed up ('grimly') by the family's old retainer, Dorcas. She observes that Rose (who likes making 'scenes') represents a type of well-manicured woman with no real life of her own, who looks young because she is selfish: "'She does it by looking after herself so carefully and lovingly…that she hasn't time to look after anybody else, not even her own children'". In contrast, Linnie looks older, but this, Dorcas tells her, does not matter: '"There's more beauty in *your* face, seems to me…and I'm not talking about skin and eyes and nose now, Mam. I'm talking about character'" (*SC*, 91).

'Character' is one of those desirable attributes which feature a good deal in Blyton's work—whether it is set in schools, on holiday or on the farm—a legacy perhaps of the war wherein it was the display of character—a kind of moral grittiness and refusal to be ground down—which saw Britain survive. It is one of the things the pupils of Malory Towers must strive for and it reappears in *Six Cousins Again* (1950) which picks up with the characters of *Six Cousins at Mistletoe Farm* eight months after the events of that novel reach a conclusion. The sequel, in which the town cousins and their parents take on the running of a new farm, comes across as a much more urgent text than its predecessor, partly because of Blyton's continued excursions into the post-war debate about 'mothercraft'. In *The Reproduction of Mothering* Nancy Chodorow explains how girls have long been 'taught to be mothers, trained for nurturance, and told they ought to be mother….They are barraged from early childhood well into adult life with books, magazines ads, school courses…which put forth pronatalist and pro-maternal sex-stereotypes'.[33] One of the giveaways at the first post-war *Daily Mail* Ideal Home Exhibition in London in March 1947 was a 'Day-to-Day Plan' for new brides, advising them not only what different household tasks needed doing (there was enough to keep one busy six-and-a-half days a week) but what to wear while doing them. In *Six Cousins* and its sequel, *Six Cousins Again*, Blyton very clearly attempts to play a part in this conditioning and enjoys the monster she has created, ensuring that the character of Rose and her particular brand of awfulness loom large. '"[S]urely, I'm the kind of mother you want, aren't I?"', she asks her children. '"Just look at me"' (*SCA*, 32). Just as the problems of the children at the beginning of the earlier novel, wherein they are spoilt, weak and selfish, are problems presented as the direct result of Rose's irresponsible parenting, so the crisis of *Six Cousins Again* comes from Rose's predisposition to siphon the farm's small profits to fund the kind of lifestyle she thinks she ought to have, despite bankruptcy looming: breakfast in bed, applying her make-up, dainty afternoon teas, and not dirtying her hands with farm work. Her husband realises, albeit rather late in the day, that the woman he has married is incapable of being supportive, not 'the kind of wife you could tell bad news to – only good news' (SCA 128). Nor, will she cook. '"I've never needed to" she explains, "…And I hope I never shall"' (*SCA*, 89). Her one foray into the kitchen results in her cutting her finger opening a tin of cold meat, 'and she sat down for another five minutes because the sight of the blood upset her' (*SCA*, 151). Rose 'could', we are told, 'be very witty and amusing when she liked, and had a pretty, silvery laugh', but, as the novel progresses, she reveals herself to be spiteful, setting her children against their father (*SCA*, 39). Chapter 22 is titled 'An Enemy at Work', the enemy being Rose and, as in the previous novel, there is the sense that both as wife and mother she is a destructive rather than constructive influence. While the life of Rose's sister-in-law, Linnie, at neighbouring Mistletoe Farm takes place within a similar cultural framework centred round family and home that Linnie both accepts and embraces, Rose is not so easily controlled and leaves a trail of destruction in her wake. Doors slam and bills are unpaid. More seriously—at least within the gendered logic of the novel—she begins to re-feminise Cyril, giving his bedroom a 'girlish' makeover (*SCA*, 45). He, in turn, has fond memories of the eight months spent at Mistletoe Farm: "'I think perhaps it was good for us, Mother," he said. "It made me tough, you know – and I think I was a bit milk-and-watery before"' (*SCA*, 51). Under Rose's influence he reverts, becoming 'rather silly', as Roddy notes, 'spouting poetry again, and going on about the wonderful music on the Third Programme' (*SCA*, 156). Lack of space prevents further examination of this interesting novel but it is worth noting that one way of reading Blyton's powerful presentation of Rose is to see her as a kind of Home Counties version of what Toril Moi describes as '[t]he monster woman…who refuses to be selfless'.[34] The majority of the most crucial incidents in *Six Cousins Again*, in terms of the narrative progression of Rose's slide into a kind of vampirism, are occasions where she is exposed—sometimes in her own words, sometimes in her behaviour—as having misjudged the extent to which she can turn her back on her responsibilities.

* * *

Although not as popular as Blyton's adventure or school stories, *House-at-the-Corner*, *Six Cousins at Mistletoe Farm* and *Six Cousins Again* invite, like the more famous series, inspection by anyone interested in the issues surrounding the topic of female voices, particularly as this relates to post-war Britain and the move to the new Elizabethan age of the 1950s. Yet, in trying to locate Blyton's writing about women within some of the contexts in which they were produced and read, the situation is complex. All of Blyton's texts stress the importance of education for girls and validate creativity and the love of learning. They suggest that fulfilment and a sense of self are desirable. In *House-at-the-Corner* Pam Farrell is represented as having lost her moral bearings but also as misunderstanding what she is expected to do in 1947, in a decade still ruled by assumptions about the home as being women's proper sphere, but which was also full of calls for women to move towards something else. Modern readers might feel that Pam is possibly deserving of more sympathy than Blyton is prepared to grant her, not least since the author's approval of her character is entirely dependent on her putting on an apron in a rather penitent way at the end of the novel. Yet this is in line with the fate of most of Blyton's female characters for whom it is suggested that they can only really be safe and fulfilled within a conventional family unit as loving wives and selfless mothers. In a curious way we can say that Blyton's stance is akin to that of the post-war Labour Prime Minster Clement Atlee in his statement about modernisation, made in 1950: 'I think', he explained, that 'the British have the distinction above all other nations of being able to put new wine into old bottles without bursting them'.[35] New ideas emerge but they are blended with existing ones and the effect is one of continuity. This seems as far as Blyton—who was in many senses a conventional woman of her time, despite her career—was prepared to go. After 1945, motherhood was loudly championed as one of the pillars of society. The images of women Blyton presented to her readers, and the plots of female destiny foisted on female characters are political in that they fit in this pattern. They also offer glimpses of the way in post-war Britain social control was maintained through representation and stereotype.

A coda to all this might be, of course, that the transgressive—'selfish'—girls and women in the stories—Amanda, Zerelda or Rose (who refuses to '"slave"' [SCA, 196])—re-represent fantasies of escape from gender roles or attacks on the subject positions available to women. Typically, of course, these interesting characters are usually squashed, contained or removed near the end as Blyton hurriedly closes up the gaps within contemporary ideologies of gender and re-establishes 'normality'. But their presence is significant. Nancy K. Miller has suggested that novels by women about women which depend on too-convenient narrative endings can also manifest 'the extravagant wish for a *story* that would turn out differently'.[36] That is, they suggest possible—unspoken—rebellion against the expectations of the conventional plot which the author—in this case Blyton—cannot bring herself to do. Thus, exactly how we might read the anti-social women who reappear throughout Blyton's work is a point of contention. Are readers expected to cheer when they are punished? Or do we sympathise with their predicament? One of our tasks in reading Blyton historically is to be alert to these seeming contradictions.

Notes

1. Vera Brittain, *Lady into Woman: A History of Women from Victoria to Elizabeth II* (London: Andrew Dakers, 1953), 8.
2. Audrey Lucas, 'Children's Shelf', *The Observer* (12 December 1943), 3.
3. Unsigned Article, 'Books for Children', *The Birmingham Daily Post* (5 December 1944), 2.
4. Unsigned Article, 'Books for Christmas', *The Birmingham Daily Post* (4 December 1945), 2.
5. Unsigned Article, 'New Books: The O'Sullivan Twins', *Coventry Standard* (12 September 1942), 7.
6. Peter, Hawley, 'Enid Blyton's Twenty Books a Year', *Reading Lamp* (1 July 1947), 12–15 (15).
7. Donald Mackenzie, 'Pot-boilers? No!', *W.H. Smith's Trade Circular* (2 December 1950), 13. See also: Enid Blyton, 'My Week', *W.H. Smith's Trade Circular* (10 September 1949), 9.
8. Barbara Creed, 'Kristeva, Femininity, Abjection', in *The Horror Reader*, ed. Ken Gelder (London: Routledge, 2000), 64.
9. Margo D. Maine, *Father Hunger: Fathers, Daughters and Food* (1991; Carlsbad, CA: Gurze Books, November 1993), xiv.
10. George Greenfield, *Enid Blyton* (Stroud: Sutton, 1998), 35; 39.
11. Donald Mackenzie, 'Pot Boilers? No!', 13; 15.
12. See Penny Tinkler, *Constructing Girlhood: Popular Magazines for Girls Growing up in England 1920–1950* (London: Taylor and Francis, 1985), 58–61; Penny Summerfield, *Reconstructing Women's Wartime Lives: Discourse and Subjectivity in Oral Histories of the Second World War* (Manchester: Manchester University Press, 1998); Helen McCarthy, *Double Lives: A History of Working Motherhood* (London: Bloomsbury, 2020).
13. Kenneth Howards, *Sex Problems of the Returning Soldier* (Manchester: Sydney Pemberton, n.d., 1945), 62–3, in Gail Braybon and Penny Summerfield, *Out of the Cage: Women's Experiences in Two World Wars* (London: Routledge, 1987), 271.
14. David Kynaston, *A World to Build: Austerity Britain 1945–48* (2007; London: Bloomsbury, 2008), 98.
15. Richard Titmuss, *Essays on the Welfare State*, 102, quoted in Helen McCarthy, 'Social Science and Married Women's Employment in Post-War Britain', *Past and Present* 233:1 (2016), 269–305 (277).
16. Rosamond Lehmann, *The Echoing Grove* (London: Collins, 1953), 311.
17. Barbara Castle, 'Women's Work: Men's Views on It and Women's', *John o'London's Weekly* (16 May 1952), 2.
18. Rosemary Auchmuty, *A World of Girls: The Appeal of the Girls' School Story* (London: The Women's Press, 1992), 15.
19. Unsigned Article, 'Girls' School Stories', *The Times Literary Supplement* (25 November 1926), 865.

20. Declan Kiberd, 'School Stories', in *Studies in Children's Literature 1500–2000*, eds. Celia Keenan and Mary Shine (Dublin: Four Courts Press, 2005), 54–69 (58–9).

21. E.W. Hildick, 'The Modern School Story', *Books and Bookmen* (October 1960), 35.

22. Unsigned Review, 'Summer Term at St. Clare's', *Coventry Standard* (1 May 1943), 4.

23. Naomi Lewis, 'Girls and Boys', *The New Statesman* (8 October 1949), 394.

24. Geoffrey Trease, *Tales Out of School* (London: Heinemann, 1949), 138–9.

25. Jeffrey Richards, 'From Greyfriars to Grange Hill', in *School Stories: From Bunter to Buckeridge, NCRCL Papers 4*, ed. Nicholas Tucker (Roehampton: National Centre for Children's Literature, 2002), 35–51 (44).

26. David Kynaston, *A World to Build*, 209.

27. Barbara Castle, 'Women's Work', 2.

28. Mavis Reimer, 'Traditions of the School Story', in *The Cambridge Companion to Children's Literature*, eds. M.O. Grenby and Andrea Immel (Cambridge: Cambridge University Press, 2009), 209–225 (216).

29. Enid Blyton, 'The Family Story', *The Author* 69:1 (1958), 11.

30. Hanly Blyton quoted in *A Child-like Person*, dir. Roger Thompson BBC Radio 4 (19 August 1975), 07.33. https://www.bbc.co.uk/archive/a-childlike-person/zvvt8xs. Accessed 14 March 2021.

31. Enid Blyton, 'The Family Story', 11.

32. Simone De Beauvoir, *The Second Sex* (1949), quoted by Ruth Robbins, '"Snowed Up": Feminist Perspectives', in *Literary Theories*, eds. Julian Wolfreys and William Baker (Basingstoke: London: Macmillan, 1996), 103–26 (118).

33. Nancy Chodorow, *The Reproduction of Mothering* (Los Angeles: University of California Press, 1999), 31.

34. Toril Moi, *Sexual/Textual Politics: Feminist Literary Theory* (London: Methuen, 1985), 65.

35. Quoted in Becky Conekin, Frank Mort, and Chris Waters, 'Introduction', in *Moments of Modernity: Reconstructing Britain 1945–1964* (London: Rivers Oram Press, 1999), xiii.

36. Nancy Miller, 'Emphasis Added: Plots and Plausibilities in Women's Fiction', in *The New Feminist Criticism*, ed. Elaine Showalter (London: Virago, 1986), 339–60 (352).

Bibliography

Auchmuty, Rosemary. *A World of Girls: The Appeal of the Girls' School Story*. London: The Women's Press.

Braybon, Gail, and Penny Summerfield. 1987. *Out of the Cage: Women's Experiences in Two World Wars*. London: Routledge.

Brittain, Vera. 1953. *Lady into Woman: A History of Women from Victoria to Elizabeth II*. London: Andrew Dakers

Castle Barbara. 1952. 'Women's Work: Men's Views on It and Women's'. *John o'London's Weekly* (16 May), 2–3.

Chodorow, Nancy. 1999. *The Reproduction of Mothering*. Los Angeles: University of California Press.

Conekin, Becky, Frank Mort, and Chris Waters. 1999. *Moments of Modernity: Reconstructing Britain 1945–1964*. London: Rivers Oram Press.

Gelder, Ken. Editor. 2000. *The Horror Reader*. London: Routledge.

Greenfield, George. 1998. *Enid Blyton*. Stroud: Sutton.

Kiberd, Declan. 2005. 'School Stories'. In *Studies in Children's Literature 1500–2000*, edited by Celia Keenan and Mary Shine: 54–69. Dublin: Four Courts Press.

Kynaston, David. 2008. *A World to Build: Austerity Britain 1945–48*. London: Bloomsbury.

Lehmann, Rosamond. *The Echoing Grove*. London: Collins.

Maine, Margo D. 1991. *Father Hunger: Fathers, Daughters and Food*. Carlsbad, CA: Gurze Books.

McCarthy, Helen. 2016. 'Social Science and Married Women's Employment in Post-War Britain'. *Past and Present* 233(1): 269–305.

———. 2020. *Double Lives: A History of Working Motherhood*. London: Bloomsbury.

Miller, Nancy K. 1986. 'Emphasis Added: Plots and Plausibilities in Women's Fiction'. In *The New Feminist Criticism*, edited by Elaine Showalter: 339–60. London: Virago.

Moi, Toril. 1985. *Sexual/Textual Politics: Feminist Literary Theory*. London: Methuen.

Reimer, Mavis. 2009. 'Traditions of the School Story'. In *The Cambridge Companion to Children's Literature*, edited by M.O. Grenby and Andrea Immel: 209–225. Cambridge: Cambridge University Press.

Richards, Jeffrey Richards. 1999; 2002. 'From Greyfriars to Grange Hill'. In *School Stories: From Bunter to Buckeridge, NCRCL Papers 4*, edited by Nicholas Tucker: 35–51. Roehampton: National Centre for Children's Literature.

Robbins, Ruth. 1996. '"Snowed Up": Feminist Perspectives'. In *Literary Theories*, edited by Julian Wolfreys and William Baker: 103–26. Basingstoke: London: Macmillan.

Summerfield, Penny. 1998. *Reconstructing Women's Wartime Lives: Discourse and Subjectivity in Oral Histories of the Second World War*. Manchester: Manchester University Press.

Tinkler, Penny. 1985. *Constructing Girlhood: Popular Magazines for Girls Growing Up in England 1920–1950*. London: Taylor and Francis.

Trease, Geoffrey. 1949. *Tales Out of School*. London: Heinemann.

10

Blyton and the 1950s

Britain in the 1950s conjures up a set of familiar images: a place where the coronation of the young Queen Elizabeth II in 1953 was watched by millions via their new television sets and in 1954 where Roger Bannister ran the first four-minute mile. The Festival of Britain had opened in 1951, its futuristic vision of the future attracting millions of visitors. An idea of progress was certainly part of the mood in post-war Britain—new towns and tower blocks were being built and by the mid-1950s there were plans to build nuclear power stations, with steam trains being gradually replaced with electric ones. In 1951 Enid Blyton, was given a gift of a biro—although she disliked it, thinking that this new kind of pen served to 'nationalise everyone's hand-writing!' (Mac, 31 January 1951). Yet for all the talk about modernity, there were areas where the country did not feel much different from the 1930s and 1940s. As Peter Hennessey has noted, the British people's 'still-vivid memory' of themselves in the war ('brave, heroic, energetic and world-saving') was clung to 'like a comfort blanket', even as the country lost world influence.[1] The Conservative victory in the General Election of October 1951, ousting the reforming Labour government and making the aristocratic pensioner and war leader Winston Churchill Prime Minister again, was a reminder, if any were needed, that in the way in which it was configured Britain was a highly class-conscious society tied to its past. In cinemas everyone was expected to stand up while 'God Save the Queen' was played. To some observers, the physical fabric of the country was also striking—not just the people still queueing for rationed food but the environment which was still bore traces of

© The Author(s), under exclusive license to Springer Nature
Switzerland AG 2021
A. Maunder, *Enid Blyton*, Literary Lives,
https://doi.org/10.1007/978-3-030-76332-9_10

the war. The bombsites which Blyton's protagonists in *The Six Bad Boys* play on in 1951 were a familiar site in Britain's cities. The German philosopher Hannah Arendt noted of Britain and the British that it was '[n]ot just what the shops look like – groceries and so on, everything scarce, everything of bad quality (which is quite new for this country), but also their genius to make life uncomfortable. Everything is set up as if expressly to make life difficult, or at least to challenge you to muster so much cheerfulness that everything can be overcome'.[2] The writer Lorna Sage (1943–2001) recalled a corresponding 'emotional claustrophobia' that enveloped the country as much as the thick grey smog belching from its coal-fired chimneys.[3]

Mustering cheerfulness while being emotionally claustrophobic was, of course, what Enid Blyton did well. It was arguably one of the reasons why the 1950s were such a good decade, especially the first half; as a woman still in tune with her time, she possessed many of its dominant characteristics in spades. If Bill Haley and Elvis Presley were the embodiment of the decade's fascination with things new (and American), then Blyton was their counterpart: familiar, polite, reliable, trustworthy. She was also, as we will examine in this chapter, ubiquitous and seemingly untouchable. In the years since the war she had, as *The New York Times* reported in November 1951, made herself 'supreme above all authors'. She was 'a category all herself' and it was not unusual for bookshops to have a designated Enid Blyton section, the result of her regularly publishing thirty or more books a year—39 in 1951 and 44 in 1952.[4] These figures were inflated by diaries, board games, jigsaws and calendars, as well regular commissions for newspapers, notably the *London Evening Standard* (from 1949). As the *National Newsagent, Bookseller, Stationer* pointed out, Blyton's coverage was such that a child of five could 'look forward to eleven years of Blytonic reading'.[5] This was confirmed in 1951 when John Menzies published *A Complete List of Books: Enid Blyton*, an (incomplete) bibliography of the 200+ titles she had published since the 1920s, intended as a way of helping readers make their way through the maze. Blyton very evidently revelled in the extent of her reach—which extended overseas to Europe and countries of the new British Commonwealth. She joked that one way of increasing sales of her books further would be to 'set up automatic machines for them & they would sell themselves' (Mac, 28 September 1950). It was not an idle boast. In 1950 David Tyrell, sales manager for the publishers Sampson Low, Marston and Co., explained that Blyton's books 'give us the easiest selling job that we have each year....Her name is the guarantee that children recognise they will enjoy every story in the book'.[6] The result was large print runs, 25,000 being the minimum Blyton would accept.[7]

Stories for Children		
Author	Copies in use	Copies on shelf
Enid Blyton	1451	117
W.E. Johns	658	191
Richmal Crompton	548	109
Alison Uttley	380	319
Louisa M. Alcott	193	180
Kathleen Fidler	149	115
Malcolm Saville	128	108
Stories for Adults		
Author	Copies in use	Copies on shelf
Dorothy L. Sayers	685	109
Hugh Walpole	596	788
Leslie Charteris	582	15
John Buchan	561	385
Agatha Christie	466	23

Fig. 10.1 'Literary Fame at the Library Counter: Census of books on loan, 13 March 1951', *Manchester Guardian* (15 September 1951), 3

Blyton also topped lists of the 'most-read' or 'most-borrowed' writers in public libraries, as shown in Fig. 10.1. In October 1951, one advertising poster carried the slogan 'The Children's Vote is for Enid Blyton – always sure of a sweeping majority in every constituency!'—a reference to the General Election of that year and it was hard not to think otherwise.[8] As a result of her ability to cast herself as the friend of children everywhere, Blyton had become wealthy. Estimates vary. In 1951 one paper suggested she was earning £10,000 a year.[9] George Greenfield, whom Blyton took on as her first (and only) agent in 1954, calculated that the figure was nearer £150,000 (4.6 million in 2021 values).[10] Blyton herself claimed not to know. Possibly she didn't. It was partly to deal with the flood of contracts and royalty cheques— as well as demands for non-payment of tax—that in 1950 a limited company was established (Darrell Waters Limited) and Blyton's copyrights given over to it.[11]

None of this was a flash in the pan. In 1956, C. Clark Ramsay suggested that the reading public's adulation of Blyton remained something very like 'deification'. 'There never was a fiction factory like it…nor is there likely to be'. Repetition was clearly powerful. It had helped make Blyton 'every child's intimate friend' and 'favourite aunt' and she was 'an irresistible personality', more famous than Stanley Matthews, Winston Churchill or Liberace. But, as Ramsay noted, she was not taking anything for granted:

Blyton never laughs at herself or her audience. She is doing a serious, full-time job, of entertaining children….She is never careless, because she could not bear to let her audience down by dropping below her own standards. She rides her bicycle eyes front – both hands – in dead earnest. She doesn't fall off![12]

It was perhaps a sign of Blyton's consciousness of her celebrity, together with the increased notion that author's faces needed to be recognisable ('an author's face should be as familiar as that of a film or TV star', was how Barbara Cartland put it in 1951), that when she decided to have new publicity photographs taken in June 1955, she did so at the Bond Street studios of Dorothy Wilding (1893–1976), long acknowledged as the country's most successful portrait photographer.[13] Wilding was the first female photographer to be granted 'by appointment' status to the Royal family following her work on the coronations of George VI in 1937 and Queen Elizabeth in 1953. The portrait is reproduced on the cover of the present book. It is difficult to think of any other twentieth-century author, other than Virginia Woolf or Rupert Brooke, whose photographic image is so identifiable as that of Blyton. In 1948 she reported having had 500 copies of an earlier photo printed 'for my fans all over the world!....I could', she commented, 'really set up quite a lucrative photographic business if I sold them at a profit' (Mac, 2 August 1948). But the Wilding portrait was clearly special. It carries many of the hallmarks of the photographer's style: clean lines, a head and shoulders close-up, bright lighting and a white background. Wilding also liked to light her subjects at a slight angle (typically forty-five degrees) in order to show up the bone structure and make them look more characterful. There is no sense that Blyton was a particularly vain woman as far as her appearance was concerned, but part of Wilding's appeal was presumably that she could make even the dowdiest of her female subjects look glamorous and modern. In her mid-fifties, Blyton was none of these things, as George Greenfield recalled:

> She wore her hair in an old-fashioned bob, with clusters of tight curls on either side of her face. She had a high complexion which increased to brick-red if she was at all nervous or excited, fine dark eyes and a prominent, somewhat bulbous, nose. No one could have classified her as beautiful or even good-looking, but in her prime there was an attractive sense of coiled energy about her. She had a chirruping quality in her voice and a strange way of eliding vowel sounds.[14]

Part of Wilding's skill was in making her subjects look younger than they had done for several years. She was unabashed in declaring that retouching was an important part of the photographic process. It stemmed from her use of harsh lighting, which inevitably meant that the sitter's blemishes and wrinkles loomed large and had to be eliminated. Before retouching the untouched studio negatives were, Wilding explained, 'grotesque', and she showed them to clients only if they had been 'very tiresome'.[15] Yet the portrait of Blyton, which is evidently retouched, was not intended to hoodwink the public; it *was* recognisably her. Blyton thought it 'quite a good likeness, for once in a way' (Mac, 8 June 1955). But the portrait also offered the public an idealised version of the famous author, a woman whose queenly beauty was what one might expect of someone ruling over several fictional 'solar systems', as a panel member on W.H. Smith's Children's Book Forum put it.[16] Gone was the clumsily permed 'wiry hair' and 'harsh red' lipstick carelessly applied (Smallwood, 115). Instead, the public saw a woman of poised sophistication, of charm but also of tough intelligence. The woman, in fact, whom Blyton wanted to be.

Yet if, during the early early-mid-fifties, Blyton was at the peak of her success, she was also discovering what other successful people had discovered—that once you become successful you have to work extremely hard to maintain your position, and that once you have hit on a winning formula it is difficult to avoid falling into the trap of repeating it. The need to keep the new company, Darrell Waters Ltd., afloat and financed did not help. Another aspect is that you also start to believe your own publicity and can take yourself too seriously. When Eileen Colwell suggested that it might be a good thing if children were exposed to books by people other than Blyton or W.E. Johns, Blyton was incandescent with rage. She accused the renowned librarian of 'defaming me & my books in public speeches' and of seeking 'to poison the minds of future book-sellers by announcing that my characters (for instance) are all puppets, [and] they have no sense of reality' (Mac, 16 November 1947). Nancy Spain, who in 1952 interviewed Blyton in her *Daily Express* column, 'Saturday Outing with Nancy Spain' (the title perhaps signals Spain's intent), set up the celebrated writer as being like Hitler and Stalin in the way she revelled in the power she wielded. This was despite being just '5ft, 4ins' and 'in appearance as sound and wholesome as a ripe apple, with masses of naturally curly hair'. Thanks to some questioning, Spain managed to draw out Blyton's occasional pomposity ('She directs all her efforts she says, towards peace') and her jingoism ('all the heroes in my stories are British...and show the truth about our Christian way of life').[17] Readers were left with the message that there was more than a touch of the humourless zealot about this particular national treasure. It was this tendency towards pomposity that led to a much-reported incident in January 1952, when a character in the BBC radio comedy sketch show *Take it From Here*

Fig. 10.2 Blyton, her daughter Gillian and Kenneth Darrell Waters outside 'Green Hedges' [c.1950]

said her son was looking forward to being 'curled up in front of the fire with Enid Blyton', while said son retorted, 'Ah, now that whacks reading any day' (quoted in Stoney, 141). Offended by the innuendo, Kenneth Darrell Waters, Blyton's 'furious' husband demanded—and received—an apology from the corporation on behalf of his famous wife. 'I really don't think they've any right to use well-known people's names just to make a low joke', Blyton wrote (Mac, 22 January 1952). Yet millions of people loved the programme. The press, too, took a robust line hinting that the famous authoress might develop a sense of humour or at least get down from her high-horse: 'We imagine that far more listeners guffawed irrepressibly…than sorrowed for the name of Enid Blyton…'.[18]

The impression of Blyton at this time is of someone who—like other creative people—was a complicated person, made up of a mixture of traits which did not sit obviously together and some of which seemed more noticeable than others: she was a natural and likeable storyteller, a humourless moralist, a public-spirited citizen, a self-effacing celebrity, a greedy opportunist, a generous and charitable friend to children—she could appear all these things. She seemed, noted Richmal Crompton, meeting Blyton for the first time, a 'most pleasant and quite un-bumptious' woman, 'rather apologetic for her vast success'.[19] But there is a sense, too that she was occasionally feeling the pressures of her remorseless workload. This, for example, is Blyton writing in January 1950 to Roland Heath, her editor at Macmillan:

> I would love to write another book for you straightaway, Roland, but I feel I really must cut down just a little on my books for a while - it's really my correspondence that gets me down, & the continual public appearances I am always pressed to make. I don't feel tired, but I feel a bit strained sometimes especially when the children are home & we have other children in the house too – it's such a strain to run the whole house, see to the children, keep my work going, & answer thousands of personal letters, which even a dozen secretaries couldn't answer without being dictated to. And I can't bear not to play golf with Kenneth on his time off, he does love me to.
>
> If I could give up all these public appearances it wouldn't be so bad – I had 4 in one week in November, all with speeches to make - & the Sunday Times Exhibition was too exciting for words, of course, & then there was the N.B.L. Exhibition, & talking to a thousand children at Leyton & dozens of other things that take precious time from my work. Nearly all my publishers urge or press me strongly to do these things, but I don't see how I can lead quite so many lives – especially as I really am not keen on much personal publicity!
>
> ....Kenneth is getting worried about my work. I haven't admitted to him that I'm feeling a bit pushed after these holidays, in case he does something drastic, so please don't tell him! (Mac, 11 January 1950)

None of this was made public, of course. Rather, in interviews Blyton continued to insist that the stories simply flowed out. 'No fumbling, no planning, no labouring, no agonising waiting for inspiration'. The process was always the same. 'Let me sit down and shut my eyes for two minutes and open the sluice gates of my imagination, reach down into my "undermind" – and out flow my characters complete in every detail'. Yet any more than this, she could not quite explain:

> What am I really, then? A vehicle for something beyond my ordinary powers, an interpreter, a spectator of something I record at top speed on my typewriter? I don't know. I only know that chance has decreed that what imagination I have shall be tapped at any moment I like, for as long as I like - and that so long as I trust to it, my story will be what the children want, and better than anything I could have planned or deliberately invented myself....[20]

The impression given out, namely that there was something magical or mystical about it all, was slightly misleading—Blyton *did* plan some of her stories—but her phraseology is striking partly for the correlations it has with arguments that critics have made for a recognisably feminine style of writing, what Hélène Cixous terms 'L'écriture féminine'. Cixous talks of 'women's imaginary' being 'inexhaustible, like music, painting, writing: their stream of phantoms is incredible'.[21] The book trade liked Blyton's productivity and took as many titles as she cared to produce, knowing that her books drew customers into shops. This at least was the impression of Catherine Gaskin (1929–2009), a novelist and occasional reporter for *W.H. Smith's Trade News* (a magazine directed at bookshops and newsagents). In October 1953, she was getting some work experience in a bookshop in the Surrey town of Rich-mond. One afternoon with the rain 'coming down in slabs', she found herself striking up a conversation with a woman ('cheerfully dyed hair showing under a headscarf') taking shelter in the shop. Their discussion got onto the topic of Blyton's books:

> She [the woman] gave me a quick scrutiny. 'There's a pile over there'. She pointed directly at it. 'You can't miss it. They always put the Blyton books where even the kids can see them'.
> She rocked back on her heels a little, eying me more carefully. 'People say there's too many Blyton books, and other authors don't get a chance. What they don't seem to see is that if Enid Blyton or any other author gives the kids the habit of coming into bookshops, then that's all that matters'.[22]

But as the unnamed woman noted, the never-ending flood of titles did not endear Blyton to other writers. Kitty Barne (1883–1961), author of the Carnegie Prize-winning, *Visitors From London* (1940), was recorded as saying that Blyton's stories were best suited 'for children who are not very *old*, or not very *clever*, or not very *well*'.[23] Noel Streatfeild was similarly caustic: 'I think one of Miss Blyton's great qualities is that she doesn't strain any child's brain', she explained. 'She uses all short words; there is nothing to look up in the dictionary'.[24] 'I think she writes good, readable children's stories but…I cannot think her stories are all *that* much better than other people's', complained another novelist for children, Arthur Groom (1904–1953), in a letter published in *W.H. Smith's Trade Circular* in December 1950. He suggested that many writers looked set to 'starve' in the face of Blyton's dominance.[25] Others spoke anonymously about Blyton's monopolising of the market, viewing her as 'an absolute curse' as she herself was well-aware and explained to Roland Heath: '[O]ne of them said in a Trade Paper the other day. "I am riding about in an old 1938 car & making do with this or that because Enid Blyton corners so much of the market!" I don't see what I'm to do about it, however' (Mac, 5 December 1951). Blyton at this stage had a chauffeur-driven Daimler and several other cars. To some, the production line of publications did not just appear greedy but the work of an obsessive or even hysterical personality. This was despite Blyton's explanations in *The Story of My Life* and elsewhere that it was simply the result of a love of storytelling (*SML*, 96). It also led to rumours that Blyton did not write all the books herself but had a team of people doing it for her. Where once people had seen only her talent, they now saw someone dishonest. Blyton was outraged by these suggestions. 'It is not', she wrote indignantly, 'in my nature to be a fraud, and certainly I could not deceive my friends, the children'.[26]

Some of these perceptions came together when they were picked up by the actress and comedian Joyce Grenfell (1910–1979). This was for her one-woman show, *Joyce Grenfell Requests the Pleasure,* which toured the country prior to a residency at London's Fortune Theatre in June 1954. It was one thing to be criticised in newspapers, which were essentially tomorrow's fish-and-chip paper, but being poked fun at every night in the West End was something else altogether. The subject of the sketch was 'Women at Work: A Lady Authoress', and no one was in any doubt who was being lampooned:

Dear Boys and Girls

I was so touched to be asked to come along and talk to you about How I Write My Books for Children.

Well of course the answer is ----I don't.

No, my books write *themselves.*

...First of all, I go up to my Hidey-Hole --- it's only a big upstairs workroom really but I like to call it my Hidey-Hole. Up there I pin a notice on my door, and it says 'Gone to Make Believe Land' which is my way off telling everybody please don't come and bother me because a book is writing itself for me and we mustn't disturb it!

Then I put down a clean white sheet of paper in my typewriter and I sit down in front of it and I shut my eyes. And what do I see?

I see a rambling olde world house in Cornwall or Devon and hark! ---I hear seagulls ---and look --- I see children ---they are *nearly* late for tea and their names are --- Jennifer Ann and Robin John and there is a wee one toiling along behind them and he is called Tiddler - because he is the littlest one...and he doesn't like porridge but don't say I said so!

I say to them 'Hullo Children' and I sit there trembling with excitement for here are three new friends and they are going to tell me all about themselves.

So, I begin to type, and I type, and I type and...then all of a sudden it is dinner time and I rub my eyes and I find myself back in my Hidey-Hole with a great pile of type-written pages beside me on the table. I must have typed it while the story told itself to me!

And so, I go on, day by day till a book is made.

And then I start a new one….It's always the same with me. No, I never revise a word, I never re-write, and I never read what I have written.

But you kiddies do. Millions and millions of you kiddies do and that is my great joy. And it is my husband's great joy too, He has given up his work to encourage me in mine and he has made Hidey-Holes for each of our five children and they are all learning to let books write for them, too. And my husband has a Hidey-Hole of his own where he spends all his day adding up things.[27]

This was quite sharp stuff in 1954. Grenfell mocked Blyton's gushing style and calculatedly babyish vocabulary, which she presents (snobbishly?) as a concerted attempt on the part of the commonplace, lower-middle-class authoress to get on the same wavelength as her readers ('the kiddies'), whom she does not so much serve as exploit. Grenfell's constructed Blyton is a hack whose main skill is writing enough pages to satisfy her publishers. Even when she reveals the harmless conceit that the characters are living, breathing people with lives off the page, 'who are going to tell me all about themselves' as she sits poised at the typewriter, Blyton's hypocritical dishonesty is, for Grenfell, all too evident. The authoress' prodigious output is the result of her and her husband's liking for money rather than any love of creative work for its own sake.

Noddy

A confusing divide in children's literature was taking shape between the 'classic' and the commercial and it was apparent which side Enid Blyton was on. Although in *Requests the Pleasure* Joyce Grenfell offered Blyton's various adventure series as exemplifying the latter trend, these were also the years during which Blyton began working on what would be the most famous character of her career: Noddy.

The broad outline of how Noddy and the first Noddy stories, *Noddy Goes to Toyland* (1949) and *Hurrah for Little Noddy* (1950), came into being is well-known: in early 1949, David White, the Managing Director of Sampson, Low, Marston wanted to create a series of picture books for younger children to be written by Blyton and to feature 'strong, central characters of a "Disney-like" type' (quoted in Stoney, 161). The invasion of American mass culture into post-war Britain did not only manifest itself in the violent magazine stories for older children but in the comics and storybooks featuring colourful cartoon characters. Noddy can be seen as a British response to this, led by the country's most famous (at that time) children's author. Blyton was amenable and, in turn, recommended that Sampson, Low, Marston invite the Dutch illustrator Eelco Martinus ten Harmsen van der Beek (1897–1953) to be her collaborator. His comic strip featuring Flipje, a little man made of berries, initially created as a mascot for a jam factory, was popular in Holland and he [van der Beek] had already supplied illustrations for one of Blyton's many seasonal anthologies, *The Fourth Holiday Book* (1949).[28] Van der Beek, who signed his work as 'Beek', joined the project as an equal partner with Blyton (both secured a 5% royalty on sales), the two of them agreeing enthusiastically with each other's vision of 'Toyland' and the look of the title character and his neighbours. Blyton produced the first two stories within four days of meeting 'Beek' and sent them off, with a promise not to interfere too much. Because she appreciated the worth of good illustrators it was a promise she seems to have kept:

> I have written them [the stories] with a view to give Van Beek all the scope possible for his particular genius – toys, pixies, goblins, Toyland, brick-houses, dolls houses, toadstool houses, market-places – he'll really enjoy himself! I don't want to tell him how to interpret anything because he'll do it much better if he has a perfectly free hand – but as Noddy (the little nodding man), Big-Ears the Pixie, and Mr and Mrs Tubby (the teddy bears) will probably feature in further books, and will be 'important' characters as far as these books are concerned, I'd be very glad if he could sketch out these characters and let me see roughs.[29]

In fact, Beek's ideas for Toyland quickly prevailed and the usual power dynamic wherein Blyton had the controlling hand over her illustrators, was not the case. Beek had enough tact to compliment Blyton, telling her how 'thoroughly' he had 'enjoyed reading them' [the stories] and how 'they are extraordinarily amusing, especially for an illustrator, because every line gives new inspiration for an illustration'.[30] By way of a try-out, Noddy was first serialised in the *Sunday Graphic* without Beek's illustrations. A version of *Hurrah for Little Noddy* was the first to appear, serialised from 5 June to 31 July 1949, followed by the story which would become *Noddy Goes to Toyland*, serialised from 7 August to 25 September 1949. *Noddy Goes to Toyland* was published in lavishly illustrated book format in November 1949.

For all that the series was later disparaged, it is not difficult to see why the books were so successful. Leaving aside the tricky question of who or what Noddy is—a fake boy? a leprechaun? a comic hero? a fool? a peculiar life form (half-living and half-mechanical)?—the stories are joyful. Their mixture of words and pictures responds to the needs and capabilities of young readers as Blyton and Beek understood them. They offer a recognisable 'grammar' but they are also the product of Blyton's belief—long held—that first-rate pictures were visual cues, a way of enabling children to recognise who characters are and what they are doing, even if they do not fully understand the words on the page.[31] (This belief extends upwards to series such as the Famous Five.) This was tied to Blyton's determination that every element of the Noddy books could be used to encourage children's enjoyment of reading and that the prospect of picking up a colourful book would be exciting. Children can draw before they can write and, in the Noddy books, Beek's pictures are used to help the child understand the words and pay attention to details. The pictures are presented in bold colours, are often meticulous and encourage close observation; the frontispiece to *Noddy Goes to Toyland* has twenty characters in it, all of them visiting the market; there is an implicit invitation for children to spot and name them. The learning offered here is a kind of game; the words are like lessons on a blackboard but when placed alongside the illustrations the two narratives complement each other.[32]

It became fashionable to downplay Blyton's contribution to the Noddy books (see Lovat Dickson's suggestion, below, that their success was thanks to 'Beek') and to suggest that the stories are highly derivative—Noddy is simply a version of Pinocchio. But Blyton's skills as a teller of tales should not be underestimated. Each Noddy book was discrete, while also being part of a larger serial story. In the first two books, readers are rapidly introduced to a seemingly limitless number of characters: a bouncing ball; a clockwork mouse, teddy bears, toy soldiers, Mr. Plod the policeman, pink cats, farmyard animals, dolls, the inhabitants of Noah's ark and 'golliwogs'. As in other Blyton stories, the animals and toys display essentially human traits. In *Noddy Goes to Toyland*, Noddy first encounters them as irritable commuters on the wooden train (blue funnel, yellow wheels):

> 'Look! We're running through Golliwog Town now', said Big-Ears.
> Sure enough, there were dozens and dozens of golliwogs to be seen. When the train stopped at Golliwog Station, three gollies squashed themselves into the same carriage as Big-Ears and Noddy.
> 'You trod on my tail,' said the pink cat, with a loud yowl.
> 'Sorry. Keep it out of the way,' said golly. 'It's silly to leave it lying about'.
> ('Enid Blyton's Story', *The Sunday Graphic* (14 August 1949), 12).

When the golliwogs first appeared, no one really commented on them. They were an accepted part of British culture. Indeed, in the same issue of *The Sunday Graphic* on 14 August, there was another golly advertising Rowntree's cocoa. What is also true, of course, is that the golliwogs demonstrate (again) Blyton's capacity for racism. It has been suggested that the golliwogs are a response on Blyton's part to West Indian workers arriving in the country to help combat the post-war labour shortage. The troopship, HMT Empire Windrush, docked at Tilbury on 21 June 1948, just fourteen months before the first Noddy story appeared. By 1950 the total number of those taking up the scheme stood at 25,000.[33] New arrivals had a mixed reception amid racism and fears that their aim was to take advantage of Britain's new welfare state, and they would sometimes see the letters 'KBW' ('Keep Britain White') on walls and bridges. It is hard not to notice that it seems central to Blyton's representation of Toyland that the place is overrun with golliwogs who are always liable to attack the town (in gangs) and that by virtue of their black faces they are indistinguishable from each other. It was a crude idea—and possibly unintentional—but effective, and over time the Noddy stories seemed in a strange way to appear as allegories of post-war Britain and not only in their racism. Toyland is full of comic and ridiculous figures of authority; Noddy is homeless and of uncertain legal status but having proved his usefulness is given a new (pre-fab) house, built in a day. Toyland uses the same currency as post-war Britain and the townsfolk's taste for consumerism is catered to in the town's market. There is also violence and, in *Here Comes Noddy Again* (1951), Noddy is car-jacked by—inevitably—a gang of delinquent golliwogs.

Another part of the success of the Noddy books was that, thanks to the highly populated world of Toyland, it could be expanded using different combinations and configurations of characters and events, rather like Blyton's book series for older children. This is what happened in the twenty-four tales in the 'Noddy Library' series, ending with *Noddy and the Aeroplane* (1963), as well as with different permutations of them: the Noddy 'Big Books' (1951–1958) and the Noddy Boxes of Books series (1951–1958). The lynchpin remained Noddy, the 'little nodding man', with the curious physical tick which he explains: "'My head is balanced on my neck in such a way that I have to nod when I speak'" ('Enid Blyton's Story', *Sunday Graphic*, 7 August 1949, 12). In the first book in the series, *Noddy Goes to Toyland*, Noddy is discovered naked in the forest by the brownie, Big Ears, having run away from his maker and keeper, Old Man Carver, in a bid to escape the growing pack of lions which the woodcarver is making. To begin with Noddy is infantile and wide-eyed and his vulnerability is that of a small child: he has basic physiological needs—food, shelter, companionship—and Blyton assumed that children would empathise with him for these reasons. Big Ears, in his role as fairy godfather, takes Noddy to Toyland buys him clothes in the market, including the soon-to-be infamous cap with a bell, and helped by Mr. and Mrs. Tubby, the teddy bears, helps him build a house. As is the way in Blyton's stories, spirits are cheered by the thought of food. Noddy, despite being made of wood, needs to eat, and discovers he can get pints of milk in exchange for allowing the milkman to touch him:

> 'Do let me tap you then,' said the milkman, and he tapped Noddy's head smartly.
> At once his head began to nod up and down very fast indeed. The milkman laughed.
> ('Enid Blyton's Story', *The Sunday Graphic* (5 June 1949), 12).

But Noddy's involuntary nodding—a sign perhaps of his good nature or of his being imprisoned in his wooden body—prompts laughter from other inhabitants of Toyland, who see him as an outsider. He is not a toy like them and should be deported. Mr. Plod thinks Noddy should be classified as an ornament—like a china pig—and it is with this threat hanging over him that Noddy is summoned before the Court of Toys where he has to prove he is deserving of leave to remain: "'I *feel* like a toy," said Noddy', but this declaration carries little weight. "'[I]s he", asks the Judge, "a GOOD toy? We don't want bad ones here"' ('Enid Blyton's Story', *The Sunday Graphic*, [25 September 1949], 16). Thankfully, because Noddy has been brave, having rescued a doll from a marauding lion (escaped from Noah's ark), he wins his case and is allowed to stay.

By the end of the initial stories—*Noddy Goes to Toyland* and *Hurrah for Little Noddy*—the stage was set for more books to follow, which they did, several times a year in various formats. The stories follow a pattern. Noddy is impressionable and passive (things happen *to* him), has an undeveloped sense of identity and easily falls prey to others. Usually Noddy learns lessons from his experiences but he remains preternaturally trusting. His adventures fall into distinct types: there are tales like *Here comes Noddy Again* (1951) and *Be Brave Little Noddy* (1956) in which Noddy works as a taxi driver in order to get money so he can buy things. Many of the adventures involve contracts in this way and it is rarer than might be supposed to see Noddy doing things purely out of a spirit of generosity. *Noddy Goes to Sea* (1959), in which Noddy sets off to find Tubby Bear Jr. who has run away, is an exception. Tony Summerfield has suggested that one of the reasons why Noddy has continued to prove so popular with young children is that (talking teddy bears aside), the character's experiences mirror that of the young reader; Noddy is like 'a child attending school, making mistakes and needing guidance from his friends'.[34]

As the 1950s progressed, the Noddy stories staked a claim to be the most widely read of Blyton's books. It was a craze that took off quickly. 'Little Noddy…now out runs every other series of mine!' Blyton reported in July

1952. 'We are in the process of making a Noddy Licensing Company, to deal with all the enquiries we get for the use of his name or character in such diverse things as soap, cotton prints, Pelham puppets, jigsaws and so on. It's really amazing' (Mac, 15 July 1952). By 1956, sales stood at 12 million (Mac, 24 April 1956); by 1962, 26 million copies of the books had been sold.[35] The series survived the death of van der Beek in 1953 and the transfer of the illustrative work to a team of other artists who followed the existing look.

Noddy's ubiquity was enhanced by his translation into other media. As we will see in Chapter 11, Blyton's pantomime, *Noddy in Toyland*, first appeared in the West End in December 1954 where it had an annual Christmas run for the six years. Later, when the BBC did not want anything to do with Enid Blyton, the corporation's new commercial rival did and *The Adventures of Noddy* began broadcasting on ITV on 25 September 1955. There were also lengthy discussions about using Noddy to 'launch' Blyton, finally, in the United States with the series presented as the 'craze' that had 'swept' through British children (Mac, 8 April 1956). In fact, it was difficult to galvanise American publishers. In New York, one publisher's reader, Margaret McElderry, who was handed *Noddy and his Car* (the third book in the series, intended as a test case) found it 'wearisome'—though 'not quite as bad' as she had feared, or as trashy as 'some comparable material…seen here'. But, she reported, the story was 'terribly manufactured and mechanical' and she doubted that it had 'any quality or characteristic that the American market has been waiting for' (Memorandum, Mac, 9 May 1956). To American eyes the books also looked old fashioned (one New York editor asked if the books had been published in 1918). The style of drawing which the British public found enchanting struck the Americans as 'immediately different visually to the American eye accustomed to contemporary American style'. Mr. Plod, in particular, looked too 'English' (Mac, 24 April 1956). There was also a feeling that the written part of the stories would need extensive revision before they could be anywhere near comprehensible. And, to look even half-attractive, the cover price would need to be set at a lowly 50 cents. An idea emerged that the books should be offered to CBS television and then launched as a television tie-in. Only then would the series look viable, but this too came to nothing. Blyton's agents gave up. 'Noddy is what he is and cannot at this stage be given a different interpretation', they wrote and, rather than waste any more time, they retreated (Mac, 24 April 1956).

Blyton's biographers and critics sometimes differ over particular details of the Noddy books and their significance, including the importance of van der Beek's illustrations to the success of the series. Lovat Dickson of Macmillan reported to his American colleague that it was the illustrations which 'have truly caught the imagination of children here and have been largely responsible for the quite phenomenal success of all the Noddy books' (Mac, 24 April 1956). There is disagreement, too, about the precise level of the books' initial success and the level of antipathy towards them on the part of librarians and educators, and about the influence of Sampson, Low, Marston in creating the finished product. It has also been suggested that Noddy 'blighted' Blyton's career, overshadowing other achievements and making her seem 'an over productive hack...'.[36]

This last point has some truth, at least if the evidence of a 1961 revue, *The Lord Chamberlain Regrets*, is to be believed. This ran at the Saville Theatre in London's West End during the summer of 1961, part of the satire boom which emerged in Britain in the early 1960s. In the offices of Biggot and Prude, Mr. Biggot ('an old-fashioned publisher') has an appointment with Beatrix Flyton, author of the bestsellers *Shoddy in Coyland*, *Still Shoddy* and *Shoddy Adventures*. She is at work on her latest story, *Carry on Shoddy*. Mr. Biggot's delicate task is to tell his client, 'a gentle lady of delicate susceptibilities' (played by the 'Carry On' films' actress, Joan Sims) that 'Little Shoddy is on the skids'. Children find him 'a little square' and he has been overtaken in popularity by the television glove-puppet, Sooty. A rethink is needed:

BIGGOT: Miss Flyton...prepare yourself for a grave shock....I have plans for Little Shoddy. Penguin Books have agreed to publish him...there will be a prosecution...Miss Flyton, Little Shoddy will be tried at the Old Bailey.
FLYTON: But Mr Biggot....
BIGGOT (*excited*): I can see it now. Professors giving evidence that Little Shoddy stands for Family sanctity....Cardinals protesting that he's the embodiment of the Christian Faith. All it needs is a little co-operation from you.
FLYTON: Co-operation?
BIGGOT: Miss Flyton, at this hour of crisis we cannot afford to mince words. We have to sex up Little Shoddy....We must concentrate on four letter words.
FLYTON. But Mr Biggot, Little Shoddy and his friends never use words of over four letters and if they do I hyphenate them.
BIGGOT: That's not quite the same thing. Miss Flyton, we have to make Little Shoddy not fit to print.
FLYTON: But what do you think he is now. Mr Biggot...have you ever *read* one of the Little Shoddy Books?
BIGGOT: Well actually no.
FLYTON: I thought not...well, you just listen to this....Yes, Little Noddy was hungry. The tart he had the night before was now forgotten. He decided he would have crumpet for breakfast. He was just going to look for some when

along came his friend Big Cheeks the brownie. He was riding his tricycle and his big cheeks wobbled from side to side.[37]

That the show's producers were able to lampoon Blyton alongside other 'Establishment' targets, including the royal family and Harold Macmillan's Conservative government, says something about her iconic status, or at least the extent to which she was a recognisable part of the cultural landscape. Although there may have been a degree of affection, the sketch's young scriptwriters, Peter Myers and Ronnie Cass, were also prepared to be cruel. They sought to mock Britain's bad taste—its 'deification of drivel', as one commentator put it—which had seen Blyton awarded the status of national treasure.[38] Then there was Blyton herself and her much-vaunted status as the servant of hard-pressed parents. Much as Joyce Grenfell had done, they did so by making her look two-faced. The scriptwriters thus single out the clash between the author's apparently genuinely felt expression of loyalty to her readers ('I will not break truth with the tiny-tots', Miss Flyton declares in a recognisably Blytonesque idiom) and her readiness to repurpose her vacuous 'Shoddy' stories into X-rated smut should there be a chance to garner publicity and enrich herself. By emphasising Miss Flyton's/Blyton's use of suggestive names for characters and places, and her fondness for the *double entendre* which they suggest is not unintentional (contrary to popular belief), the producers made the point that Blyton's use of language was crude—in both senses of the word. In what was a topical reference, they also raise the tantalising possibility of this distinguished writer being put on trial charged with crimes not just against decency but literature as well. As the audience would know, this was a nod to the *Lady Chatterley's Lover* obscenity trial of November 1960 in which Penguin Books was prosecuted for seeking to publish D.H. Lawrence's banned novel and called in the most respectable writers and academics they could find as "expert" witnesses for the defence, something which caused some unintentional hilarity. (As we shall see in Chapter 11, Blyton was one of those invited, but had refused.) Above all though, Miss Flyton's literary career is also, of course, an outlet for her greed and her eye for the main chance is all too evident. The scriptwriters thus made the veteran author look opportunistic and cynical while also making the British public look foolish and gullible for being taken in by her. It was an unsubtle reminder, if anyone was in any doubt, that Flyton's/Blyton's success did not—at this stage of her career at least—have a great deal to do with thoughtfulness or a desire to publish quality work.

* * *

It should be clear that while Enid Blyton remained a formidable presence in 1950s Britain, she had lost some of the critical respect that she had earned in the 1930s and 1940s. Her reputation became more unstable and she sought to protect it. Although she was unappreciated by many critics, she retained her hold on the 'masses'. (A poll of 1957 put her top of the list of the authors most popular with girls aged eleven and over.)[39] She also remained resolutely defensive about the honesty of her books and their value to children, as well as continuing to take herself seriously as a writer. But there were hints, too, that hers was not always the healthiest way to live. Visiting Blyton at Green Hedges in the mid-1950s, George Greenfield came away with 'the increased impression she was living sealed off, going round and round like those blindfolded donkeys in Middle Eastern countries, drawing up water from a deep well as they tramped in circles, imagining they were making progress'.[40] It was a perceptive comment, the truth of which would become more evident as the next decade loomed.

Notes

1. Peter Hennessey, *Having It So Good: Britain in the Fifties* (2006; London: Penguin, 2007), 622.
2. David Kynaston, *Family Britain, 1951–1957* (London: Bloomsbury, 2009), 104.
3. Lorna Sage, *Bad Blood* (2000; London: 4th Estate: 2001), 99.
4. Heather Bradley, 'A Letter from London', *The New York Times* (13 November 1949), BR32.
5. R.M.H., 'The Bountiful Miss Blyton', *National Newsagent, Bookseller, Stationer* (6 September 1947), 1557.
6. Unsigned Article, 'Sales Talk', *W.H. Smith's Trade Circular* (1 July 1950), 21.
7. George Greenfield, *A Smattering of Monsters* (2005; London: Little Brown and Company, 1997), 115.
8. Advert, 'The Children's Vote Is for Enid Blyton', *W.H. Smith's Trade Circular* (20 October 1951), 19.
9. Unsigned Article, '10,000 Words a Day Bring in £10,000 a Year', *Irish Times Pictorial* (14 July 1951), 6.
10. George Greenfield, *A Smattering of Monsters*, 116.
11. See George Greenfield, ibid., 121. Greenfield describes how the company's team, solicitor Arnold Thirlby, accountant John Basden, stockbroker Eric Rogers, together with Kenneth Darrell Waters appeared to benefit more than Blyton. Yet it was on her 'creative flair' that the company's success depended. Rogers, in particular, is marked out as sharp and unscrupulous, taking control of the business deals and manipulating Waters.

12. C. Clark Ramsay, 'You Can't Ignore Enid Blyton', *Illustrated* (December 1956), 49.

13. Barbara Cartland, 'Publishers, Bookseller and Librarians', *W. H. Smith's Trade Circular* (17 May 1951), 17–18.

14. George Greenfield, *A Smattering of Monsters*, 113–4.

15. Terence Pepper, *Dorothy Wilding, The Pursuit of Perfection* (London: National Portrait Gallery, 1991), 7; 25; 18.

16. Unsigned Article, 'Children's Book Forum', *W.H. Smith's Trade Circular* (25 August 1951), 11.

17. Nancy Spain, 'Saturday Outing with Nancy Spain', *The Daily Express* (27 September 1952), 4.

18. Unsigned Article, 'Take It from Here', *The Evening Post* (21 January 1952), 6.

19. Kay Williams, *Just Richmal. The Life and Work of Richmal Crompton Lamburn* (Guildford: Genesis, 1986), 198.

20. Editorial Note, 'Around the Bookshops', *W.H. Smith's Trade Circular* (7 July 1951), 34.

21. Hélène Cixous, 'The Laugh of the Medusa', in *Feminisms*, eds. Robyn R. Warhol and Diane Price-Herndl (New Brunswick: Rutgers University Press,1991), 334–49 (334).

22. Catherine Gaskin, 'Conversation with a Customer', *W.H. Smith's Trade News* (17 October 1953), 32.

23. Quoted in Geoffrey Trease, *Tales Out of School* (London: Heinemann, 1949), 158.

24. Unsigned Article, 'The Children's Book Forum', *W.H. Smith's Trade Circular* (25 August 1951), 11.

25. Arthur Groom, 'Authors Will Starve If...', *W.H. Smith's Trade Circular* (30 December 1950), 23.

26. Unsigned Article, 'Around the Bookshops', *W.H. Smith's Trade Circular* (7 July 1951), 34.

27. Joyce Grenfell, *Joyce Grenfell Requests the Pleasure*, British Library Add Ms, Lord Chamberlain's Collection. LCP 1954/26, 20 April 1954. A recording by Grenfell of a version of the full sketch is available at https://www.youtube.com/watch?v=WSsmWbf8gaQ. Accessed 17 June 2021.

28. Brian Stewart and Tony Summerfield, *The Enid Blyton Dossier* (Penryn: Hawk, 1999), 64.

29. Enid Blyton to David White, quoted in Brian Stewart and Tony Summerfield, *The Enid Blyton Dossier* (Penryn: Hawk, 1999), 65.

30. Orla Hughes, 'Noddy's Other Half—Harmsen van der Beek' (8 November 2015) http://nerdalicious.com.au/books/noddys-other-half-harmsen-van-der-beek/#fnref-21494-3. Accessed 8 March 2021.

31. Mel Gibson, 'Picturebooks, Comics and Graphic Novels', in *The Routledge Companion to Children's Literature*, ed. David Rudd (London: Routledge, 2010), 100–111.

32. This is the point made by Lesley Delaney, *Walter Crane: Promoting Visual Literacy in Nursery Picture Books, Children's Books History Society Occasional Paper IX* (Buckfast: Children's Books History Society, 2011), 2; 8.
33. Peter Hennessey, *Never Again*, 442.
34. Tony Summerfield, quoted in Julie Harding, 'The Little Man with the Red and Yellow Car', *Country Life* (17 July 2019), 108–9 (109).
35. Brian Stewart and Tony Summerfield, *The Enid Blyton Dossier*, 66.
36. David Rudd, quoted in Julie Harding, 'The Little Man with the Red-and-Yellow Car', 109.
37. Peter Myers and Ronnie Cass, 'Kids' Stuff', *The Lord Chamberlain Regrets*, British Library Add Ms, LCP 1961/31, No. 1804. A recording of the production is available on You Tube https://youtu.be/3gdjCo7Mn0M. Accessed 27 June 2021.
38. C. Clark Ramsay, 'You Can't Ignore Enid Blyton', 49.
39. R.H. Langbridge, 'Reading—Top Hobby for Girls', *W.H. Smith's Trade News* (25 May 1957), 26–7.
40. George Greenfield, *A Smattering of Monsters*, 114.

Bibliography

Cixous, Hélène. 1991. 'The Laugh of the Medusa'. In *Feminisms*, edited by Robyn R. Warhol and Diane Price-Herndl: 334–49. New Brunswick: Rutgers University Press.

Delaney, Lesley. 2011. *Walter Crane: Promoting Visual Literacy in Nursery Picture Books. Books History Society Occasional Paper IX*. Buckfast: Children's Books History Society.

Gibson, Mel. 2010. 'Picturebooks, Comics and Graphic Novels'. In *The Routledge Companion to Children's Literature*, edited by David Rudd: 100–11. London: Routledge.

Greenfield, George. 1995; 1997. *A Smattering of Monsters*. London: Warner.

Grenfell, Joyce. 1965. *Joyce Grenfell Requests the Pleasure*. British Library Add Ms, Lord Chamberlain's Collection. LCP 1954/26.

Harding, Julie. 2019. 'The Little Man with the Red and Yellow Car'. *Country Life* (17 July): 108–9.

Hennessey, Peter, 1992; 2006. *Never Again: Britain 1945-1951*. London: Penguin.
———. 2006; 2007. *Having It So Good: Britain in the Fifties*. London: Penguin.

Hughes, Orla. 2015. 'Noddy's Other Half-Harmsen van der Beek' (8 November). http://nerdalicious.com.au/books/noddys-other-half-harmsen-van-der-beek/#fnref-21494-3. Accessed 8 March 2021.

Kynaston, David. 2009. *Family Britain, 1951–1957*. London: Bloomsbury.

Pepper, Terence. 1991. *Dorothy Wilding, The Pursuit of Perfection*. London: National Portrait Gallery.

Sage, Lorna. 2000; 2001. *Bad Blood*. London: 4th Estate.

Stewart, Brian Stewart, and Tony Summerfield. 1999. *The Enid Blyton Dossier*. Penryn: Hawk.

Williams, Kay. 1986. *Just Richmal. The Life and Work of Richmal Crompton Lamburn*. Guildford: Genesis.

11

Blyton and the Theatre

Throughout her life Blyton was fascinated by the theatre. Aged five she played the heroine in a school production of *Alice's Adventures in Wonderland* and, as a teenager, she and some friends formed *The Mauve Merriments*, a Pierrot troop which performed skits and songs at the end of the school term (Stoney, 23). Her interest was formed as well by regular visits with her parents to the theatre attached to the Crystal Palace (six miles from Beckenham). It was one of a large number of venues which offered London suburban audiences the chance to see high-quality touring productions at cheap prices: the sword-and-sandals epic *The Sign of the Cross*, the musicals *The Quaker Girl* and *The Maid of the Mountains*, the pantomime *Peter Pan* and Frank Benson's Shakespearean company were amongst the things Blyton saw (*SML*, 101–102). As an adult in the 1920s, she extended her knowledge by taking advantage of the West End theatres and, in her 'From My Window' column in *Teacher's World* (from 1923), would occasionally write about what she had seen. She also began to write plays herself. One of her earliest books was *The Play's the Thing* (1927) [with Alex Rowley], followed by *Six Enid Blyton Plays* (1935), which dramatised fairy and folk tales and was eagerly adopted by schools and youth groups, not least because, as Blyton explained to would-be directors, 'the parts are easy to learn, and the scenery and properties are articles in everyday use, and easily obtainable' (*Six*, 7). When Blyton published her 'Empire play', *The Union Jack*, as part of the coronation festivities for King George VI in May 1937, this was widely performed as well. Most successful of all, however, were Blyton's later adaptations, *Noddy in Toyland* (1954) and

A. Maunder, *Enid Blyton*, Literary Lives, https://doi.org/10.1007/978-3-030-76332-9_11

Famous Five Adventure (1955), which ran concurrently in the West End, a feat Blyton described as 'rather fun... especially as it never occurred to me that I could write proper stage plays' (Mac, 8 April 1955). There are thus short periods where Blyton diverts some of her energies from pure story-telling. In an interview with *The Stage* in 1955, she confided that it was in 'the hectic, warm and friendly life of the theatre' that she 'felt at home'.[1]

Blyton's move towards the theatre took place during what is generally seen as an important moment in British cultural history. Thanks to plays like Samuel Beckett's *Waiting for Godot* (1952), John Osborne's *Look Back in Anger* (1956) and Shelagh Delaney's *A Taste of Honey* (1958), the 1950s is seen as a transformative decade. In fact, for much of the time the theatre industry was notoriously unadventurous. In 1954, *Theatre World Annual* described the British stage as 'sterile', noting that the 'great upsurging of dramatic creativeness appropriate to a second Elizabethan age' showed little sign of materialising. The sole exception had been the coronation of Elizabeth II in 1953 and its 'superb pageantry and drama'.[2] The theatre offered nothing comparable. The following year, Frances Stephens lamented 'the lack of serious plays – old or new -produced in the West End'.[3] The problem, as the young playwright Christopher Fry explained, was the British theatre industry's crippling conservatism: 'the busy sound of men knowing what they like'.[4] Producers fell back on a diet of genteel comedies and thrillers with 'all-star' casts. The veteran producer Bertie Meyer defended this approach on the basis that managers 'must be guided by public taste', which was not that much different to what it was before the war: 'At the present time it is still very unsophisticated, and the long runs are all light-hearted plays'. Sounding rather like Blyton when she was called upon to pronounce on the dangers of comics, Meyer explained how he was 'a believer in clean plays; those dealing with sordid problems usually have a very limited appeal'.[5]

Although she had ceased to be a regular theatregoer—her husband's deafness ruled it out—Blyton was presumably aware of some of these trends and the opportunities available if she was able to get her work staged. As well as giving her the chance to try something new, there was the potential for increasing her sales. Her books, along with *Enid Blyton's Magazine*, could be sold in the theatre foyer and advertised in the programme and she could use the magazine to plug the play. What also drew her in was frustration at other avenues closed to her, most notably broadcasting, which, before the launch in 1955 of independent commercial television, meant the BBC, which had a monopoly. One of the ways in which authors for children could be expected to capitalise on their popularity and expand their reach was by having their stories transmitted on BBC radio or dramatised in the *Children's Hour* slot. Blyton's rivals, Alison Uttley, W.E. Johns, Malcolm Saville, Barbara Euphan Todd and Noel Streatfeild all benefitted in this way. The latter's plays about the Bell Family set in Deptford, billed as 'an absolutely ordinary family of children who don't catch burglars, find jewels down wells, or have any of those adventures peculiar to children in books', were regularly on radio from 1949 to 1953.[6] In contrast, and despite Blyton's popularity, the BBC refused to have anything to do with her work. Whatever explanations she received never convinced her and (not unreasonably) she interpreted the BBC's intractable attitude towards her as being borne out of snobbery or jealousy and certainly not what was due to her. In October 1947, describing a literary luncheon organised by Foyle's Bookshop at which she was the main speaker, she explained her unease at finding out that the organisers had tactlessly—but presumably unintentionally—invited the popular BBC presenter 'Uncle Mac', aka Derek McCulloch (1897–1967), the BBC's head of children's broadcasting, to be master of ceremonies (McCulloch was also famous in the early 1950s for providing the voice of 'Larry the Lamb' in the radio series *Toytown*). As Blyton reported of the lunch, 'he does dislike me & my work so much, so made me feel very uncomfortable - & introduced me as churlishly as he possibly could!' The experience left her convinced that, 'if he has anything to do with it, I shall NEVER get any books broadcast by the B.B.C. Not that I mind, because I don't think my books can stand any more publicity at present' (Mac, 1 October 1947). Whether or not, McCulloch was behind things, he was certainly influential. A BBC memorandum dated 1950 shows him reminding colleagues that the decision not to broadcast material by Miss Blyton was now department policy. In 1954 it was something encountered by Janet Quigley, a new producer for the magazine programme, *Woman's Hour*. Quigley did wonder if the BBC was being 'rather stuffy and dictatorial in not allowing listeners to hear somebody whose name is a household word', but was reassured with advice from a senior colleague, Jean Sutcliffe, who had been Head of the BBC Schools department in the 1940s:

In my view if the invitation is simply to meet her and she be asked to give her views on Horror comics or hats or anything under the sun except her own methods and aims in writing for children – no harm could be done.

But if she is allowed to lay down the law on aims and methods of writing for children – unchallenged by really good writers or parents and educationalists of wide and deep experience in the field of children's literature, the BBC becomes just another victim of the amazing advertising campaign which has raised this competent and tenacious second-rater to such astronomical heights of success.[7]

Sutcliffe continued:

> No writer of real merit could possibly go on believing that this mediocre mate-
> rial is of the highest quality and turn it out in such incredible quantities. Her
> capacity to do so amounts to genius and it is here that she has beaten everyone
> to a standstill. Anyone else would have died of boredom long ago.[8]

Thus by the 1950s there was consensus at the BBC that it was undesirable to
encourage Blyton any further. Even when Blyton offered—as she had in the
1940s—to take on a Christian theme—there was no give. The corporation's
mission to improve public taste would not allow it. The BBC epitomised
the role of the public service broadcaster obliged to disparage much of what
Blyton, a writer of mass appeal who was not—in their eyes—terribly good or
dynamic, stood for. 'It really is odd', observed one executive, 'to think that
this woman is a best-seller'.[9] Meanwhile, the message that there was a deliberate attempt to keep her off the airwaves gradually sank in and deepened
into permanent resentment on Blyton's part. 'I and my stories are completely
banned by the BBC as far as children are concerned', she was quoted as
saying, 'not one story has ever been broadcast, and, so it is said, not one
ever will be'.[10]

It was against this backdrop that Blyton began to think about theatre as
the medium through which she would reach out further. She knew that other
writers of books for children, most notably Edith Bagnold (1889–1981) and
Dodie Smith (1896–1990), doubled as dramatists and Blyton saw no reason
why she should not do something similar. Nor was she short of offers. She
was asked by the manager of London's Empress Hall to write a play to form
the basis for an ice show, but declined: 'I really think I've enough on my plate
at the moment!' (Mac, 2 November 1954). Still, theatre drew her in. It was
possibly because she was bored and liked a challenge, but she also wondered
if her 'imagination, apparently harnessed only to the writing of books' could
'adapt' itself to drama (quoted in Stoney, 222). Her agent, George Greenfield, boosted her confidence: 'I reckon that if you put your mind to it, you
could write pretty well anything' (quoted in Stoney, 165). She also took—
or pretended to take—soundings from her readers: 'Would you like me to
write you a play…that can be acted in a theatre for you at Christmas-time?'
she asked in *Enid Blyton's Magazine* ('Green Hedges', *EBM*, 7 July 1954,
3). The response was heartening enough for her to go ahead. However, she
decided to put off adapting one of her adventure books. A pantomime based
on Noddy, she decided, would be the medium most sympathetic to her own
style and she constructed one in two weeks, providing the magazine's readers
with a running commentary on the progress from page to stage.

In opting to write a pantomime, Blyton was obviously choosing to exploit what was a long established and familiar genre. When, as a child, Blyton encountered pantomimes at the Crystal Palace Theatre, productions had developed a set of distinctive, slapstick and humorous characteristics mixed with a storyline taken from a well-known fairy-tale. A series of spectacular hits in the early 1900s at London's Drury Lane Theatre, featuring popular music hall comedians and singers, helped cement pantomimeas a Christmas tradition. In the post-war West End, the London Palladium, which in December 1954 offered Max Bygraves and Peter Sellers in *Mother Goose*, had become the leading venue, but it had to compete with other theatres, including the Scala Theatre, which in 1954 presented the fiftieth-anniversary production of *Peter Pan*, starring the American actress, Barbara Kelly; the Empress Hall, showing *Aladdin on Ice*, with comedian Tommy Trinder; a revival of A.A. Milne's adaptation of *Toad of Toad Hall* (originally presented at the Royal Shakespeare Memorial Theatre); *Puss in Boots* at the Fortune Theatre, as well as the rank-and-file suburban theatres that continued to try to attract local audiences. But there was also a sense that pantomime was under threat. Celebrity casting (pop singers and television personalities) was rife, while traditionalists lamented the disappearance of 'proper' stories. As *The Stage* observed in 1954, pantomime was turning 'into just another form of variety bill, full of jokes about politics, income tax and mothers-in-law'. Children lacked 'real plays of their own.'[11] If this is the way pantomime is going', remarked one reviewer faced with the crooner, Frankie Vaughan at the Palladium, 'it will speedily become a yearly parade of television performers going through their usual paces...[and] there will be little point in taking the children along'.[12] Thus, there was a sense of a gap (at least in the West End) which the launch of an Enid Blyton show might fill. This, at least, came to be the view of *The Stage*, which argued that if children enjoyed the 'party atmosphere of joining in', they would 'become life-long habitués'.[13] Who better to provide this than the woman who, more than anyone, appeared to have a pass key to children's hearts?

Blyton's own recorded thoughts on her theatrical ventures can seem bland or circumspect but there is a case for arguing that some of her dramatic ambitions matched those of *The Stage*. In January 1924, describing in *Teacher's World* a visit to see a children's show, *The Windmill Man*, she wrote of glancing 'round the child-crowded theatre...to see nothing but entranced wonder on every face' (*TW*, 23 January 1924, 855). It was presumably something of this that she hoped to recapture, a version of what the comedian, Eric Morecambe, later called the 'emotional rapport' unique to live performance.[14] What also emerges is that writing a play was more demanding than she anticipated. This was something Blyton admitted in January 1955, in a letter to Peter McKellar, a New Zealand psychologist with whom she corresponded about her creative methods:

> For the first two days I endeavoured to use the same process of writing as I use for my books – finding characters and settings and then using the 'cinema screen' in my mind, on which the whole story seems to be projected from beginning to end without any active volition from me. This method was a *complete* failure for the writing of the play....I stumbled...Then like a flash I seemed to discard the old way of writing, and instead of needing to see characters in their story setting and using the 'cinema screen', into my mind came the stage itself, all set with scenery. And then in came the characters on this stage, singing, talking, dancing – and once again something went 'click' and the whole writing of the play went out of my hands and was taken over by my imagination again. I no longer stumbled, puzzled, tried to invent. There were the characters, all dressed for their parts, there were their houses and their 'props' (car, bicycle, etc.) and on they came, talking, dancing, singing... (quoted in Stoney, 165–66)

In pinpointing the moment at which her play came together, Blyton re-emphasised her need to give visual life to her characters before anything else could happen (this was the technique mocked in the revue, *Joyce Grenfell Requests the Pleasure*). More significantly perhaps, Blyton seems to imbue her characters, at least those in the Noddy books, as performers anyway. They appear on the page (or stage), do their familiar 'turns', then make an exit. What was also easy, once she got under way, was fitting Noddy into the familiar framework of pantomime. Summarising the genre's characteristics, critics have also noted the form's emphasis on 'good' overcoming 'evil' and the quest which must be completed by the hero: Aladdin must find the magic lamp; Jack must climb up the beanstalk to kill the giant. Set usually in an unnamed time and place, the emphasis is invariably on an exciting plot, constructed around characters coping with highly pressurised situations, the result of malevolent schemes set in motion by people more powerful than themselves; false imprisonment; a heroine who needs rescuing. The characters are likely to include a young hero (traditionally played by a woman) forced to endure a range of trials and with whom the audience is supposed to identify, a beautiful heroine of unimpeachable virtue and a predatory (upper-class or magically empowered) villain. As Millie Taylor has noted, pantomime also promise resolution; 'The [show's] two halves...are reflections of each other, an arch-like structure, where the journey away from, and back to, equilibrium is mirrored to reflect the stability and fixity or society'. This is also part of the genre's 'incentive to goodness' and its accompanying message that 'even the meekest can succeed'.[15]

Reporting her play finished on 18 August 1954, Blyton fed her readers titbits about its contents: there would be a 'real' steam train on stage and, on 24 November, she explained in *Enid Blyton's Magazine* how delighted she was to be able to cast a boy 'EXACTLY like Noddy!' She continued: 'I cannot tell you how excited I am over the Play I have written for you to see', and reminded her readers that she would be one of the attractions: 'I shall often be at the theatre and shall see so many of you!' ('Green Hedges', *EBM*, 24 November 1954, 3). Meanwhile, Bertie Meyer was lined up to produce, together with André van Gyseghem, as director, a surprising choice given his association with left-wing agitprop. Blyton was flattered that these celebrated men of the theatre wanted to be involved. A lease was taken on the Stoll Theatre, on Kingsway, a big venue (too big perhaps) with a capacity of 2400, long associated with large-scale musicals, operettas and star vehicles (Ingrid Bergman, in *St Joan at the Stake*, had performed there earlier in the year). A designer, Richard Lake, who fitted the essential requirement of being able to recreate Beek's colourful illustrations on stage, and a congenial composer, Philip Green, able to work with Blyton to set her songs to music, were also recruited. The production was announced in the press in October. By the following month Blyton was reporting not only that 'the bookings are very good (touch wood!)' but also that she was heavily involved. 'Rehearsals are now in full swing & I cannot resist going to as many as possible!' she wrote (Mac, 30 November 1954). Part of this was policing. She was adamant that 'there must be nothing adult, vulgar or frightening or this will taint the quality of the play and spoil its essential child-likeness'. She did not *quite* trust the professionals to whom she had handed over her work (*NT*, 62).

It is possible to get a sense of *Noddy in Toyland's* production because, when it opened for matinees on 23 December 1954, it was clearly an 'event' and responses to it featured across the press. The familiarity of the characters, or 'creatures', as the *Guardian* rather ambiguously termed them, was part of its appeal. Its reviewer, despite being reduced to despair by the play's running time (two-and-half hours), noted that the look of the play was 'true-to-book'.[16] Others observed not only the delighted shouts of recognition when the curtain was raised or as characters made their entrance but also the way in which the production team had structured the play so that it did not simply appear to be a bestselling children's series lazily replicated on stage. Rather, the audience was presented with, or assaulted by (as some reviewers put it), familiar stage formulas drawn from other pantomimes, including *Peter Pan*, a work Blyton greatly admired. In the opening scene, the inhabitants of Toyland are shown going about their daily business but break off to sing the opening number ('Oh sing the song of Toyland Town') before Noddy makes a noisy entrance in his (by now famous) car, beeping 'Parp-parp-parp-parp!' The tendency in pantomime to halt the action with musical interludes is maintained as Noddy sings his own song, 'I'm the little nodding man,/I always nod my head', a song repeated throughout the production. Meanwhile, Mr. Plod's pompous rule over the town is established; one running joke is how his inability to distinguish between the golliwogs Gollie, Woggie and Nigger allows them to play tricks on him. After an interlude of tap dancing, the audience rewarded by seeing another Blyton landmark recreated on stage: the Magic Faraway Tree.

Noddy in Toyland's plot centres on a panic about red goblins (Communists?) in the Enchanted Wood, who have escaped from a witch. A bag of money is offered as a reward to the Toyland resident who catches them, a challenge which the usually timid Noddy takes up, rather like the titular hero of 'Jack and the Beanstalk'. Like any self-respecting pantomime hero, he asks the audience for their help: 'I DO want that bag of money – so, listen – if any of you see a red goblin coming here, just whistle to me – like this (*Gives a loud whistle*). Will you do that?' (*NT*, 11). This is an example of the "ghost gag" as it is known in pantomime. It is also an instance of Blyton, the schoolteacher, establishing rules of engagement for the afternoon as well as trying to encourage the audience to feel they are participants in the world of Toyland, rather than passive spectators. They would, Blyton hoped, identify with an everyman figure like Noddy, not with the goblins, whose nastiness is shown by the way they vandalise Toyland—running riot, pushing over lampposts and stealing clockwork keys (which cause the clowns to stop working). It is when Mr Plod, who is as dim-witted on stage as he is in the books, accuses Noddy of the thefts, that the hero (rather like a character in a Victorian melodrama) has to prove his innocence. The audience, meanwhile, were instructed to nod their heads if they believed him. Noddy's task thus becomes that of tracking down the goblins: 'If we can't get them, and make them give back those clockwork keys, I'll never be able to go back to Toyland again! If I don't, I'll have to go to prison for something I didn't do' (*NT*, 56). With a sense of jeopardy established, Noddy summons Big-Ears (portrayed with a Scottish accent) and Mr Pinkwhistle, and they board the Toyland train (whose arrival on stage puffing out real steam is the finale of the first act). Their destination is the Magic Faraway Tree, at the top of which Goblin Land is resting temporarily. Once Noddy has bested the goblins, he returns to Toyland, reprises his solo, and is rewarded with money, which he uses to fund a party while the goblins are carted off to prison. Unlike many traditional pantomimes, the audience were not rewarded with a lavishly costumed wedding. Instead, they were invited to shout 'we want Noddy', at which point the hero, having been granted his wish to fly—something most of the audience would like to be able to do—hovered spectacularly above them. By this point, the audience—at least those under five—were also grabbing the sweets, crackers and balloons being tossed from the stage. One of the observations made by reviewers was that the audience was rarely silent, rather, they were excitedly and noisily enraptured throughout, leaning dangerously over the balconies to get closer. It was a foretaste, perhaps, of the teenage fans who would scream during the Beatles' concerts a decade later (possibly they *were* the same people). It was pandemonium but, to Blyton, this did not matter: 'the children took over the play at times and even held up the action', she reported proudly (quoted in Stoney, 166).

Noddy in Toyland's mixture of familiar ingredients received generally positive reviews—some saw it as testament to Blyton's ability to move seamlessly between genres and the show, whilst overpopulated with characters, was reckoned to have been cleverly tailored for the audience who tuned in to the BBC's *Listen with Mother* radio programme. Writing for the *Daily Mail*, Cecil Wilson reported that the show 'abounds in perky charm', thanks 'to Miss Blyton's knack of making childish absurdities sound so sensible'.[17] For *The Stage*, it was proof that 'the best way to make youngsters take a lasting interest in the theatre is to offer them real plays of their own'.[18] *The Times* predicted a 'turn of the tide', announcing how '[f]or the first time since the war the prospect for children being taken to the theatre this Christmas is brighter'.[19] Even Kenneth Tynan—a declared enemy of things twee and formulaic—offered the production some praise in his *Observer* column ('mildly pleasing') and compared it favourably to the star-studded pantomimes elsewhere, full of 'radio comedians…condemned to fidget uneasily in doublet and hose'. As Tynan noted, *Noddy in Toyland*, which had no 'stars' amongst its cast, kept things simple.[20] Simplicity was, of course, part of Blyton's stock-in-trade and, in the case of *Noddy in Toyland*, was part of its appeal. The show was easier to follow than other pantomimes: it blended fairies, goblins, talking animals, humans and toys together with music to make up a world that made sense to its young audience and gave them the opportunity to enter it through audience participation. Thus, it seemed to fill a need—especially for preschool children. As *The Times* later noted, there was a 'myth'-like quality to it all; it promised another way of living beyond the everyday which even to under-fives who (one might suppose) had not lived long enough to be weary or jaded, was beguiling. A more earthy aspect of the show's appeal was, as *The Times* pointed out, its ability to provide plenty 'of the falling-over and bonkings on the head that are the acme of humour for any child'.[21]

What is also apparent is that, as she had promised, Blyton, the celebrity, was one of the attractions. She attended many of the performances and publicised the fact to her fans in *Enid Blyton's Magazine*. 'I think you will recognise me, won't you', she wrote prior to *Noddy in Toyland's* first revival in December 1955. 'I am very like the picture [the Dorothy Wilding photograph] at the top of this letter!' (*EBM*, 21 December 1955, 3). Children were asked to wear their 'Busy Bee' or 'Famous Five' club badges as identification and Blyton promised that, if the audience waved to her, she would wave back. Shortly after Christmas, a gossip columnist for the *Daily Mail* spotted Blyton taking her place in her regular box to the right of the stage. What struck him, though, was not her expensive fur coat or her regal demeanour as she acknowledged the crowd from the royal box, but her behaviour as the show got under way. There was, he reported, '[n]o doubt at all that these characters of her imagination – Mr Plod…Noddy…Moonface - come alive for her on the stage.…She was leaning forward, studying the stage, intent on every word'.[22] There was something about this powerful woman, seemingly lost in the world of her own play, that the observer found rather touching.

All this was very gratifying for Blyton, of course, and doubly so when *Noddy in Toyland* looked like becoming a fixture in the West End during the Christmas season: the production was revived at The Prince's Theatre (1955–6), The Stoll (1956–7), The Prince's (1957–8), The Victoria Palace (1958–9), The Prince's (1959–60) and The Scala (1962–3), each iteration becoming more elaborate: flying ballets and pantomime horses were amongst the new additions. By the time *Noddy* moved triumphantly to The Scala, which had long been the traditional home of productions of *Peter Pan*, critics had started to compare Blyton's creation with Barrie's ageless flying boy. Both were 'landmarks' and, along with Lewis Carroll's Alice, were a permanent part of the theatrical scene.[23]

The success boosted Blyton's belief in her playwriting skills. She decided that she wanted her dramatic work to 'cover the whole of my age group', as she told Lewis E. Carroll, and so decided to focus on older children, 'the nines to fifteens'. Initially, she planned to write an adaption of one of the 'Adventure' stories but the logistics of having a parrot on stage put her off (Mac, 11 May 1955). Instead she wrote the *Famous Five Adventure*, as she explained:

> I've written a play based on the books I do for Hodders, the 'Famous Five'.…There's a dog there, of course, but I feel he would be easy to manage

compared with a parrot! It's been accepted, & will be on in London at the same time as 'Noddy in Toyland'– rather fun to have two plays running - especially as it never occurred to me that I could write proper stage plays. It is probably <u>opening</u> in the summer as we had had some enquires for an E.B. play from holiday resorts - & it would, I think, be a good idea to let it run for a few months in big provincial towns so that it will be absolutely slick when it opens in London. I do hope you'll come and see it – it's quite different from Noddy! (Mac, 8 April 1955)

Although the summer season never happened, the new play seemed guaranteed a good audience, not least because in telling her fans about it, Blyton was deliberately vague about its source and hinted that it was an original story. As she explained: 'I have written a Famous Five play at last!…It is what you asked me to make it—funny—exciting—and real!…[W]on't it be exciting' ('Green Hedges', *EBM*, 11 May 1955, 2–3). But she also confessed coyly to the readers of *Enid Blyton's Magazine* that, although the play was a 'new adventure', it was also 'just a little bit like one or two of the books, as you will see'. As she had done with *Noddy*, she dangled the prospect of seeing her famous characters in the flesh. 'How', she asked, 'will you like to see the…- Five come alive—to see old George losing her temper, and to see Timmy trying to help when danger comes?' ('Green Hedges', *EBM*, 23 November 1955, 3).

In the event, the play's mixture of intrigue, cross-dressing, American thugs and fairground folk was adapted mostly from *Five Have Plenty of Fun*, the fourteenth adventure in the series, published in July 1955.[24] The book features a spoilt and nervous American girl (Berta) daughter of an atomic scientist, who is billeted secretly in Kirrin Cottage and, as a means of protecting her from kidnap, is disguised as a boy. In contrast, in the stage version, the young American is a cocky boy who is disguised as 'Susan'. In other respects, things are familiar. The Famous Five are as socially insular on stage as they are in the books and George, in particular, comes across as egotistical and unpleasant as she stamps round the stage before being kidnapped by mistake. With the help of a runaway circus girl, Polly, who has been sleeping rough in the garden shed, Julian and Dick track down the fairground caravan where George is being held. Polly's uncle seems to be involved. Anne, meanwhile, is given little to do. In a cleverly creepy move, the play's climactic scenes take place in the dungeons on Kirrin Island (as with *Noddy*, one of the 'treats' of the production was for the audience to see familiar landmarks realised on stage) where the children outwit the American mobsters by slamming doors on them and climbing up hidden well shafts. This part of the play introduced a panoply of special effects, including a chase scene where the stage was plunged into darkness and the audience could only see torch-lights moving across it. The play's conclusion seemed to be a way of reassuring the audience that English children—these middle-class children at any rate—were still essentially brave and good. While Britain might be losing its way in the world, Blyton's famous characters were not.

Other influences were at work, too. *Famous Five Adventure* was the Famous Five series re-visioned—or regurgitated—for the stage by its money-spinning creator. But Blyton referred to it as 'a straight play' (quoted in Stoney, 167). In some ways, the treatment given the book had links back to the plays of Blyton's youth: the Five are squeezed into the framework of the 'well-made' thriller, not least in the emphasis on action rather than character and in the climatic final scene and patriotic resolution. Comparisons could also be made with another play featuring child adventurers, *Smugglers Beware* by Eleanor Whitcombe, which had run in London a year earlier in 1954.

Famous Five Adventure opened at the Prince's Theatre (now the Shaftes-bury Theatre) on 23 December 1955 where it ran in the evenings alongside the revival of *Noddy* (staged in the afternoons). It proved a commercial success and played to crowded houses, but critical reactions were often luke-warm. The *Birmingham Daily Post* admitted that, with the play's display of 'racing and chasing, kidnapping, fairground and caravan…the twelves and thirteens are [as intended] kept on the end of their seats…[w]hatever adults may say of it'.[25] But others thought the play had been thrown together and better suited to radio, and a frequent observation was that the dog playing Timmy was wont to distract by doing his own thing.

Despite the mixed reviews, it must have seemed to Blyton in December 1955 that there were no more triumphs to be had. Critics were indulgent about her being as much a fixture of the West End as she was everywhere else. Reporting on the theatrical year 1956 *Plays and Players* noted how, at a time when the 'present-day, post-war, Welfare State-aided average child is distinctively "age-grouped"…clever Miss Blyton rides a tandem – offering us a *Noddy and the Famous Five* to meet all demands'.[26] For Blyton, the activity had been a happy experience and her letters celebrate her success: 'They say it's the first time it's ever happened that an author has 2 plays in the same theatre at once', reported Blyton, 'but I'm pretty sure Agatha Christie has done this! It's all great fun, of course' (Mac, 1 November 1955). But although *Famous Five Adventure* was successful, it did not conquer in the way *Noddy* had done and ran for only two seasons (1955–1956 and 1956–1957). Part of the problem was the play felt dated. The *Daily Mail* approved of its cast of 'nicely brought up child characters' using '"topping"' as an exclamation but, to other commentators, they seemed old-fashioned and quaint.[27] By the end of the second season, there was also perhaps a growing sense that its ingredients had become too familiar and almost parodic. As *Plays and Players* reported, even 'Blyton devotees' had been heard to say, '"Gosh, I'm getting tired of the same sort of thing happening"'.[28] The impression one gets is that Blyton—Noddy aside—needed to find another play if she wanted to continue to appeal to her older readers, at least on stage. In fact, despite her new-found confidence, *Famous Five Adventure* represented the peak of her theatrical success and Noddy was her final significant new character. In May 1956 she found it impossible to get her play for adults, *The Touchstone* (also titled *Out of the Blue* and *Summer Storm*), taken on by Bertie Meyer or any other producer. The play, by 'Justin Geste' (just in jest?), had a plot centred on sibling disagreement and family squabbles. In its favour was the fact that it was the kind of politely strained, upper-middle-class drama, with French windows as part of the set, which dominated the West End during the 1950s. But it was also limp and amateurish. The best that could be said was that it teetered on the brink of competence. The younger Enid Blyton might have tried to revise it, but her sixty-year-old self was too tired, or too busy to do so, and her creative energies were running low. *The Touchstone* was never produced or published.

* * *

The extent of Blyton's theatrical ambitions and how successful she was at achieving them remain a matter of dispute. On the one hand, she was clearly successful within the limits she set herself. Watching a matinee of *Noddy of Toyland* in 1962, reporter Jean Stead took the audience reactions to it as confirmation that Blyton had now become 'one of the great monopolistic figures of the age. She appears in person at the end to wave vigorously to her worshippers'.[29] *Noddy in Toyland* and *Famous Five Adventure* gave the Blyton cult more space to flourish. On the other hand, it was felt by some, as *The Guardian* put it in 1954, that while Blyton's work gave 'great pleasure', her 'touch' was 'less sure as a dramatist than as a writer', that a text which might work as a bedtime story looked over-extended on stage.[30] There was also a feeling that a major part of her success was largely due to the expert staging of her texts by experienced professionals. A resisting observer might therefore claim there was something grandiose about Blyton's increasing tendency to describe herself as a West End playwright. 'I could write another in a week', Blyton boasted in 1955, 'now that I know how to harness my imagination to the new medium' (quoted in Stoney, 222). However, she was not a Dodie Smith, a Joan Temple (1887–1965) or an Esther McCracken (1902–1971), female playwrights who in the 1950s achieved long runs with well-crafted plays for grown-up audiences. Blyton's attempt to expand her range further did not take off.

Nonetheless, it is also possible to detect a more adventurous spirit and coherent purpose in Blyton's plays than she is given credit for; she wanted to push the boundaries of how she might tell her stories and used her plays to connect with her audiences and further create a sense of shared experience. There is also a case for arguing that it was the success in theatre which was responsible for Blyton's works finally being taken up by television and film. (In 1944–45 Blyton had conversations with Gaumont-British Studios about adapting some of the 'Adventure' series for the cinema but nothing had ever come of it). It was on 25 September 1955, following the acquisition of the Noddy books by the new independent ATV (the creation of which broke the monopoly of the BBC), that Blyton's achieved her longed-for foothold in broadcasting. Television was recognised as the 'coming medium' and, by the end of the 1950s, there were 10 million televisions in use, watched each evening by roughly half the country's population. Acquiring Enid Blyton made sense for commercial television's investors and advertisers and the little nodding man and his friends (now puppets), found a place alongside the cowboy, Roy Rogers and quiz shows like *Double Your Money* and *Take Your Pick*, as well as being used to advertise 'Kellogg's Sugar Ricicles' in the ad breaks.[31] '[T]hey have offered me the peak half hour', Blyton explained, '& give me an absolutely free hand' (Mac, 25 November 1954). The first season of *The Adventures of Noddy* (1955–56) was broadcast in competition with the BBC's puppets, Muffin the Mule, Andy Pandy and Bill and Ben. As conceived by ATV, Noddy was no less bland than these offerings and the fifteen-minute programmes were deemed suitable for Sunday viewing. As *Picture Post* told parents: 'It should help the young and point to values and ideals which are neglected by many other media of entertainment'.[32] A second series followed.

Nor was this the only means by which Blyton sought to move herself and her work into other media. In August 1956, work began on a film adaptation of *Five on a Treasure Island*, under the auspices of the Rank Organisation and on location at Corfe Castle and Studland Bay. Two years later, EMI brought out four extended-play records featuring Blyton reading Noddy stories. The series producer, Robert Tredinnick, wrote of how Blyton, whom he judged an 'honest' and likeable hard-worker, did not arrive grandly at the recording studios 'with a preconceived notion of how the job would be tackled' but rather 'with a genuine desire to learn something of the technique'.[33] With such comments, the narrative that casts Blyton as a controlling attention-seeker is derailed again and the complexities of her responses to different aspects of her writing life are highlighted. The presence of these overlapping activities is also typical of the way Blyton juggled her professional life more generally, of course, and, as the 1960s loomed, she regarded all of them as important ways of strengthening her prestige.

* * *

As a coda to this chapter on Blyton and the theatre, it is worth noting a performance that did not take place. As mentioned in the previous chapter, in August 1960, Blyton was asked to appear as a witness for the defence at the trial of publishers Penguin Books. They were being prosecuted under the Obscene Publications Act for seeking to publish D.H. Lawrence's sexually explicit novel *Lady Chatterley's Lover* (1928). The trial placed Britain's archaic decency laws under the spotlight and its titillating content received considerable press attention. One of the points of interest was Penguin's decision to call some of the country's leading authors, academics and clerics as "expert" witnesses who would support their [Penguin's] case. Those who appeared in court included E.M. Forster, J.B. Priestley and Helen Gardner. They were cross-examined by the Crown's lawyer, Mervyn Griffith-Jones, whose old-fashioned assumptions about society were captured in his much-mocked question as to whether Lawrence's novel was something 'you would even wish your wife or servants to read'. The jury judged the book not to be obscene, Penguin went to press and, within three months, three million copies had been sold in a cheap paperback edition.

When Michael Rubenstein, Penguin's solicitor, asked Blyton to appear, she was 'astonished' and flattered but refused, on the grounds that as a 'small fry' children's writer nothing she had to say on the subject of a 'pornographic book' would carry much weight with the public. She was perhaps unduly modest here but realised that the spectacle would be incongruous. 'Don't you think there is something slightly comic about E.B. solemnly declaring that L.C. Lover is a fit & proper book for everyone's reading?':

I'd love to help Penguins Ltd. – they are doing a fine job with their publications – but I don't see how I can. For one thing I haven't read the book - & for another thing my husband said NO, at once. The thought of me standing up in court solemnly advocating a book 'like that' (his words, not mine – I feel he must have read the book!) made his hair stand on end. I'm awfully sorry – but I don't see that I can go against him. I feel impelled to read the book now, of course (what MARVELLOUS publicity it is having, & how pleased Penguin's must be!) though a woman author (for adults) once told me that it was dull & badly written.

Can you manage to convey my apologies to Penguins, & let them know that while I <u>am</u> against too much censorship of books, I really cannot go against my husband's most definite wishes in this.[34]

It is an interesting glimpse into Enid Blyton as the 1960s began. She is charming, lively, cheerful and broad-minded but the mention of Kenneth Darrell Waters (channelling Mervyn Griffith-Jones) reminds us again that, in some respects, she was a woman of her time. Sixty years on, we can only regret that she did not say 'yes' and take part in an event that proved a symbolic moment in Britain's cultural history.

Notes

1. Enid Blyton, 'Writing for Children's Television', *The Stage TV Supplement* (22 September 1955), x.
2. Frances Stephens, 'Review of the Year', *Theatre World Annual* 5 (1953–4), 7.
3. Frances Stephens, 'Review of the Year, *Theatre World Annual* 6 (1954–55), 7.
4. Christopher Fry, *An Experience of Critics,* quoted in Frances Stephens, 'Review of the Year', *Theatre World Annual* 5 (1953–4), 7.
5. Unsigned Article, 'Bertie Meyer's Jubilee', *The Stage* (31 January 1952), 10.
6. Quoted in Angela Bull, *Noel Streatfeild* (London: Collins 1984), 252.
7. Unsigned Article, 'BBC Archive releases new documents about Enid Blyton and her tempestuous relationship with the BBC' (15 November 2009). http://www.bbc.co.uk/pressoffice/pressreleases/stories/2009/11_november/15/blyton.shtml. Accessed 26 June 2021.
8. Quoted in Tom Sutcliffe, 'Commercial juggernaut at its best', *The Independent* (17 November 2009) https://www.independent.co.uk/voices/columnists/thomas-sutcliffe/tom-sutcliffe-the-over-complicated-life-of-belle-de-jour-1821768.html. Accessed 14 June 2021.
9. Unsigned Article, 'BBC Archive releases new documents about Enid Blyton and her tempestuous relationship with the BBC'.
10. Unsigned Article, 'Small beer' Blyton banned by BBC' (15 November 2009). http://news.bbc.co.uk/1/hi/uk/8361056.stm. Accessed 8 March 2021.
11. Unsigned Article, 'New Fashioned Christmas', *The Stage* (31 December 1954), 18.
12. Quoted in Norman Robbins, *Slapstick and Sausages: The Evolution of British Pantomime* (London: Trapdoor, 2002), 210.
13. Unsigned Article, 'The Christmas Shows of 1959', *The Stage* (7 January 1960), 9.
14. Eric Morecambe, 'Views', *The Listener* (21 December 1972), 849.
15. Millie Taylor, *British Pantomime Performance* (London: Intellect, 2007), 82–3.

16. J.F.B., 'Christmas Shows for Children: Miss Blyton's Toys Come to Life', *Guardian* (24 December 1954), 2.
17. Cecil Wilson, 'Little Noddy Keeps his Fans Buzzing', *Daily Mail* (24 December 1954), 3.
18. Unsigned Article, 'New Fashioned Christmas', 18.
19. Unsigned Article, 'Christmas in the Theatres', *The Times* (20 December 1954), 9.
20. Kenneth Tynan, 'Winter Fuel', *The Observer* (26 December 1954), 7.
21. Unsigned Article, 'The Stoll Theatre', *The Times* (24 December 1956), 10.
22. 'Tanfield's Diary', *Daily Mail* (28 December 1955), 10.
23. Unsigned Article, 'Blyton Country Does not Date', *The Times* (22 December 1962), 3.
24. Enid Blyton, *Famous Five Adventure*. British Library Add Mss, Lord Chamberlain's Collection of Plays 1955/67.
25. Unsigned Article, 'Pantomime Has Little chance in London', *The Birmingham Daily Post* (28 December 1955), 13.
26. Leslie Daiken, 'But once a Year', *Plays and Players* (February 1957), 13.
27. E.G, 'For Blyton Fans', *Daily Mail*, (24 December 1955), 5.
28. Leslie Daiken, 'But once a Year', 13.
29. Jean Stead, 'More Noddy', *Guardian* (22 December 1962), 4.
30. J.F.B, 'Christmas Shows for Children', 2.
31. Peter Hennessey, *Having it So Good: Britain in the Fifties* (2006; London: Penguin, 2007), 230; 535; 536.
32. Peter Eadie, 'What the Children will be Seeing', *Picture Post* (3 February 1955), 44.
33. Cave of Books: *Audio Section* www.enidblytonsociety.co.uk. Accessed 8 March 2021.
34. Enid Blyton to Michael B. Rubenstein, 20 August 1960. University of Bristol Special Collections DM1679/Box 7, 'Witnesses unhelpful or rejected'. Also quoted in *Penguin Portrait, Allen Lane and the Penguin Editors*, ed. Steve Hare (London: Penguin, 2005), 243–4.

Bibliography

Bull, Angela. 1984. *Noel Streatfeild*. London: Collins.
Hare, Steve. Editor. 1995. *Penguin Portrait, Allen Lane and the Penguin Editors*. London: Penguin.
Robbins, Norman. 2002. *Slapstick and Sausages: The Evolution of British Pantomime*. London: Trapdoor.
Stephens, Frances. 1955. 'Review of the Year'. In *Theatre World Annual* 5 (1953–4): 5–8. London: Rockliff

———. 1956. 'Review of the Year'. In *Theatre World Annual* 6 (1954–5): 5–8. London: Rockliff.

Taylor, Millie. 2007. *British Pantomime Performance*. London: Intellect.

Unsigned Article, 'Enid Blyton and the BBC: Revealing the Writer's Troubled Relationship with the BBC'. *BBC Archive*. http://www.bbc.co.uk/archive/blytonand thebbc/. Accessed 1 September 2016.

Unsigned Article. 2009. 'BBC Archive Releases New Documents about Enid Blyton and her Tempestuous Relationship with the BBC'. http://www.bbc.co.uk/presso ffice/pressreleases/stories/2009/11_november/15/blyton.shtml. Accessed 8 March 2021.

Unsigned Article. 2009. 'Small beer' Blyton banned by BBC'. http://news.bbc.co. uk/1/hi/uk/8361056.stm. Accessed 8 March 2021.

12

Final Years

After her theatrical successes, Blyton expected to carry on with the same routines she had followed since the 1930s. For a while, this was indeed the case. The seventeenth Famous Five adventure, *Five Get into A Fix*, was published in 1958. So too was *Puzzle for the Secret Seven*, the tenth book in that series. There were new stories about Bom (a toy drummer), Scamp (a puppy) and more about Noddy. But it became clear to those around Blyton that she was finding it difficult to work at the same pace or with the same consistency. Up until this point, her health had generally been good, apart from an attack of pneumonia in 1954 and an attack by a dog two years earlier, which had required surgery. But, in May 1957 (aged fifty-nine), she suffered what was assumed to be a 'minor' heart attack while playing golf. She was slow to recover and began to feel anxious and depressed. It was evident that she needed to reduce her workload (Stoney, 176–7). *Enid Blyton's Magazine* continued to appear for two more years but became burdensome. Blyton announced its closure on 9 September 1959, explaining:

> It is because of two things. The first is that all kinds of interesting work keeps coming along which unfortunately no one but myself can do [here she mentions the Noddy TV series, films, records, stage productions, and overseas radio broadcasts]....And going all the time is my magazine, of which, as you know, I write practically every word....The second reason is to do with my husband, who, now that he has decided to retire, naturally wants me to go about with him a good deal, and share the things he loves so much – his farm down in Dorset, golf, and travelling here and there about the world. Well, I

A. Maunder, *Enid Blyton*, Literary Lives, https://doi.org/10.1007/978-3-030-76332-9_12

must be with him, of course, and so, with much sadness, I have decided to give up the thing that ties me down the most – our magazine, the work I love best. I am sad because it has kept me in such close touch with all you boys and girls for so long, and we have shared so many things together. ('Green Hedges', *EBM*, 9 September 1959, 2–3)

Possibly the magazine could have continued but it relied heavily on Blyton's personality—or what passed for it—and it is difficult to imagine anyone else taking over. Meanwhile Blyton spent time focusing on the last of her series books. The final 'Barney' story, *The Ragamuffin Mystery*, was published in July of the same year. It revealed a distinct 'falling off' in Blyton's powers and craftsmanship. She, meanwhile, remained keen to try and crack the U.S. market. She pushed Paul Hodder-Williams to try to place *Five on a Treasure Island* and *Five Go Adventuring Again* with an American publisher. Eleven firms were approached but Williams reported that 'they [the books] met with such a bad reception' that it was hopeless to continue.[1] However, back in Britain, Blyton remained 'ubiquitous', as Walter Allen, the American critic living in London reported in 1960, constituting 'a whole children's mass-entertainment industry in her own person'.[2] The previous year, Alison Uttley, guest of honour at a garden fete in July 1959, was irked to discover that, while they listened politely enough, what the attendees *really* wanted to know was '[d]id I know Enid Blyton?'.[3]

Yet the start of the new decade was also the time in which responses to Blyton and her work underwent a negative turn. She experienced rejection from her long-standing publisher Macmillan when their reader turned down *The Mystery that Never Was* (1961). What struck the reader, Phyllis Hart-noll, was the 'faint but unattractive touch of old-fashioned xenophobia in the author's attitude' and also the story's 'painfully thin' characterisation.[4] As we saw in Chapter Two, Blyton also began to encounter resistance from educationalists and librarians who started to talk about Blyton being overrated and complained about her vice-like grip on the nation's children and their parents. Other criticisms of her were that she was mediocre and self-serving, her vision was narrow and commonplace and her social politics was glib and outdated. The Find-Outers series, which ended in desultory fashion in 1961 with *The Mystery of Banshee Towers*, was a case in point. Blyton's world was one of cooks, gardeners, summer-houses and deferential shopkeepers seen through the elderly author's rarefied pre-war lens. Similar complaints were levelled at Agatha Christie. Yet to criticise Blyton (or Christie) on her inability to provide a gritty portrayal of 1960s Britain was—and is—to miss the point. The Find-Outers stories are not mimetic. Blyton was more inclined to shield her readers from the disturbances of the modern world than plunge them into it. Others, however thought she should be doing something different. 'We know that from the very beginning of life…the phantasies of the child's mind are by no means the pretty stories which Miss Blyton regales us with', announced Anthony Storr in *The New Statesman* in November 1960. 'They are both richer and more primitive and the driving forces behind them are those of sexuality and the aggressive urge to power'.[5] Critical appreciations of her work thus became rare. Profiles of her that did appear were sometimes derogatory and condescending. As we saw in Chapter 9, sneering at Blyton became something of a habit, a first step towards extolling the new, making oneself seem better attuned to children and being more 'with it'.

While Blyton seemed to be stuck in the past, her earnings were not. In 1959 the *Financial Times* estimated that amongst living British authors she was second only to Agatha Christie (who earned £75,000 a year, mostly from her stage plays) and far ahead of Daphne du Maurier, Graham Greene and Somerset Maugham.[6] The British sales for the Famous Five 'are quite stupendous', reported George Greenfield in April 1959. He was speaking in particular of *Five Get into a Fix* and its first-year figure of 93,491. Blyton's royalty for the same period was £4481.[7] (By way of comparison, a clerical officer in the civil service could expect to receive an annual salary of around £525.) Other works, too, continued to make a mark. In 1959, thirteen cartoon films based on the toy soldier, Bom, were made by World Wide Pictures. The BBC—seemingly reconciled to Blyton—bought them, paying £150 per film, a sum which was, as Philip Hodder Williams noted, 'top of the market price'.[8] In 1963, journalist Simon Kavanaugh described Blyton as the 'highest paid woman in Britain', whose work had been translated into over twenty languages, whose Noddy books alone had sold 26 million copies and whose total sales were clearly far in excess of this: 'What sort of woman is Enid Blyton to have chalked up this remarkable record?' he asked. He went to investigate:

She is a modest, uncomplicated person who lives comfortably with her husband and her cats in a pleasant house in Beaconsfield….Her home gives a good clue to her personality. It is the sort of setting beloved by the authors of light comedy about English middle-class life. There is an air of tranquillity and good taste worn discreetly.

Inevitable income considered, it is a modest ménage that does not even hint at being the fountainhead of what is in fact a thriving commercial enterprise with tentacles reaching into publishing, theatre, television, toys and toilet requisites. (Noddy toothbrushes, Noddy nursery soap etc.)

Kavanagh's impression of the Enid Blyton of 1963 as a genteel lady novelist was not far off the mark and his visit to her was clearly useful in correcting some of the ideas about her which had sprung up. People who hadn't met Blyton had come to visualise her either as a female Walt Disney *or* a latter-day Beatrix Potter, 'fluttering captive of a lifelong childish dream'. In fact, as Kavanagh explained, Enid Blyton was 'neither'. She was not, as popularly supposed, a 'type':

> While she is no cold-eyed exploiter of childish fancy, at the same time she is not naïve. She is a good business-woman in that she knows what her public wants and provides it for them in good measure.
>
> No more is she fey and other worldly. After all she is the wife of a surgeon and the mother of two grown daughters, the sort of background that fosters a certain cynicism about the existence of fairies at the bottom of the garden.

Yet the woman who wrote stories about teddy bears, goblins, child detectives and midnight feasts was also sincere—a trait which impressed itself. Blyton was not, as Kavanagh had expected, a fake but rather an unusual person with an 'uncanny access to the childish mind, a faculty lost to most adults or overlaid beyond recall'. Admittedly, Blyton's self-identification with readers—her manifesto—was harder to digest than it had been twenty years before—at least for her detractors, who remained suspicious. It was also at odds with the cynicism of 1960s Britain which, as Kavanaugh noted, 'tends to raise an incredulous eyebrow at such characteristics and wonder "what is her gimmick?"' After meeting the sixty-five-year-old authoress, Kavanagh came away charmed, thinking she was somewhere 'in her fifties'; Blyton was obviously not about to disabuse him.[9]

These kinds of encounters—which appear intermittently in newspapers and magazines in the early 1960s—are a reminder that forty years after she had begun, Blyton was still occasionally able to negotiate images of herself that accommodated conflicting and changing views about writers and women. She was proud to be receiving 300 letters a month from her readers who, as she put it, guided her in what she wrote, and whose letters were their own reward. They were validation and proof that, even in her sixties, she could fill her self-designated role as teacher and protector: '"I am a contented and happy person", she told Lewis De Fries in June 1962, "because I have done the one big thing I have always wanted to do – and am still doing it"'. But it was not just about the children. '"I have many interests outside my work – I like to knit, to read, to play chess and bridge, paint flowers, potter about in the garden. And I adore golf"'.[10]

Fig. 12.1 Enid Blyton in the porch at Green Hedges, 1963 © Alamy

She may have been semi-retired but, as people in the 1960s said, Blyton always seemed to be there. Annuals, reprints, revivals on stage of *Noddy in Toyland*, ensured she remained part of the fabric of popular culture. In May 1966, the BBC children's drama series *Quick Before They Catch Us* was clearly indebted to her—right down to the pet monkey kept by one of the three child detectives in their bid to expose a Peter Rachman-type villain (Rachman had been a notorious racketeer and slum landlord in the 1950s). Earlier, Blyton had made her way onto the stage of London's most progressive theatre, the Royal Court. Their 1965 Christmas show *Clowning*, a typically avant-garde mix of mime and improvisation, showed how hero and heroine, Jim and Enid, escape from the machinations of the wicked 'Big Nose' and become clowns in the circus. As we saw in Chapter Two, moves in 1967 by publishers such as Hamlyn and Armada and Knight (an imprint of Hodder) to reissue part of Blyton's back catalogue in paperback helped keep her works visible and, at 2 shillings and sixpence, her books were accessible to children looking to spend precious pocket money.

Yet, by the middle of the decade, Blyton was struggling. In 1957, she had written to Peter McKellar, a psychologist, about the nature of creativity and about her fears of not being able to function: 'I dread the feeling of losing my identity, of not being able to control my own mind!' (quoted in Stoney, 182).

By the start of the 1960s there were signs that her memory *was* failing. She became disorientated and became confused about times and places. Gradually she found it difficult to live in the present and would sometimes imagine that she was back in her childhood home in Beckenham (Stoney 183). Writing became harder. She completed *Fun for the Secret Seven* over five weeks in January and February 1963 but she also found it difficult to concentrate. George Greenfield recalled how she would take a previously published story, type it out afresh and present it to him as new, not realising what she was doing. Greenfield, a loyal and kindly man, continued to keep Blyton up to speed with how her books were selling, but meetings were less about business and were increasingly held at her home rather than in London. Public appearances, too, began to dwindle. In January 1963 she was present at the final performance of the Christmas season of *Noddy in Toyland* at the Scala Theatre (*D*, 19 January 1963). In 1964, Hodder and Stoughton suggested that she attend the World Book Fair to be held at Earl's Court Exhibition Centre on 10 June. The week-long event would be an opportunity for Blyton to reconnect with her fans now that *Enid Blyton's Magazine* was no longer published. Greenfield, however, dismissed the idea of such a high-profile public appearance. It might, he explained, be a success if Blyton was having a 'good' day (which was possible). She might sign some autographs for an hour. Yet anything else presented too great a risk. It was certainly out of the question that she be asked to talk or tell stories to the crowd as she once had done.[11]

There is a sense of Blyton's world—which had never been wide—shrinking. In her diary for February 1964 she records feeling depressed and having trouble sleeping (*D*, 24 February 1964). By this time, most of the titles published under her name were reprints—or were anthologies like *Enid Blyton's Storytime Book* or *Enid Blyton's Bedtime Book*, the titles of which disguised the fact that this was not new work. Blyton's final, new title, *The Man Who Stopped to Help*, a re-telling of the Biblical tale of the good Samaritan, was published by Lutterworth in 1965. It was clear that her wish to write another Famous Five book was not going to happen. It became apparent, too, that the business side of publishing—the contracts, agreements, rights—which she had once managed with aplomb, was beyond her. 'I don't really understand it all' she confided to her diary (*D*, 27 April 1966).

During all this, Kenneth Darrell Waters, who was also in poor health, tried to shield Blyton and remove anything which could tarnish the carefully wrought image, including burning diaries. His efforts were noted during Blyton's last interview, which was for BBC *Woman's Hour* and recorded in January 1966. Sue MacGregor, the interviewer, recalled it as a disconcerting experience. She had already met Blyton's contemporary, Richmal Crompton, 'an amusingly sharp - elderly lady…warmly humorous and very civilised company'. The meeting with Blyton, whose works she had devoured as a small child in South Africa, was less enjoyable, largely on account of Darrell Waters:

> After each of my questions he raised an admonishing hand, preventing his wife from saying anything until he had decided what the answer should be….One of the most startling responses my questioning elicited was the calm revelation that Miss Blyton's writing method consisted of thinking a bit, and then 'typing out the story without a stop'.[12]

Like other worshippers who find their idols have feet of clay, MacGregor struggled to hide her disappointment.

Events moved rapidly in summer of 1967 when Darrell Waters was admitted to hospital with kidney failure (partly a side effect of his dosing himself with powerful painkillers for his arthritis). His last days were spent worrying about his wife. One of his final acts was to ask George Greenfield to take a letter to Blyton who, confused and needing care, had been admitted to a nursing home. As Greenfield tells it, the nursing home was grim and cheerless, and Blyton barely knew where she was, but Greenfield helped her to write a reply. When, on 15 September 1967, Kenneth passed away, the blow was devastating. Blyton scrawled in her diary: 'My darling Kenneth died. I loved him so much. I feel lost and unhappy'—sentiments which capture the last year of her life (D, 15 September 1967). Blyton's daughter Gillian noted in a letter how, from this point, life seemed to lose its interest.[13] Meanwhile Blyton's health declined rapidly. By January 1968 she had stopped answering letters herself; Eric Rogers took over her affairs, liaising with Blyton's publishers. A long-term associate, Ewart Wharmby, who had worked with the novelist at Brockhampton Press, reported that it was becoming evident that she could no longer cope. A plan for Blyton, who felt cut off and lonely, to move to Yorkshire and live with her daughter Gillian, came to nothing.[14] Instead, Blyton was looked after on a day-to-day basis by her long-serving housekeeper, Doris Cox, before being admitted into a Hampstead nursing home where she died in her sleep on 28 November 1968. The death certificate for Enid Mary Darrell Waters, aged seventy-one, gave coronary thrombosis as the cause of death. There were no recorded last words or last wishes.

News of Blyton's death was filtered through to the public by newspapers, but there were no big headlines as there might have been fifteen years before.

The papers were preoccupied with other things. The funeral of the assassinated U.S. Attorney General, Robert Kennedy, had just taken place. This was alongside reports of John Lennon, Yoko Ono and Georgie Fame being tried at a London court for drugs possession. The death of an old-fashioned elderly author was not something for the front pages. '[H]er world', *The Newcastle Journal* noted of Blyton, 'and the world of her fictitious child characters, was basically narrow' and 'belonged to another age. She wrote of children who went to pay schools and never lacked for money, who had healthy outdoor adventurous school holidays and an unconquerable devotion to tracking down evil-doers. In her world there was no pop and no teenage romance'.[15] *The Times* noted that the average age of Blyton's readers had fallen since the 1940s; no self-respecting sixteen-year old would be seen dead reading one of her books, while the 'cold war' that Blyton conducted with librarians had revealed someone whose ideas about children had not changed much over the years and who was unwilling to adapt.[16] She was in essence, the *Newcastle Journal* explained, '[a] shy retiring woman who had servants that she called by their surnames, a habit of talking about "our kind of people" and an unfortunate tendency to make her fictional villains golliwogs'—all things which helped ensure that she had outlived her usefulness.[17] It was widely noted that she had 'made many enemies by her prolific pen, and her jumbo, long-lasting success' as *W.H. Smith's Trade News* put it.[18] Yet while there was agreement that Blyton had written too much it was conceded that her best books were quite good, notably *The Enchanted Wood* and the Famous Five series, stories which gave joy to children growing up on war-time austerity.

What most papers *were* forced to acknowledge was that the extent of Blyton's success was unlikely to be seen again. No one was quite sure how many books she had written (even she had lost count). Was it 350? 400? 700? Some notices reported that she had left behind several unpublished works that would add to the tally in due course. *W.H. Smith's Trade News* reported that her total sales in English stood at 85 million.[19] The *Daily Mail* reported that she still sold 5 million books a year.[20] Meanwhile, the *Birmingham Daily Post* suggested that her total sales (30 million in their estimate) were at least 8 million more than Ian Fleming's James Bond novels, proof that she had managed to enchant readers who 'knew better what they wanted than her critics....Not least of their attractions were the clearly defined moral precepts which some parents and teachers probably distrust as being unrepresentative of the moral complexity of the world the children are going to face. But children are all-natural moralists and Enid Blyton...knew this well'.[21] In the *Daily Mail*, Diana Norman admitted Blyton's limitations, including the tendency not to 'challenge' readers, but noted, too, the sense of 'security' offered by her books: 'for more than 40 years, in a frightening and perplexing world, her books remained the same'. Norman compared Blyton's appeal with that of Georgette Heyer, the celebrated author of historical romances. Readers 'knew exactly what they were going to get'. 'Opening an Enid Blyton book was like getting into a warm bath or starting a box of chocolates - it might not be good for you, but…it was a luxury…She never gave children what they should have. She gave them what they wanted'.[22]

Of Blyton herself, the obituarists had less to say. Several explained that she had been a recluse who lived in 'complete seclusion'—a statement which might have been true for the last two years of her life but was certainly not the case for most of it.[23] All the obituaries mentioned that she had two daughters, although the impression given to readers was that they were the result of Blyton's marriage to Kenneth Darrell Waters rather than Hugh Pollock. The *Daily Mail* was amongst the papers that had to retract this claim. Occasionally writers tracked down people who had known her—or not. The *Daily Record* quoted Blyton's housekeeper, Doris Cox who described her former employer as "'a wonderful woman'". A 'neighbour', who was also quoted, reported that Blyton was "'a quiet woman who rarely went out and kept very much to herself'".[24] In a similar vein, *The Buckinghamshire Advertiser* titled its report, 'Enid Blyton – the quiet author of Beaconsfield', and described her as one of the town's 'most famous and best-loved residents'. It offered a titbit given by a Mrs B. Atkinson, who had known (via Blyton's next-door neighbour) that the celebrated author was 'a very pleasant person'. This rather mundane recollection was followed by a more peculiar one from Alison Uttley (aged eighty-three), still living less than a mile away. Finally able to have the last word, she explained (untruthfully) that she had only met Blyton once (at 'a social evening') and found her behaviour odd: "'Enid Blyton picked up a little painting book of mine and looked at it intently from cover to cover. I remember I couldn't understand why. I thought it was a grown-ups' party. Normally people will just flick through the pages of a child's book'".[25] It is hard to work out what Uttley was implying here: Blyton's interest in all things relating to children? Her social ineptitude? Her eccentricity? Or was that this was the only comment from Uttley that was fit to print?

Not surprisingly, the other aspect of Blyton's life that interested the newspapers was her wealth. There was a consensus that she was 'among the best known – and richest authors in the world' but that, despite being a wealthy woman, had chosen to live modestly, her luxuries being restricted to a golf course and several luxury cars.[26] As always, there was speculation about how much she actually earned. Some journalists claimed that it was £50,000 a year.[27] Others suggested that her earnings were much higher: £150,000 in a 'good' year and £100,000 in a 'bad' one (£150,000 is worth roughly 2.6 million in 2021 values). Four days after Blyton's death *The Daily Express* used the headline 'Where Noddy's Earnings Go' as a prelude to assessing the 'fascinating' state of Blyton's finances and went as far as it dared to hint at money laundering. It was reported that Kenneth Waters had left 'more than £250,000', an unusually substantial sum for a retired surgeon. There was no evidence that Blyton's income was being invested in other businesses. She had sold her golf course some years previously. *The Daily Express* ended its speculation by drawing attention to the existence of Darrell Waters Ltd., the company run by Blyton's 'old friend and executor', Eric Rogers, described as a 'city stockbroker'. Rogers was quoted as explaining that, '"Nothing was ever further from her [Blyton's] understanding than finance"', a statement which *The Express* presented in such a way as to imply that the elderly authoress—a national treasure—had been duped by unscrupulous people—Rogers foremost amongst them. It was possible, of course, that there *was* no secret. The paper quoted Rogers describing how interests in Noddy were now invested in a company called the British Printing Corporation and in an offshoot called 'Noddy Subsidiaries', which was '"very profitable"'. When Blyton's will was announced in January 1969, it was explained that she had left personal wealth of £283,598 net which would go primarily to her daughters.[28]

Alongside the personal recollections and financial discussions, there were also attempts to decide on Blyton's literary legacy. How many of her books would last? Several journalists noted her similarities to A.A. Milne and Arthur Ransome but concluded that while the formers' books would come to be regarded as 'classics'—not least because they took trouble with them, whereas Blyton, for whom writing was 'like spinning cotton off a reel', did not.[29] Her stories were unsophisticated, very predictable and instantly forgettable and, being 'readable', did not count for much. But at the same time, she seemed critic-proof and sold well.[30] As William Feaver noted in 1974, following the publication of Barbara Stoney's biography: '[B]y the time the critic has cleared his throat and voiced his complaint about poverty of speech, imagination and characterisation, the storyteller and her fans have hurried on, volumes ahead'.[31] There was widespread recognition, too, that her death represented the passing of an era—something compounded in January 1969 with the passing of Richmal Crompton. W.E. Johns had died in June 1968. Who, it was asked, would take over?

* * *

Although Blyton has not, of course, disappeared, the sense of her belonging to a very specific time and place is something which remains strong. As has been seen, her career as an author spanned more than fifty years, from the end of the First World War through to the 'swinging' 1960s. During this period, Blyton's writings offer witness to the emergence of different phases of the development of writing for children. In the early 1920s, fairy poems, school stories and talking animals dominated children's publishing and Blyton rose quickly in this environment. In Blyton's last years, her relevance could seem less obvious and she was eclipsed in critics' minds by younger writers like Robert Westall, Leon Garfield, Nina Bawden and Susan Cooper whose works were more obviously 'grittier'. Novels like *Tom's Midnight Garden* by Philippa Pearce (1958), *The Wolves of Willoughby Chase* by Joan Aiken (1962) and *Charlie and the Chocolate Factory* by Roald Dahl (1964), while not obviously more forward-looking, possessed more ambition and flair than the stories Blyton had long been content to publish. But, in between these times, Blyton's ability to work in different genres, her mastery of the children's adventure and detective story, the boarding school story and the family story, her editorships and her ability to establish a close bond with her audience, were more important than any other author's in encouraging literacy and a love of reading.

What, then, of Blyton in the twenty-first century? I began this book by noting that Blyton has not gone away. The company she was involved in setting up, Darrell Waters Ltd. continued to operate extremely profitably before being sold to Trocadero plc for £14.6 million in 1995. In 2012, the rights to Blyton's published works were purchased by Hachette UK (with the exception of the Noddy books, which were bought by Classic Media). 'For more than 60 years, Noddy has helped bring the magic of toys to life and we're going to keep passing that along to fans and new generations', Classic Media's CEO Eric Ellenbogen explained.[32] Yet, to log on to those parts of cyberspace hosting the Enid Blyton Society, World of Blyton or Enid-Blyton.net, is to realise that appreciation is not confined to businessmen or the under twelves. Blyton also figures in academe; she has been the subject of PhD studies in addition to featuring on courses devoted to children's literature. Moreover, although not all of Blyton's 700 or so books (figures remain vague) are in print, there are over two hundred titles available.[33] Many of them have been updated (a process begun with the Famous Five series during the 1970s) with vocabulary changed to give them a more 'modern' feel but as was noted at the beginning of this book, they continue to sell in large quantities. Add to this the revisiting of Blyton's characters in new stories including Pamela Cox's six Malory Towers sequels (2009), Pamela Butchart's *The Secret Seven: Mystery of the Skull* (2018), Claude Voilier's long-running *Le Club des Cinq* series, the German films *Funf Freunde* (dir. Mike Marzxuk,

2012; sequels 2013, 2014; 2015), Christine Hartmann's *Hanni & Nanni*, based on the St Clare's stories (2010; sequels 2012; 2013; 2017), the Dreamworks' series *Noddy: Toyland Detective* (2016), which followed Chorion's GCI animated *Make Way for Noddy* (2002–3), the 'Enchanted World' series by Elise Allen (2008–9) which continued the Magic Faraway Tree tales and *Five on a Great Western Adventure* by Mandy Archer (2019), a tie-in with the railway company's advertising campaign, there is plenty to suggest Blyton's wide appeal.[34] In 2018 Jacqueline Wilson and Michael Morpurgo were amongst those selecting their favourite Blyton stories for a new anthology.[35] If nothing else, this continuing presence is testimony to a desire to keep the author and her characters—or at least versions of them—alive and talking and suggests that her influence on later generations of writers has not gone away entirely.

Yet what Blyton actually 'means' is complicated. To recognise her achievements and give her a central place in twentieth-century literary history is not to stabilise her or excuse the less appealing parts of her work. She was a flawed personality (like all of us). She remains inherently contradictory and frustrating. She is at once devoted daughter, genius, ambitious careerist, opportunist, outsider, insider, the epitome of a recognisable type of 1930s, no-nonsense, middle-class womanhood, repressed, neurotic, casually racist and epitome of the literary hack. Although she may seem to fit awkwardly within any of the tropes of successful waves of feminist biography, it is also the case that she confounded many of the expectations of her time(s), at least as far as women were concerned. She was not a literary rebel—although she gained considerable power and influence for herself both in and outside the publishing world—and the critics of the day and her readers found her fiction morally unimpeachable. Above all she was a writer, someone whose diverse output is indelibly linked to the popular genres of the early mid-twentieth century, most notably those tailored for children, to trends in publishing practices and literary fashion. Considering where she started from, her success was all the more remarkable. The Blyton revealed in this context is thus a figure whose rehabilitation is long overdue, not least because her literary life offers an unparalleled case study of literary professionalisation in the twentieth century.

Notes

1. Paul Hodder-Williams to George Greenfield, 20 March 1959, London Metropolitan Archives/Hodder and Stoughton Archives, M.16352A.

2. Walter Allen, 'A London Father Tells of His Children's Literary Taste', *The New York Times* (13 November 1960), CBS30.

3. Quoted in Dennis Judd (ed.), *The Private Diaries of Alison Uttley* (Barnsley: Pen and Sword, 2009), 228.

4. Quoted in Chris Hastings, 'Publisher Rejected Blyton Tale for Being "Xenophobic"', *The Sunday Telegraph* (20 November 2005), 5.

5. Antony Storr, 'The Child and the Book', *The New Statesman* (12 November 1960), 741–2.

6. Unsigned Article, 'A Writer's Rewards', *Financial Times* (12 December 1959), 6.

7. George Greenfield to Paul Hodder-Williams, 24 April 1959, Hodder and Stoughton Archives/London Metropolitan Archives, M.16352A/MS16313.

8. George Greenfield to Paul Hodder-Williams, 11 June 1959, Hodder and Stoughton Archives/London Metropolitan Archives, M.16352A. Blyton's fee was £1324.

9. Simon Kavanaugh,' No Gimmicks for Noddy Books Author', *Coventry Evening Telegraph* (9 February 1963), 6.

10. Lewis De Fries, 'Saturday Miscellany: World's Children Are Her Readers', *The Belfast Telegraph* (23 June 1962), 4.

11. George Greenfield to Paul Hodder-Williams, 19 May 1994, London Metropolitan Archives/Hodder and Stoughton Archives, M.16352A.

12. Sue MacGregor, *Woman of Today* (Bath: Chivers, 2002), 108.

13. Gillian Baverstock to Paul Hodder-Williams, 30 November 1968, London Metropolitan Archives/Hodder and Stoughton Archives, M.16352A.

14. Ewart Wharmby to Paul Hodder-Williams, 2 February 1968, London Metropolitan Archives/Hodder and Stoughton Archives, M.16352A.

15. Anne Valery, 'Blyton-Land Will Now be a Sadder Place', *The Newcastle Journal* (29 November 1968), 8.

16. Unsigned Article, 'Miss Enid Blyton', *The Times* (29 November 1968), 12.

17. Anne Valery, 'Blyton-land will now be a sadder place', 8.

18. Unsigned Article, 'Whitefriar Talking', *W.H. Smith's Trade News* (7 December 1968), 21.

19. Ibid., 22.

20. Diana Norman, 'Noddy Loses His Oldest Friend', *Daily Mail* (29 November 1968), 5.

21. Keith Brace, 'The Innocent Notoriety of Enid Blyton', *Birmingham Daily Post* (29 November 1968), 11.

22. Diana Norman, 'Noddy Loses His Oldest Friend', 5.

23. Anne Valery, 'Blyton-Land Will Now Be a Sadder Place', 8.

24. Unsigned article, 'Enid, the Child's Friend Dies in a Nursing Home', *Daily Record* (29 November 1968), 3.

25. Unsigned Article, 'Enid Blyton—The Quiet Author of Beaconsfield', *Buckinghamshire Advertiser* (5 December 1968), 1.

26. Diana Norman. 'Noddy Loses his Oldest Friend', 5.

27. Unsigned Article, 'Writer Enid Blyton Dies', *Belfast Telegraph* (29 November 1968), 2.
28. Willian Hickey, 'Where Noddy's Earnings Go', *Daily Express* (2 December 1968), 3.
29. Unsigned Article, 'Enid Blyton', *The Bookseller* (7 December 1968), 1917.
30. This was also the message of Roy Clarke's television play *Will Amelia Quint Continue Writing 'A Gnome Called Shorthouse'?* (1971). Amelia Quint, a loosely disguised version of Blyton (played by Beryl Reid) is lured back from her retirement in Italy and the life of alcohol and gigolos she is now enjoying. A former teacher, Miss Quint (her name deliberately recalling the ghost in Henry James' *The Turn of the Screw* [1898]) has become very wealthy by writing lots of books about goblins and elves for "'kiddies to cut their teeth on'" (00.05.50). Her work has been dismissed as old-fashioned and overly moral and her campaigning against on-screen violence out of date. Parents, however, like it and her former publishers want her to start writing again. Miss Quint, intelligent and self-aware, agrees to come back but the venture is not a success and the novelist expresses her hatred for her characters and her regret at not using her talent for more challenging writing.
31. William Feaver, 'The Naughtiest Girl in the Library', *The Listener* 92 (29 September 1974), 415.
32. Jesse Whitlock, 'Classic Media Snaps Up Noddy', *C21Media* (7 March 2012). https://www.c21media.net/news/classic-media-snaps-up-noddy/. Accessed 30 March 2021.
33. These figures are taken from the Hachette UK website, the company which bought the rights to Blyton's published work in 2012. They also note that there are 2000 short stories. https://www.hachette.co.uk/contributor/enid-blyton-2/. Accessed 30 March 2021.
34. For a fuller list of sequels see the World of Blyton site https://worldofblyton.com. Accessed 3 July 2021.
35. See *Favourite Enid Blyton Stories: Chosen by Jacqueline Wilson, Michael Morpurgo, Holly Smale and Many More* (London: Hodder Children's Books, 2018).

Bibliography

Judd, Dennis. Editor. 2009. *The Private Diaries of Alison Uttley.* Barnsley: Pen and Sword.
McGregor, Sue. 2002. *Woman of Today.* Bath: Chivers.

Chronology

This chronology is necessarily selective and does not list all the stories, poems and articles by Blyton published in a given year.

Year	Life and work	Notable events
1897	11 August: Born at 354 Lordship Lane, Dulwich, to Thomas and Theresa Blyton. The family moves to 95 Chaffinch Road, Beckenham (–1902)	Queen Victoria's Diamond Jubilee; Bram Stoker, *Dracula*
1899	Brother Hanly born	First motor bus in London
1902	Family move to 35 Clock House Road. Brother Carey born. Attends 'Tresco' nursery school	Arthur Conan Doyle, *The Hound of the Baskervilles*
1907	Attends St Christopher's School (–1915)	Robert Baden-Powell forms the Boy Scouts
1910	Thomas Blyton leaves the family	Edward VII dies; accession of George V
1911	Enid enters a poetry competition for children run by Arthur Mee editor of *The Little Paper*	Troops defeat alleged Russian anarchists in Sidney Street; Frances Hodgson Burnett, *The Secret Garden*
1912	Moves with mother and brothers to 4 Elm Road, Beckenham	Captain Robert Scott's expedition reaches the South Pole. RMS Titanic sinks
1915	Family moves to 13 Westfield Road, Beckenham. Enid leaves school and moves into the home of a friend, Mary Attenborough. Intends to apply for the Guildhall School of Music	Herbert Asquith forms coalition wartime government; First Zeppelin air-raid on Britain; Ocean liner *Lusitania* is sunk by German submarines

(continued)

© The Editor(s) (if applicable) and The Author(s) 2021
A. Maunder, *Enid Blyton*, Literary Lives,
https://doi.org/10.1007/978-3-030-76332-9

(continued)

Year	Life and work	Notable events
1916	Enrols on a Froebel teacher training course at Ipswich High School (–1918)	Battles of Verdun and the Somme; David Lloyd George is Prime Minister
1917	Publishes poem 'Have You…?' in *Nash's Magazine* (March)	Russian revolution; United States declares war on Germany
1918	Completes Froebel training course	11 November Armistice signed
1919	January: Teaches at Bickley Park School	Nancy Astor elected MP
1920	Works as governess for the Thompson family, Surbiton. July: Thomas Blyton dies of a heart attack aged 50. Blyton receives legacy of £500	League of Nations established. Communist Party of Great Britain established; Katherine Mansfield, *Bliss;* D.H. Lawrence, *Women in Love*
1921	February: Wins an essay competition in *The Saturday Westminster Review:* 'On the Popular Fallacy that to the Pure All Things are Pure.'	Irish Free State established; Marie Stopes open first Mothers Clinic; John Galsworthy *To Let;* Lytton Strachey, *Queen Victoria*
1922	February: story, 'Petronel and His Pot of Glue', *Teacher's World;* June: *Child Whispers*	Benito Mussolini leads fascist march on Rome; Tomb of Tutankhamun discovered T.S. Eliot, *The Wasteland*
1923	July: 'From My Window' column begins in *Teacher's World*. Meets Hugh Pollock. Earns £300 from her writings	Conservatives led by Stanley Baldwin win Election. Arnold Bennett, *Riceyman Steps* (reviewed by Blyton in *Teacher's World*). Elinor M. Brent-Dyer, *The School at the Chalet*
1924	August: Marries Hugh Pollock, moves to a flat at 32 Beaufort Mansions, Chelsea. October: *The Enid Blyton Book of Fairies.* Earns over £500 from her writing	Ramsay MacDonald becomes Prime Minister of the first Labour government E.M. Forster, *A Passage to India* Noel Coward, *The Vortex*
1925	*The Enid Blyton Book of Bunnies; Silver and Gold.* Income from writing reaches £1,095	Adolf Hitler, *Mein Kampf;* Virginia Woolf, *Mrs Dalloway*
1926	February: Moves to Elfin Cottage, Beckenham. July: Becomes editor/sole-contributor to *Sunny Stories* (250 issues) November: Acquires Bobs, a fox-terrier	3–12 May, General Strike; birth of Princess Elizabeth; Rudolph Valentino dies; A.A. Milne, *Winnie-the-Pooh*; Fritz Lang, *Metropolis* [film]
1927	Learns to type and drive. August: 'Letters to Children' column begins in *Teacher's World* (–1929)	A.A. Milne, *Now We are Six* Charles Lindbergh flies solo from New York to Paris

(continued)

(continued)

Year	Life and work	Notable events
1928	Consults a gynecologist about her apparent difficulties in conceiving a child *Tales of Brer Rabbit Retold*	Women's suffrage extended to women over twenty-one. A. Milne, *The House at Pooh Corner*. Jean Rhys, *Quartet*
1929	August: Moves to "Old Thatch", Bourne End; *Nature Lessons*, with illustrated by Blyton published. September: Begins children's page (*Teacher's World*)	Ramsay MacDonald, Prime Minister of Labour government. Wall Street crash Virginia Woolf, *A Room of One's Own*
1930	Cruise to Maderia and the Canary Islands	Aviator Amy Johnson flies solo to Australia; Arthur Ransome, *Swallows and Amazons*
1931	July: Gives birth to daughter, Gillian	Ramsay MacDonald's National Government
1932	February: Submits novel for adults, *The Caravan Goes On* but fails to find a publisher	First airline service; Aldous Huxley, *Brave New World*; Stella Gibbons, *Cold Comfort Farm*
1933	October: *Letters from Bobs*. Sales reach 10,000 in the first week	Hitler becomes German Chancellor F.D. Roosevelt becomes U.S. President
1934	Suffers a miscarriage; Hugh Pollock works with Winston Churchill editing *The Great War*	British Union of Fascists rally attracts 10,000 Geoffrey Trease, *Bows Against the Barons*
1935	October: Gives birth to daughter, Imogen. A residential nurse, Dorothy Richards, is employed to help. She and Blyton form a close friendship. November: Bobs dies	L.C.C. establishes 'Green Belt' to halt spread of London; Edith Bagnold, *National Velvet*; T.S. Eliot, *Murder in the Cathedral* Penguin books founded
1936	*The Yellow Fairy Book; The Famous Jimmy*	December: abdication of Edward VIII; accession of George VI
1937	January: Relaunch of *Sunny Stories* as *Enid Blyton's Sunny Stories*. Blyton writes the contents of 552 issues. Uses it to publish longer stories as serials including *Adventures of the Wishing Chair*	J.R. Tolkien, *The Hobbit;* Walt Disney, *Snow White and the Seven Dwarfs* [film] Noel Streatfeild, *Ballet Shoes;* The Carnegie Medal for Children's Literature established; Arthur Ransome is the first winner
1938	August: moves to "Green Hedges". September: *The Secret Island*; *Mr. Galliano's Circus*	German troops enter Austria Neville Chamberlain signs Munich Agreement with Germany
1939	May: *The Enchanted Wood;* October: *Naughty Amelia Jane!*	3 September: Britain declares war on Germany; *The Wizard of Oz* [film]

(continued)

(continued)

Year	Life and work	Notable events
1940	May: Hugh Pollock joins Home Guard. November: Writing as 'Mary Pollock' publishes *The Children of Kidillin*	Rationing; Italy declares war on Britain Charlie Chaplin, *The Great Dictator* [film] Kitty Barne, *Visitors from London*
1941	May: *The Adventurous Four;* on holiday with Dorothy Richards in Budleigh Salterton, Enid meets Kenneth Darrell Waters. November: *The Twins at St Clare's.* Five further titles follow (– 1945). December: *Sunny Stories Calendar 1942*	United States and Soviet Union enter the War. Morrison shelters distributed Noel Coward, *Blithe Spirit* Virginia Woolf, *Between the Acts* Mary Treadgold, *We Couldn't Leave Dinah* *The First of the Few* [film]
1942	First use of the Blyton logo-signature. Publishes twenty-two books. September: Gillian sent as a boarder to Godstowe School. September: *Five on a Treasure Island* (Hodder & Stoughton). December: Divorces Hugh Pollock citing his adultery	Japan takes control of Singapore RAF bombers attack Cologne Beveridge Report advocates a scheme of social welfare. Walter de la Mare, *Collected Poems*. T.S. Eliot, 'Little Gidding'. *In Which We Serve* [film]
1943	April: *Seven o'clock Tales;* June: *The Children's Life of Christ.* October: *The Magic Faraway Tree;* marries Kenneth Waters. December: *The Mystery of the Burnt Cottage*	Allied invasion of Italy RAF bombing of Hamburg
1944	March: *Tales from the Bible;* April: *The Three Golliwogs;* July: *The Boy Next Door;* September: Imogen (aged 8) sent to Godstowe school; November: *The Island of Adventure*	Normandy landings; final heavy bombing raids on London. *Henry V* [film]; L.P. Hartley, *The Shrimp and the Anemone;* Joyce Cary, *The Horse's Mouth* *The Way Ahead* [film]
1945	Blyton suffers a miscarriage. January: *Round the Clock Stories; The Family at Red-Roofs;* June: *The Caravan Family;* July: *Enid Blyton Nature Readers* Nos 1–10 [Nos. 11–20 published in October]; *Hollow Tree House.*	8 May: Victory in Europe Day; 15 August: Victory of Japan Day; Labour government elected; Nancy Mitford, *The Pursuit of Love;* George Orwell, *Animal Farm;* Evelyn Waugh, *Brideshead Revisited; Brief Encounter* [film]
1946	Doris Cox begins work as a maid at Green Hedges (–1968). March: *The Put- 'Em-Rights* (Lutterworth); July: *First Term at Malory Towers* (Methuen). November: Enid Blyton's *Gay Story Book* (Hodder); December: *The Enid Blyton Holiday Book* (Samson, Low, Marston)	Nuremberg war crimes trials. Major industries nationalised. First session of UN Assembly. Heathrow Airport opens Television resumes (suspended since 1939) J.B. Priestley, *An Inspector Calls* Terence Rattigan, *The Winslow Boy* BBC Third Programme begins

(continued)

(continued)

Year	Life and work	Notable events
1947	August: *House at the Corner.* October, *Little Green Duck.* December: *Before I Go to Sleep*	Partition of India; Princess Elizabeth marries Prince Philip of Greece; Rogers and Hammerstein, *Oklahoma;* Christian Dior's 'New Look'
1948	May: *Let's Garden;* June: *Brer Rabbit and His Friends.* July: *Come to the Circus.* October: visits New York to meet publishers. November: *Six Cousins at Mistletoe Farm.* The board game, *Journey Through Fairyland* is issued	Mahatma Gandhi assassinated; National Health service created; Gas industry nationalised; Olympic Games, London John Betjeman, *Selected Poems;* Alan Paton, *Cry the Beloved Country;* Terence Rattigan, *The Browning Version*
1949	Publishes thirty-two books; March: *The Rockingdown Mystery* (5 more titles – 1959). July: *A Story Party at Green Hedges.* September: *Enid Blyton Bible Stories: Old Testament* (14 titles). November: *The Secret Seven* (14 further titles –1963); *Those Dreadful Children*; *Noddy Goes to Toyland* (Noddy Library series: 24 books –1963)	NATO founded; end of sweet and clothes rationing; first flight of DH Comet, first jet airliner; the Goon Show begins on radio; George Orwell, *Nineteen Eighty-four;* Dodie Smith, *I Capture the Castle;* T.S. Eliot, *The Cocktail Party;* Simone de Beauvoir, *The Second Sex*
1950	March: Darrell Waters Ltd is set up. 31 October: Theresa Blyton dies, Enid does not attend funeral. November: *The Pole Star Family; Faraway Tree*, the first Enid Blyton card game is issued	General Election reduces Labour majority; petrol rationing ends; anti-apartheid demonstration in South Africa; C.S. Lewis, *The Lion, the Witch and the Wardrobe;* Doris Lessing, *The Grass is Singing*
1951	Blyton purchases a golf course at Studland Bay, Dorset; October: *The Six Bad Boys*; November: *The Proud Golliwog*	Festival of Britain; Conservatives win General Election; J.D. Salinger, *The Catcher in the Rye*
1952	44 titles published. September: *The Story of My Life*; November: *Enid Blyton's Animal Lover's Book;* Famous Five Club formed	Death of George VI; accession of Elizabeth II. Smog in London blamed for over 2000 deaths; Agatha Christie, *The Mousetrap;* Mary Norton, *The Borrowers*
1953	George Greenfield becomes Blyton's agent. February: steps down from *Sunny Stories; The Story of Our Queen*; March: launches *Enid Blyton's Magazine*(–1959)	Everest is climbed; Death of Stalin; 2 June: Queen Elizabeth is crowned; Samaritans founded; end of sugar rationing; Ian Fleming, *Casino Royale*

(continued)

(continued)

Year	Life and work	Notable events
1954	Rumours continue to circulate that Blyton does not write her own books. January: *Enid Blyton Bible Stories: New Testament* (nos 1–14). December: Blyton resigns her directorship of Darrell Waters Ltd; *Noddy in Toyland* opens at the Stoll Theatre	Food rationing ends; Television Bill paves way for a commercial channel Kingsley Amis, *Lucky Jim* William Golding, *Lord of the Flies* J.R. Tolkien, *The Fellowship of the Ring*
1955	September: Noddy puppets appear on ITV. December: *Famous Five Adventure* opens in London (revived in 1956)	General election won by Conservatives; dock and print strikes; Samuel Beckett, *Waiting for Godot*
1956	September: *A Story Book of Jesus.* October: *Bom, the Little Toy Drummer* (7 further titles –1961); *Tales from the Bible* (Muller). Completes a play for adults, *The Touchstone,* but it is never performed	First Aldermaston march; Suez crisis; John Osborne, *Look Back in Anger;* Patricia Highsmith, *The Talented Mr Ripley;* Dodie Smith, *One Hundred and One Dalmatians*
1957	Darrell Waters retires. May: Blyton is taken ill whilst playing golf; *Five on a Treasure Island* film is made by Children's Film Foundation. July: *Enid Blyton New Testament Picture Books*	Harold Macmillan becomes Prime Minister Wolfenden Commission recommends legalization of homosexual acts between consenting adults. John Osborne, *The Entertainer*
1958	July: *Enid Blyton's Tenth Bedside Book.* August: *Enid Blyton's Bom Annual*	C.N.D. launched. Racial violence in Notting Hill. Shelagh Delaney, *A Taste of Honey.* Philippa Pearce, *Tom's Midnight Garden*
1959	September: Blyton announces closure of *Enid Blyton's Magazine*	Obscene Publications Act becomes law Conservatives win General election Alan Sillitoe, *Loneliness of the Long-Distance Runner*
1960	Blyton is asked by Penguin Books to be a defence witness at the *Lady Chatterley's Lover* trial; *Adventure of the Strange Ruby*	J.F. Kennedy becomes U.S. president; Harper Lee, *To Kill a Mockingbird;* Alan Garner, *The Weirdstone of Brisingamen*
1961	October: *The Mystery that Never Was; The Big Enid Blyton Book.* It becomes noticeable that Blyton is beginning to suffer from memory loss	Berlin Wall built; Britain applies for EU membership; Muriel Spark, *The Prime of Miss Jean Brodie;* Roald Dahl, *James and the Giant Peach*

(continued)

(continued)

Year	Life and work	Notable events
1962	Noddy book sales reach 26 million July: *The Four Cousins* (Lutterworth)	Commonwealth Immigration Bill removes right of free entry for Commonwealth citizen. Cuban Missile Crisis. *That Was The Week That Was* broadcast [watched by Blyton]
1963	February: Existing Blyton series (St Clare's, Malory Towers, the Find-Outers,) released as paperbacks by Armada. July: *Five are Together Again* (final story in the series; *Fun for the Secret Seven.* November: *Noddy and the Aeroplane,* the last of 24 titles in the 'Library' series	Profumo Scandal; Macmillan resigns. J.F. Kennedy assassinated. Beeching Report recommends closing 2000 railway stations; Sylvia Plath, *The Bell Jar;* Sam Selvon, *The Lonely Londoners;* The Beatles, *Please, Please Me* [album]; Clive King, *Stig of the Dump*
1964	Blyton's agent and publishers decide she is not well enough to undertake public appearances	Vietnam War (–1975); General election won by Labour under Harold Wilson; Roald Dahl, *Charlie and the Chocolate Factory*
1965	August: *The Man who Stopped to Help; The Boy who came Back* - believed to be the last books written by Blyton	Abolition of Death Penalty. Relations Act prohibits racial discrimination. Mary Whitehouse founds the National Viewers and Listeners Association campaigning against 'bad taste.'
1966	*The Dog that Would Go Digging.* Part of the "John and Mary" series; eight further titles (–1968)	General Election increases Labour majority; Aberfan disaster kills 144; Eight new universities created
1967	Contacts her brother Hanly for the first time in many years. February – May: Knight Books (a division of Brockhampton) publish the Famous Five series in paperback. September: Kenneth Waters dies	Road Safety Act provides penalties for drink-driving. National Front founded; Tom Stoppard, *Rosencrantz and Guildenstern are Dead;* Angela Carter, *The Magic Toyshop*
1968	28 November: dies in her sleep in a Hampstead nursing home aged 71	Martin Luther King assassinated; Theatres Act abolishes censorship
1969	January: memorial service held at St James's Church, Piccadilly	Neil Armstrong and Buzz Aldrin land on the moon
1970	Darrell Waters Ltd has an estimated turnover of £500,000	
1971	Green Hedges is sold (demolished in 1973). November: Hugh Pollock dies	

Sources

Brian Stewart and Tony Summerfield. 1999. *The Enid Blyton Dossier*. Penryn: Hawk Books.

Enid Blyton Society Chronology. https://www.enidblytonsociety.co.uk/chronology.php. Accessed 27 February 2021.

Tony Summerfield. 2002. *Enid Blyton: An Illustrated Bibliography*. Part 2: 1943–1952. Salisbury: Milford Books.

Tony Summerfield. 2002. *Enid Blyton: An Illustrated Bibliography*. Part 3: 1944–1952. Salisbury: Milford Books.

Tony Summerfield. 2005. *Enid Blyton: An Illustrated Bibliography*. Part 2: 1953–1974. Salisbury: Milford Books.

Bibliography

Works by Enid Blyton

Adventures of the Wishing Chair. 1937. London: Newnes.
The Adventurous Four. 1941. London: Newnes.
The Boy Next Door. 1944. London: Newnes.
Child Whispers. 1922. London: J. Saville.
The Children of Kidillin. 1940. London: Newnes.
Circus Days Again. 1942. London: Newnes.
Claudine at St. Clare's. 1944. London: Methuen.
Famous Five Adventure. British Library Add Mss, Lord Chamberlain's Collection of Plays. 1955/67.
Fifth Formers' at St. Clares. 1945. London: Methuen.
First Term at Malory Towers. 1946. London: Methuen.
Five Go off in a Caravan. 1946. London: Hodder and Stoughton.
Five Go to Billycock Hill. 1957. London: Hodder and Stoughton.
Five on a Treasure Island. 1942. London: Hodder and Stoughton.
Five on Finniston Farm. 1960. London: Hodder and Stoughton.
Five Run Away Together. 1944. London: Hodder and Stoughton.
Hollow Tree House. 1945. London: Lutterworth Press.
House-at-the-Corner. 1947. London: Lutterworth Press.
Hurrah for the Circus! 1939. London: Newnes.
In the Fifth at Malory Towers. 1950. London: Newnes.
The Island of Adventure. 1944. London: Macmillan.
Last Term at Malory Towers. 1951. London: Methuen.
The Magic Faraway Tree. 1943. London: Newnes.

© The Editor(s) (if applicable) and The Author(s) 2021
A. Maunder, *Enid Blyton*, Literary Lives,
https://doi.org/10.1007/978-3-030-76332-9

The Mystery of Tally-Ho Cottage. 1954. London: Methuen.
The Mystery of the Disappearing Cat. 1944. London: Methuen.
The Naughtiest Girl in the School. 1940. London: Newnes.
Noddy in Toyland. British Library Add Mss, Lord Chamberlain's Collection of Plays.
    1954/17
Real Fairies. 1923. London: J. Saville.
The River of Adventure. 1955. London: Macmillan.
The Rockingdown Mystery. 1949. London: Collins.
The Rubabdub Mystery. 1952. London: Collins.
The Secret Island. 1938. Oxford: Basil Blackwell.
The Secret Mountain. 1941; 1947. Oxford: Basil Blackwell.
The Secret of Killimooin. 1943. Oxford: Basil Blackwell.
Shadow, The Sheep Dog. 1942. London: Newnes.
Shock for the Secret Seven. 1961. Leicester: Brockhampton Press.
The Six Bad Boys. 1951. London: Lutterworth.
Six Cousins Again. 1950. London: Evans.
Six Cousins at Mistletoe Farm. 1948. London: Evans.
Six Enid Blyton Plays. 1935. London: Methuen.
The Story of My Life. 1952. London: Pitkins.
Third Year at Malory Towers. 1948. London: Methuen.
Three Cheers Secret Seven. 1956. Leicester Brockhampton Press.
The Twins at St. Clare's. 1941. London Methuen.
Upper Fourth at Malory Towers. 1949. London: Methuen.

Articles by Blyton

Blyton, Enid. 'Writing for Children's Television'. *The Stage TV Supplement* (22
    September 1955): x.
'Changes in Children's Reading'. 1955. *The Sunday Times* (18 November): 6.
'The Enjoyment of Poetry'. 1951. *The Voice of Youth,* 1.1 (Spring): 4–7.
'The Family Story'. 1958. *The Author* 1: 11.
'My Week'. 1949. *W.H. Smith's Trade Circular* (10 September): 9.
'No Violence Please'. 1950. *W.H. Smith's Trade Circular* (4 March): 9–10.
'Writing for Children'. 1959. *The New Statesman* (9 May): 649–50.

Archives

British Library. Lord Chamberlain's Collection of Plays.
British Library. Macmillan and Company. Special Correspondence: Enid Blyton.
    Add Ms: 89262/1/5; 89262/1/6; 89262/1/7; 89262/1/8.
City of London, London Metropolitan Archives/Hodder and Stoughton. M
    16312/313; M.16352A.

Seven Stories [National Centre for Children's Literature]. Enid Blyton Diaries. EB/02/01/01- EB/01/01/23.

University of Bristol Special Collections. Lady Chatterley materials. DM1679.

Media

———. *Home for the Day: Enid Blyton.* 1963. Interview with Marjorie Anderson, BBC Light Programme (13 January). https://www.bbc.co.uk/archive/home-for-the-day--enid-blyton/zvy6kmn. Accessed 1 March 2021.

———. *Queen of Adventure: Enid Blyton.* 1997. BBC Radio 4 (31 July). https://www.bbc.co.uk/archive/queen-of-adventure-enid-blyton/zjjcpg8. Accessed 14 March 2021.

Connolly, Steve. Director. 2016. 'Staggering Storytellers' Song'. *Horrible Histories.* CBBC (11 July). https://www.bbc.co.uk/cbbc/watch/staggering-storytellers-special-sneak-peek?collection=international-womens-day. Accessed 13 March 2021.

Dyson, Jeremy. Director. 2013. 'Psychobitches: Enid Blyton'. Series 1: 2. Tiger Aspect Productions/Sky Arts (6 June). https://youtu.be/nX3LPe9jd7U. Accessed 13 March 2021.

Seven Stories. 2013. *The Blyton Legacy.* https://youtu.be/lTEjM2xLtTM. Accessed 3 March 2021.

Thompson, Roger. Director. 1975. *A Child-Like Person.* BBC Radio 4 (19 August). https://www.bbc.co.uk/archive/a-childlike-person/zvvt8xs. Accessed 14 March 2021.

Websites

Enid Blyton. https://www.enidblyton.net/.
Enid Blyton Society. http://www.enidblytonsociety.co.uk/.
Hachette Blyton website. https://www.enidblyton.co.uk/.
World of Blyton. https://worldofblyton.com/updates-to-blytons-books/.

Other Works Cited

———. 1951. *Complete List of Books: Enid Blyton.* Edinburgh: John Menzies.

Addison, Paul. 1975; 1977. *The Road to 1945. British Politics and the Second World War.* London: Quartet.

Aldgate, Anthony and Jeffrey Richards. 1986. *Britain Can Take It.* Oxford: Basil Blackwell.

Attenborough. John. 1975. *A Living Memory: Hodder and Stoughton Publishers 1868–1975.* London: Hodder and Stoughton.

Auchmuty, Rosemary. 1992. *A World of Girls: The Appeal of the Girls' School Story.* London: The Women's Press.

Baxendale, John. 2007. *Priestley's England: J. B. Priestley and English Culture.* Manchester: Manchester University Press.

Beetham, Margaret. 1989. 'Open and Closed: The Periodical as Publishing Genre'. *Victorian Periodicals Review* 22(3): 96–100.

Belsey. Catherine. 1998. 'Popular Fiction and the Feminine Masquerade'. *European Journal of English Studies* 2(3): 343–58.

Bennett, Tony, Colin Mercer and Janet Wollacott. 1986. *Popular Culture and Social Relations.* Milton Keynes: Open University.

Bensoussane, Anita. 2018. 'Enid Blyton and Edith Nesbit'. *Blyton Society Journal* 66 (Summer): 50–66.

Benton, Michael. 2009. *Literary Biography. An Introduction.* Chichester: Wiley Blackwell.

Berresford, Peter and Jennifer Schofield. 2003. *By Jove, Biggles! The Life Story of Captain W.E. Johns.* Watford: Norman Wright.

Bingham, Adrian. 2009. *Family Newspapers? Sex, Private Life and the British Popular Press 1918–1978.* Oxford: Oxford University Press.

Bluemel, Kristen. Editor. 2009. *Intermodernism: Literary Culture in Mid-Twentieth Century Britain.* Edinburgh: Edinburgh University Press.

Boston, Anne. 1989. *Wave Me Goodbye.* Harmondsworth: Penguin.

Bourdieu, Pierre. 1993. *The Field of Cultural Production: Essays on Art and Literature.* Oxford: Blackwell.

Braybon, Gail and Penny Summerfield. 1987. *Out of the Cage: Women's Experiences in Two World Wars.* London: Routledge.

Bressey, Caroline. 2008. 'It's Only Political Correctness—Race and Racism in British History'. In *New Geographies of Race and Racism,* edited by Claire Dwyer and Caroline Bressey: 29–41. Aldershot: Ashgate.

Brittain, Vera. 1953. *Lady into Woman: A History of Women from Victoria to Elizabeth II.* London: Andrew Dakers.

Brogan, Hugh. 1985. *The Life of Arthur Ransome.* London: Hamish Hamilton.

Buckingham, David. 'The Blyton Enigma'. https://davidbuckingham.net/growing-up-modern/the-blyton-enigma-changing-critical-perspectives-on-childrens-popular-culture/. Accessed 8 March 2021.

Bull, Angela. 1984. *Noel Streatfeild.* London: Collins.

Cadogan, Mary. 2004. 'Richmal Crompton Lamburn'. *New Dictionary of National Biography* https://doi.org/10.1093/refodnb/34386. Accessed 1 January 2021.

Caine, Barbara 2010. *Biography and History.* London: Palgrave.

Cairns, J.A.R. Editor. 1928. *Careers for Girls.* London: Hutchinson.

Carey, John. 2014. *The Unexpected Professor.* London: Faber.

Carpenter, Kevin. 1984. *Desert Islands and Pirate Islands.* Frankfurt: Peter Lang.

Castle, Barbara. 1952. 'Women's Work: Men's Views on It and Women's'. *John o'London's Weekly* (16 May): 2–3.

Cederwell, William. 2017. *Reading London in Wartime: Blitz, the People and Propaganda in 1940s Literature*. London: Routledge.

Chambers, Aidan. 1985. *Booktalk*. London: Bodley.

Childs, David. 1979. *Britain Since 1945: A Political History*. London: Methuen.

Chodorow, Nancy. 1999. *The Reproduction of Mothering*. LA: University of California Press.

Citron, Marcia. 2000. *Gender and the Musical Canon*. Urbana: University of Illinois Press.

Cixous, Hélène. 1991. 'The Laugh of the Medusa'. In *Feminisms*, edited by Robyn R. Warhol and Diane Price-Herndl: 334–49. New Brunswick: Rutgers University Press.

Clay, Catherine. 2006. *British Women Writers 1914–1945: Professional Work and Friendship*. Aldershot: Ashgate.

———. Maria DiCenzo, Barbara Green and Fiona Hackney. Editors. 2018. *Women's Periodicals and Print Culture in Britain 1918–1939: The Interwar Period*. Edinburgh: Edinburgh University Press.

Coetzee, Liesel. 2011. 'Empowering Girls? The Portrayal of Anne and George in Enid Blyton's Famous Five Series'. *English Academy Review* 28(1): 85–98.

Collier, Patrick Collier. 2006. *Modernism on Fleet Street*. Aldershot: Ashgate.

Colwell, Eileen. 1947. 'Twenty Eventful Years in Children's Books'. *Library Association: Papers and Summaries of Discussion at the Brighton Conference* (June 1947): 55–9

Conekin, Becky, Frank Mort and Chris Waters. Editors. 1999. *Moments of Modernity: Reconstructing Britain 1945–1964*. London: Rivers Oram Press.

Connolly, Cyril. 1938. *Enemies of Promise*. London: Routledge.

Cook, Daniel. Editor. 2002. *Symbolic Childhood*. New York: Peter Lang.

Cosslet, Tess. 2017. *Talking Animals in British Children's Fiction, 1786–1914*. London: Routledge.

Cragoe, Hugh. 2001. 'Enid Blyton: The Greatest Adventure of Her Life'. In *Utter Silence: Voicing the Unspeakable*, edited by Alice Mills and Jeremy Smith: 157–82. New York: Peter Lang.

David, Deirdre. 2002. 'Empire, Race and the Victorian Novel'. In *A Companion to the Victorian Novel*, edited by Patrick Brantlinger and William Thesing: 84–100. Oxford: Blackwell.

Delaney, Lesley. 2011. *Walter Crane: Promoting Visual Literacy in Nursery Picture Books*. Buckfast: Children's Books History Society.

Dinnage, Rosemary. 2004. *Alone! Alone! Lives of Some Outsider Women*. New York: New York Review of Books.

Dixon, Bob. 1974. 'The Nice, the Naughty and the Nasty: The Tiny World of Enid Blyton'. *Children's Literature in Education* 5(3): 43–61.

Duffy, Maureen. 1989. *A Thousand Conspicuous Chances. A History of the Methuen List, 1889–1989*. London: Methuen.

Federico, Annette. 2000. *Idol of Suburbia: Marie Corelli and Late Victorian Literary Culture*. London: University Press of Virginia.

Fisher, Margery. 1961. *Intent upon Reading: A Critical Appraisal of Modern Fiction for Children*. Leicester: Brockhampton Press.

Floridi, Luciano. Editor. 2016. *The Routledge Handbook of Philosophy of Information*. London: Routledge.

Fraser, Antonia. Editor. 2015. *The Pleasures of Reading*. London: Bloomsbury.

Gallop, Jane. 1982. *The Daughter's Seduction*. Basingstoke: Macmillan.

Garbett, Cyril. 1945. *Reading in War-Time*. Oxford: Oxford University Press.

Gardiner, Juliet. 2004. *Wartime Britain 1939–1945*. London: Headline.

Gelder, Ken. Editor. 2000. *The Horror Reader*. London: Routledge.

Gibson, Mel. 2010. 'Picturebooks, Comics and Graphic Novels'. In *The Routledge Companion to Children's Literature*, edited by David Rudd: 100–11. London: Routledge.

Giles, Judy Giles and Tim Middleton. Editors. 1995. *Writing Englishness 1900–1950: An Introductory Sourcebook*. London: Routledge.

Gillett, Philip. 2020. *Reading Enid Blyton*. Cambridge: Cambridge Scholars Publishing.

Greenfield, George. 1995; 1997. *A Smattering of Monsters*. London: Warner.

———. 1998. *Enid Blyton*. Stroud Sutton.

Grenfell, Joyce. 1954. *Joyce Grenfell Requests the Pleasure*. British Library Add Ms, Lord Chamberlain's Collection. LCP 1954/26.

Grier, Katherine C. 2006. *Pets in America: A History*. Chapel Hill: University of North Carolina Press.

Hadley, Elaine. 1995. *Melodramatic Tactics: Theatricalized Dissent in the English Marketplace, 1800–1885*. Stanford: Stanford University Press.

Hall, Christine and Martin Coles. 1999. *Children's Reading Choices*. London: Routledge.

Hankin, Cherry A. Editor. 1988. *Letters between Katherine Mansfield and John Middleton Murray*. London: Virago.

Harding, Julie. 2019. 'The Little Man with the Red and Yellow Car'. *Country Life* (17 July): 108–109.

Hardy, Dennis. 2000. *Utopian England: Community Experiments, 1900–1945*. London, Routledge.

Hawley, Peter. 1947. 'Enid Blyton's Twenty Books a Year'. *The Reading Lamp* 1 (July): 12–15.

Hennessey, Peter. 1992; 2006. *Never Again: Britain 1945–1951*. London: Penguin.

———. 2006; 2007. *Having it So Good: Britain in the Fifties*. London: Penguin.

Hildick, E. Wallace. 1970. *Children and Fiction*. London: Evans.

Hill, Susan. 2009. *Howard's End is on the Landing*. London: Profile Books.

Hilliard, Christopher. 2006. *To Exercise Our Talents: The Democratization of Writing in Britain*. London: Harvard University Press.

Houghton, Robert. 2014. 'The Railway Children and the Family at Red-Roofs'. *The Enid Blyton Society Journal* 54 (Summer): 4–10.

Hughes, Orla. 2015. 'Noddy's Other Half—Harmsen van der Beek' (8 November). http://nerdalicious.com.au/books/noddys-other-half-harmsen-van-der-beek/#fnref-21494-3. Accessed 8 March 2021.

Humble, Nicola. 2001. *The Feminine Middlebrow Novel, 1920s to 1950s*. Oxford: Oxford University Press.

Hunt, Peter. 1994. *An Introduction to Children's Literature*. Oxford: Oxford University Press.

———. 1995. 'How Not to Read a Children's Book'. *Children's Literature in Education* 26: 231–40.

———. 1995. *Children's Literature: An Illustrated History*. Oxford: Oxford University Press.

———. Editor. 2001. *Children's Literature. An Anthology*. Oxford: Basil Blackwell.

———. 2001. *Children's Literature*. Oxford: Blackwell.

Jauss, Hans Robert. 1982. *Toward an Aesthetic of Reception*. Minnesota: University of Minnesota Press.

John, Angela V. 2013. *Turning the Tide: The Life of Lady Rhonda*. Cardigan: Parthian.

Johnson, Alan. 2014. *This Boy: A Memoir of Childhood*. London: Corgi.

Joseph, Michael. 1922. *Short Story Writing for Profit*. London: Hutchinson.

Judd, Dennis. 1986. *Alison Uttley: The Life of a Country Child*. London: Michael Joseph.

———. Editor. 2009. *The Private Diaries of Alison Uttley*. Barnsley: Pen and Sword.

Kadar, Marlene. Editor. 1992. *Essays on Life Writing: From Genre to Critical Practice*. Toronto: University of Toronto Press.

Kiberd, Declan. 2005. 'School Stories'. In *Studies in Children's Literature 1500–2000*, edited by Celia Keenan and Mary Shine: 54–69. Dublin: Four Courts Press.

Knight, Stephen. 1980. *Form and Ideology in Crime Fiction*. Basingstoke: Macmillan.

Koste, V. Glasgow. 1987. 'Mere Giants: The Child Protagonist in Drama for Intergenerational Audiences'. *Children's Literature Association Quarterly* 12(1): 33–5.

Kynaston, David. 2007; 2008. *A World to Build: Austerity Britain 1945–48*. London: Bloomsbury

———. 2010; 2011. *Family Britain, 1951–1957*. London: Bloomsbury.

Larson, Erik. 2020. *The Splendid and the Vile: A Saga of Churchill, Family and Defiance during the Blitz*. London: Collins.

Leavis, Q.D. 1932; 1978. *Fiction and the Reading Public*. London: Bellow Publishing.

Leeson, Robert. 1985. *Reading and Righting: The Past, Present and Future of Fiction for the Young*. London: Collins.

Lehmann, Rosamond. *The Echoing Grove*. London: Collins.

Liggins, Emma, Andrew Maunder and Ruth Robbins. 2010. *The British Short Story*. London: Palgrave.

Lloyd, Marjorie. 1937. *Buckinghamshire: An Illustrated Review of the Holiday, Sporting and Industrial Facilities of the County*. London: E. J. Burrow & Co.

Loomba, Ania. 2002. *Shakespeare, Race and Colonialism*. Oxford: Oxford University Press.

Lustig, T. J. 2014. 'Enid on Enid: Blyton's Use of Arthurian Narratives in *The Knights of the Round Table*'. *Children's Literature in Education* 45: 89–100.

Macaulay, Rose. 1925. *Casual Commentary*. London: Methuen.

Mackenzie, Donald. 'Pot Boilers? No!'. *W.H. Smith's Trade Circular* (2 December 1950): 13; 15.

Maine, Margo D. 1991; 1993. *Father Hunger: Fathers, Daughters and Food*. Carlsbad, CA: Gurze Books.

Mangum, Teresa. 2002. 'Dog Years, Human Fears'. In *Representing Animals*, edited by Nigel Rothfels: 35–47. Bloomington: Indiana University Press.

Manlove, Colin. 2003. *From Alice to Harry Potter: Children's Fantasy in England*. Rochester: Lisa Loucks Christenson Publishing.

Maslen, Elizabeth. 2001. *Political and Social Issues in British Women's Fiction, 1928–1968*. Basingstoke: Palgrave.

McAleer, Joseph. 1992. *Popular Reading and Publishing in Britain 1914–1950*. Oxford, Oxford University Press.

McCarthy, Helen. 2016. 'Social Science and Married Women's Employment in Post-War Britain'. *Past & Present* 233(1): 269–305.

———. 2020. *Double Lives: A History of Working Motherhood*. London: Bloomsbury.

McConachie, Bruce A. 1989. 'Using the Concept of Cultural Hegemony to Write Theatre History'. In *Interpreting the Theatrical Past: Essays in the Historiography of Performance*, edited by Thomas Postlewait and Bruce A. McConachie: 37–58. Iowa City: University of Iowa Press.

McGarry, Mike and Sally Walker. 2014. *Malcolm Saville. An Illustrated Bibliography*. Harpenden: Malcolm Saville Society.

McGregor, Sue. 2002. *Woman of Today*. Bath: Chivers.

McLaren, Duncan. 2008. *Looking for Enid: The Mysterious and Inventive Life of Enid Blyton*. London: Granta.

Melman, Billie. 1988. *Women and the Popular Imagination in the Twenties: Flappers and Nymphs*. Basingstoke: Macmillan.

Miller, Kristine. 2009. *British Literature of the Blitz: Fighting the People's War*. Basingstoke, Palgrave Macmillan.

Mills, Cyril Bertram. 1967. *Bertram Mills Circus: Its Story*. London: Hutchinson.

Milne, A.A. 1939. *It's Too Late Now: The Autobiography of a Writer*. London: Methuen.

Moi, Toril. 1985. *Sexual/Textual Politics: Feminist Literary Theory*. London: Methuen.

Morse, Deborah Deneholz and Martin Danahay. Editors. 2007. *Victorian Animal Dreams*. Ashgate.

Myers, Peter and Ronnie Cass. 1961. *The Lord Chamberlain Regrets*. British Library Add Ms, LCP 1961/31.

Nicolson, Nigel Joanne Trautman. Editors. 1979. *The Letters of Virginia Woolf*. New York: Harcourt Brace Jovanovich.

O'Hanlon. 2001. *Beyond the Lone Pine: A Biography of Malcolm Saville*. Worcester: M. O'Hanlon.

O'Malley, Andrew. 2012. *Children's Literature, Popular Culture and Robinson Crusoe*. Houndsmills: Palgrave Macmillan.

Oram, Richard. 2014. 'Writers' Libraries'. In *Collecting, Curating and Researching Writer's Libraries*, edited by Richard W. Oram and Joseph Nicholson: 1–28. Lanham: Rowman and Littlefield.

Orwell, George Orwell. 1940. *Inside the Whale and Other Essays*. https://www.orw ell.ru/library/essays/boys/english/e_boys. Accessed 4 March 2021.

———. 1947. *English People*. London: Collins.

———. 1986. *Decline of the English Murder and Other Essays*. Harmondsworth: Penguin.

Pennethorne, R. A. 1940. 'Children in Wartime'. *The Parents' Review* 51 (July–August): 380–3.

Pepper, Terence. 1991. *Dorothy Wilding, The Pursuit of Perfection*. London: National Portrait Gallery.

Pollock, Ida. 2009. *Starlight*. Hertford: Authors online.

Pumphrey, George H. 1949. 'Children's Periodicals—Some Disturbing Developments'. *Junior Bookshelf* 24(4): 194–201.

R.H.M. 1947. 'The Bountiful Miss Blyton: News of Her Latest Books'. *National Newsagent, Bookseller, Stationer* (6 September): 1554–8.

Reimer, Mavis. 2009. 'Traditions of the School Story'. In *The Cambridge Companion to Children's Literature,* edited by M.O. Grenby and Andrea Immel: 209–25. Cambridge: Cambridge University Press.

Rennell, Tony. 2007. 'Britain 1947: Poverty, Queues, Rationing—And Resilience'. *Daily Mail* (20 November), 24.

Reynolds, Kimberley. 2009. 'Changing Families in Children's Fiction'. In *The Cambridge Companion to Children's Literature*, edited by M.O Grenby and Andrea Immel: 193–204. Cambridge University Press.

———. 2011. *Children's Literature: A Very Short Introduction*.

Richards, Jeffrey Richards. 1999; 2002. 'From Greyfriars to Grange Hill'. In *School Stories: From Bunter to Buckeridge*, NCRCL Papers 4, edited by Nicholas Tucker: 35–51. Roehampton: National Centre for Children's Literature.

Richardson, Phyllis. 2017. *House of Fiction: From Pemberley to Brideshead, Great Houses in English Literature*. London: Unbound.

Robbins, Norman. 2002. *Slapstick and Sausages: The Evolution of British Pantomime*. London: Trapdoor

Robbins, Ruth. 1996. '"Snowed Up": Feminist Perspectives'. In *Literary Theories*, edited by Julian Wolfreys and William Baker: 103–26. Basingstoke: Macmillan.

Royce, Marjory and Barbara E Todd. 1925. *The Very Good Walkers*. London: Methuen.

Rudd, David. 1995. 'Five Have a Genderful Time: Blyton, Sexism, and the Infamous Five'. *Children's Literature in Education* 26(3): 185–96.

———. 2000. *Enid Blyton and the Mystery of Children's Literature*. London: Palgrave.

————. 2004. 'Blytons, Noddies and Denoddification Centers: The Changing Construction of a Cultural Icon'. In *Change and Renewal in Children's Literature*, edited by Thomas van der Walt: 111–8. London: Praeger.

————. 2004. Gollywog: Genealogy of a Non-PC Icon'. In *Studies in Children's Literature, 1500–2000*, edited by C. Keenan and Mary Shine Thompson: 70–7. Dublin: Four Courts.

————. 2005. 'Island and i-lands in Enid Blyton'. In *Treasure Islands in Children's Literature*, edited by Mary Shine Thompson and Celia Keenan: 72–8. Dublin: Four Courts.

————. 2008. 'Froebel Teacher to English Disney: The Phenomenal Success of Enid Blyton'. In *Popular Children's Literature in Britain*, edited by Julia Briggs, Dennis Butts and M.O. Grenby: 251–69. Aldershot: Ashgate.

————. 2009. 'In Defence of the Indefensible? Some Grounds for Enid Blyton's Appeal'. In *Children's Literature: Approaches and Territories*, edited by J. Maybin and N. Watson: 168–82. London: Palgrave Macmillan.

————. 2010. 'The Development of Children's Literature'. In *The Routledge Companion to Children's Literature*, edited by David Rudd: 1–13. London: Routledge.

Ruppel, Richard. 1993. '*The Lagoon* and the Popular Exotic Tradition'. In *Contexts for Conrad*, edited by Keith Carabine, Owen Knowles and Wieslaw Krajia: 177–87. New York: Columbia University Press.

Sage, Lorna. 2000; 2001. *Bad Blood*. London: 4th Estate.

Saunders, N. J. 2001. 'Apprehending Memory: Material Culture and the War, 1919–1939'. In *The Great World War*, edited by J. Bourne, P.H. Liddle and H. Whitehead: 476–8. London: Harper Collins.

Scholes, Robert. 1985. *Textual Power: Literary Theory and the Teaching of English*. London: Yale University Press.

Seago, Edward. 1933. *Circus Company*. New York: Putnam.

Sevareid, Eric. Editor. 1967. *All England Listened. The War-Time Broadcasts of J.B. Priestley*. New York: Chilmark Press.

Shaw, Valerie Shaw. 1983. *The Short Story: A Critical Introduction*. London: Longman.

Skeggs, Beverley. 2003. *Class, Self, Culture*. London: Routledge.

Smallwood, Imogen. 1989. *A Childhood at Green Hedges*. London: Methuen.

Smith, May. 2010. *These Wonderful Rumours: A Young Schoolteacher's Wartime Diaries, 1939–1945*. London: Virago.

Smith, Angela Smith. 2000. *The Second Battlefield. Women, Modernism and the First World War*. Manchester: Manchester University Press.

Spaas, Lieve and Brian Stimpson. Editors. 1996. *Robinson Crusoe. Myths and Metamorphoses*. Basingstoke: Macmillan.

Stanley, Liz. 1995. *The Auto/Biographical I: The Theory and Practice of Feminist Auto/biography*. Manchester: Manchester University Press.

Stevenson, Robert Louis. 1922. *Memories and Portraits*. In *The Works of Robert Louis Stevenson*: XII 188–9. New York: Charles Scriber's Sons.

Stewart, Brian Stewart and Tony Summerfield. 1999. *The Enid Blyton Dossier.* Penryn: Hawk.

Stoney, Barbara. 1974; 1992. *Enid Blyton: A Biography.* London: Hodder and Stoughton.

Streatfeild, Noel. 1958. 'The Book and the Serial'. *The Author* 68(3): 63–7.

Summerfield, Penny. 1998. *Reconstructing Women's Wartime Lives: Discourse and Subjectivity in Oral Histories of the Second World War.* Manchester: Manchester University Press.

Summerfield, Tony. 2002. *Enid Blyton. An Illustrated Bibliography: Part 2: 1942–1952.* Salisbury: Milford Books.

———. 2003. *Enid Blyton. An Illustrated Bibliography: Part 3: 1953–1962.* Salisbury: Milford Books.

———. 2005. *Enid Blyton. An Illustrated Bibliography: Part 2: 1963–1974.* Salisbury: Milford Books.

Taylor, D.J. 2016. *The Prose Factory: Literary Life in England since 1918.* London: Chatto and Windus.

Taylor, Millie. 2007. *British Pantomime Performance.* London: Intellect.

Thornton, Kristen. 'Arthur Mee's "Children's Encyclopaedia"'. https://www.dea kin.edu.au/library/special-collections/collections/mee-encyclopaedia. Accessed 10 March 2021.

Tinkler, Penny. 1985. *Constructing Girlhood: Popular Magazines for Girls Growing up in England 1920–1950.* London: Taylor and Francis.

Towheed, Shafquat, Andrew Nash and Claire Squires. 2019. 'Reading and Ownership'. In *The Cambridge History of the Book in Britain, Volume 7: The Twentieth Century and Beyond,* edited by Andrew Nash, Claire Squires and I.R. Willison: 231–76. Cambridge: Cambridge University Press.

Trease, Geoffrey. 1949. *Tales out of School.* London: Heinemann.

———. 1974. *Laughter at the Door: A Continued Biography.* London: Macmillan.

Trotter, David. 1994. *The English Novel in History. 1895–1920.* London: Routledge.

Tucker, Nicholas. 1975. 'The Blyton Enigma'. *Children's Literature in Education* 6(4): 191–7.

Tucker, Nicholas and Kimberley Reynolds. Editors. 1997. *Enid Blyton. A Celebration and Re-appraisal.* London: National Centre for Research in Children's Literature.

Unsigned Article. 2009. 'Small beer' Blyton banned by BBC'. http://news.bbc.co. uk/1/hi/uk/8361056.stm. Accessed 8 March 2021.

Unsigned Article. 2009. 'BBC Archive Releases New Documents about Enid Blyton and Her Tempestuous Relationship with the BBC'. http://www.bbc.co.uk/presso ffice/pressreleases/stories/2009/11_november/15/blyton.shtml. Accessed 8 March 2021.

Unsigned Article 2016. Enid Blyton and the BBC: Revealing the Writer's Troubled Relationship with the BBC'. BBC Archive, http://www.bbc.co.uk/archive/blyton andthebbc/. Accessed 1 September 2016

Varlow, Sally. 2011. *A Brush with Enid Blyton: The Life and Work of Marjorie L. Davies.* Lewes: Pomegranate Press.

Wagner Martin, Linda. 1994. *Telling Women's Lives: The New Biography*. New Brunswick: Rutgers.

Wall, Barbara. 1991. *The Narrator's Voice. The Dilemma of Children's Literature*. Basingstoke: Macmillan.

Watson, Victor. 2000. *Reading Series Fiction*. London: Routledge.

Welch, Colin. 1958. 'Dear Little Noddy: A Parent's Lament'. *Encounter* (January): 18–23.

Williams, Kay. 1986. *Just Richmal. The Life and Work of Richmal Crompton Lamburn*. Guildford: Genesis.

Wilson, Jacqueline. 2001. 'Preface'. Eleanor Graham. *The Children Who Lived in a Barn:* i–x. London Persephone Books.

Wolfreys, Julian. 2001. *Victorian Hauntings: Spectrality, Gothic, the Uncanny and Literature*. London: Palgrave.

Woolf, Virginia. 1942; 2011. 'Middlebrow'. In *The Essays of Virginia Woolf*, edited by Stuart N. Clarke. Vol. 6, Appendix II: 470–9. London: The Hogarth Press.

Wootton, David. 1995. *The Art of George and Eileen Soper*. London: Chris Beetles.

Young, Iris Marian. 1997. *Intersecting Voices: Dilemmas of Gender, Political Philosophy and Policy*. Princeton: Princeton University Press.

Index

© The Editor(s) (if applicable) and The Author(s) 2021
A. Maunder, *Enid Blyton*, Literary Lives,
https://doi.org/10.1007/978-3-030-76332-9

Printed by Printforce, United Kingdom